TYCOON'S WAR

TYCOON'S WAR

How Cornelius Vanderbilt
Invaded a Country to Overthrow America's
Most Famous Military Adventurer

STEPHEN DANDO-COLLINS

DA CAPO PRESS
A Member of the Perseus Books Group

Set in 10.75 point Fairfield Light by the Perseus Books Group

Library of Congress Cataloging-in-Publication Data

Dando-Collins, Stephen.
  Tycoon's war : how Cornelius Vanderbilt invaded a country to overthrow America's most famous military adventurer / Stephen Dando-Collins.
      p.   cm.
  Includes bibliographical references and index.
  ISBN 978-0-306-81607-9
  1. Nicaragua—History—Filibuster War, 1855–1860. 2. United States—Military relations—Nicaragua. 3. Nicaragua—Military relations—United States. 4. Vanderbilt, Cornelius, 1794–1877. 5. Businessmen—United States—Biography. 6. Compañía Accesoria del Tránsito—History. 7. Nicaragua Canal (Nicaragua)—History. 8. Walker, William, 1824–1860. 9. Filibusters—Nicaragua—Biography. 10. United States—Foreign relations—1815–1861. I. Title.
  F1526.27.D36 2008
  972.85'044—dc22
                                            2008014632

Published by Da Capo Press
A Member of the Perseus Books Group
www.dacapopress.com

Da Capo Press books are available at special discounts for bulk purchases in the United States by corporations, institutions, and other organizations. For more information, please contact the Special Markets Department at the Perseus Books Group, 2300 Chestnut Street, Suite 200, Philadelphia, PA 19103, or call (800) 810-4145, ext. 5000, or e-mail special.markets@perseusbooks.com.

10 9 8 7 6 5 4 3 2 1

CONTENTS

ACKNOWLEDGMENTS

OVER THE YEARS THAT THIS book has come together, many people have provided sincerely appreciated help and advice. I want to thank Clyde Prestowitz Jr., President of the Economic Strategy Institute, Washington, D.C., for advice on the U.S. economy in the 1850s and 1860s. Also, Chris Morrison of the Historical Office of the U.S. Department of State, Washington, D.C., provided invaluable information on the U.S. State Department and its workings in the mid-nineteenth century. My gratitude also goes to Dr. Erika Cox, Pathology Department, Launceston General Hospital, in Tasmania, Australia, for advice on contagious diseases common to Central America. And Marco A. Argotte, formerly of Chile, now of Sydney, Australia, for translation assistance.

For their enthusiastic assistance with my on-the-ground research in Nicaragua, I thank Juan Carlos Mendosa of Managua, Nicaragua, and Major John Seldomridge (U.S. Army, retired) of Elisabethtown, Kentucky. And for path-finding help on the Vanderbilt trail on Staten Island, the intrepid Robert and Alison Simko of Lower Manhattan.

I especially want to thank Bob Pigeon, Executive Editor with Da Capo Press, who has supported my ambitions for this book for a number of years, as I molded it into the tale it has become, and his efficient assistant, Ashley St. Thomas. My New York literary agent, Richard Curtis, the general of my campaigns in American, Roman, British, Australian, and French historical territory, has never doubted the importance of this book; without both his belief and his knowledgeable guidance, it would never have seen the light of day.

And, as always, my thanks go to my wonderful wife, Louise. She has marched at my side every step of the way on this book, in museums, libraries, and archives and on battle sites in the United States, Central America, and elsewhere, then encouraged, assisted, and advised me as I worked through the drafts. What a lonely, boring life it would be without my "Dona Louise."

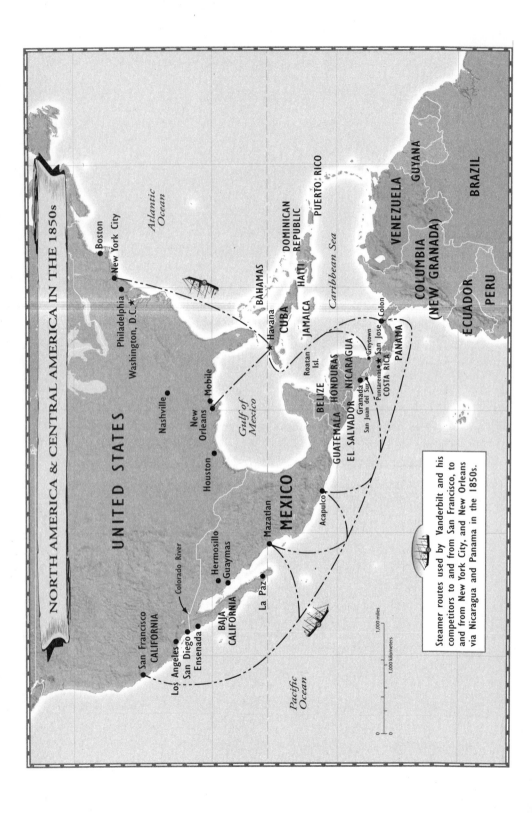

NORTH AMERICA & CENTRAL AMERICA IN THE 1850s

Steamer routes used by Vanderbilt and his competitors to and from San Francisco, to and from New York City, and New Orleans via Nicaragua and Panama in the 1850s.

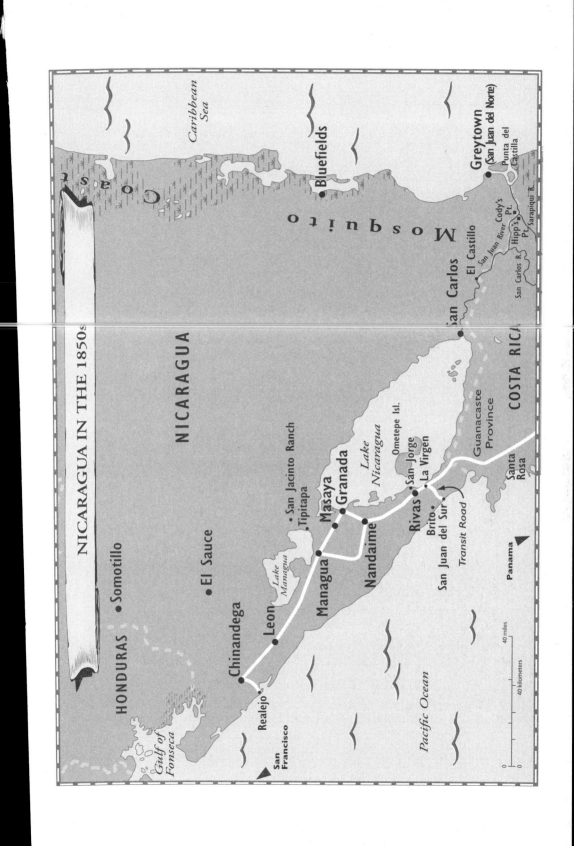

NICARAGUA IN THE 1850s

HONDURAS

Somotillo

Gulf of
Fonseca

San
Francisco

Realejo

Chinandega

Leon

El Sauce

NICARAGUA

Lake
Managua

Managua

San Jacinto Ranch
Tipitapa

Masaya
Granada

Nandaime

Lake
Nicaragua

Ometepe Isl.

San Jorge
La Virgen

Rivas

Brito

San Juan del Sur

Transit Road

Guanacaste
Province

Santa
Rosa

COSTA RICA

Panama

Pacific Ocean

San Carlos

El Castillo

San Juan River Cody's
Pt.

Hipp's

San Carlos R.

Sarapiqui R.

Greytown
(San Juan del Norte)

Punta del
Castilla

Mosquito

Coast

Caribbean
Sea

Bluefields

40 miles

40 kilometers

0

0

INTRODUCTION

IN THE SPRING OF 1849, two men arrived in Washington, D.C., by carriage from New York City. One was fifty-five-year-old shipping magnate Cornelius Vanderbilt, "the largest steamship owner in the world, one who commenced his career by commanding a small schooner, and who is known moreover wherever commerce spreads a sail, as Commodore Vanderbilt."[1] This description of Vanderbilt was part of rhetoric from a pamphlet issued by one of his shipping lines, but every word happened to be true.

The carriage drew up at the Fifteenth Street entrance to the Northeast Executive Building, a squat, thirty-year-old, two-story structure, its leaden-gray paintwork leavened with white trim. Designed by James Hoban, architect of the white-painted Executive Mansion, or the White House as it has become known, which stood just two hundred yards away, the gray building had an imposing, north-facing front entrance with an ornate pediment topping six grand white Corinthian columns. But anyone who did business with the U.S. State Department in 1849 knew to use its Fifteenth Street side entrance.

Cornelius Vanderbilt stepped down from the carriage and arched his back to shake off the stiffness of the journey. He was an imposing man, lanky, lean, and handsome. His hair was thick and gray; he was clean-shaven but for luxuriant, gray pork-chop side whiskers. His mouth was tight, his eyes assessing. Vanderbilt, impatient to do business, strode forward and tramped up four steps and passed in through the Executive Building's side door. The second traveler, hurrying to follow his long-legged companion, was Joseph L. White, Vanderbilt's efficient lawyer and business partner.

Hard-swearing, frugal-living Cornelius Vanderbilt, the descendant of poor Dutch immigrants, the Van der Bilts, would die in 1877 possessing more money than was held by the U.S. Treasury. By one estimate, his fortune

1

exceeded $96 billion in present-day dollars.[2] Far and away America's richest
man, he built his massive fortune on steam—first, his fleets of steamboats
and ocean steamers plying North American rivers and the world's oceans, and
later, after the American Civil War, steam trains on his ever-expanding net-
work of North American railroads. "I have been insane on the subject of
money-making all my life," Vanderbilt would tell the *New York Daily Tribune*
shortly before his death.[3]

When gold was discovered in California in January 1848, Vanderbilt was
already a multimillionaire, but the immense wealth he would amass by the
time he died was then still only the stuff of dreams. Within a year, the
Forty-Niners—the first wave in a sea of gold-seeking immigrants who would
flood California—were heading west, hoping to swiftly make their fortunes
in the gold fields. Vanderbilt had figured out another way to make a fortune
from the gold rush. And that was why he had come to Washington. Ironically, this Washington meeting would create the circumstances that would,
within seven years, bring Vanderbilt to the brink of financial disaster and
send him to war to save his business empire.

Passing clerks on the staff of the Fifth Auditor of the Treasury, who occupied the first floor, Vanderbilt reached a wide south-side staircase. Topping the stairs, he waited for White to join him. A former Washington
politician, White knew his way around this building; the State Department
occupied the fifteen offices on this second floor and the six offices on the
attic floor above. White led the way to the northeast corner, opening a door
and ushering Vanderbilt into the reception room of the secretary of state.
Through an open doorway, Secretary of State John M. Clayton, working at
his desk in the adjoining office, saw the pair, rose to his feet, and came out
to greet them.

A solid man with bristly gray hair and probing eyes, fifty-two-year-old
Clayton was a Delaware native and Yale graduate who, in 1829, had become the youngest member of the U.S. Senate. Considered one of the
finest orators in the country and one of the nation's best minds, Clayton
had been secretary of state for barely a month, having resigned from the
Senate to accept the appointment from President Zachary Taylor. The State
Department that Clayton administered had 218 personnel at twenty-seven
embassies and 197 consulates around the world. Here in Washington,

Clayton administered the foreign interests of the United States with a total of twenty-two staff.[4]

Clayton warmly greeted White, an old friend, and then shook the hand of Cornelius Vanderbilt. To close friends, Vanderbilt was "Corneel." To mere acquaintances such as Clayton, he was "Mr. Vanderbilt." Clayton was a nationalist and an ardent advocate of America's commercial expansion beyond its borders. The State Department had been abuzz with national sentiment ever since the United States won the Mexican War the previous year and came out of the conflict with half a million acres of Mexican territory stretching from the Rio Grande to the Pacific Ocean. This victory had come on the back of the 1845 U.S. annexation of the independent Republic of Texas, with the approval of the Texans. Despite these successes, Clayton was wary of further U.S. involvement in Mexico or the rest of Central America yet was just as wary of the ambitions of European powers in the region.

The Spanish, who were thrown out of Central America in 1821 by the locals, seemed content to focus on their Caribbean territories—the islands of Cuba and Puerto Rico. But Britain and France, both of which had extensive Caribbean island possessions, had been sending expansionist signals concerning Central America. In 1838, the French had planned to build a railroad across the Central American isthmus, only for the project to die for lack of funds. And in 1848, the French government had discussed with a Nicaraguan government envoy an agreement that would have allowed the French to develop a canal across Nicaragua to link the Caribbean Sea and the Pacific Ocean.

Meanwhile, in January 1848, coinciding with the discovery of gold in California, Britain had landed Royal Marines at San Juan del Norte, a settlement on San Juan Bay at the mouth of San Juan River, on Nicaragua's Caribbean coast—a region known as the Moskito, or Mosquito, Coast, because it is the home of the Moskito Indians. The British took control of that Nicaraguan settlement, renaming it Greytown, and British warships frequently dropped anchor there and at Bluefields, another British settlement farther up the Mosquito Coast. To cover their territorial grab, the British set up the protectorate of the Mosquito Shore and said they recognized the Moskito king's sovereignty over the Mosquito Coast. In some U.S. circles, there was concern that the British planned to extend their influence in Central America from this Mosquito Coast jumping-off point, and Clayton shared that concern.

In his modestly furnished reception room, the secretary of state listened intently to the business tycoon and the lawyer. Clayton and White were members of the same political party, the liberal-minded Whigs, and had been members of Congress at the same time—White had represented Indiana in the House of Representatives prior to his recent move to New York. As for Vanderbilt, Clayton did not know him personally, but he knew of him. Who in America then didn't?

Unschooled Vanderbilt may have been—he left school at the age of eleven to work as a laborer on vessels plying the East River. But he was notoriously street-smart. "If I had learned education," Vanderbilt once said, "I would not have had time to learn anything else."[5] Vanderbilt wrote nothing down, reputedly keeping every detail of his business dealings in his head, and at any given time knew his income and expenditures down to the last cent. So, while the colorful businessman might inject a curse word or two into every sentence, what he had to say was of keen interest to the secretary of state.

Vanderbilt spoke of California and the gold rush. Only a small percentage of the thousands of Americans and immigrants from Europe flooding west with the hope of making their fortunes in California made the journey overland in covered wagons. Their route cut through dangerous Native American homelands and clawed over treacherous mountain passes and took as long as six months. Hundreds of travelers died each year as a result of accidents, exposure, starvation, or Indian attacks. The alternative route was by sea. Some sailed down to the bottom of South America, rounded Cape Horn, then sailed up the Pacific side to California. The graceful clipper *Flying Cloud,* the largest American merchant ship built to that time, would in 1851 set a new record of eighty-nine days for the voyage from New York to San Francisco via Cape Horn. This sea route was quicker than the Oregon Trail, and safer. But it was expensive, costing six hundred dollars a head for a one-way ticket, in steerage, the cheapest and most uncomfortable class of ocean travel.

Several American shipping companies had spotted another way to cash in on the California gold rush. For the past two years, the shipping line operated by George Law, and the Pacific Mail and Steamship Company—

known as the Pacific Mail Line—headed by William Aspinwall, had been running steamer services to and from the United States and Panama, which was then part of Colombia. Law's United States Mail Company, operating as the U.S. Mail Line, had a contract from the U.S. government to carry the U.S. mails to and from Panama and the East Coast. Aspinwall's line, which had steamships running on the Pacific side and conveyed passengers from Panama to San Francisco, had the U.S. mail contract from Panama to San Francisco. A third operator, Charles Morgan, had ships of his Empire City Line on the route from New Orleans to Panama, via Cuba.

Six hundred dollars would take you, via Cuba, from New York to Chagres on the east coast of Panama; put you on a horse or mule; take you on a weeklong trek across the Panamanian isthmus along muddy tracks and over flooding rivers, hopefully avoiding local bandits; and then, on the Pacific side, put you aboard another steamer, which conveyed you up to San Francisco, with refueling stops at Acapulco or Mazatlan along the way. This route took just four weeks. Six hundred dollars was the equivalent of several years' salary for a laborer, yet thousands of passengers were lining up to take the Panama route to "Californy," as Cornelius Vanderbilt called it.[6] William Aspinwall also intended to build a railroad across Panama; Aspinwall's engineering team, headed by John L. Stephen, was at this very moment surveying the route.

This was where Cornelius Vanderbilt came in. He'd run ferries up and down the Hudson River and across New York Harbor to Staten Island before graduating to large side-wheel ocean steamers. He could easily put existing ships onto the California trade, could quickly have new ships built. But, he told Secretary Clayton, he would not use the Panama route. And he scoffed at the six hundred dollars being charged by the operators who did use Panama.

"I can improve on that," Vanderbilt assured Clayton, spreading a map of Central America in front of them. "I can make money at three hundred dollars, crossing my passengers by Lake Nicaragua, a route six hundred miles shorter."[7]

It wasn't just California passengers the Commodore was after. Vanderbilt wanted the U.S. mail contracts—jointly worth $365,000 a year, or several hundred million dollars in today's money. He could also see an even larger pot of gold in the future. Vanderbilt tapped his map, pointing to Nicaragua, or "Nicaraguey," as he called it.[8] Vanderbilt proposed to build a canal across the country—in fact, two short canals, combining them with the existing waterways, Lake Nicaragua, the largest lake in Central America, and the San Juan River. Just twelve miles of land on the west coast separated the lake and the Pacific. A large lock would be necessary in the twelve-mile west coast canal to bring vessels down to sea level from the lake, which was ninety-five feet above sea level. The task on the eastern seaboard would be more challenging, for via several sets of rapids, the San Juan River dropped in stages from Lake Nicaragua to the Caribbean. Vanderbilt proposed to build an eighty-mile-long canal from the Mosquito Coast, to join the San Juan above the rapids, with several locks along the way.

Vanderbilt told Clayton he wanted exclusive rights from the Nicaraguan government to build his canals across Nicaragua. In the meantime, he said, he would run steamships to and from Nicaragua from New York and San Francisco, conveying his passengers up the San Juan and across Lake Nicaragua by river and lake steamers and across the twelve-mile stretch from the lake to the Pacific by mule. This would cut hundreds of miles and several days off the journey from New York to San Francisco.

The secretary of state wanted an American company to build any Nicaraguan canal and so was warm to Vanderbilt's request that the U.S. government support his bid to win exclusive rights from the Nicaraguan authorities. This would serve both of Clayton's Central American objectives: excluding the British and expanding American interests. Already, Clayton was thinking about how to use the Vanderbilt initiative in planned talks with the British government. Although the secretary of state told Vanderbilt he would think on the proposal for a time, Vanderbilt and White returned to New York confident that their Nicaragua plan would receive government backing.

At around the time that Vanderbilt and White met with the secretary of state in Washington, in New Orleans, a city that had just experienced a deadly cholera epidemic, another American was overcome with grief. William Walker was a boyishly handsome twenty-four-year-old. Five foot seven, wiry, with dark hair and piercing gray eyes, he was the editor of the

Daily Crescent, a New Orleans newspaper making a name for itself crusading against crime and corruption in Louisiana. Walker's fiancée of twelve months, Ellen Martin, had just died in the cholera outbreak, her fever culminating in fatal "congestion" according to attending physician, Dr. Kennedy.[9] Walker was mortified. The epidemic seemed to have passed when Ellen fell ill. Walker, a qualified doctor himself after studying medicine in the United States, France, Germany, and Britain, had been unable to save the woman he loved. Ellen's death would shape the rest of his life.

Walker was born in Nashville, Tennessee, in 1824. His father, James Walker, a native of Glasgow, Scotland, had migrated to the United States after his uncle died and left him a dry-goods business in Nashville. James had made a success of that small business, using it as the foundation of a highly profitable insurance company. The wealthy young Scotsman had subsequently married local girl Mary Norvell. Her family, considered one of Nashville's best, could trace its lineage back to seventeenth-century English colonists who founded Williamsburg, Virginia. Mary's father, Lipscombe Norvell, served as a lieutenant under George Washington during the Revolutionary War, and her brother John Norvell was a former U.S. senator and founder of the *Pennsylvania Inquirer* newspaper in Philadelphia (which became the *Philadelphia Inquirer* in 1860). James Walker built his bride a brick mansion in the best part of Nashville, and there they'd raised their children— three boys, including William, and a girl, Alice.

James Walker was a member of the Disciples of Christ, a Protestant sect whose members lived their lives according to strict biblical interpretation. He had expected eldest son William to become a minister of the church, but the boy had other ideas. Mary Walker had been ailing for several years, and the local physicians were unable to diagnose her condition. Devoted to his mother, William determined to become a doctor and cure his mother's mystery illness. He had started reading and writing while very young and consumed books from the family's well-stocked bookshelves, often reading aloud to his bedridden mother. By age twelve, William had mastered Greek and Latin, and his father took him to the University of Nashville, proposing that the boy be admitted. When skeptical college authorities put the boy to the test, young William effortlessly translated the Latin tests of Caesar's *Commentaries* and Cicero's *Orations* and did the same with Greek passages of the New Testament. Twelve-year-old William was admitted to the university and, two years later, graduated *summa cum laude*. He had already begun to read medicine with the family's physician, and within months of graduating, he moved to Philadelphia, home of his uncle, newspaper publisher John Norvell. At fourteen, William enrolled at the medical school of the University of Pennsylvania, and by eighteen, William Walker had his M.D. Not satisfied with that, young Dr. Walker set off for Europe to further his studies.

After a year at the Medical Faculty of the University of Paris, Walker took himself to Heidelberg in Germany, another leading center of medical instruction, attending lectures from top German doctors and participating in fencing contests. He emerged skilled at both saving life and taking it. During his time in Europe, too, Walker added French, German, and Spanish to the languages in which he was fluent. In Scotland, he attended lectures at the University of Edinburgh, which had been made famous by the likes of Joseph Lister, an early proponent of the use of vaccination against infectious disease.

Walker had arrived back in Nashville a highly skilled physician, only to find his mother on her deathbed. Despite all his training, Walker was unable to save her; Mary Walker died soon after. Devastated, Walker set off for New Orleans. With his faith in medicine destroyed by his mother's death, Walker threw himself into legal studies and, with the help of tutor Edmund Randolph, whose grandfather had been George Washington's attorney general, obtained a law degree within two years. He had not long been practicing law in New Orleans as Randolph's partner when he was approached by local businessmen A. H. Haynes and J. C. McClure. Intending to set up a new daily newspaper, the *Crescent,* the pair proposed that Walker come in as a partner and the paper's editor.

By this time, Walker's best friend Edmund Randolph had introduced him to a beautiful local girl, Ellen Galt Martin. A year younger than Walker, with silky dark hair and an angelic face punctuated by large eyes and a small, pert mouth, Ellen was reputedly the belle of New Orleans. Scarlet fever at the age of five had left her totally deaf, but her affluent parents, leading members of New Orleans society, had sent her to a special school in Pennsylvania, where she had received an excellent education and been taught the new sign language for the deaf recently introduced into the United States from

France. Ellen, who had grown into a dark-eyed beauty, had a lively mind and was determined to socialize despite her deafness. She had gone to balls and parties equipped with a tiny pad and a pencil, with which, said a family member, she would "exchange lively repartee with many" a budding suitor.[10]

And then William Walker came along. With his facility for languages, Walker quickly made himself fluent in sign language. Ellen lived at home with her widowed mother, Clarinda Glasgow Martin, who welcomed the accomplished and gentlemanly young Tennesseean, especially when she saw how devoted and tender Walker was with her daughter. Ellen and Walker became virtually inseparable, and Ellen encouraged him to take on the editorship of the *Crescent*. Quite probably influenced by his newspaperman

mightier than either the scalpel or the gavel, became a newspaper editor. Among his staff members was a young Walt Whitman.

With Walker at the helm, the *Crescent* gained a strong readership with its liberal stance. Walker particularly relished taking on corrupt politicians, judges, and police. One of his stinging editorials condemned proslavery North Carolina senator and former U.S. vice president, John C. Calhoun: "We do not rank among his admirers."[11] Walker himself had been raised in a household where slavery was abhorred—James Walker had employed several free blacks for many years, and on the *Crescent*'s pages, his son expressed the belief that slavery should be abolished in the United States, state by state.

Ellen had proudly supported Walker's crusades, even when they twice led to challenges to duels from affronted New Orleans power brokers. One challenge even led him to the field of combat, where Walker and his opponent each fired a single shot before walking away unhurt and with honor intact. Walker had been devoted to Ellen, just as he had been devoted to his mother. Ellen was a Catholic, and on the day in 1848 that they had become engaged, she gave William a gold crucifix on a chain. He would wear it around his neck until the day he died.

For weeks following Ellen's death, Walker could not bring himself to write a word for the *Crescent*. But eventually, to escape his grief, the embittered twenty-five-year-old threw himself into his work, never imagining that before too many years had passed, he would be the most famous man in

America, with people calling him "Mr. President." Or that he would take on Cornelius Vanderbilt in an unparalleled duel for power.

It seems that in August, Secretary of State Clayton tipped off Cornelius Vanderbilt, via old friend Joseph White, that the secretary was about to send a new ambassador to Central America to negotiate a treaty between the United States and Nicaragua. The treaty would, among other things, give exclusive rights to an American company to build a canal across Nicaragua.

On August 27 in New York City, while the new ambassador, Ephraim George Squier, a twenty-seven-year-old journalist and archaeologist, was en route to Nicaragua, Cornelius Vanderbilt signed a contract as president of the newly formed Atlantic and Pacific Ship Canal Company. Lawyer and fellow director Joseph L. White also signed, as did the company's vice president, Daniel B. Allen, a Vanderbilt son-in-law. Another director was a prominent New York businessman, Nathaniel J. Wolfe.

Joseph White immediately gave the signed contract, which was to become known as the Transit charter, to his brother Colonel David L. White and sent him hurrying off to Nicaragua with it. On reaching Granada, the Nicaraguan capital, Colonel White was welcomed by the government, which was worried about the British presence on the Mosquito Coast; an American presence in their small country would, they hoped, counter British expansionism. In March, the Nicaraguan government had attempted to negotiate a canal treaty with David Brown, a representative of the New York and New Orleans Steam Navigation Company. But the British consul general to Central America, Frederick Chatfield, who was based in nearby Guatemala, thwarted the contract by warning the Nicaraguan government that Britain would deny Nicaragua the right to grant concessions in territory that did not belong to it—reminding the Nicaraguans that, apart from the new British-sponsored Mosquito Shore Protectorate, both Costa Rica and Honduras had long-standing claims to parts of the Mosquito Coast.

While the Nicaraguans didn't want to be dominated by any foreign power, they preferred to get into bed with economic powerhouse America rather than empire-building Britain. So, in desperation, Nicaraguan envoy Buenaventura Selva was sent to negotiate a treaty with Elijah Hise, the American chargé d'affaires in Guatemala City. On June 21, although possessing no authority from Washington to do so, Hise had signed a treaty between the United States and Nicaragua. Hise and Selva also signed a secret agreement, which became known as the Hise-Selva Convention; this gave the American government or any company it endorsed a monopoly on a canal in Nicaragua. Hise sent the two agreements to Washington, but Secretary Clayton would not submit them to Congress for ratification. Instead, the secretary sent new U.S. envoy Squier to negotiate a treaty incorporating terms that were acceptable to Clayton and to Cornelius Vanderbilt.

government. Article 35 of the treaty preserved the exclusive right of an American company to build a canal across Nicaragua. Within days, as if by coincidence, Colonel David White arrived in Granada while ambassador Squier was still in town, bearing the Atlantic and Pacific Ship Canal Company contract for canal and transit rights.

The contract provided for an immediate payment of $10,000 (several million in today's dollars) to the Nicaraguan treasury, plus $200,000 in canal company stock and $10,000 a year until construction was completed. The contract required the canal to be built within twelve years, and once it was operational, the Nicaraguan government would receive 20 percent of net profits. After eighty-five years, ownership of the canal would pass to the Nicaraguan government.[12] Unafraid of Britain now that they had a treaty with the United States, the Nicaraguans signed without hesitation, giving Cornelius Vanderbilt the exclusive right to build and operate his Nicaraguan canal.

Early in 1850, the enormity of the task of raising the money to build the canal, which, if it proceeded, would be one of the largest civil engineering projects in the world up to that time, caused Vanderbilt and his directors to send Colonel White back to Granada to negotiate a slight amendment. This provided exclusive rights for the Canal Company or a company authorized by it "to construct a rail road, or rail and carriage road, and water communication between the two oceans" and to convey passengers via that route from ocean to ocean.[13] In return, the Nicaraguan government was guaranteed 10 percent of the annual net profits from that trans-Nicaragua operation. While in Granada, Colonel White registered a new company, the Accessory Transit Company, with Cornelius Vanderbilt as president.

In Washington, Clayton began a series of long and sometimes rocky negotiations over Central America with the new British ambassador to Washington, Sir Henry L. Bulwer. Clayton was aided at times during the negotiations by his lawyer friend Joseph L. White, who, according to the press, played "a very conciliatory part throughout."[14] While these negotiations continued, the Canal Company hosted a dinner in New York at which the Nicaraguan chargé d'affaires to the United States, Eduardo Carcache, was guest of honor. Vanderbilt's son-in-law and company vice president, Daniel Allen, presided, and Joseph L. White gave the keynote speech, lauding the canal project as if it was a fait accompli.

After the U.S.-British negotiation reached mid-March without a resolution, President Zachary Taylor denounced the British government in a March 19 message to Congress and sent the Senate several pertinent documents, including the previously secret and unratified Hise-Selva Convention. By early April, with the United States seemingly about to break off negotiations, the pragmatic Sir Henry Bulwer came to see the positive side of the Canal Company's contract with the Nicaraguans. Bulwer expressed the view that the prospects of building a Nicaragua canal would be vastly improved with an injection of British capital, and he encouraged Clayton to urge the Canal Company to seek British financial support. Clayton, seeing the diplomatic benefits of such a concession, agreed, and treaty drafting began.

The secretary of state and the British ambassador signed the Clayton-Bulwer Treaty on April 19, 1850. That treaty provided a "Convention for facilitating and protecting the construction of a ship canal between the Atlantic and Pacific Oceans," and recognized the primacy of the contract between the Atlantic and Pacific Ship Canal Company and the government of Nicaragua. But there was an important condition—within one year, Vanderbilt's company must show its good intentions regarding the project, or lose its rights in Nicaragua. In addition, the United States and Great Britain agreed not to fortify, colonize, or settle in Central America and agreed that the ports used as the Caribbean and Pacific termini of the planned canal would be free ports, with no customs duties, and that both countries would act as middlemen in any regional territorial disputes that might frustrate the canal project. Both sides also agreed not to allow the relations that either country might have with political entities of the region to interfere with the canal project.

The Clayton-Bulwer Treaty was a total victory for Cornelius Vanderbilt and his business partners. The New York *Herald* saw the fingerprints of Van-

"concocted" by White and foisted on a "weak" and "ignorant" Clayton.[15] Clayton denied having been influenced by White or anyone else, but Vanderbilt knew who to thank for his new Nicaraguan gold mine—he would give the names *John M. Clayton* and *Sir Henry L. Bulwer* to two steel-hulled stern-wheel river steamers he ordered from Wilmington boat-builders Harlan and Hollingsworth for use in Nicaragua.

To meet treaty requirements and ensure the continued backing of the U.S. and British governments, Vanderbilt dispatched Colonel White to Panama to buy a river steamer, which White was then to take to the San Juan and use on a survey of the river. Vanderbilt also engaged Colonel O. W. Childs, a highly respected engineer responsible for recently enlarging the Erie Ship Canal, to conduct a detailed feasibility study for the trans-Nicaragua canal, requiring engineering plans and an estimate for the cost of construction and for operating the completed waterway by the following April. This would allow Vanderbilt to comply with the deadline set down by the Clayton-Bulwer Treaty for evidence of the Canal Company's good intent.

In June, Colonel White, who had arrived at Greytown in the newly acquired Panamanian river steamer *Orus,* obtained permission from James Green, the British consul at Greytown, for the Canal Company to set up a depot on Punta Arenas, a point of land on the southern side of the mouth of the San Juan River. Stocks of coal and equipment were soon ferried to Punta Arenas from Greytown.

When, on August 5, the SS *Prometheus,* the first of several new ocean steamers commissioned by Vanderbilt for the planned Nicaragua run, slid down the stocks of the New York shipyard of Vanderbilt's nephew Jeremiah Simonson, and took to the water, there could be no doubting the Commodore's seriousness about his Nicaraguan venture. In late September, Vanderbilt and Joseph White set off for England by transatlantic steamer. Arriving on October 5, they conducted a whirlwind series of meetings. In one of those meetings, British foreign secretary, Lord Palmerston, promised every assistance from the British government on the canal project. Palmerston also guaranteed that, in accordance with the Clayton-Bulwer Treaty, customs duties currently levied on every merchant ship that dropped anchor at Greytown would be abolished. The foreign secretary kept his word, at the end of that month issuing to Her Majesty's Consul James Green at Greytown an instruction that duties must cease to be imposed there, beginning next January 1.[16]

Vanderbilt and White also met with numerous financiers to discuss British investment in the canal project. Bankers including Lord Percy, the Rothschilds, and the Baring brothers gave the pair cordial hearings, and on September 15, the *Times* of London announced that satisfactory financial arrangements for the canal had been completed by the two Americans.[17] In reality, Vanderbilt and White returned to the United States empty-handed; the British money men, while interested in the canal project, would not make any commitment to finance it until they had assessed the results of Colonel Childs's feasibility study.

But Vanderbilt wasn't waiting. His contract with the Nicaraguans permitted him to carry passengers across Nicaragua at once, and he intended making money out of the right without delay. In the second week of December, with the two giant paddlewheels on her sides churning, the brand new *Prometheus* steamed out of New York, towing an equally brand new river steamer, the side-wheeler *Director,* another product of the Simonson yard. The *Prometheus* turned south. Apart from her crew, she carried just a single passenger, her owner, Cornelius Vanderbilt. The purpose of the voyage was so secret that not even Vanderbilt's wife, Sophia, knew that her husband had left town, let alone where he was going. Left to spend Christmas with her thirteen children and their spouses, Sophia only learned where Cornelius was three weeks later, in a letter from her husband that reached her via Panama.

Vanderbilt was on a mission. The news from Colonel David White in Nicaragua had not been good. The little steamer *Orus* had been wrecked on rapids in the San Juan River. The rapids were impassable, said a frustrated Colonel White, who declared that the Commodore's dream of conveying passengers up the river to the lake was unrealizable. Cornelius Vanderbilt would see about that. He would not let a few rocks stand in the way of making a fortune in Nicaragua.

❦ 1 ❦

GUN-BARREL DIPLOMACY

ON THE LAST DAY OF DECEMBER 1850, IN THE BAY OFF THE RAMSHACKLE settlement of Greytown on Nicaragua's Caribbean shore, the shiny new fifteen hundred–ton ocean steamer SS *Prometheus* dragged at anchor like an eager puppy straining at the leash. The *Prometheus* had a wooden hull, two decks, two masts, and two central steam engines that drove the massive paddlewheels on her sides. She had been launched just eleven weeks back, and this shakedown run to Nicaragua's Mosquito Coast had been her maiden voyage. It was a nine-day trip made with just a single passenger, the *Prometheus*'s owner, shipping magnate Cornelius Vanderbilt—"the Commodore," as he was known to friend and foe.

Up on the ship's main deck, tall, gray-haired, handsome Vanderbilt was cursing loudly. That was not unusual; every sentence that came out of his mouth was generally peppered with a cussword or two, even when he was happy. But today, the Commodore was a far-from-happy man. The *Prometheus* was all Vanderbilt's; he'd paid the hundreds of thousands of dollars she cost to build out of his own pocket. And by Vanderbilt's estimation, she was costing him five thousand dollars a day just sitting here doing nothing while his engineers thrashed around the rapids up the San Juan River like timid children at the beach.[1]

For a week, Colonel David White and Vanderbilt's engineers had been aboard the river steamer *Director*, trying to force a passage over numerous sets of rapids that stood like walls in their path on the San Juan. To open up a passenger route from the Caribbean to Lake Nicaragua, those rapids had to be conquered. But White had returned defeated; it couldn't be done, he said.

16

Vanderbilt had endured enough of this child's play. "I'm going up to the lake, without any more fooling!" he declared.[2]

He had several lengths of stout rope loaded onto the river steamer *Director*, which was moored alongside her larger sister ship, then clambered down the ladder to the *Director* and took charge. He had designed the *Director* especially for the San Juan, with a shallow draught and a solid oak hull. She had two decks; the upper deck was open to the elements, but a canvas awning made it comfortable for passengers. Fully loaded, the *Director* could accommodate 150 passengers, but for this mission, she would carry just thirty—the Commodore, White and his engineers, the *Director*'s crew, and some brawny members of the *Prometheus*'s crew, hand-picked by Vanderbilt. With her thirty-horsepower steam engine driving her paddlewheels, the *Director* pulled away from the *Prometheus*, turned her prow west, and, parting the thick, humid air, left the ocean steamer, the cove, and Greytown behind.

Entering the world of the jungle, the *Director* chugged up the silent, green-brown San Juan River. A passenger on the San Juan a little over a year later described the scene that met Vanderbilt's eyes as he headed inland: "The banks of the river were one dense, impenetrable jungle of trees, with vines intertwining their branches. Alligators could be seen watching their chances for prey, lizards climbing in the branches of the trees, at least four feet long, flights of parrots screaming at the tops of their voices."[3]

The further she went up the river, the more the *Director*'s progress was impeded by an increasingly strong current. But after several hours, she rounded a bend, and her passengers were met by the sight of the Machuca Rapids and the old Panamanian riverboat *Orus*, sitting where Colonel White had left her months before, wedged between the rocks in the middle of the rapids. Vanderbilt ignored the *Orus*; someone else could salvage her. The Commodore's time was money, and that time was otherwise engaged.

One of the engineers on board the *Director* later told the New York *Herald*: "The Commodore insisted upon 'jumping' all the obstacles, and tied down the safety valve, put on all steam, and compelled the little steamer to scrape and struggle over the obstructions and into clear water again."[4] With Vanderbilt at the controls, the *Director*, looking like some strange dinosaur, literal walked over the rocks, using her paddlewheels for feet. With the engineer shaking their heads in wonderment, the *Director* made it over the Machca Rapids.

The expedition met a much more formidable obstacle farther upriver, at the Castillo Rapids. Overlooking the surging rapids from atop a grassy hill stood an abandoned two-hundred-year-old Spanish fortress. At the foot of the hill lay the village of El Castillo—just twenty huts with roofs of thatched palm leaf. Not even Cornelius Vanderbilt could jump these rapids; here, the river dropped eight feet in as many rocky yards. Yet the Commodore was undaunted; he showed his companions one of the tricks he'd learned during fifty years in the river navigation business. The ropes were broken out; one end was attached to trees upstream, the other to a capstan on the boat. With the *Director* lightened of all but essential hands, with everyone else in the surging water putting their shoulders to the hull, and with the engine straining, the *Director* was "warped" up and over the "impassable" rapids, to the astonishment of barefoot native Indians watching from the shore. Reloaded, the boat continued on her way northwest up the San Juan, as the sun went down ahead of it.

In moonlit darkness, the party reached the final obstacle, the Torro Rapids. These rapids were not as formidable as the last, and, as he had at the Machuca Rapids, Vanderbilt slowly, laboriously "jumped" the rocks in the *Director*, following the least craggy course, close to the shore. In clear water once more, the little craft steamed a dozen more placid river miles west, passing through country that was hilly but less wild than that below the rapids; here bananas and oranges were seen growing.

As dawn broke behind it, the *Director* drew level with San Carlos, "a small village, containing twenty or twenty-five houses, or huts, made of poles, covered with palm," which occupied the northern bank of the river.[5] Like El Castillo, San Carlos had an old, ruined Spanish fortification on a hill above. The fort was occupied by white-clad Nicaraguan soldiers, who looked down from their vantage point in surprise as the steamer chugged by. San Carlos sat at the head of the river, where it drained from Lake Nicaragua, a vast expanse of water 110 miles long from north to south and 31 miles across, covering more than 3,000 square miles. The Spanish had called it Mar Duce, the Freshwater Sea, but according to legend, the locals had named it after Nicaroa, long ago a chief of an Indian tribe that lived on the lake shores. It was the lake that in turn gave Nicaragua its name.

Cheers rose from Vanderbilt's companions as the *Director* steamed out onto the lake. It was New Year's Day 1851, and Cornelius Vanderbilt had just piloted the first steam-powered vessel to have negotiated the entire 119-mile length of the San Juan River and reached Lake Nicaragua from the Caribbean Sea. Not for the first time in his life, or the last, Vanderbilt had said that something could be done and then had gone out and proven it. In the process, he opened up the way to California via Nicaragua—a path that would soon be followed by tens of thousands of his countrymen.

In San Francisco, on January 12, less than two weeks after Cornelius Vanderbilt conquered the San Juan River in Nicaragua, two men stood facing each other on Mission Road armed with revolvers, waiting to commence firing at one another. One combatant was Will Hicks Graham, a fiery local official. The other was William Walker, former editor of the New Orleans *Crescent*.

Walker had come to California the previous year, sailing from New Orleans for Panama aboard the Law Line's SS *Ohio* on June 15.[6] The New Orleans *Crescent* had gone out of business by the summer of 1850, and Walker had followed his good friend and law partner Edmund Randolph to booming San Francisco. Here, Randolph had set up a law practice, and as soon as Walker arrived in San Francisco after a rough passage via Panama, the editor had looked up his friend. Randolph had subsequently introduced Walker to John Nugent, a director of Toy, Nugent and Company. Just weeks before Walker's arrival, the company had begun publishing the *San Francisco Herald*, one of seven new newspapers to go on sale in San Francisco in 1850. Nugent, a fiery young Irishman, was the paper's editor, but, impressed with Walker and his newspaper background and liberal views, Nugent had immediately employed him as his coeditor.

Just several months after this, Lieutenant George Crook, fresh out of the U.S. Military Academy at West Point, would pass through San Francisco on the way to join his West Point roommate Lieutenant Philip Sheridan at their new posting in Oregon. Crook said that the gold rush had made San Francisco unlike any city on earth at the time: "It was hard to realize I was in the United States. Everything was excitement and bustle, prices were most exorbitant, common laborers received much higher wages than officers of the Army." It was a melting pot of humanity: "People had flocked there from all parts of the world; all nationalities were represented there. Sentiments and ideas were so liberal and expanded that they were almost beyond bounds." In other words, vice and corruption abounded. "Money was so plentiful amongst citizens that it was but lightly appreciated," said Crook, who, like his friend Sheridan, would go on to become a famous U.S. Army general.[7]

Newspapermen William Walker and John Nugent quickly stirred up a hornet's nest in San Francisco. The town had grown from a population of eight hundred in 1847, prior to the gold rush, to fifty thousand. San Francisco's infrastructure struggled to cope, and crime was rampant. A vigilante group would soon take the law into its own hands, lynching two men in one of San Francisco's main streets for all the world to see. Walker and Nugent pulled no punches when it came to blaming town officials and members of the judiciary for permitting the crime wave, and Will Hicks Graham had taken such umbrage at what Walker had written about him in the *San Francisco Herald* that he challenged him to a duel, and Walker accepted the challenge.

Had the chosen weapons been swords, Walker, a skilled swordsman after fencing training in Nashville and Germany, would have made mincemeat of his opponent. But this was the West, and here a man used a gun to settle differences. In New Orleans, Walker had fought a gentlemanly duel with single-shot dueling pistols. But this was not starchy New Orleans; here, five-shooters and six-shooters were the common weapons of choice.

Graham's idea of a duel was that you kept blazing away at your opponent until he went down. Only then would Graham feel satisfied. So, watched from a distance by a large crowd, the pair stood with loaded Colt Dragoon .44 revolvers at their sides. No Hollywood quick-draw nonsense here. On the word of the referee, they would raise their gleaming Samuel Colts and open fire. Perhaps disconcertingly for Graham, a crack shot, William Walker showed no fear as they prepared to do battle; his gray eyes were clear and intense, his face impassive. There was a fearlessness about Walker that would characterize the rest of his life. It was as if, ever since the death of Ellen Martin, the love of his life, he didn't care whether he lived or died.

The referee raised a hand containing a handkerchief. The crowd fell silent. "Upon my signal, gentlemen," said the referee. He dropped his hand. "Fire!"

Up came the two heavy revolvers. Trigger fingers flexed. Both men fired at the same time. Walker missed with his round but immediately took a .44 slug in the leg. Walker staggered, then straightened; he refused to go down voluntarily. Steely-eyed, again he raised his pistol. Graham cursed. Again both men fired. Walker was hit a second time in the leg, which collapsed under him. He went down. His second, lawyer Edmund Randolph, a tall, handsome Virginia native not many years older than Walker, strode over to him, concern flooding his face. The referee called to Graham to put up his weapon. Graham turned and walked away, and the crowd surged around the downed man to see how gravely he'd been hurt.

Walker was lucky; his wounds were not serious. In September, Graham would fight a duel with another opponent, outside the military barracks at Benicia. After seven shots were fired, Graham's adversary, George F. Lemon, would go down seriously wounded. The following year, Walker's boss and coeditor John Nugent would fight two duels; in the second, with a U.S. senator for California, the duelists would face off armed with rifles, and one of Nugent's arms would be shattered in the exchange, terminating his dueling career.[8]

Twelve weeks after Walker's duel with Graham, an angry crowd of four thousand San Francisco residents surrounded the county jail, demanding the release of the coeditor of the *San Francisco Herald*, who had been lodged inside for refusing to pay a fine. That coeditor was William Walker. He had recovered from the wounds he had suffered in the gunfight only to find himself in a duel of a different kind with San Francisco judge Eli Parsons, with words for weapons. The judge had told a grand jury that "the press is a nuisance."[9] Walker answered this with a stinging attack on the judge in the *Herald*. In response, Parsons had Walker arrested and hauled before the court, found him guilty of contempt of court, and levied a fine of five hundred dollars. Walker, on principle, refused to pay, so the judge put him behind bars.

Walker quickly became such a popular figure in San Francisco, with his views widely shared by locals and with his courage much admired, that these thousands of supporters turned out to demand his release and to demand Judge Parson's impeachment. Meanwhile, Walker's friend Edmund Randolph, a clever and charismatic attorney, had no trouble quickly convincing another judge to issue a writ of habeas corpus. Walker was released to appear in the Superior Court. There, on constitutional grounds that protected the freedom of the press, the presiding judge found that Judge Parsons had erred in convicting Walker. To the cheers of his thousands of supporters, crusading William Walker emerged from the San Francisco courthouse a free man.

Cornelius Vanderbilt was experiencing a standoff of his own. It was late November, and the SS *Prometheus* again lay at anchor on San Juan Bay, off Greytown, Nicaragua. On the ship's bridge, Vanderbilt and the master of the *Prometheus*, Captain Henry Churchill, were being confronted by a stubborn British official and a party of armed Greytown police.

Back on July 14, Vanderbilt had inaugurated the first services to and from California via Nicaragua, sailing aboard the *Prometheus* that day as she set out from New York bound for Greytown and crowded with passengers on their way to San Francisco. Although the *Prometheus* had been ready for business in January, the Commodore had waited several months to launch his Nicaragua service, until more new ocean steamers designed, commissioned, and financed by him had come rumbling down the stocks of New York and Boston shipbuilders.

By late spring, Vanderbilt had been able to send his new SS *Pacific* and SS *Independence* around the cape to California, to operate from Long Wharf at the bottom of San Francisco's Sacramento Street along with the chartered SS *Monumental City*. Meanwhile, Vanderbilt already had the *Prometheus* and yet another new ship, the SS *Daniel Webster*, operating from Number 2 Pier on New York's North River (as the lower Hudson River was then known).

When his new steamers, the *Northern Light* and *Star of the West*, were launched in the new year, they would join the Vanderbilt fleet on the Atlantic run. In 1852, Vanderbilt would purchase the SS *Brother Jonathon* from Edward Mills and the SS *Samuel S. Lewis* from the failed New England Ocean Steamership Company, sending them both to San Francisco to operate on the Pacific run to Nicaragua.

With four steamers eventually servicing each side of Nicaragua, Vanderbilt aimed to offer intending passengers a departure from New York and San Francisco once every two weeks. During this same period, the Commodore had a number of river and lake steamers constructed in New York and on the Delaware River for service in Nicaragua. Like the *Director*, they had been progressively towed to Nicaragua—the 180-passenger stern-wheeler *Central America*, for example, went down with the *Prometheus* on her October 21 sailing, to become the largest steamer on Lake Nicaragua. Several more wooden river steamers had been built locally at the Punta Arenas depot across the bay from Greytown. Meanwhile, facilities had been thrown up along the land route across Nicaragua.

Once the service began in July, Vanderbilt and partner Joseph White took it in turn traveling on the line's sailings from New York to ensure that teething problems were ironed out. That's what brought Vanderbilt down to Greytown on the *Prometheus* on her most recent run from New York. And that was why he was present for what turned out to be a major international incident.

In the early afternoon on November 21, gray coal smoke wafted from the *Prometheus*'s pair of tall red funnels as she raised steam in preparation for getting under way for the return to New York. A Vanderbilt river steamer was alongside, disgorging baggage belonging to 510 New York–bound passengers who had just come across Nicaragua after sailing down from San Francisco aboard the SS *Pacific*. Among that baggage was sack after sack of California gold dust—$120,677 worth (the equivalent of tens of millions of modern-day dollars), consigned as freight bound for the U.S. Mint in New York, plus another $500,000 worth, which the *New York Times* estimated to be in the hands of the ship's passengers.[10]

A little after 1:00 P.M., Englishman Robert Coates, Greytown's port captain, or harbormaster, had clambered up the side of *Prometheus* from a rowboat, followed by a party of armed black policemen of the Greytown constabulary—Jamaicans, the sons of former slaves, these policemen were well-trained former soldiers from Britain's West Indian Regiment. On four previous occasions, Coates had demanded that the *Prometheus* pay harbor duties, and on each occasion, the ship's master had ignored him, quoting the Clayton-Bulwer Treaty, which made Greytown a free port. Coates and his constables made their way to the *Prometheus*'s bridge, where they found the steamer's master, Captain Churchill and owner Cornelius Vanderbilt. There, Coates handed Churchill a written demand for $123 in unpaid port duties, together with a "process of attachment": On the orders of his superior onshore, consul James Green, Coates intended to seize the *Prometheus*, which was worth some $300,000, until the $123 debt was paid.

"Let them seize the vessel, if they can," growled Cornelius Vanderbilt.[11]

Captain Churchill, who had only recently taken over command of the *Prometheus*, would later tell the *New York Times* that the port dues were, "we supposed, to be illegally demanded, and had consequently refused to pay them, as I did in this present instance."[12] Churchill asked the Englishman on whose authority he was acting.

"The city authorities of Greytown," Coates replied, "constituted by the authority of the Musketo [sic] King."[13]

Cornelius Vanderbilt shook his head. "I cannot nor will not recognize any authority here. And I will not pay unless I am made by force."[14] Turning to Captain Churchill, Vanderbilt instructed him to have these impudent fellows escorted from his American vessel.

Coates realized that he and his men were greatly outnumbered by the ship's crew and the American passengers—the vast majority of them hardened former gold miners who were all too ready to join in any fight with British officials. So Coates departed the steamer. Hurriedly rowing ashore, he reported to Consul Green. The consul immediately penned a note to Captain William Fead, master of the British brig-of-war *Express*, which was anchored in the cove, requiring him to provide the physical assistance of the Royal Navy in the collection of the outstanding port duties.[15]

In the meantime, Vanderbilt had ordered Churchill to get under way. Little more than a year before, Britain's foreign secretary had personally given Vanderbilt his word that port duties would not be charged at Greytown, and

Vanderbilt did not believe that Green had any authority to enforce his $123 demand, let alone involve the British navy. Green was in fact deliberately disobeying Lord Palmerston, possibly because the consul knew that Palmerston and his prime minister, Lord John Russell, were at odds—Palmerston would be forced to resign within weeks of this incident, over another matter—and Green believed that the prime minister would back the tough line he was taking with the American magnate.

Consul Green then had himself rowed out to the warship. According to the log of the *Express*, at 1:30, the *Prometheus* slipped her moorings.[16] With her two giant paddlewheels turning slowly, the steamer eased down the bay on the current entering from the San Juan River. The river steamer was still attached to the *Prometheus*'s side, like a limpet, as her crew frantically tried to complete the transfer of baggage before the big ship cleared the harbor. Five minutes after the steamer began to move, Green clambered aboard the *Express* and handed his note to Captain Fead. Once the British commander read the note, he gave orders for his vessel to get under way. Unlike the *Prometheus*, the warship could only rely on the wind for motive power; with a light onshore breeze behind her, she moved across San Juan Bay toward the steamship, but at the speed of a tortoise.

The steamer's rails were lined with passengers and crew, who watched the warship make a leisurely pursuit. Meanwhile, the river steamer was still attached to the *Prometheus*'s side, making it impossible for the larger vessel to make any speed. By two o'clock, the *Prometheus* had reached the mouth of the bay, with the *Express* just a quarter of a mile away and moving parallel with her. A British voice hailed from the warship, requiring the *Prometheus* to stop. Captain Churchill ignored him. Soon after, there was a puff of smoke from one of the brig's cannon. It was a harmless blank cartridge, a warning shot. Again Churchill took no notice. Now a voice called across the water, requiring the steamer to anchor. Still the master of the *Prometheus* treated Britain's Royal Navy with disdain.

There was another booming detonation. With a whoosh, a cannonball flew over the *Prometheus*'s forecastle. Captain Churchill looked up to see the projectile pass over his head, and estimated that it cleared the ship's wheelhouse by less than ten feet. There was a gasp from the shocked passengers. Moments later, another gun aboard the *Express* fired; this time,

Churchill later said, the cannonball "passed over the stern so near that the force of the ball was distinctly felt by several of the passengers."[17]

Begrudgingly, Vanderbilt ordered the *Prometheus*'s engines stopped, but he didn't drop anchor. As the *Prometheus* drifted toward the open sea, Vanderbilt sent a junior officer in the ship's quarter boat to the *Express*, "to inquire the cause of firing into us."[18]

"It was to protect the authorities of Greytown in their demands," Captain Fead informed the steamer's officer, with a nod toward Consul Green. "And if you do not immediately anchor I will fire a bomb-shell into you." As the *Prometheus*'s officer looked at him in disbelief, Fead gave orders to his gunnery officer: "Load the guns with grape and canister shot."[19]

After the American officer hurried back to Captain Churchill and the Commodore, both agreed they had no choice but to comply, rather than risk the lives of their passengers. So, with the river steamer completing her business and peeling away, the *Prometheus* proceeded under steam back to her original anchorage and compliantly dropped anchor. The *Express* followed, anchoring close by, still with her guns trained on the passenger ship. At 3:00 P.M., a small boat from the warship brought written instructions from Captain Fead, requiring Captain Churchill to extinguish his engine room fires. Shortly after, a victorious Robert Coates returned to the *Prometheus*, to again demand payment of the outstanding $123.

A New York *Herald* correspondent living at Greytown wrote that Commodore Vanderbilt, "having a large number of passengers on board, who had become very gritty at being brought up by 'John Bull,' came ashore, and paid the charges, under protest."[20] At four o'clock, once the money had been handed over, Captain Fead gave permission for the *Prometheus* to sail, and fifteen minutes later, the steamer weighed anchor and headed for the open sea.[21]

Vanderbilt was seething as his ship plowed north through the blue Caribbean, heading for a refueling stop at Havana on her ten-day voyage back to New York. That evening, he had Captain Churchill write a letter for delivery to the New York press the moment the ship reached home port, describing "the circumstances of the English brig of war *Express* firing into the *Prometheus*."[22] As soon as the *Prometheus* docked in New York, Vanderbilt called a meeting of the Atlantic and Pacific Ship Canal Company board. The board resolved to seek the aid of the U.S. State Department in guaranteeing the terms of the Clayton-Bulwer Treaty and urged John Clayton's successor as secretary of state, Daniel Webster, to send U.S. Navy ships to Greytown to enforce the treaty and to protect American shipping from British aggression.

After the news of the *Prometheus* incident broke in the United States, newspapers were up in arms that a British warship fired on an American passenger vessel and insulted the U.S. flag. If Britain did not make an apology and pay reparation, American papers demanded "application of the Jacksonian doctrine of retaliation and reprisals," as the New York *Herald* put it.[23]

Vanderbilt was determined to see the British reined in, but at the same time, he wanted to protect his immediate financial interests. So, on December 1, the same day that Joseph White wrote a strongly worded letter to the secretary of state on behalf of the Canal Company, calling for government action, Vanderbilt dictated a letter to the editor of the *New York Times*, which reported the next day, "A letter from Mr. Vanderbilt states that everything was quiet at San Juan del Norte (Greytown), and that no war, riot or disturbances of any kind existed on that route." A day later, Secretary Webster wrote to Abbott Lawrence, America's ambassador in London, instructing him to demand an unqualified apology from the British government for firing on the Vanderbilt ship.

On December 15, the U.S. Navy's Commodore Foxhall Parker was ordered to immediately sail for Greytown with the U.S. steam frigate *Saranac* and the sloop-of-war *Albany*. When Commodore Parker reached Greytown on January 1, he found Captain Fead's *Express* still in port, along with two other British warships, the steam frigate *Arrogant* and sloop-of-war *Calypso*. Parker learned that, when Cornelius Vanderbilt's SS *Daniel Webster* had arrived at Greytown earlier in December, it, too, had been forced to pay port duties under threat of the *Express*'s guns. Parker informed the Greytown town council that the United States would not tolerate the collection of port duties by the British navy.

But the feared confrontation between the ships of the two navies at Greytown did not happen. On the contrary, the opposing commanders showed each other extraordinary courtesy and even flew each other's colors as a mark of respect. "The most friendly feeling existed between the officers of both countries," the *New York Times* reported in its January 31 issue, under the headline "The Prometheus Difficulty Settled."[24]

The bilateral furor caused by the *Prometheus* incident prompted Captain Fead's superior, Vice Admiral George Seymour, to reprimand him for his actions. At the same time, the British embassy in Washington wrote to Consul Green, instructing him not to do anything that discriminated against the Canal Company, and the British foreign secretary formally apologized to the U.S. ambassador in London.

For the moment, a crisis had been averted. For the moment, the United States, and Cornelius Vanderbilt, had won the argument.

ᗘ 2 ᗘ

DOWN, BUT NOT OUT

I N THE DARKNESS OF THE EVENING OF MAY 20, 1853, THE *NORTH STAR,* the world's largest private steam yacht, cleaved through the waters of New York Harbor, heading for the Narrows and the sea. At twenty-three hundred tons and 270 feet long, she was larger than most ocean steamers. Delivered brand spanking new from Jeremiah Simonson's New York yard just weeks before, the *North Star* was even grander than the queen of England's royal yacht *Victoria and Albert,* which was less than half the American yacht's tonnage. The *North Star* had a saloon that extended over half the main deck and was decorated with satinwood relieved with rosewood. The ship's rosewood furniture, designed in the Louis XV style and covered with plush green velvet, had been made especially for her. The dining room, forward of the saloon, was lined with Pyrenees marble and Naples granite, while in the dining room ceiling there were portraits of Washington, Franklin, Webster, Clay, and other famous Americans. The staterooms, each a different color, were decorated with silk and lace.

The *North Star* was Cornelius Vanderbilt's private pleasure ship, his statement to the world that he had made it. The cost to build and fit her out, combined with the cost of the four-month cruise to Europe on which he and his family were now embarking, would total $500,000.[1] On this, her maiden voyage, she carried just twenty-three passengers. In addition to Vanderbilt and his wife, Sophia—who had convinced the Commodore to make this trip—those passengers included eleven of the thirteen Vanderbilt children and seven sons-in-law. Vanderbilt had even brought along his own physician, and a chaplain, John O. Choules. The minister would later say of the trip, "The Commodore did the swearing and I did the preaching, so we never disagreed."[2]

As Vanderbilt prepared to embark on this luxurious excursion, the first vacation he had ever taken in his life, he was asked by Jacob Van Pelt, a friend of fifty years standing, if he had "everything fixed"—meaning, were his investments in good enough shape to allow him to turn his back on business for such an extended period? Vanderbilt had nodded. "Van, I have got eleven millions invested better than any other eleven millions in the United States," he told his friend. "It is worth twenty-five per cent a year without any risk."[3]

To the astonishment of many observers, the Commodore had recently sold his controlling interest in the Atlantic and Pacific Ship Canal Company and the Accessory Transit Company, resigning as director and president of both. Yet no one could deny he had sold those shares exceptionally well, for the two companies had become the highest traded securities on Wall Street. Their value skyrocketed as the Nicaraguan Transit business proved hugely profitable for almost all concerned. Carrying two thousand passengers a month and billions of dollars' worth of gold as paying freight, it delivered Vanderbilt a personal profit of a million dollars (tens of millions in today's dollars) in just the first twelve months of operation, despite cutting its through fares to three hundred dollars to take passengers away from competitors that were using the Panama route.[4]

One party not making a large profit from the deal was the Nicaraguan government. It was receiving its annual fee of ten thousand dollars, as provided by the contract with Vanderbilt, but Nicaragua had not seen a penny of the specified 10 percent of profit. That was because Vanderbilt claimed there was no profit. He slyly billed everything possible to the Accessory Transit Company—the cost of Colonel Childs's canal survey, the cost of the trip Vanderbilt and Joseph White made to England seeking canal financing, even the mortgage payments of ships he had put on the Nicaragua run. In June, the Nicaraguan government had sent two commissioners, Gabriel Lacayo and Rafael Tejada, to the United States to demand payment of the outstanding commissions. The Transit Company had appointed two commissioners of its own to confer with Lacayo and Tejada, but when they met, on the advice of Transit Company general counsel Joseph White, the American representatives claimed that as the company was registered in

Nicaragua, there was nothing that U.S.-based officers of the company could do to help the Nicaraguan commissioners. U.S. ambassador to Central America at the time, Ephraim Squier, later described the Transit Company's dealings with the Nicaraguan government as "an infamous career of deception and fraud."[5]

Vanderbilt even sold his seven new ocean steamers to the Accessory Transit Company, for $1.4 million in cash and bonds; he no longer owned a single ship on the Nicaragua run. With Vanderbilt's withdrawal from the business, the Accessory Transit Company set up the Nicaragua Steamship Line to operate its ocean steamers. Transit Company director Charles Morgan was running the business, and Vanderbilt seemed to have lost all interest in Nicaragua. That attitude was attributed by many to the fact that the Canal Company had yet to raise the finance for the Nicaragua canal project. In April 1852, Colonel Childs had delivered his feasibility study, together with an estimate of $33 million to build the necessary canals, locks, and other facilities. British bankers the Baring brothers had not been impressed with Childs's report—they said his proposed canal was too expensive and too narrow for large vessels. The fees that the company would need to charge ships to make the canal a viable proposition would be too high and would scare off most shipping companies. Since then, other financiers had been equally dubious, and the canal project was very much in limbo.

Yet, Vanderbilt did not entirely sever his links with Nicaragua. He still had a minority shareholding in the Accessory Transit Company and was the largest holder of the company's bonds. He was still the New York shipping agent for the sale of tickets to and from Nicaragua, and in his absence overseas, his clerk Lambert Wardell would continue to invoice the company for 2.5 percent commission on every ticket to California sold in New York. And then there was the secret arrangement whereby Vanderbilt received 20 percent of the Transit operation's turnover, an arrangement that he, as company founder, expected to continue.

As the *North Star* glided by Staten Island in the May moonlight, rockets screamed from her deck and streaked into the night sky. The ship was even equipped with several small cannon, and these boomed a loud blank-cartridge salute. This was all in honor of Vanderbilt's mother. She lived there on Staten Island, in a little brown house. Staten Island was where Vanderbilt was born and raised, where he went to work at the age of eleven for his father. And it was through his half share in the Staten Island ferry, from Manhattan to the island, that he'd created the foundation of his fortune. He still had a financial interest in the New York and Staten Island Ferry Company, but just a year or so back he sold his ferries and most of his shares to competitor "Live Oak" George Law.

Vanderbilt himself had a large mansion on Staten Island. A three-minute walk from his mother's house, it was a showplace with a grand portico equipped with tall Corinthian columns. That house stood empty. His wife Sophia would have gladly lived out her days in its placid surrounds, but not the Commodore. When Cornelius built his Manhattan mansion at Washington Place in 1848, Sophia had hysterically refused to move from the island house she loved. So Vanderbilt put her in a private mental asylum for three months until she changed her mind. When Sophia's daughters warned her that their father was having an affair with a governess, Sophia quickly agreed to move to Washington Place. As much as Cornelius liked Staten Island, it was too far away from the city and too far away from the heartbeat of commerce—which made this European trip all the more surprising to most observers.

The *North Star* steamed on, past Sandy Hook and out into the Atlantic. In the wheelhouse, Captain Asa Eldridge set a course for Southampton, England. For the passengers relaxing in the palatial saloon below, ahead lay fifteen thousand miles of steaming and sixteen weeks of playing the part of curious rich American tourists in Europe. For Europeans, who had never seen the likes of them before, this American millionaire, his large family, and his fabulous yacht would also be curiosities.

And while the Commodore was away, his own business partners would stab him in the back.

On June 15, just weeks after Cornelius Vanderbilt sailed for England aboard the *North Star*, William Walker set sail from San Francisco aboard the chartered brig *Arrow*, heading south for Mexico. Walker had resigned from the *San Francisco Herald* to set up a law practice in Marysville, California, in partnership with Henry P. Watkins, and the two lawyers had been commissioned by California residents to negotiate with the governor of the Mexican state of Sonora to obtain land at Arispe for an American mining and cattle-raising colony.

Walker and Watkins came ashore at Guaymas on the Gulf of California on July 3. But the town's prefect, Captain Cayetano Navarro, and the port captain, Antonio Campuzano, were suspicious of the American duo. The Mexican officials sought instructions from the commandante general of Sonora, Manuel Maria Gandara, in Hermosillo, 150 miles to the north, at the same time forbidding the Americans to travel to the interior. Campuzano wrote to his superior: "Your Excellency will perceive that there is undoubtedly an intention to invade this portion of the Mexican territory," naming Walker as a principal promoter of this feared American invasion.[6] Commandante General Gandara responded by ordering the detention of Walker and Watkins.

Walker had a reputation for having a silver tongue. "He arrested your attention with the first word he uttered," said a San Franciscan who knew Walker at this time. "And as he proceeded, you felt convinced that he was no ordinary person. To a few confidential friends he was most enthusiastic upon the subject of his darling project."[7] The American consul in Guaymas, Juan A. Robinson, was won over by Walker and had become a convert to that project—an American colony in Sonora—and he argued strenuously with the local officials on behalf of the two Americans and kept them out of jail.

Commandante General Gandara suddenly changed his mind—he invited Walker and his colleague to come overland to see him in Hermosillo. But with Apaches rampaging close to Guaymas and massacring all the men at a nearby ranch, and with no Mexican escort on offer, Walker realized that such an invitation was calculated to lead to their deaths. He and Watkins boarded their vessel on July 16 to return to San Francisco.

Despite the failure of his mission, Walker had seen enough to believe that, in his own words, "a comparatively small body of Americans might gain a position on the Sonoran frontier . . . whether sanctioned or not by the Mexican Government."[8]

While growing up, Walker had read Julius Caesar's memoirs about his conquest of Gaul. In Sir Walter Scott's *Morte d'Arthur*, he had read of the kingdom created by King Arthur and his knights of the round table. Walker would also have grown up with Sam Houston as a hero. Like Walker, Houston had been born and raised in Nashville, then had become a lawyer. He had gone on to serve as a U.S. congressman representing Tennessee and had also been governor of Tennessee. In 1833, Houston had settled in the Mexican state of Texas, and two years later, he became general of the army of Texas settlers that defeated Mexico's president, General Santa Anna, and created the new Republic of Texas. In 1836, Houston had become the first president of the Republic of Texas. If General Sam Houston could carve a new nation out of Mexican territory, so, William Walker believed, could he.

The Commodore was back. It was September 23, and the *North Star* lay anchored off the northeast corner of Staten Island while Vanderbilt was rowed ashore to see his aged mother and regale her with all that he had seen and done on his European tour.

There was much to tell. After landing at Southampton, the party had visited London, where Vanderbilt, who seemed not to have given up on the Nicaragua canal idea after all, inspected the new Thames Tunnel, a similarly audacious civil engineering project. The Vanderbilts attended a reception held by the Lord Mayor of London, and while British nobility ignored them, they were made welcome by the American ambassador. They made excursions to Windsor, Bristol, Bath, and elsewhere. The Commodore, a horse fancier, took the gentlemen to the Ascot races, and the entire party went to Covent Garden to see an opera, with Queen Victoria and her husband, Prince Albert, sitting in the royal box opposite. After the Lord Mayor of Southampton hosted a civic reception for the Vanderbilts, the Commodore reciprocated by taking five hundred British guests on a sail around the Isle of Wight aboard the much admired *North Star*—"This yacht is a monster steamer," the London *Daily News* had gushed on June 4.

And then the Commodore's floating palace had sailed on, first to Le Havre, from where the party visited Paris, and then to the Baltic, with stops at Copenhagen and then Petershof, from where the Vanderbilts visited St. Petersburg. The czar's second son, Grand Duke Constantine, paid the *North*

Star a visit and asked permission for his naval architects to copy her design. Vanderbilt, who had designed the ship himself, was delighted to agree. After that, the *North Star* headed for the Mediterranean and an exotic list of stopovers—Gibraltar, Malaga, Florence, Pisa, Naples, Malta, Constantinople, Tangiers. And then they headed home across the Atlantic, via the island of Madeira.

Once the *North Star* docked on the North River, Cornelius and Sophia returned to the plain four-story brick Vanderbilt mansion at Manhattan's 10 Washington Place, a stone's throw from Washington Square and Broadway. And it was the next day, at his West Fourth Street office behind 10 Washington Place, that Vanderbilt learned from his clerk Wardell that, just ten days after he had begun his transatlantic jaunt, the directors of the Accessory Transit Company had shafted him.

The assault on the Commodore had been led by Transit Company director Charles Morgan. A fifty-eight-year-old, self-educated native of Connecticut and the owner of the Crescent City Shipping Line operating out of New Orleans, Morgan had, like Vanderbilt, made a fortune from the shipping business. By the time he died in 1885, Morgan had owned or co-owned 117 steamships during his career, starting with a little steam packet in 1833. He also operated the Morgan Iron Works on the New York City waterfront, manufacturing many of the steam engines and boilers and much of the machinery that drove his own steamships and those of numerous other operators, including Vanderbilt.

Morgan's chief collaborator in the conspiracy against Vanderbilt was fellow Transit Company director Cornelius Kingsland Garrison. Born near West Point, New York, Garrison, now forty-four, had started out as a cabin boy on sloops working the Hudson River. A boat and bridge builder in Buffalo and in Canada for a time, Garrison had gone on to make a pile of money building and running Mississippi River steamboats. Once the California gold rush began, Garrison had taken his money to Panama and set up a flourishing bank there with partner Ralph Fretz. They were soon joined in the business by a young friend from their Mississippi River days, twenty-eight-year-old William C. Ralston, who had been engaged to Louisa Thorne, a granddaughter of Cornelius Vanderbilt. To Ralston's everlasting sorrow, his fiancée had died shortly before they were to be married.

Earlier in the year, Cornelius Garrison had relocated to San Francisco, where, with Vanderbilt's approval, he had been appointed the Transit Company's shipping agent. Garrison earned a whopping sixty thousand dollars a year from that contract, but Vanderbilt hadn't complained—the efficient Garrison reorganized the West Coast operation with very profitable results. The line's Pacific run had previously been far less well managed than Vanderbilt's East Coast operation, with complaints about overcrowding, careless crew, poor food, and timetables that were ignored. Garrison very quickly changed that. The San Francisco locals, too, had been impressed by the garrulous Garrison, electing him mayor of San Francisco in November, after he had spent just nine months in the city.

During Vanderbilt's European absence, Morgan and Garrison collaborated to manipulate Transit Company stock in their favor. And, on May 30, they had held a board meeting at which Morgan was elected to the vacant company presidency and was appointed the company's New York agent, replacing Vanderbilt in that role. The board had also voted to cease Vanderbilt's 20 percent skim of company revenue. Vanderbilt's clerk told him that the Transit Company's office at 5 Bowling Green had refused to pay the accounts that he had sent for the Commodore's commissions. Even Vanderbilt's attorney and business partner Joseph L. White, who sold his stock and resigned from the board at the same time that Vanderbilt had, not only bought new company stock on the cheap in Vanderbilt's absence but accepted a Transit Company directorship from Morgan and Garrison.

Vanderbilt's cash flow from the Transit Company was choked off. The New York *Herald,* when it learned what Morgan and Garrison were doing, had declared, "Trouble is anticipated upon the return of Commodore Vanderbilt."[9] How right the paper was. Vanderbilt was livid. He immediately dictated a short letter to Wardell, addressed to both Morgan and Garrison: "Gentlemen, you have undertaken to cheat me. I won't sue you, for the law is too slow. I'll ruin you. Yours truly, Cornelius Vanderbilt."[10] This was a declaration of war. The press would call what followed "The War of the Commodores."[11]

Offshore at La Paz, Mexico, Juan Robinson's schooner *Caroline* swung at anchor with a Mexican flag flying. It was November 4, 1853, six weeks since Cornelius Vanderbilt had arrived back in New York. Longboats from the schooner ground into the beach, and forty-four well-armed Americans jumped out and splashed ashore. Most of these Americans were in their twenties; some, in their teens. They were all, in the words of William Walker, "full of military fire and thirsting for military reputation."[12]

They made for the residence of Rafael Espinosa, governor of the state of Baja California. Weapons at the ready, the invaders trotted along a dusty street of low adobe buildings. In the shade of a portico on the town's plaza, three men were waiting—William Walker, his deputy, and the master of the *Caroline*. Young "Colonel" Walker, as he now styled himself, led the way into the governor's residence. Walker had originally been heading for Guaymas, on the other side of the Gulf of California, but at the last moment had decided to land at La Paz. For eighteen months during the Mexican War, La Paz had been occupied by a garrison of U.S. Army troops who had beaten off sustained attacks from the Mexican Army. Ironically, La Paz means "the peace." Walker and his men were about to shatter that peace.

The Americans placed Espinosa under arrest. The few sleepy Mexican police in the town were quickly disarmed. The Mexican flag was hauled down, and in its place, another, of Walker's design, was run up. Comprising three red horizontal bars on a white field and two stars representing the states of Baja California and Sonora, this was the flag of the new Republic of Lower California—Walker's new republic. Walker's men fired a salute. The boom echoed around the town, setting off a cacophony of barking dogs. A proclamation was issued: "The Republic of Lower California is hereby declared Free, Sovereign and Independent, and all allegiance to the Republic of Mexico is forever renounced." It was signed "William Walker, President."[13]

Walker then prepared to wait for his law partner Watkins to arrive from San Francisco with 200 reinforcements. Several years before, 260 Frenchmen led by Count Gaston Raoulx de Raousset-Boulbon had attempted the same sort of colonizing venture in Sonora. "A young man of large ideas" and a "gentleman adventurer," Boulbon had been a newspaper publisher and novelist in Paris before he came to North America.[14] In Mexico, he had proved a failure as both a soldier and a colonizer. His expedition had been routed by

the Mexican Army. The count had been shot by firing squad, and his fol-
lowers ejected from the country. William Walker, who had met Boulbon in
San Francisco in 1852, had no intention of emulating the Frenchman's fate.
Full of self-belief, Walker was determined to do things differently.

By January 1854, Commodore Vanderbilt's assault on Morgan, Garrison,
and the other rogue directors of the Accessory Transit Company had gathered pace. A new steamship operator, the combatively named Independent
Opposition Line, was advertising in the New York press. For $150 in a cabin
and $75 in steerage, Commodore Vanderbilt's new line would take you to
California via Panama. On the run from New York to Panama, the Independent Line was using the *North Star*. Vanderbilt had stripped his beautiful
private yacht and fitted her out to carry six hundred passengers. He would
never again trifle with such a fabulous toy and would never again take an extended vacation.

To augment the *North Star*, Vanderbilt had purchased the year-old SS
Cortes from the New York & San Francisco Steamship Line. And he brought
in as his partner in the Independent Line Edward Mills, who was "justly entitled to be described as the pioneer of ocean steam navigation," according
to a leading San Francisco newspaper.[15] Mills, who had years before established a transatlantic steamship line from New York to Bremen, Germany,
put his ocean steamers *Uncle Sam* and *Yankee Blade* on the Independent
Line's route from Panama to San Francisco. Setting up the Independent Line's
New York ticket office at 9 Battery Place, not far from the Transit Company's ticket office, Vanderbilt installed son-in-law James Cross as the Line's
New York agent.

The Independent Line's four ships were immediately filled to capacity on
every trip. Vanderbilt had halved the fare offered by all his competitors, including the Transit Company. He was also offering travelers a chance to sail
on his world-famous former private yacht, plus the fastest trip to California
available. The *North Star* turned out to be the greyhound of the seas, en-
abling the Independent Line to quickly boast a new record for the trip from
New York to San Francisco—under twenty-three days, despite using the

longer route via Panama. By the summer, this would be lowered to twenty-one days, fifteen hours. The Commodore, determined to put the Transit Company out of business and ruin Morgan and Garrison, announced plans to construct more steamers for the Independent Line fleet.

In January, too, Vanderbilt offered a block of five thousand Accessory Transit Company shares for sale at twenty-five dollars each. The stock had recently been selling for above thirty. The Vanderbilt offering was snapped up—the buyer was reputed to be Charles Morgan.[16] To observers, the Commodore was clearly dumping his Transit Company shares. With the Independent Line increasingly biting into the Transit Company's business, and its profits, the stock market price of the Accessory Transit Company, already on the slide since Vanderbilt ceased to be president, continued to decline.

It should have been a day for William Walker to celebrate—May 8, 1854, his thirtieth birthday. But it was a day on which he was forced to surrender. Walker's Lower California experiment had proven a failure. It almost cost him his life.

After receiving two hundred reinforcements and leaving twenty men to garrison Ensenada, he had marched into Sonora to annex it to his republic, driving a herd of cattle ahead of him. Trying to cross the Colorado River on rafts, Walker lost his cattle, the column's food supply. Many of his reinforcements subsequently lost heart and deserted, heading north for Fort Yuma, in U.S. territory. With his original men and forty from the second party, Walker had turned back for Ensenada. But when he reached the town, it was to find that his garrison had been wiped out by Mexican irregulars led by Colonel Guardalupe Melendres, a wealthy local landowner. Realizing the game was up, and fighting off the Mexicans and Apaches along the way, Walker had led his bedraggled survivors toward the U.S. border south of San Diego. Near the village of Tia Juana, three miles from the border, Walker had found Colonel Melendres and hundreds of Mexican militia in his path.

Melendres had sent a message to the U.S. military commander at San Diego, then just a rundown mission with a U.S. Army camp garrisoned by eighty troops, telling the commander that he, Melendres, was chasing Yankee bandits toward the border. Melendres had asked the U.S. Army not to intervene, and the American commander had assured Melendres he would not cross the border. When Walker's motley band appeared, Melendres sent them an offer of free passage to the border—if Walker was handed over. But the exhausted men who for a solid year had "fought and starved for Walker," had refused to give up their leader. They had fought their way through the Mexicans, making a dash for the United States.[17]

At the border, a stone monument marked the invisible line that separated Mexico and the United States. A party of U.S. Army infantrymen from San Diego waited in wagons on the American side of that monument. The soldiers had been told that Colonel Walker and the last of his "filibusters" were approaching. Filibusters—it was a term that Walker abhorred. Based on the Dutch word *vijbuiter*, meaning "freebooter," it was applied to Frenchmen, Spaniards, Cubans, and Americans who had tried to colonize parts of Mexico and liberate Cuba with force of arms in recent times. Walker, an idealist who didn't see himself in the filibuster mold, led thirty-five exhausted, starving survivors to the border marker and crossed back into the United States.

These men were sallow-faced, with tattered clothes and bushy beards. Most sported wounds. Charles Gilman, one of the oldest men in the party— he had a teenage son back in San Francisco—had to be carried back into the United States. Gilman had lost a leg, which had been amputated out in the desert by Walker after Gilman took a bone-shattering Mexican bullet. According to Walker, Gilman suffered "long and cruelly."[18] As Walker himself limped onto U.S. soil with one foot bandaged, Major Justes McKinstry, district quartermaster from the post at San Diego, who had orders to apprehend these men for breaching the U.S. Neutrality Act of 1818 by occupying foreign territory using force of arms, now called on them to surrender.

Just thirteen days before, the governments of Mexico and the United States had ratified the Gadsden Purchase agreement, via which the United States would pay Mexico $10 million to acquire thirty thousand square miles of Sonora to add to what would eventually become the American states of Arizona and New Mexico. The agreement had originally been signed back on December 30, when William Walker and his little army were in control of Baja California and threatening Sonora, and many people would credit Walker's presence there as the reason the Mexicans proved so eager to sign the Gadsden Purchase. For, as a codicil to that agreement, the U.S. government had undertaken to strictly police its Neutrality Act and actively prevent American citizens like Walker from entering and occupying Mexican territory.

But instead of placing Walker and his men in custody, McKinstry allowed them to give their parole and proceed to San Francisco to await legal proceedings against them under the Neutrality Act. That same day, the party continued north, with their arms and without an escort.

After Walker and his companions arrived, sick and sorry, back in San Francisco in mid-May, they learned that a civil war had broken out in Nicaragua between the conservative Legitimista party, which was in power, and the liberal Democratico party, whose exiled leaders landed from Honduras on May 5, just three days prior to Walker's surrender at the Mexican border, with a small armed force. The Democraticos had since captured several key towns in northern Nicaragua.

Soon after returning to San Francisco, Walker was employed by young newspaper publisher and merchant Byron Cole to edit his *Commercial-Advisor*. Far from soured by the outcome of the Sonoran enterprise, in hindsight Walker saw it as "an opportunity of tremendous experience" and a valuable learning exercise.[19] Walker and his employer, Cole, a restless New Englander not much older than Walker, held similar expansionist views about extending American influence south of the border, and they took a keen interest in news coming out of war-torn Nicaragua over the next few months, agreeing that perhaps it was not to Mexico, but farther south, to Central America, that they should be directing their thoughts for the future.

Nicaragua particularly appealed. At fifty-seven thousand square miles, it was the largest Central American nation. It was a country rich in natural resources, yet its population of just 260,000 had not exploited the country's potential—less Nicaraguan land was being farmed now than thirty-five years back, when the Spanish were still in charge. Perhaps, Walker and Cole concluded, this Nicaraguan civil war might open the door to strong American leadership in the region.

The U.S. Navy's sloop-of-war *Cyane* sat off Greytown, on Nicaragua's Caribbean coast, with her guns aimed at the town. It was July 13, 1854, and at 9:00 A.M., the warship's captain, Commander George H. Hollins, gave the order to commence firing. Her cannon boomed, and cannonballs whirred across the bay. A day earlier, Hollins had given the 440 residents of Greytown twenty-four hours to evacuate. Now the *Cyane* lobbed 177 projectiles into the deserted town, which consisted of just two streets of wooden buildings thatched with palm leaves. When the bombardment ended, Greytown had been leveled

This astonishing act was in response to an assault, in Greytown, on America's latest chargé d'affaires to Central America, Solon Borland. After a collision on the San Juan River, a black boatman had been shot dead by the American captain of a Transit Company riverboat. The Greytown authorities had attempted to arrest the steamboat skipper, who had taken refuge at the house of the U.S. commercial agent in Greytown. When Ambassador Borland arrived in the town on May 16 to escort the riverboat captain to safety, there was a riot and Borland was hit on the head with a bottle. When town authorities failed to arrest anyone for this assault, the U.S. government had dispatched the *Cyane* to Greytown, with Commander Hollins under orders to take appropriate action.

Some would suggest that the Greytown unrest had been sparked by anti-U.S. feeling going back to an April 1852 agreement between the U.S. secretary of state, Daniel Webster, and the new British ambassador to the United States, John M. Crampton. The agreement had guaranteed the rights of the Canal Company in Nicaragua and provided for British withdrawal from Greytown, after which the town would be returned to the control of the Nicaraguan government. The residents of Greytown—mostly British and American—much preferred an efficient British administration to sloppy Nicaraguan management. But, by the time of Borland's 1854 visit to Greytown, the Webster-Crampton Agreement was more than two years old, and still Britain had shown no inclination to withdraw from the Mosquito Coast.

The Greytown affair worked in Cornelius Vanderbilt's favor. For the civil war now raging in Nicaragua had not prevented the Accessory Transit Company from continuing to convey thousands of passengers across the country, as both sides in the conflict recognized the neutrality of Transit Company travelers and guaranteed their safety. But once the news reached New York that a U.S. warship had flattened the town at the Caribbean terminus to the Nicaraguan Transit, the fear of being caught up in military action caused many travelers to bypass Nicaragua and use ships on the Panama route operated by Vanderbilt, Law, and others. The Accessory Transit Company's business went into decline, and as a result, its share price slumped even further. It was almost as if Vanderbilt had engineered the whole affair.

Of course, contriving an attack on a U.S. ambassador was quite illegal, but a comment attributed to Vanderbilt sums up his attitude to the law. "What do I care about law?" he reputedly said. "Hain't I got the power?"[20]

To win back business, the Accessory Transit Company dropped its fare from New York to San Francisco to one hundred dollars, and thirty dollars in steerage. Vanderbilt immediately matched the fares.

While Vanderbilt had little time for the law, to beat Morgan and Garrison he even took them to court, suing the Accessory Transit Company for his outstanding commissions. But when the case came before a judge and Transit Company legal counsel Joseph L. White reminded the court that the company was registered in Nicaragua, the judge decreed that Vanderbilt would have to contest his claims there. The Commodore then sought to place an attachment on the SS *Prometheus,* which was now Accessory Transit Company property, with the object of selling it to obtain the money the company owed him. If the court went against him and ruled the ship to be Nicaraguan, he said, then the *Prometheus* had no legal right to operate in U.S. waters. Attorney White responded that while the company was registered in Nicaragua, its ships had been registered in the United States, in the names of the officers of the company, so, technically, they were American. Again, the court ruled against Vanderbilt. The Commodore went away empty-handed and permanently soured toward the law as a remedy. A decade later, he would growl, "By God, I think I know what the law is. I have had enough of it."[21]

But Vanderbilt's other measures were biting—by the fall of 1854, the price of Transit Company shares had dropped to twenty-one dollars. Morgan and Garrison were then approached by Marshall Roberts, astute operator of George Law's U.S. Mail Line. Like the Transit Company, Roberts's line and William Aspinwall's Pacific Mail Line had been suffering from the stiff competition from Vanderbilt's Independent Line. Roberts proposed that, to get the Commodore off all their backs, the Transit Company pay Vanderbilt's outstanding financial claims for commissions and buy the *Uncle Sam* and *Yankee Blade* from Edward Mills. Meanwhile, in the same deal, Aspinwall's Pacific Mail Line would buy the *North Star* and the *Cortes* from Vanderbilt. It would be costly, but the existing operators would end up with some fine ships, and most importantly, Vanderbilt and Mills's Independent Line would cease to be.

The proposal was put to Vanderbilt, and to the surprise of many, he accepted it. When the deal was finalized in January 1855, the *New York Tribune* reported that the settlement had been "amicably arranged."[22] This deal signaled, so Morgan and Garrison believed, that Vanderbilt had given up on his plan to ruin them. But the Commodore had done no such thing. Having wrung his outstanding commissions from his enemies— money few observers thought he had any hope of recovering—Vanderbilt would embark on a fresh campaign to ruin the pair, cashed up with their money.

For two months, nothing was heard from Vanderbilt. Meanwhile, the hard-pressed Accessory Transit Company failed to deliver a dividend in January, due to the cost of the settlement with Vanderbilt and Mills. But with the Independent Line no longer competing for its passengers, the Transit Company issued an optimistic forecast for the coming year's earnings. Then, in March, Vanderbilt's son-in-law Daniel Allen, former Transit Company vice president, launched a legal action against the current directors, accusing them of incompetent management, misappropriation of funds, and the illegal issuing of forty thousand new shares in the company in 1853 to finance the purchase of Vanderbilt's seven ships. Allen succeeded in convincing Judge John Duer, chief judge of the New York Superior Court, to issue against Morgan and Garrison an injunction that prevented them from issuing more stock or entering into new contracts with the company.

The market rated Morgan and Garrison good managers, with many observers expressing the belief that the Transit line had actually been better run during their reign than during Vanderbilt's. The pair had also added New Orleans to the East Coast points of departure, with a monthly service from New Orleans to Greytown, and this had helped increase passenger numbers. Shareholders had been particularly impressed with Garrison's management of the West Coast operation, and they were worried that, because of the injunction, Garrison's contract with the company would not be renewed. The uncertainty caused shareholders to dump Transit Company stock—its value plummeted to fifteen dollars.

With the share price down, Vanderbilt began to acquire Accessory Transit Company stock, a parcel here, a parcel there, frequently using friends as the buyers. Meanwhile, with the Commodore designing new ocean steamers to take on the Cunard Line and the Collins Line on the transatlantic run to Europe, Morgan and Garrison were totally blindsided. Month by month, Vanderbilt discreetly rebuilt his stockholding in the company he'd tried to destroy, working toward the day when he could again boast a controlling interest and could kick out Charles Morgan and Cornelius Garrison.

An old adage warns us to beware what we wish for. The company that Vanderbilt was determined to reclaim would prove something of a poisoned chalice. The Transit Company, and a gray-eyed native of Nashville, would soon make the Commodore's life hell.

3

ENTER THE COLONEL

ALL WAS SILENT BUT FOR THE SWISH OF THE PADDLES DRAGGING through the water and the raucous call of a macaw from the jungle on shore. It was midafternoon on June 16, 1855, and a small fleet of long, slim bungoes, native dugouts, had pulled away from the 155-ton Californian brig *Vesta* as she lay off Point Ycaco on the Pacific coast of Nicaragua.

In single file, the slender craft made their way up a narrow inlet, heading north. In the dugouts, seated between the bronze-skinned Indian paddlers, sat a uniformed Nicaraguan officer and fifty-eight Americans. Most of the Americans were armed with holstered pistols and sheathed bowie knives. Some also had swords. All possessed long-barreled rifles, with the barrels pointing skyward. From a distance, the rifles looked like a forest of dead trees floating across the water.

Several of the riflemen wore the Mexican War vintage uniform of U.S. Army officers—dark blue, with stiff, high collars, red piping, and gold epaulettes—and peaked caps of the kind associated with naval officers. Others wore dark frock coats, waistcoats, and broad-brimmed black felt hats. In the first bungo, the thirty-one-year-old, frock-coated leader of the band sat bareheaded and poker-faced, his gray eyes studying the shore, his nostrils taking in the sweet-scented tropical air. His hair was neatly cropped and combed, and unlike most of his men, some of whom had mustaches, the rest, beards, he was perfectly clean-shaven. There was something of the look of a clergyman about William Walker.

The Nicaraguan Indians paddling the lead canoe chattered away in Spanish among themselves. Walker understood every word, but kept his lips buttoned. He was pretending to Colonel Ramirez, the Nicaraguan officer in one of the following canoes, that he could speak no Spanish. It was a pretense he would keep up for some time, knowing that the locals might talk unguardedly in his presence if they thought that, like most North Americans, he couldn't speak their language.

A little before 4:00 P.M., four miles from the *Vesta's* anchorage, the bungoes slid into a wooden jetty. Some occupants climbed onto the jetty. Those still in the boats handed up weapons and belongings, then joined the others. The Americans assembled in ranks on the jetty with bedrolls and haversacks on their backs, rifles on their shoulders, and bags in their hands. Felix "Madregil" Ramirez, the Nicaraguan officer, a swarthy Democratico army colonel who only spoke when he had to, led the way down the jetty to solid ground followed by the American commander and his solid, middle-aged deputy, Achilles Kewen. Behind them, Timothy Crocker, a slight but handsome young man barely into his twenties, snapped an order and led the men in ranks of two at the march behind the senior officers.

The San Francisco newspaper the *Daily Alta California* had recorded the Americans' departure with a brief comment datelined May 3, 1855, five weeks before, reporting that Walker and his party had sailed for Nicaragua "to assist the government there in establishing peace." There were elements of truth in the report, if it is accepted that to make peace, Walker and his fellow soldiers of fortune had come fully prepared to first make war. Nicaragua, being in the middle of a civil war at this moment, had two opposing governments, and Walker and his companions planned to help one and overthrow the other.

As the American contingent marched by a guardhouse at the roadside, the neat, slim, young Democratico officer of the guard, resplendent in high boots, white trousers, and jacket, and with a sword at his side and a short, red cloak slung over one shoulder, called out the guard. A drummer boy tapped a tattoo on an aged kettle drum, and a dozen men turned out and formed a line. These soldiers were local peasants, conscripts. Like most adult males in Nicaragua, they had mustaches, and some, goatees. Their hair was untidily long. All wore grimy, loose-fitting white jackets and white trousers that were rolled up past their knees. Every man wore a wide-brimmed straw hat bearing a wide red hatband—red being the color of the Democratico faction—on which was printed the words *Ejercito Democratico,* "Democratic Army." These draftees were all barefoot, but on their officer's command, they came to attention like regular soldiers and presented their ancient flintlock muskets to the passing officers.

Colonel Ramirez led the Americans along a dirt street, past houses where attractive, dark-haired, dark-eyed Nicaraguan women in colorful dresses lounged barefoot in doorways and at open windows, smiling an enticing welcome at *los Yanquis* as they passed. There were far more women and children to be seen than men—many of the town's men were either serving in the army or had died in the thirteen-month-old civil war. Ramirez guided the Americans to quarters in the heart of the town, then bade them a good night.

Walker allowed his men to purchase *aguardiente,* or *guaro,* as it was nicknamed, the cheap but highly potent local liquor, not unlike rum, made from the sugar cane. Guaro was sold by the town's *pulperias,* or grocery stores, and the storekeepers gladly remained open half the night to do a brisk trade with the Yankees. At their quarters, the Americans swigged their guaro and chattered and joked well into the warm tropical night.

Soon after sunrise the next morning, Colonel Ramirez reappeared, bringing two Americans with him to escort Walker to a meeting with the Democratico leadership in León, the Democratico capital, farther to the south. One of the Americans, Dr. Joseph W. Livingston, was a resident of the city of León and onetime U.S. consul there, having lived in Nicaragua for nine years.[1] The other man was twenty-six-year-old Charles W. Doubleday. English-born, Doubleday had migrated to the United States at age three with his parents and had been raised on a farm in Ohio. Like thousands of other adventure seekers, Doubleday had been drawn to California by the gold rush, but by mid-1854, he had been returning home, via Nicaragua, when the civil war broke out. After losing the trunk containing the gold he was taking home, Doubleday, game for anything, had thrown in his lot with the Democraticos and, because he spoke good Spanish, had been commissioned a captain in their army. He had first commanded a gringo unit comprised of twenty Americans, Britons, and Irishmen, but after most had been killed or wounded, he had led a company of Nicaraguan troops.

Not having mixed with Americans for a year, Doubleday was delighted to see the Walker party. But when introduced to their leader, he was a little surprised, even disappointed. Doubleday had never previously met Walker but had known of him in San Francisco. "Colonel" Walker's reputation had made him sound, to Doubleday, a big man, in more ways than one. But in the flesh, Walker "did not, at the time, impress me as the man of indomitable will and energy which I afterwards found him to be. He was quiet and unassuming."[2]

For the thirty-mile ride to León, Walker chose to take along young Tim Crocker, one of seven men in his band who had survived the Sonoran expedition with Walker and unhesitatingly signed up to follow him again. Crocker didn't say much and seemed mild enough to the casual acquaintance, but, said Walker, "he was a man to lead others when danger was to be met."[3] Before he left Realejo, Walker took aside his deputy, Achilles Kewen, a large, chivalrous, and fearless character, and told him to march the Americans ten miles to the regional capital of Chinandega, there to wait for Walker to either return or send for them.

Walker, Crocker, Doubleday, Livingston, and Ramirez then set off, riding east. It was the rainy season, which lasts from May to October in Nicaragua, and it had rained overnight so the dirt road was muddy and heavy going, but otherwise, this leg was uneventful. The church bells of staunchly Democratico Chinandega welcomed the horsemen as Walker took in the dramatic scenery, noting, in the distance, the picturesque cone of the extinct volcano El Viejo rising up to dominate the landscape. Beyond Chinandega, villagers came out of moss-encrusted stone cottages fronted by cacti fences to smile and wave to the passing horsemen—word had gone before them that Yankee soldiers had arrived at Realejo to help the Democraticos win the war.

The narrow road cut through thick vegetation that occasionally yielded to fields of corn and plantations of plantain—the potato of Latin America. Several times, the riders passed groups of idle, white-clad Democratico soldiers shading themselves at the roadside beneath the branches of ceibas, the sprawling silk-cotton tree of the tropics. Many of the local soldiers were smoking cigarillos. And, Walker noted, the sergeants and corporals in charge seemed always on their guard in case any of their men tried to run off. As Walker quickly learned, few of the common people in this country took part in the civil war by choice. In fact, the peasants dreaded military service. Desertion from the ranks was rife on both sides.

As the party of riders neared León, a vast plain opened before them; a plain, Walker would write, that "seems almost boundless in extent as you look toward the south, while gazing northward you perceive the lofty line of volcanoes—Viejo on one flank and Momotombo on the other—stretching from the Gulf of Fonseca to the Lake of Managua."[4] The city of León, with a population of fifty thousand, was the second-largest in Central America. It had been established in the sixteenth century by Spanish conquistadors from Panama City, who had surrounded it with thick stone walls—not to keep out the locals as much as protection against Cortes's Mexico-based conquistadors who had come south looking for Nicaragua's famed but often elusive gold and silver deposits. The conquistadors not infrequently fought their own countrymen for the spoils of Nicaragua. The León that Walker found was a city of graceful Moorish architecture. From the tower of the city's massive cathedral of San Pedro, Charles Doubleday told him as they rode, it was possible to see thirteen volcanoes and, to the west, the gleaming Pacific.

Outside a large house fronting the city's central plaza, the riders dismounted. There was a Democratico detachment standing guard over the house, while above it flew the drab Democratico flag: three horizontal bars of yellow, white, and beige. Colonel Ramirez led the Americans into the house. Middle-aged provisional director, Don Francisco Castellon, came to greet them. A short man, clean-shaven, with thick gray hair, and of Spanish descent, he looked more like a musician than a politician. "It did not require many minutes," Walker would note, "to see that he was not the man to control a revolutionary movement."[5]

Walker kept up the pretense of having no Spanish. Even Doubleday believed that Walker "did not yet speak Spanish" and so acted as interpreter.[6] Castellon did not hide his delight at seeing the Americans. Back on December 29 of the previous year, he had signed a contract with Byron Cole, Walker's former employer. That contract had called for two hundred North American mercenaries and a mortar to be dispatched at once to join the Democratico army's siege of the Legitimista capital, Granada. The fact that neither Yankees nor mortar had turned up had influenced Castellon's decision to abandon the protracted and fruitless siege. Since then, the war had gone badly for the Democraticos. The Legitimistas had gone on the offensive, winning a battle in the field and driving the Democratico forces back. Legitimista armies now hemmed the Democraticos in from the northeast and the south.

Still, even though the Americans were six months late, Castellon could certainly use them. Walker had in fact been responsible for their delayed arrival. In the fall of 1854, Byron Cole had sold the *Commercial-Advisor* and headed for Central America. In December, Walker had moved to Sacramento to become editor of the *State Democratic Journal*. Two months later, out of the blue, Cole had sent Walker the signed contract from Nicaragua, urging him to use his reputation gained from the Sonora venture to recruit the two hundred men the contract specified and lead them down to Nicaragua at once.

But Walker, the trained lawyer, knew that Cole's contract infringed the U.S. Neutrality Act. Following the Sonora debacle, a friendly San Francisco jury had acquitted Walker of breaking the Neutrality Act in Mexico, and he was determined not to infringe it again. So Walker had sent a new contract down to Castellon, this time specifying the recruitment of "colonists," with no mention of arms. Castellon had signed and returned this second contract, but when Walker still did not come, Castellon had felt that the American had only been toying with him, with no Yankee mercenaries likely to come to his aid after all.

Walker, in turn, had been frustrated by difficulties in raising money to pay for weapons and ammunition and in chartering a ship to take the "colonists" to Nicaragua. Just one major investor, San Francisco merchant Joseph Taylor, had been found, contributing $1,000. Walker's former legal tutor and firm friend Edmund Randolph had put up a little cash, as did another lawyer friend, A. Parker Crittenden. Crittenden also agreed to act as Walker's San Francisco agent and recruit more men to serve in Nicaragua once Walker had become established there. Walker also added his own meager savings to the fund. But the money-raising had consumed valuable time.

As the León meeting progressed, the provisional director told Walker that he wanted the American volunteers to form a separate corps within the

Democratico Army, the *Falange Americana,* or "American Phalanx," under Walker's command. Walker did not agree right away; he wanted to meet the Democraticos' commanding general before he and his men finally committed themselves to this war. Walker had learned that Castellon had removed General Maximo Jerez from command of the Democratico Army following his wounding by a French sniper during the aborted siege of Granada. Not that Jerez would be any great loss. Walker had also learned that General Jerez, educated in France and a doctor before the civil war, had neither the experience nor the aptitude to successfully lead an army. Most important of all, Jerez had never commanded the respect of his men. It hadn't helped that he had once fallen off his horse in front of his troops. According to the cynical locals, Jerez couldn't ride, couldn't shoot, and couldn't win a battle.

After dinner, the new commander in chief, General Don José Trinidad Munoz, arrived at the provisional director's house to meet Walker. Despite Charles Doubleday's assertion that Munoz was thought by many "to be the ablest soldier in Central America," critics said that the general was afraid of committing to battle.[7] Others suggested that Munoz had political ambitions— instead of fighting the Legitimistas, he would prefer to see a compromise deal done between the two warring parties, one that left him in a position of power. Born in El Salvador, Munoz had fought in wars in several Central American countries and had once tried unsuccessfully to overthrow the Nicaraguan government. Tall and handsome, "a man of the most striking physical beauty" in Doubleday's estimation, Munoz arrived wearing the flashy uniform of a major general.[8] As Castellon introduced him, Munoz gave Walker an extravagant salute.

Walker was unimpressed with General Munoz from the start. Barely acknowledging Walker's companions, the pompous, conceited Munoz launched into an extraordinary dissertation about the comparative merits of American generals Winfield Scott and Zachary Taylor in the Mexican War, "expressing his ignorance in every sentence," as far as Walker was concerned.[9] Doubleday saw immediate antipathy bloom between Walker and Munoz, likening it to the kind of reaction "exhibited in the sudden encounter between a dog and a cat."[10]

To make matters worse, Castellon and Munoz did not much like each other either, and Castellon had not warned Munoz that the Americans had landed in the country. It was in this meeting that Munoz first learned of his provisional director's plan to employ American mercenaries. When Castellon informed Munoz that he had proposed to Colonel Walker that the Americans form a separate unit within the Democratico Army, the general was not happy. Munoz suggested that Walker's American riflemen be distributed among his Democratico units, to stiffen the less-than-ardent fighting spirit ' of his native conscripts, but seeing that neither Castellon nor Walker liked that idea, he excused himself and departed.

After Munoz left, Walker gave the provisional director, through Doubleday, an ultimatum. "If my comrades and myself are to enter the service of the Provisional Government, it must be with the distinct understanding that we are not put under the orders of General Munoz."[11]

The next morning, after spending the night at the director's house, Walker surprised Castellon by proposing that the Americans immediately launch a campaign against the Legitimista city of Rivas, in the Meridional Department, a southwestern province well behind Legitimista lines. Rivas commanded the Transit Road, the route via which Accessory Transit Company passengers crossed from Lake Nicaragua to San Juan del Sur on the Pacific coast, and over which, twice a month, gold shipments from California passed.

Walker pointed out that, if successful, such an operation behind enemy lines would have two benefits—tax moneys raised in the Meridional Department could be sent to the cash-strapped Democratico government in León, and more Americans could potentially be recruited into Walker's unit from among the thousands of travelers who used the Transit Route. All Walker asked for was two hundred Nicaraguan troops to back up the American Falange. Give him those men, said Walker, and he would take Rivas and the Meridional Department for the Democraticos.

This was no spur-of-the-moment idea; Walker had obviously planned this operation against Rivas well in advance, before he left the United States. The plan was undeniably novel, if not brilliant, but the thought of the Americans leaving the north and operating independently well to the south worried Castellon. He much preferred to keep the Yankees close by, to act as his personal bodyguard if worse came to worst. But Walker had no intention of allowing his men to serve as the provisional director's bodyguard unit—like the Praetorian Guard of ancient Rome, he would later write.[12] Nor would Walker contemplate dividing his men among the Democratico Army's untrained, ill-disciplined Nicaraguan peasants, as Munoz wanted. As the provisional director stalled, Walker continued to push for the Rivas operation. This strike behind enemy lines, he said, had the capacity to secure the Transit lifeline and put Democratico forces in a position to strike at the Legitimista capital, Granada, from the rear, leaving Legitimista armies stranded in the north. If successful, it could bring about a swift end to the war.

With Castellon prevaricating, Walker informed him that his Americans would only become involved in this war if the Rivas operation was given the go-ahead. It had to be Walker's way, or none at all. As the Tennesseean rose to leave, the suddenly worried provisional director hurried to say that he would get back to him as soon as he'd spoken with his war minister. Walker replied that he was rejoining his men. He and Timothy Crocker set off for Chinandega, leaving Castellon with no doubt that if Walker's daring Rivas operation did not receive approval and support, the Americans would return to the United States.

4

LANDING BEHIND
ENEMY LINES

THE WALKER COLUMN HAD NOT MOVED MORE THAN HALF A MILE inland from the landing site before rain came lashing down in torrents, drenching every man within minutes. Before long, in the sheeting rain and the dark, Walker's guide, the elderly Don Maximo Espinosa, who owned a valuable cacao estate at Rivas, had lost the trail, forcing Walker to call a halt. The men of the column gladly moved into the surrounding trees looking for shelter as Walker ordered Colonel Ramirez to send several of his Nicaraguans scouting around to find the lost trail.

Walker had won his way with Provisional Director Castellon, and the behind-the-lines operation against Rivas was going forward. In the moonlight on June 27, 1855, four days after sailing from Realejo aboard the *Vesta*, Walker's small force had come ashore on the southwest coast of Nicaragua. They had landed at a small beach near El Gigante Point, out of sight of the nearby village of Brito and eighteen miles north of San Juan del Sur, the town that served as the Pacific terminus for Accessory Transit Company steamers from San Francisco.

Castellon had scraped up 110 barefoot Democratico conscripts for the operation, putting Colonel Ramirez in charge of them. Walker's own little unit had been depleted when four Americans had walked away at Realejo. But at least the *Falange Americana* had been bolstered by the addition of the handy Charles Doubleday, who had volunteered to join Walker as a private. Walker had divided his Americans into two companies, commissioning a captain to command each. His senior captain was Charles C. Hornsby, from Columbus, Mississippi. In his forties, Hornsby was well over six feet tall, with jet black hair, a bushy black beard tinged with gray, sunken cheeks, intense eyes, and a military bearing. An "upright honorable soldier" and "a man of great dignity" who neither drank nor gambled, he was a crack shot with a rifle and served as a captain in the U.S. Army during the Mexican War.[1]

Hornsby had sailed down from New Orleans with two colleagues, Thomas E. Fisher and Julius De Brissot, and had been in Nicaragua when Walker was in Sonora. The three of them had tinkered with the idea of becoming involved in the civil war, offering to raise a force of Americans back in the States to join the Democratico side. But the disorganized nature of the Democratico army had persuaded Hornsby and De Brissot otherwise. They had traveled on to San Francisco, where both had subsequently joined Walker's expedition on condition that they be given the rank of captain. De Brissot was something of a romantic; he had been on his way to Ecuador's Galapagos Islands the previous year when he had joined up with Hornsby and Fisher on a steamer heading to Nicaragua from New Orleans. In Walker's estimation, De Brissot sometimes tried too hard to impress but could be trusted to do his best.[2]

Thomas Fisher, a native of New Orleans, was one of several men Walker commissioned as lieutenants. Another was Francis "Frank" P. Anderson, from New York State. Brash and brave, Anderson, who had served in the New York Regiment during the Mexican War, was passionate about good horses and good brandy and was popular with the other men. For his other lieutenants, Walker selected the quick-tempered but tough-as-nails John R. Markham and the no-nonsense youngster Robert Gay, both of whom also had U.S. Army experience. Like Hornsby, Markham and Gay were wearing their old U.S. Army uniforms on this mission. All the officers were armed with swords and pistols—Colt navy revolvers in most instances, although Tim Crocker favored a six-barreled pepperbox pistol. And, like all the members of the force, Walker's officers wore red Democratico army ribbons tied around their hatbands.

Most of the rank-and-file members of the American Falange were, in Walker's words, "men of strong character, tired of the humdrum of common life, and ready for a career which might bring them the sweets of adventure and the rewards of fame."[3] Among them was the resilient Kanaka John, a powerfully built native of the Hawaiian Islands—no one knew his last name.

Then there were the eager teenagers, including J. Calvin O'Neal, who was barely eighteen, and Benjamin Williamson. Walker had also recruited a doctor. While he himself was a qualified physician, Walker had seen during the Sonoran venture that the commander could not always spare the time to tend to the wounded. Prior to signing on with Walker, Dr. Alex P. Jones had been searching for buried treasure in the Cocos Islands. While he had the medical credentials for the job, Jones also had no qualms about using a rifle if he had to.

Each Falange member marched with an ammunition pouch packed with large-caliber .758 rifle rounds, and his canteen was full—in most cases, full of brandy, whiskey, or wine. Every Nicaraguan soldier had a *jicara* swinging from a buttonhole. These elaborately carved clay bottles contained *tiste,* a mixture of chocolate, sugar, and cornmeal diluted in water. In his haversack, every man carried enough rations for just two days— Walker intended taking Rivas within forty-eight hours. But already that timetable seemed optimistic.

The landing had not gone well. Julius De Brissot had steered their largest boat onto the rocks, wrecking it. Doubleday, who was already unwell, had been tipped into the water and had only just been saved from drowning. It had taken hours to ferry men and stores ashore. Then, after midnight, when the column was at last on the march, with the Falange leading and most of Ramirez's Nicaraguans in the rear and some in the center carrying their heavy ammunition boxes, down came the rain. And then they had lost their way. Doubleday had felt so feeble he had to lie down. "It would be hard to imagine a more miserable object than I felt myself to be as I lay on the bare, sodden ground," he later reflected.[4]

Before long, the rain ceased, just as instantly as it had begun. Then the scouts returned, reporting that they had relocated the trail. The march resumed, now with a soldier at each of Doubleday's arms, holding him up. But on the muddy ground, "the walking was fearfully bad."[5] The column's progress, as men slipped and slid in the darkness, was at a snail's pace. But when the sun rose on the morning of June 28, its heat was immediately felt and the men of the slow-moving column quickly dried out. Spirits lifted, as did the rate of march. Keeping to the woodland and avoiding farmhouses, they pushed on toward the village of Tola. Walker had it in mind to spend the next night there, before continuing on to Rivas the following day in time to surprise the Legitimista garrison on the night of the twenty-ninth.

By 9:00 A.M. the column found a deserted adobe house, and there, with sentries posted, the troops breakfasted. Sitting on the ground, the North Americans brought out crackers and cold meat. The Nicaraguans had cheese and tortillas. The North Americans washed down their meal with water or liquor from their canteens, the Nicaraguans with a little sweet *tiste*. Strolling around the gypsylike encampment, Walker eyed his command with paternal pride. "The felt hats of the Falange showed, in their drooping brims, the effects of the night's rain; and the thick, heavy beards gave to most of the body a wild and dangerous air," he would note.[6] After the meal, Walker allowed the column to catch a few hours' sleep. The energetic colonel himself didn't need much sleep.

As the men rested, Walker eyed Colonel Ramirez. Doubleday had alerted Walker to Nicaraguan friends' warnings that Ramirez "was not only a man of inferior capacity and courage," which Doubleday knew from experience to be true, having seen him in action at Granada, "but was also a tool of Munoz."[7] Walker had heard that General Munoz was totally against the Falange's Rivas operation, probably because he feared that if Walker succeeded, the American could usurp him as Democratico commander in chief. While Colonel Ramirez had obeyed Director Castellon's order to raise recruits for the Rivas operation, he had done so without enthusiasm, quite blatantly telling Walker that he considered the mission "hazardous and ill-advised."[8] Walker had decided not to place too much reliance on Ramirez or his men.

By early afternoon, the march to Rivas was under way again. The air was balmy and mild. "You felt," Walker said later, "as if a thin and vapory exhalation of opium, soothing and exhilarating by turns, was being mixed at intervals with the common elements of the atmosphere."[9] Shortly after sunset, the rain returned, again bucketing down. The rain-soaked Americans were dragging their feet when Don Maximo Espinosa led the weary column to a property outside Tola owned by Democratico sympathizers. From the farmers, Walker learned that a detachment of twenty Legitimista lancers had that same day arrived in Tola and occupied the town's previously deserted *quartel*, or military barracks.

This news was disconcerting enough, but Walker also received a warning from the Democratico family that they'd heard that the Legitimista commander in chief at Granada, General Ponciano Corral, was expecting Walker's American Falange to turn up in the south. Corral had sent a force under Colonel Manuel Bosque to strengthen the Rivas garrison, and another to San Juan del Sur. Colonel Bosque had in turn sent the lancers to Tola with orders to be on the lookout for Democraticos landed from the sea.

Clearly, someone on the Democratico side, either a spy or a traitor, had sent the Legitimistas a warning about Walker's Rivas operation. At this point, knowing that his mission had been compromised and that he had lost the element of surprise, another commander might have aborted the mission. But not William Walker.

In the darkness, the rain resumed—"Harder than I ever saw it," Doubleday was to recall.[10] Cursing the weather, the sodden members of the column splashed on along a road running with water like a small river. Half a mile out from Tola, with thunder rumbling in the heavens and lightning flashing in the distance, Walker dispatched twenty of his own men to locate the Legitimista lancers and deal with them. The chosen men handed their knapsacks and bedrolls to colleagues, then moved out on the double through the rain with rifles under their coats to keep the ammunition dry. Behind them, Walker led the column forward at a brisk walking pace.

Built on the ruins of the once great capital of the Toltec Indian empire, Tola was a humble adobe village set around the usual Central American plaza. Along the deserted cobbled main street, the twenty men of the advance party trotted, their muscles tensed for action. The quartel was easy to locate; it was the only building in Tola with a sentry posted outside. The other lancers advertised their presence indoors by noisily playing cards in the light of burning tallow dips. As laughter floated out from inside and the rain beat down on the roof tiles and cobblestones, the twenty Americans flattened themselves against the adobe wall next door to the quartel, pausing with pounding hearts to listen for sounds of discovery. But the lone

Legitimista sentry was skulking back out of the drumming rain and hadn't seen or heard them. As one, the Americans rushed the quartel's double doors.

"*Quien vive?*" came the startled sentry's challenge, as he leveled his musket at the shapes appearing from the darkness.[11] He didn't wait for an answer, loosing off a shot. There was a clap of thunder from nearby at the same moment that the lancer's smooth-bore musket boomed. The shot was instantly met by the characteristic whiplike crack of an American's Minié rifle. Though fired on the run, the reply was accurate—the sentry went down. His own shot missed the mark; the ball flew harmlessly out into the night.

Stepping over the wounded sentry, the Americans kicked in the quartel doors, and in through the opening they barged, rifles at the ready. A black-coated Legitimista lieutenant of lancers ran down the corridor toward them, drawing a sword as he came. A handful of his white-clad enlisted men were behind him. Several Americans fired at once, dropping the officer and two of his men. There was another clap of thunder. Yelling in terror, the surviving lancers turned and fled out the back way. Some Americans gave chase; others burst into the front room, where more than a dozen terrified card players threw up their hands.

Walker studied the wounded Legitimista lieutenant and the other Nicaraguan prisoners.

"Shoot them, Colonel!" urged Captain Tejada, one of Ramirez's officers. Short, dumpy, pompous Tejada had been given the nickname "Napoleon" by the Americans, for his outlandish uniform and ridiculous bicorn hat. "Shoot them!"[12]

As the Americans soon learned, there was an unwritten rule in Central America—in war, all prisoners were shot. Ramirez's deputy, Colonel Mariano Mendez, a bloodthirsty Mexican in his sixties, was nodding; he knew enough English to loudly concur with Tejada. "Keel them!"[13]

Walker ignored the pair, ordering Dr. Jones to tend to the wounded Legitimistas as if they were his own men. During the night, Walker quietly talked with the captured Legitimista officer and several of his men, in Spanish. Grateful to have been spared, they spoke freely, revealing that a German merchant from León had turned up at Granada and told General Corral of a planned Falange operation against Rivas. The German had been able to leave León and pass through Democratico lines because he carried a passport—newly issued by none other than General Munoz. To Walker, the conclusion was inescapable: Munoz had deliberately sent the German to Granada to warn the Legitimistas of Walker's mission.

Yet, despite the fact the Legitimistas were expecting an attack on Rivas, Walker was determined to proceed next day, June 29, as planned.

Under a dry sky, they began the march at 8:00 A.M. With Don Maximo and his young nephew remaining at Tola to guard the prisoners, the columns' new guides were a courtly Rivas resident, Don Cleto Mayorga, once a captain in the Democratico army, and his son, a boy of twelve. Walker had divided the lancers' twenty captured horses among his American officers and an advance guard. Mariano Mendez, the Mexican colonel, managed to also find a horse for himself in the village; eager for action and equipped with a captured seven-foot lance, he rode with the advance guard.

Just as northern Nicaragua was dominated by one political faction and the south by another, even the agriculture of Nicaragua was different in north and south. Unlike the cane fields of the north, the countryside that Walker and his men now passed through was dominated by cacao plantations; the cocoa bean from the cacao tree fueled the flourishing local chocolate-making industry.

An hour out of Rivas, the column met a stream of Nicaraguan women walking along the road from the city. Mostly young, they had empty, hand-woven fruit baskets on their heads. The ethnic mix in Nicaragua took in the original Indian inhabitants, the descendants of African slaves brought in to work the plantations by the Spanish overlords of Nicaragua, a very small percentage of landed gentry of pure Spanish ancestry, and subgroups created by intermarriage between the other groups. Most Nicaraguans, like these women fresh from the morning market where they had sold and bartered their farm produce, were poor subsistence farmers or the employees of the few major landowners.

As they passed either side of the column, the women, chattering and giggling, quickly overcame their initial surprise and gave the Yanquis warm smiles and cheerful greetings, sometimes also calling out to men they recognized in the Democratico ranks at the rear of the column. Walker's Americans, charmed by the attractive senoritas, tried out their limited Spanish, telling the women how beautiful they looked. "The girls," Walker was to record, "seemed pleased with the compliments of the men from the land of gold."[14] Walker himself could appreciate the beauty of the local women, but only one woman had ever turned his head—his late fiancée, Ellen Martin, to his mind the most beautiful woman in all of New Orleans, if not the world. Around his neck, he continued to wear the simple gold crucifix that Ellen had given him when they had become engaged.

Amid the banter and "interchange of civilities" between members of the column and the passing women, Spanish-speaker Doubleday overheard Colonel Ramirez questioning the females about the number and disposition of Legitimista troops at Rivas. But Ramirez didn't pass on to Walker what he learned. "The full significance of this was revealed by subsequent events," Doubleday later wrote.[15]

The women were soon left behind. The Americans' smiles faded, their heart rates increased, as they drew closer to Rivas and the fight they expected must soon erupt. As the advance guard topped a rise four miles from Rivas, there was a gasp from the men riding with Walker. Lake Nicaragua spread before them and, in it, quite near, an island from which sprouted a pair of volcanoes—Concepcion, the taller of the two, and Madera. Shooting up three thousand feet from the island, the conical mountains were symmetrical and almost identical. "Dark forests of the tropics clothed the sides," Walker noted of the volcanoes. To Walker, who, like most of his men, was seeing it for the first time, this was "a vision of enchantment." Such was its beauty, he said, "The first glimpse of the scene almost made the pulse stand still."[16]

To the locals, it was a commonplace scene. "Ometepe," said Mariano Mendez matter-of-factly, identifying the island for the Yankees.

The road now curved around to the north, following the lake, and the Americans could hardly take their eyes from the scenery as they continued the march. The guide told Walker that a mile from Rivas, the road joined the main highway to Granada. Walker took this route so that he could enter Rivas from the north, avoiding pickets likely to be on the lookout for him to the south and west, and putting himself between the city and any rein-forcements coming from the Legitimista capital.

Colonel Bosque, the Legitimista commander at Rivas, had set up barri-cades on all the roads leading into the city. At a farmhouse beside the road less than half a mile out from Rivas, Walker called a halt. Ahead, a typical breast-high barricade of dried mud and tree branches could be seen stretch-ing across the road, from one house to another, blocking the Granada road. The heads of Legitimista troops could be seen above the top of the barri-cade, while the barrel of a large cannon, a twenty-four-pounder, jutted through a gap in the mud wall. Ordering the mounted members of the Falange to dismount, Walker summoned his senior American and Nicar-aguan officers to a conference.

In discussions with the Espinosas on the voyage down from Realejo, Walker had formed a clear picture of the layout of Rivas, and this picture had been confirmed by Mayorga. In good times, the city of Rivas held a pop-ulation of twenty-five thousand. Civil war casualties, conscription, and the flight of Democratico supporters had reduced that to eleven thousand, leav-ing many empty buildings in the suburbs. On the northern outskirts of the city, there were cacao plantations on either side of the road—the Maleano estate and the Santa Ursula estate. Santa Ursula was Don Maximo Es-pinosa's property, now in the hands of the Legitimista government. The ad-joining Maleano estate was the property of Don Juan Ruiz, a member of the Legitimista government. There had been a long-standing feud between Es-pinosa and Ruiz, and this had been the motivation for Espinosa's taking the Democratico side in the civil war.

Characterized by rising ground and numerous adobe buildings, the two cacao plantations offered good defensive positions, and Walker decided that if the need arose, he could fall back to one of those. His plan was to quickly drive over the barricades and through the suburbs to the central plaza of Rivas before the Legitimista garrison had time to organize. Explaining his plan of attack to his officers, Walker assigned half the men of the Falange to Lieutenant Colonel Achilles Kewen and half to Major Crocker. Their orders were to push Legitimista troops from the streets and rapidly advance to the plaza. Colonel Ramirez was instructed to follow close on the heels of the Falange and protect its flanks and rear by covering the Granada and San Juan del Sur roads.

Walker still had not let on that he could speak Spanish and passed on his instructions to the Nicaraguan commander via Captain "Napoleon" Tejada, who spoke relatively good English. But Tejada balked, asking Walker to repeat the orders. Tejada seemed to think it unwise to allow Ramirez to stay in the rear and stubbornly declined to translate the orders, shrugging and pretending not to understand. Exasperated, Walker sent Tejada to the rear and had Doubleday pass on the orders to Ramirez. Doubleday noted that "the eyes of Ramirez sparkled" when he heard his instructions.[17]

Although Doubleday had immediately passed on Walker's orders, Doubleday, like Tejada, had his suspicions about Ramirez's reliability, and he, too, voiced his concern to Walker, suggesting it would be a mistake to let the Americans take the brunt of the assault on their own. He added, "It would be better not to send our native troops too far out of reach, Colonel."[18]

A myth would later grow that William Walker never smiled, but Doubleday made a lie of that in his memoirs. Of Walker's response to his suggestion about Ramirez's troops, he wrote: "With a smile which we afterwards learned to understand the meaning of so well, he replied that I had not yet seen what fifty-six such men as he had, and so armed, could do."[19] Bowing to his superior, Doubleday offered no more advice.

"Do you fully understand your orders?" Walker now asked his officers. When all acknowledged that they did, Walker sent them to their troops.[20] As the Mayorgas led away all but Walker's horse, Walker took out his fob watch and checked the time—it was just going on noon. He pulled himself up into the saddle. "Advance!" he called.

5

THE BATTLE OF RIVAS

THE FALANGE WENT FORWARD TO THE ATTACK AT A BRISK WALK. Kewen and his men were on the left of the road, Crocker on the right, in columns of two. All Walker's men were, in Walker's words, eager for the "strife in which they expected to soon mingle."[1] He himself rode immediately behind them. A little way further back came Ramirez and his Nicaraguan troops, but the closer they came to the city outskirts, the more they lagged behind.

Walker called for a charge, and the Americans leaped forward with a bloodthirsty yell. Their approach had been observed, and, belching smoke and flame, the big gun at the barricade boomed a welcome. Its aim was too high—grape and canister designed to cut infantry to pieces went whistling over the ducking heads of the Falange members. Before the gunners had time to reload, the Americans scaled the barricade, only to see a second barricade ahead. Walker's men didn't waste ammunition on fleeing Legitimistas, instead sprinting to the next barricade. This was quickly abandoned by the enemy.

Clearing the first barricade on his horse, Walker came galloping up behind his troops as they mounted the second barricade. On the far side, Walker could see the summit of Santa Ursula Hill in the near distance. The road ahead, up which Legitimista troops were fleeing, was dotted with adobe houses. Excitedly the Americans pushed forward, up the hill, toward the city center. But as they reached a cross street, they ran into a hail of musket fire from loopholes strategically cut into the walls of buildings at the intersection. Rather than pause and be bogged down, the Americans ran by

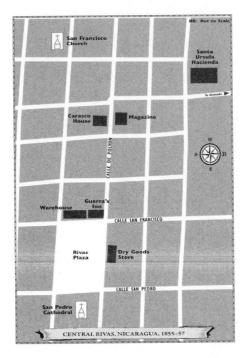

as the Legitimistas at the loopholes were reloading, leaving these troops for Ramirez to deal with when his men came up.

The Falange breasted the crown of the Santa Ursula Hill, only to be met by lethal, concentrated fire from virtually invisible opponents in buildings to their front and flanks. Doubleday recorded, "We kept close to the houses either side" of the street, hugging the adobe walls for cover in what had become a deadly shooting gallery. But, he said, "Already we were counting our dead and wounded."[2]

On the summit of Santa Ursula Hill, Achilles Kewen, seeing the futility of trying to push farther forward in the face of murderously accurate Legitimista fire coming from close range, ordered his men to break into the large house surrounded by a veranda beside them. After using rifle butts to smash open wooden gates and crash down front doors, his men dragged and carried their wounded into cover, taking possession of the empty hacienda. On the other side of the road, Major Crocker's men followed suit, crashing their way into several smaller houses.

Walker rode up just as the houses were being occupied. Continuing on past, he saw Tim Crocker ahead in the street, alone. Young Crocker was panting. His eyes were wide with excitement. His right arm hung uselessly at his side, for his shoulder had been shot through, and his sword lay where he'd dropped it. Blood ran from a wound on his chin. Three of the six barrels of the smoking pepperbox pistol in his left hand had been discharged.

Walker, knowing that the Rivas Plaza was just three blocks west and two blocks north, called from the back of his horse, "Crocker, how far have the men got toward the Plaza?"

"Colonel, the men falter," Crocker returned in a despairing voice. "I can't get them on!"[3]

Walker, hoping to restart the drive toward the plaza by now introducing Colonel Ramirez's men into the fray, looked around to see how close the Democratico troops were. But of Ramirez and most of his command, there was no sign. A handful of Nicaraguans were coming up with ammunition boxes offloaded from their mules, and off to the right Walker could see mad Mariano Mendez and a handful of Democratico troops pushing forward down a side street. But that was all.

Looking to the front again, Walker spotted a mass of Legitimista infantry moving forward to outflank the Americans through the undergrowth on their left. These were eighty men of a Legitimista company commanded by Colonel Manuel Arguello, who had just arrived in Rivas after being urgently summoned from San Juan del Sur. Arguello's men fired as they advanced, and musket balls whizzed all around Walker. He calmly dismounted and joined Kewen's men.

Kewen had occupied the Hacienda Santa Ursula, home of Don Maximo Espinosa, who waited back at Tola for news of Walker's victory. It was a spacious, airy house with large rooms and high ceilings. Two hundred years old, it had been built in classic Mediterranean Spanish style, with shading, pillared verandas on all sides. And unlike the homes of the common people, which generally had dirt for floors, the hacienda's floor was tiled. Don Maximo's more valuable and portable contents had long ago been looted by the Legitimistas, but the larger furniture remained, and Walker, Kewen, and Doubleday dragged heavy, baronial-style tables and sideboards to the wide-open doorway to barricade it, for the Americans had destroyed the doors when they'd broken in.

As the three of them toiled to create a barricade, there were shouts from Americans in the houses across the street—Major Crocker had been killed, and the Legitimistas could be seen massing for an assault on the houses. The trio closed off the hacienda's doorway just in time—a wave of bellowing Legitimistas came charging up onto the veranda with bayonets fixed, and Walker, Kewen, and Doubleday stood shoulder to shoulder at the doorway behind their temporary barricade, desperately batting away thrusting bayonets with their swords. In the nick of time, Captain Charles Hornsby and several others came running to join Walker and the others and, poking rifles over the shoulders of the three Americans in the doorway, fired point-blank into the mass of attackers.

As soon as Hornsby and his companions fired, they stood aside to reload their single-shot rifles, allowing more Americans to take their places and loose off another deadly volley. Then Hornsby and his men stepped up with reloaded weapons and fired again. The combined result was carnage—a pile of white-clad Legitimistas, some lifeless, others savagely wounded, and all covered in blood, lay in front of the doorway. The remaining attackers withdrew, turning and firing the occasional shot as they went.

As the assault petered out, big, bushy-bearded Kewen, standing right beside Doubleday, clutched at the air with both hands, staggered, and fell; he had been hit by a parting shot. "I caught him and laid him gently on his back," Doubleday wrote. Blood was running from the corner of Kewen's mouth, and there was a red spot on his breast, from which blood also flowed freely. "He had been shot through the lung," Doubleday would record, "and smilingly sank into death."[4]

By the time that Kewen breathed his last, Colonel Arguello had put his Legitimista company between Colonel Ramirez's Democratico troops and the Falange and had also regained the cannon abandoned at the first barricade. When Ramirez saw this, he briskly marched his troops away from the battle. Skirting Rivas, he headed south to take his men across the frontier into neighboring Costa Rica. Ramirez left Walker and his small American band of little more than fifty men surrounded by twelve hundred Legitimista troops.

As exhausting hours passed and rain came and went, the Legitimistas launched attack after attack on the houses being held by the Americans, only to be driven back each time. Inside the Santa Ursula hacienda, Doubleday noticed that many fellow Americans were sitting on the floor with their backs to the wall by window or door. Their rifles were loaded, ready in case the enemy broke into the house, but no one was making a target of himself.

After surviving a year of fighting as a member of the Democratico army prior to Walker's coming to Nicaragua, Doubleday had come to think of himself as leading a charmed life. Convinced that he was indestructible, he now crawled around the men, taking their loaded rifles, poking them out an opening, and firing as soon as he saw the head of an enemy. Doubleday had done this several times and was just drawing a bead on a fresh target when "a ball struck me in the right temple, and I dropped to the floor."[5] Later, he would recollect a flickering sensation as he lay there on the tiles. Then he heard the voices of two men who had come to kneel beside him.

"He's gone," said Charles Hornsby.

"It is a pity," said Walker with a sigh.

Doubleday opened his eyes and looked up at the pair. "I'm not gone yet!" he declared, pulling himself to his feet, where he stood, swaying, noticing that his clothes were damp with his own spilled blood.[6] Dr. Jones wound a bandage tightly around Doubleday's skull, telling him that he was lucky to be alive—the temporal artery had been severed, and the Legitimista musket ball had lodged in his skull, behind the ear. Later, when the surgeon had the opportunity, said Dr. Jones, he would dig the ball out.

Walker was relieved that Doubleday had survived. He had already lost his most senior officers, Kewen and Crocker, "the two men upon whom [I] chiefly depended." Walker had formed a close relationship with young Tim Crocker; they'd become like brothers. "The fellowship of difficulty and danger had established a sort of freemasonry between (us)," Walker would later remark. Their joint experience in Mexico had convinced Walker that cool, calm Crocker had a peculiar ability to get himself, and the men he led, out of even the tightest scrape.[7] Yet now, Crocker was dead.

Five of Walker's men had been killed, but it was the loss of the two senior officers that hurt most. He would later say that the spirits of his men began to droop once it was known that Crocker and Kewen were dead.[8] Walker's own spirits seem to have also taken a tumble—Doubleday wrote that for a time, his commander appeared in a daze and incapable of deciding what to do. Walker told Doubleday that the Falange should wait for nightfall and might then try to launch an assault on the city plaza.[9] Doubleday thought this insane. To him, the Falange was in no shape to try anything other than escape—if they lived long enough. Dizzy from loss of blood, sitting with his back to a wall and looking around the room, Doubleday took in the sight of wounded Americans all around him. Among them were rash Captain Julius De Brissot and tight-lipped Lieutenant Frank Anderson, both with leg wounds and in considerable pain, and Hughes, a rifleman who had fought under Doubleday at the siege of Granada. The glassy-eyed Hughes looked in a bad way.[10]

Someone called a warning: Legitimista soldiers could be heard, and soon seen, punching a hole in an adobe wall opposite the Espinosa hacienda, using picks and crowbars. And through the growing gap in the wall, the ominous shape of a four-pound field gun was spotted. Its cannonballs could soon demolish the walls of the Espinosa house, if the gun was allowed to open fire. This threat jerked Walker from his malaise. He called for volunteers to join him in a charge to put the cannon out of commission.

Minutes later, as the Legitimista gun crew was trying to bring the gun to bear, half a dozen Americans come hurdling over the barricade at the hacienda door, yelling ferociously, charging the gun position. Bareheaded Colonel Walker was in the lead, sword in one hand, pistol in the other. The others carried rifles. The men of the gun crew, caught with ram, gunpowder cask, and cannonballs in hand, dropped everything and turned to flee. Some, too slow, were cut down. Wielding rifle butts like sledge hammers, Walker's men smashed the spoked wheels of the cannon's carriage; the barrel crunched to the ground. Walker and his companions then dashed back the way they had come, reaching the Espinosa hacienda unscathed.

Legitimista commander Colonel Manuel Bosque surveyed the scene with sour dissatisfaction. From a loophole in the house where he had set up his headquarters, he could see at least thirty bodies lying in the open, between his position and the buildings occupied by the Yankee *filibusteros*. One or two of the dead were Americans, but most were Bosque's own men. Littering the ground around the bodies were rifles, muskets, pistols, hats—the detritus of war. Bosque had been born in Spain. Normally, in Nicaragua, a Spaniard was hated, just as all Spanish had been hated ever since their countrymen were thrown out of Central America by the local people in the 1820s. Spanish overlords had been cruel and arrogant during their three centuries of occupation. But Bosque was a capable, determined, no-nonsense soldier, and that made him valuable to the Legitimistas.

Nothing Colonel Bosque tried in his effort to dislodge the Americans had worked. Repeated frontal assaults had failed. And his attempt to employ a field gun to blast the *filibusteros* out had been foiled. Bosque had by this time suffered more than one hundred casualties. Determined still, he tried something new, sending runners around his positions with a message—he would pay fifty pesos to the man who set fire to the Espinosa house. Not only would this tactic serve a strategic end, but it would also have the symbolic purpose of destroying the hacienda of the Democratico "traitor" Don Maximo Espinosa.

Two men answered the call. Emanuel Mongolo had been a Rivas schoolteacher before joining the Legitimista army. In his twenties, he was fit and an excellent runner. The other volunteer was Nery Fajardo, a Rivas laborer. When Colonel Bosque pulled out his purse and repeated his offer of fifty pesos if they set fire to the Espinosa hacienda, both men declined the money—they would do this for patriotism, not for pesos, they said.

So, Bosque had a makeshift torch prepared: A bayonet was tied to the end of a long, wooden pole, straw was wrapped around the bayonet, and this was covered with tar. A little before 3:00 P.M., Mongolo and Fajardo burst into the open, with Mongolo holding the burning torch, as Legitimista troops let fly with covering fire aimed at the doors and windows of the buildings sheltering the *filibusteros*. Mongolo reached the rear of the Espinosa house unscathed. Inside, the Americans were hunkered down to avoid the concentrated musket fire coming from Legitimista lines. Fajardo came panting close behind and, grabbing Mongolo's legs, hoisted his companion up. Frantically, Mongolo used one hand to rip away roof tiles. Even today, in rural Nicaragua, the roofs of Nicaraguan homes are constructed in the same manner as that of the Espinosa house in 1855. Rough-hewn wooden rafters were laid from wall to wall. Sugar cane was laid over the rafters to create the ceiling, and over the cane lining went the outer covering of baked, red clay roof tiles.

Once Mongolo had removed several tiles, he was able to thrust the torch into the cane lining. The torch lay there burning; the ceiling smoldered until it caught fire. Mongolo and Fajardo scampered back to Legitimista lines, to receive the congratulations of Colonel Bosque and their Legitimista comrades. In its July 10 issue, the Granada-based Legitimista newspaper *Defender of Order* would laude their courageous deed, quoting Minister for Foreign Relations and the Interior Mateo Mayorga, who would say that the pair was all the more worthy of public admiration because they turned down the fifty-peso reward.[11] For their act, Mongolo and Fajardo were elevated to the sparse ranks of Nicaragua's national heroes, where they remain to this day.

Don Maximo's hacienda was burning. The fire at the back of the house had slowly spread through the ceiling. Because there was no water within the house, the Americans inside had no means of fighting the fire. As the flames licked and spread, choking smoke began to fill the air. With the hacienda soon untenable, Walker issued orders for everyone in it to transfer to the nearest house across the street occupied by Crocker's men. Confirmation of the plan was yelled across to the Americans holding that building, warning them to expect visitors.

All the wounded were lifted up and carried on shoulders or assisted to run, as in a single mad dash, Walker and his surviving men fled the burning Espinosa house, crossed the body-strewn street, and crushed through the doorway of the house opposite. In this crowded, smaller house, with the hacienda across the street gripped by fire, Walker took stock of his situation. It was obvious even to the stubborn Tennesseean that any notion of taking Rivas with the men he had left was unachievable. In addition to losing five men, twelve of his followers were wounded, some seriously. Just thirty-seven men remained fit to fight. Better to break out now and live to return and fight another day.

Walker called the men in the building next door to join him, and in ones and twos, they scuttled to him. Once all his men were concentrated in the one house, he told them they would bayonet-charge a narrow front, attacking the Legitimista encirclement to the west, where there was "a kind of moat or ravine bordered by trees." "Although the intervening space was crowded by the enemy," Walker told his men, the element of surprise should allow them to drive through the Legitimistas and break out of the encirclement. Walker's men would then keep going through the cacao plantations to the Transit Road, before following that to San Juan del Sur, where they would find a boat. The plan was "received with a shout" of approval by Walker's followers.[12]

But, Walker warned them, for the breakout to succeed, every participant must be able to defend himself, must be able to fight his way out, and had to run unassisted. No one could be spared to carry the wounded. With the detached coolness of a physician, he said that any man unable to run would have to be left behind—with the hope the Legitimistas would provide them with medical treatment. The Americans knew what the Legitimistas did with prisoners, but no one argued with their colonel. As the able-bodied men loaded weapons and slid bayonets from scabbards and fastened them in place on the end of their rifles, Walker and Dr. Jones moved around the wounded. The most severely injured men were unconscious—their fate was sealed.

The thigh muscles of both Frank Anderson and Julius de Brissot had been shot through. In addition, one of Anderson's feet was bandaged and he had another bandage over a bayonet slash on the scalp. But both Anderson and De Brissot were adamant that they could run and fight, and they were determined to take their place in the breakout. Admiring their courage and knowing how popular Anderson was with the others, Walker decided to give the pair a fighting chance and agreed to their participation.

Private Hughes, sitting propped up in a corner, called Doubleday to his side. Colonel Walker and Dr. Jones had told him he would have to remain behind. Hughes couldn't stand, let alone walk or run, but still he begged Doubleday not to leave him here. "Any hesitation at this moment would have been fatal to all, besides being useless to him," Doubleday would later guiltily remark.[13] He didn't bother to lie to the man—Hughes had been en-gaged in this civil war longer than most of the men in the room, and he of

all people knew from personal experience what Nicaraguans did with prisoners. But when Doubleday firmly said that Hughes must stay behind—for
the good of them all—Hughes didn't make a fuss and accepted his
sacrifice. Hughes, one of five wounded Americans left to the mercy of the
Legitimistas, watched with empty eyes as the other men made their silent
preparations to depart, avoiding his gaze.

Walker checked his watch. It was a little before 4:00 P.M. They had been
fighting for their lives here in Rivas for close to four hours. The little colonel
now quietly told his men it was time to go. As the Espinosa house across the
street burned fiercely and attracted the eyes of the Legitimista troops in
the encirclement, in the way that a house fire always becomes a beacon to
spectators, the forty-five Americans taking part in the desperate escape bid
came to their feet. Walker glanced at the men crowded behind him. Dr. Jones
had dumped his medical bag and was equipped with rifle and bayonet.
Hornsby and Markham looked cool and determined. Most of the others were
tense; wide eyes flashed from one to another. They knew that if this breakout
attempt failed, they would all be dead by the time the sun went down.

Walker nodded to the man on the other side of the doorway, who drew
back the door. Out into the open dashed Walker. On his heels came the un-
wounded men. Doubleday, De Brissot, Anderson, and four other wounded
brought up the rear. All yelled as if possessed by demons. It was every man
for himself. As they ran, they fired rifles and pistols at Legitimista soldiers in
their path and were prepared to bayonet any man who stood in their way.
Surprise was with the Falange. "We were firing our revolvers into our opponents' faces and thrusting our way through their ranks before they had any
notion of what we were about," Doubleday later recalled.[14] A few Legitimistas got off a shot. A young American private fell, mortally wounded. But the
power of the charge swept the others into the Legitimista line, and through
it. "Before the enemy could disengage themselves from us we had passed
through their midst."[15]

On reaching the lip of the ravine, the Americans swung around to
counter any attempted pursuit. But the Legitimistas were fleeing in all directions in panic. Walker quickly led the party along the top of the ravine to
open country and the beckoning trees of a distant cacao plantation. With
Hornsby and several of his best men as rear guard, the party moved into the

plantation. Not a single Legitimista followed. It seemed to Walker's Americans that the Nicaraguans were glad to see the back of them.

The news that reached Colonel Bosque at his command post was confused. He was told that some of the Yankees had managed to escape by charging through the western side of the encirclement. When he asked who was giving chase to the fleeing filibusters, he was sheepishly informed that no one was. But, he was assured, most of the Yankees were still holed up in two houses at the top of Santa Ursula Hill. Their false belief had been created by the enormous firepower that the Americans demonstrated throughout the afternoon. The Legitimistas were convinced that, to deliver such devastating rifle fire, many more Americans must have been involved in the attack on Rivas than had actually been the case.[16]

For a time, the Legitimistas tensely waited for the other Americans they imagined to still be in the two houses to attempt another breakout. But when nothing stirred and there was no answering fire, Colonel Bosque ordered an all-out assault on the buildings. Hearts in mouths, hundreds of white-clad Legitimista troops charged the houses the Yankees had occupied half an hour before. Meeting no resistance, they burst inside.

When Bosque arrived at one house, he found his men glaring at five seriously wounded Yankee prisoners on the floor. These filibusters had killed their friends and relatives in the battle—the final Legitimista casualty count would be seventy killed and a similar number wounded. Bosque ordered a pile of wood to be raised in the Rivas Plaza. The bodies of the dead Americans—Crocker, Kewen, and four others, including the young private killed during the breakout—were taken on a cart to the plaza and irreverently tossed onto the pile. The Spanish colonel then ordered that Hughes and the four other wounded Americans also be placed on the woodpile and chained in place. On Bosque's order, the log pile was set alight. With leering Legitimista troops and thousands of Rivas residents silently filling the plaza to watch, the Yankee wounded were burned to death on the pyre.

In the cacao plantation, the Falange linked up with Mayorga their guide, who led them west along a little-used track. It was soggy from the rains, and before long, the Americans were struggling in mud halfway up to their knees. Cursing, using their rifles as walking sticks, giving each other a hand, with some of them, including Doubleday, losing boots to the clawing mud and having to go on in bare feet, they struggled through the darkness. Close to midnight, they reached a hilltop hut on a small cattle ranch cleared from the forest. The Transit Road to the Pacific Coast, said Mayorga, was about two miles farther on. The terrified *ranchero* and his wife, who occupied the hut, were placed under guard, and here the weary Americans grabbed a few hours sleep.

With the dawn of June 30, Walker's survivors ate and drank the last of their rations. This was the first meal they'd had since breakfast the previous day in Tola, seemingly a lifetime before. Using a jackknife that he sharpened on a pebble, surgeon Jones took the opportunity to remove the musket ball lodged in Doubleday's skull, without anesthetic. With a triumphant smile, Dr. Jones held a bloodied one-ounce ball of lead under Doubleday's nose. "He managed the operation skillfully," Doubleday later remarked of the painful procedure.[17]

Resuming the march, the column reached the Transit Road by 9:00 A.M.—the same road personally mapped out by Cornelius Vanderbilt. After he had jumped the rapids in the steamboat *Director* on his history-making trip up the San Juan River to Lake Nicaragua, Vanderbilt had crossed the lake to Virgin Bay, which was selected as the lake terminus for the road to San Juan del Sur on the Pacific coast. Vanderbilt's original road, hacked through the forest, had been the source of much complaint from early Transit Route travelers. "Pleasant enough in dry weather but horrible when wet," noted Dr. William Rabe, a New York passenger who traveled the road in August 1851.[18] "It was one giant mudhole," reported Lieutenant George Crook after his passage along the road in 1852. "Places where mule and rider would almost sink out of sight." As for his friend Lieutenant Dutch Kautz, "the last he saw of his mule was its ears sticking out of the mud."[19]

Commodore Vanderbilt had promised to improve the road, and he had. First he covered it with planks, and then he covered the planks with white gravel. He turned it into reputedly the best road in Central America. By 1855, Transit passengers were traveling the road in the comfort of stagecoaches brought in by Vanderbilt. Of American construction and painted blue and white, the national colors of Nicaragua's Legitimista government, the coaches were light and fast. Midway along the road stood the American hotel—universally known as the Half Way House—where the coaches paused to change horses.

Walker led his grateful men onto the Transit Road and began to follow it west, but only a few minutes after they set off toward San Juan del Sur, the sound of a tinkling mule bell met their ears, coming from around a bend.

"It is the Treasure Train, Colonel," said guide Mayorga. "Steamer passengers from California crossed from San Juan del Sur to Virgin Bay yesterday. This will be the mule train carrying the treasure shipment from the steamer."[20]

Having heard that the Treasure Train was usually accompanied by an armed escort, Walker quickly ordered his men off the road, and they dove for cover in the undergrowth. The Treasure Train soon passed by at a leisurely pace, but apart from unarmed muleteers, the train, carrying millions of dollars in California gold, had no escort. Once the mule train was out of sight and out of earshot, the Falange reformed on the road and continued west. They were approaching the Half Way House when a rider came galloping up to them from the direction of San Juan del Sur.

Doubleday recognized the horseman, a native of Kentucky named Dewey who had served under him at Granada. Dewey had gone into business at San Juan del Sur, primarily as a saloon cardsharp fleecing passengers just off the San Francisco steamers. As Dewey reigned in his horse, Walker noted that the man wore a pair of holstered .36 Colt Navy revolvers. After Dewey and Walker introduced themselves, Dewey said, "I'm just from San Juan del Sur, Colonel."[21] As he spoke, he cast an eye over the battered and bleeding Falange. Recognizing Doubleday, his former commander, he gave him a friendly nod. Dewey went on to tell Walker that, after Colonel Arguello's hurried departure for Rivas early the previous morning, there wasn't a single Legitimista soldier in San Juan del Sur. "Some of your native Democrats, including Mariano Mendez, passed through the town last night," Dewey added. "On their way to Costa Rica, I do believe."[22]

Dewey linked up with the column, and seeing Doubleday both wounded and barefoot, he dragged him up onto his horse behind him.[23]

A little after sunset, the column reached San Juan del Sur. The town had been renamed Pineda City in 1852, but the name never stuck; San Juan del Sur it had remained. In 1855, it had a population of several thousand. Its wooden buildings and small farming lots spread along a strip of flat ground between a beach of volcanic gray sand fronting the cove and the hills behind. Those hills rose sharply for a hundred feet and were covered with thick, lush vegetation. Most of the land here was owned by the Legitimista government, to which the landholders paid rent. The majority of the businesses in the town, including its saloons, were owned by foreigners—Americans, French, British, and Germans, in the main. The town had no port facilities, not even a jetty. Passengers and freight were all brought to the beach from Transit Company steamers in small boats. There had been a few government officials, including a Collector of Customs, based at San Juan del Sur, but they had all cleared out of town and fled to Rivas when Walker's Americans appeared in the Meridional Department.

Beside the beach, Walker and his men took over the military barrack vacated by Colonel Arguello's company only the previous day. Seeing a handsome schooner, the seventy-five-ton *San José*, a former San Francisco pilot boat now flying the Costa Rican flag, dropping anchor in the cove, Walker sent a detail under Captain Hornsby out in a rowboat to take possession of her.

In case he had to make a hurried retreat from southern Nicaragua, Walker had arranged with the skipper of the *Vesta*, Gilbert Morton, to sail the brig up and down the coast for several nights. If Morton spotted a pre-arranged light signal from Walker, he was to put in to rescue the Falange. But now, once he had control of the *San José*, Walker knew that if he failed to make contact with the *Vesta* in the night, he could use the schooner to take his battered little force back to Realejo.

But even while he was thinking about escaping from San Juan del Sur, Walker was planning his return, with more troops, and with reliable Democratico officers. A new plan of attack was forming in his mind. And it was quite brilliant.

Walker and the savaged Falange arrived back at Realejo on July 1. After failing to attract the attention of the *Vesta* with their light signals, they had used the *San José* to depart San Juan del Sur, only to encounter the *Vesta* off the coast and transfer to her at sea. And they had come back with their depleted numbers slightly increased by the addition of two Americans who had been in San Juan del Sur and had opted to join Walker's little band despite the failure at Rivas.

Within days of returning to the north, Walker had put a new plan to Provisional Director Castellon and a new demand for two hundred Democratico troops to join his next attempt to take Rivas and the Transit Route. This time, he wanted Democratico officers he could trust. He very quickly accused General Munoz of betraying his previous plan to the Legitimistas and demanded that Castellon remove the general. But the provisional director stalled over both Walker's demands. The Legitimista commander in chief, General Ponciano Corral, had marched his army to Managua, within striking distance of León. He was expected to attack the Democratico capital soon, and Castellon wanted the Americans to help defend León. As for General Munoz, he had too much support among leading Democraticos, and Castellon would not, or could not, remove him.

For weeks while he was based at Realejo and then Chinandega, Walker negotiated at a distance with Castellon in León, threatening to pull out of Nicaragua if the provisional director failed to support his latest plan. General Munoz, meanwhile, sang a familiar song, agitating to have the Falange disbanded and the Americans spread through his units. But Walker did achieve one success, convincing the provisional director to sign a contract authorizing Walker to recruit for service in the *Falange Americana* an additional three hundred Americans, men who would each be paid a hundred dollars a month and granted five hundred acres of land in Nicaragua on the cessation of hostilities. Tellingly, the contract also empowered Walker to settle all differences and outstanding accounts between the government of Nicaragua and the Accessory Transit Company. Castellon, not realizing the significance of Walker's Transit Company clause, did not question any aspect of the contract.

As the weeks passed, two of Walker's men, Turnbull and McNab, became restless and quit. Walker didn't stand in their way, but the pair's departure had a negative effect on the morale of the remaining Americans, many of whom saw this as the beginning of the disintegration of the Falange. So, Walker called his men together and delivered a speech. Accounts of Walker's speeches tell of him talking in a firm but modulated voice, without excessive emotion or grand gestures. Yet, he was uncommonly persuasive; there was something about both what he said and the way he said it that could rekindle sagging spirits and fire dampened enthusiasm in even the most dire of circumstances.

And so it was on this occasion. Walker told his men that they were there to "regenerate" the civilization of Latin America—not just Nicaragua, not just Central America, but all of South America. They were there to introduce American values and democracy, to replace a worn-out Old World social and political order. These fortunate few, these original men of the Falange, were the first of many, he said, "the precursors of a movement destined to affect materially the civilization of the whole continent of South America."[24]

This term, "regeneration," would quickly gain currency, and soon, in the United States, men who signed up to follow Walker would be referred to by their admirers not as filibusters but as regenerators. As for these Originals, as the men of the first enlistment of the Falange became known, they were inspired by Walker's address, which, in their eyes, elevated them above the caliber of mere mercenaries and gave them a broader vision and a new purpose. There was no more talk of disintegration, only of regeneration.

An outbreak of cholera in Managua forced General Corral to withdraw his Legitimista army to Granada, but in early August, when General José Santos Guardiola left Granada and marched north toward Condega with a small but well-equipped Legitimista force of several hundred men, General Munoz finally took his Democratico army into the field. Munoz's orders were to prevent Guardiola from linking up with Legitimista irregulars in the province of Tegucigalpa to the northeast, from where he could threaten León and all the Democratico northwest. General Munoz left León, taking with him six hundred men and all the best equipment and supplies.

Walker was, in the meantime, looking for a local officer he could rely on. He found his man at Chinandega—the town's subprefect, Don José Maria Valle. A colonel in the Democratico army, Valle had been badly wounded during the siege of Granada. The injury had left him with a stiff knee and forced him into the Democraticos' civil service. Mostly of Indian stock, Colonel Valle could neither read nor write, yet he had a nobility and an eloquence that endeared him to the local people. Valle was also a gifted troubadour. "When he took the guitar in hand he would carry the women away with his songs of love or of patriotism," Walker said with admiration.[25]

Walker liked Valle immediately and found in him a man he could trust. The feeling was mutual—Valle, or Chelon as he was known familiarly by the locals, liked and respected Walker. It was not Walker's habit to tell even his closest friends everything that was in his mind, and he only told his subordinates what they needed to know. But to win Valle over and in strictest confidence, Walker told him of his new plan, a plan that went well beyond anything he had proposed to Castellon. If it could be pulled off, the civil war would be over within weeks. Valle was so taken by this audacious secret plan that he immediately and excitedly committed to commanding the Democratico troops involved in Walker's return to the south, at the same time giving Walker his solemn promise not to breathe a word to anyone about what Walker really intended. Walker's trust was not misplaced—from this moment on, Valle was one of Walker's most loyal Nicaraguan supporters.

Valle was an old friend of Provisional Director Castellon, and inspired by Walker's plan, the subprefect traveled down to León to convince Castellon to support Walker's return to the Meridional Department with men and matériel. When Castellon resisted and spoke against the operation, Valle argued all the harder, for, determined to avenge the death of a brother in the siege of Granada, Valle could not wait to come to grips with the Legitimistas again. While Walker was awaiting Valle's return, the colonel was joined by an unexpected American recruit—his brother Lipscomb Norvell Walker. Two years younger than Walker, Norvell, as he was known, served as a U.S. Army lieutenant during the Mexican War. Walker immediately commissioned his brother into the Falange with the rank of captain. But when William Walker later spoke about Nicaragua, he would never mention Norvell; his brother would become a liability and a source of embarrassment. As one of Walker's later recruits would say, when Norvell wasn't talking, he was drinking, and when he wasn't drinking, he was talking.[26]

By the middle of August, Castellon caved in to Valle's arguments and agreed to support Walker's stated mission. Walker immediately marched the Falange to Realejo to board the *Vesta*. But when the promised troops and supplies failed to materialize, Walker wrote to Castellon, telling him he planned to sail for Honduras to enter the service of the president of Honduras, Trinidad Cabanas, an elderly Democratico under threat from the Legitimista government of neighboring Guatemala. Spurred by this threat, Castellon gave the necessary orders.

Colonel Valle soon arrived with 170 local recruits. But in the third week of August, as Walker was loading supplies aboard the *Vesta* and a Costa Rican ketch he had hired for the mission, cholera arrived at Realejo. Valle's Nicaraguan recruits were quickly infected, but not a single North American came down with the disease. Walker, with all his medical training, was unable to account for the total immunity of the Americans. So deadly was this strain to the Nicaraguans that a man who was healthy one day could be dead three days later. A number of Valle's men perished, while others deserted to escape the disease.

But Walker would not be put off his mission, not by cholera nor by an urgent dispatch that arrived from Director Castellon. This dispatch advised Walker that there had been a bloody battle near the town of El Sauce in Nicaragua's central north, between General Munoz's Democratico army and General Guardiola's Legitimista army. After several hours' fighting, the Democraticos had won. But General Munoz was dead—either as the result of a battle wound or, as another account had it, after being shot in the back by one of his own men once victory had been gained.

"Now, Munoz being out of the way, all will be well," Castellon wrote to Walker, as he urged the American to abandon his mission to the south and come directly to León with his troops.[27] Munoz's army, while victorious, had suffered heavy casualties; without a commander, it limped into the town of Pueblo Nuevo, licking its wounds and reluctant to take any further offensive action. Although the defeated Legitimista commander, General Guardiola, was said to be riding hard for Granada with just a single companion, the provisional director feared that the Legitimistas might send a new army from

Granada against León while Munoz's army was immobilized. But stubborn William Walker ignored Castellon.

On August 23, the *Vesta* and the chartered Costa Rican ketch upped anchor and set sail, the word having spread around Realejo that, now that the Democraticos had been victorious at El Sauce, Walker and his Americanos were sailing for Honduras to help President Cabanas. Once the vessels were out of sight of land, they turned south, not north as Legitimista spies back at Realejo would report in expectation of *los Yanquis* sailing for Honduras. This time, the Legitimistas in the south would receive no warning that William Walker was coming.

VICTORY AT LA VIRGEN

A FTER A SIX-DAY RUN DOWN FROM REALEJO, THE *VESTA* BOLDLY dropped anchor in the cove at San Juan del Sur in the darkness. On the way south, the brig had lost contact with the Costa Rican ketch carrying most of Valle's troops, while aboard the *Vesta,* cholera had killed several more Nicaraguans in the first days of the journey. But by the time the brig arrived off San Juan del Sur on August 29, the epidemic had run its course on board.

Lanterns twinkled in the town. San Juan del Sur was peaceful. But the *Vesta* had been recognized as William Walker's vessel, and a rowboat came pulling out from the shore, bringing two locally resident Americans who informed Walker that the Legitimista garrison that had reoccupied the town since June had vamoosed as soon as the *Vesta* was sighted—the town was now undefended and open to Walker's occupation. The pair also informed Walker that a one-armed U.S. citizen by the name of Parker H. French had recently arrived from Granada and was waiting to catch the next Transit Company steamer when it arrived, to go up to San Francisco. French's loud-mouthed mulatto servant had told the two Americans that French had offered his services to the Legitimistas at Granada as an artillery officer.

Walker was acquainted with Parker H. French. The one-armed man—a *coto,* in the local parlance—had arrived in San Francisco in 1851 saying he'd lost his right arm fighting the Mexicans. Only in his twenties, French had set up in business as a lawyer and, with an outgoing personality, had made friends easily. He had gone on to serve in the new California legislature, occupying the seat of his law partner when he died suddenly, and had run a short-lived newspaper in Sacramento. When Walker was recruiting for the Falange in San Francisco back in February, French had said he would come down to join Walker's venture in Nicaragua once Walker initiated the affair.

Walker had French brought out to the *Vesta* to answer some questions. After greeting Walker warmly, French told him that he had actually gone to Granada to spy on the Legitimistas, pretending to be on their side while he assessed the strength of their forces and defenses, information that he passed on to Walker. While Walker would later say he did not altogether trust French at the time, the commander trusted him enough to give him a commission to raise more men for the Falange in San Francisco. Returning to California with French went the injured Frank Anderson, who was still limping badly as a result of the wound sustained at Rivas.

Walker established quarters in several buildings in San Juan del Sur on August 30, and later that day, the Accessory Transit Company's metal dinghies ferried hundreds of passengers the half mile from a freshly anchored ocean steamer to shore. Walker hoped to recruit some fit, young Americans into the Falange from among these travelers, but to his disappointment not one accepted his invitation to join the adventure. In a hive of activity, blue and white Transit Company stagecoaches carried the passengers away, over the Transit Road to Virgin Bay, while mule trains prepared to transport their luggage and the latest gold shipment from San Francisco.

Just before midnight, Valle arrived on the Costa Rican ketch, and with daylight, he and his Democratico soldiers came ashore. Walker now had a force of 43 North Americans and 120 Nicaraguans, Valle having lost 50 men to cholera and desertion. Information coming from Rivas via Transit Company personnel at Virgin Bay had it that General Guardiola had volunteered to take command at Rivas and had marched down from Granada with 200 of the Legitimistas' best men to bolster Colonel Bosque's garrison. Walker's informants put the size of Guardiola's total command at Rivas at 1,000 fighting men. But Walker considered that figure exaggerated, calculating that his expeditionary force of 163 men would be up against 500 to 600 Legitimistas.[1] The actual number of able-bodied Legitimistas at Rivas was, with Guardiola's reinforcements, 1,200.[2]

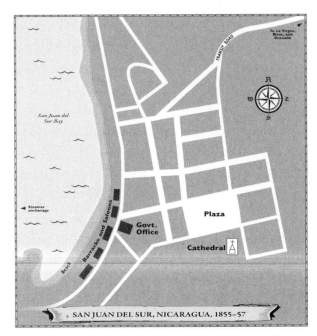

SAN JUAN DEL SUR, NICARAGUA, 1855–57

Walker waited at San Juan del Sur for the passengers from the latest Atlantic steamer to arrive from across the lake, which they did on September 2. But again he was unable to attract a single recruit—the passengers had heard about Walker's defeat at Rivas in June, and there was nothing attractive about failure. When the San Francisco–bound steamer sailed that same day, taking French and Anderson with it along with the hundreds of passengers from the East, Walker's force was loading mules and carts for an advance inland. In the middle of the night, Walker set out along the Transit Road with his little army.

At 9:00 A.M. on September 4, the column reached Virgin Bay, where Lake Nicaragua spread placidly before them. This lakeside place, called La Virgen, was a Transit Company depot personally established by Cornelius Vanderbilt. The Commodore had even gone sailing in a local boat here in 1850 and had almost capsized when a storm had sprung up out of nowhere, as frequently happened in these latitudes.

The La Virgen settlement had consisted of eight wooden accommodation huts in the fall of 1851, when the first Transit passengers had come through.

By 1855, the company bunkhouses had been joined by privately run hotels, and a number of other buildings had sprung up a little way back from the narrow beach that ran along the lakeshore—stables and horse corrals, a coach house, a blacksmith's workshop, staff quarters, and a commodious headquarters building occupied by Cortlandt Cushing, the Accessory Transit Company's manager in Nicaragua. The location chosen by Vanderbilt for the way station was poor in one sense, because, for a distance of half a mile out, the lake was quite shallow and travelers had to transfer from lake steamer to beach by rowboat. With Charles Morgan and Cornelius Kingsland Garrison running the Transit Company, work had begun on the construction of a long wooden jetty out into the lake.

Walker introduced himself to Transit manager Cushing, finding him a deliberate, even-tempered man. From others, Walker learned that Cushing was not known to either exaggerate or invent news. As he must, operating a business in the middle of civil war, Cushing kept his ear close to the ground. So when Cushing informed Walker that his contacts told him General Guardiola had marched south from Rivas the previous afternoon with a large force, apparently aiming to intercept Walker's column, but then had inexplicably turned his army around and returned to Rivas, Walker believed the manager.

After posting pickets around the settlement, Walker sent Commissary Doubleday to find beds and food at the town's hotels. These hotels did a fine trade when the Transit passengers came through every second week, but were virtually empty the rest of the time. On the strength of Cushing's information, which put the enemy many miles away, Walker allowed his men to fall out for breakfast.

But Cushing's intelligence was faulty. General Guardiola was on the march, and drawing closer by the minute.

When the small Legitimista garrison from San Juan del Sur had reached Rivas wide-eyed with the report that Yankees had arrived aboard the *Vesta*, General José Santos Guardiola had ordered six hundred of his best men to march on San Juan del Sur at once to confront the filibusters at the port.

Ambitious, arrogant, energetic, restless to the point of recklessness, and notoriously moody, thirty-eight-year-old Guardiola, a native of Honduras, had
fought in revolutions, counterrevolutions, and cross-border wars all his adult
life. But as a confirmed right-wing conservative, he always fought under the
Legitimista banner.

Most recently, Guardiola had fought against Honduras's Democratico
government of President Trinidad Cabanas, with only limited success.
It had taken the ascendancy of the Legitimistas in Nicaragua to lure Guardiola south to accept a command against Castellon's Democraticos. Guardiola's
defeat by General Munoz at El Sauce had stung his pride. "Brooding over
his ill-luck in the north," William Walker would write of him, "and anxious
to regain his lost fame, he leaped at the chance of going to Rivas." Guardiola had in fact come to Rivas declaring that he would "sweep the filibusters
into the sea."[3]

Supremely confident in his own abilities and blaming the troops then
under him for the defeat at El Sauce, Guardiola fully believed he would
crush the Americans. He knew that the Yankee numbers were small, and
that the last time William Walker ventured into the Meridional Department,
the Democratico soldiers had deserted Walker. If Walker was again supported by Democraticos, it was questionable whether those men could be
relied on when the time came to put their lives on the line. Guardiola,
meanwhile, had every confidence in his own officers, several of whom "were
reputed to be of skill and courage, and desirous of more active service than
was to be had under (General) Corral" at Granada.[4] But Guardiola was less
confident of his rank and file. So, in his baggage train, among vehicles carrying supplies and ammunition, oxcarts traveled loaded with wicker-covered
glass bottles filled with guaro. It was Guardiola's intention that, when his
troops went into action, they would be primed with generous amounts of
the local liquor.

Guardiola had found a six-pound field gun at Rivas. Cast in Spain and a
leftover from the Spanish occupation, the old cannon didn't even have a lim-
ber and consequently could not be hauled by horses or mules. Determined
to use the cannon against the Americans, Guardiola had ordered a detachment of his men to haul it. Hitched to its human beasts, the cannon had
taken pride of place in his column when he marched from Rivas on the

afternoon of September 3. Later that same day, General Guardiola's column joined the Transit Road and tramped west toward San Juan del Sur along the white gravel highway.

As darkness fell, Guardiola left the road and set up camp at the hacienda on the Jocote cattle ranch, one and a half miles from the Half Way House. Guardiola at that point believed Walker to still be at San Juan del Sur and intended to attack him soon after daylight. At daybreak on September 4, Guardiola resumed his march, but when he reached the Half Way House, he learned from servants there that the Americans and their Democratico allies had passed by in the night on the way to La Virgen and had even been provided with water by the inn's American owner. Because Guardiola had failed to leave pickets on the road, Walker and his column had marched right past the Jocote in the darkness, without the Legitimistas even noticing. Guardiola immediately swung his army around and marched for Virgin Bay, six miles away.

Now, with La Virgen just beyond a rise ahead, Guardiola called a halt. The short, squat general looked along the military column from the back of his horse. With thick black hair, a round face, and small eyes, the man had a thin, pencil-straight nose and pudgy cheeks. His dark beard was thick, but neatly trimmed, while the ends of his mustache twirled in the Spanish fashion. With satisfaction, Guardiola noted that the men hauling his lone field gun were making good progress. The gun's attendants knew what to expect from their unforgiving commander if they faltered. Guardiola was proud of his nickname, "the Butcher"—gained from his habit of executing his prisoners. It was a nickname that put fear into the hearts of both his Central American opponents and his own men.

With the column stationary, Guardiola had the guaro distributed. Empty wicker-encased bottles littered the roadside when cavalry scouts came trotting from the east to excitedly report that the Yankees were at La Virgen. Cursing that the filibusters had the advantage of the settlement's buildings for cover, the general ordered his field gun brought up. But as the troops assigned to the cannon labored to drag and push it up to a firing position on the hill ahead, from where it could shell the settlement, the aged gun's weathered carriage suddenly gave way. With cries of alarm from its crew, the artillery piece crashed uselessly into the dirt, where it lay like a dead whale.

Guardiola cursed his men as buffoons and useless sons of bitches, but possessing neither the time nor the skills to repair the gun carriage, he regretfully had its touch hole spiked to prevent the weapon's being of use to the enemy, then abandoned it.

The Legitimista army was formed up in companies. The enlisted men were in universal white, with white ribbons on their straw hats. The officers were clad in more elaborate uniforms—trim black jackets; white breeches; and flat, broad-brimmed, Spanish-style hats circled by white ribbons. General Guardiola also wore a flat hat and a black uniform, but his tunic shone with gold epaulets and a profusion of gold braid. At the front of the column, the color party surrounded the blue and white Legitimista flag as it fluttered from its staff. A troop of lancers stood behind General Guardiola with long, white cloth pennons trailing from their seven-foot-long lances.

Guardiola knew that the Yankees over the hill were totally unaware that Legitimista troops were close by—the scouts had reported that most of the enemy could be seen sitting around breakfasting. General Guardiola gave his officers their battle orders, assigning several units to each wing to outflank the settlement. The remaining units would make a frontal assault. When his officers, on horseback, had returned to the head of their troops, Guardiola gave the order to fix bayonets. Officers and sergeant majors repeated the order, and through the ranks, the troops drew their bayonets and slotted them onto the end of their loaded muskets. Guardiola ordered the advance. Bugles trilled, and the army moved forward. Guardiola kicked his horse into the walk, and the lancers of his bodyguard followed close behind.

As the Legitimista infantry came up and over the hill, those units assigned to the assault in the center received sporadic but inaccurate fire from Colonel Valle's startled pickets posted in their path. The Battle of La Virgen had begun.

Commissary Doubleday was leaning on the porch rail outside the Transit Company headquarters at La Virgen, talking with company manager Cortlandt Cushing. Falange members had just finished eating a hearty breakfast and were thinking about catching some shut-eye. Doubleday frowned, seeing a puff of white smoke on the rise to the west of the town, where the Transit Road came in from San Juan del Sur. At first, Doubleday couldn't make out what the smoke meant. Then he saw a mass of Legitimista troops come over the hill.

William Walker was in the open. The first hint of trouble was a dull popping sound from the direction of the Transit Road. Looking to the west, Walker could see Colonel Valle's pickets withdrawing in good order ahead of a white mass of Legitimista troops flooding over the rise, firing as they came. As the pickets backpedaled down the slope toward the town, they paused to reload, fired again, then continued to pull back. Walker saw hundreds of Legitimista infantrymen spreading along the edges of the settlement, aiming to seal off his flanks. Hundreds more Legitimistas were advancing from the west in a body to make a frontal assault, walking in step to rattling kettle drums played by fresh-faced drummer boys. Officers in black rode with them.

As Valle's drummer rapped out the call to arms, Walker's Americans rushed to where their rifles stood neatly stacked outside the hotels. In their rush, they took the first weapon they laid their hands on. The men of Valle's western picket reached the settlement without loss, and Walker, calm and confident, quickly assessed the threats and issued clear, concise orders for the defense of the settlement. Twenty Americans under Captain Charles Hornsby were dispatched to secure the right flank, where rising ground would give the Legitimistas the advantage if they were permitted to occupy it. Fifteen more Falange members under Lieutenant John Markham were sent to the left flank, where the ground was flat. The remaining handful of Americans hurried off with Lieutenant Robert Gay to take up a defensive position at the lake beach, behind the settlement, to prevent the Legitimistas from coming along the beach and attacking Walker from the rear.

Colonel Valle's Democraticos, ordered to hold the center, quickly spread across the Transit Road. Walker himself drew sword and pistol and, concerned that his Democraticos might not stand up to the Legitimista frontal attack, joined Colonel Valle and his aide Captain Luzarranga in the center, taking personal command there. Doubleday, who had become Walker's chief aide and interpreter, hurried along on his commander's heel.

The residents of the settlement, many of them the wives and children of the American employees of the Transit Company working at Virgin Bay and crewing the lake steamers, ran to the cluster of buildings to the left of the Transit Road and close by the Virgin Bay jetty. The largest of these structures housed the Accessory Transit Company warehouse and office. Here, Transit Company manager Cortlandt Cushing and half a dozen American staff frantically piled up trunks and boxes, creating a protective wall at the door. It was there that the civilians took shelter. Despite the frightening situation, the women and children appeared remarkably calm, as if this was an everyday occurrence.

On the right, Hornsby and his men advanced to occupy the high ground. Keeping low, they crept through the undergrowth, firing only when they had a good target, and quickly reloading. As the Legitimista troops on this flank pushed toward Hornsby, the Americans formed a line of lying and kneeling men, using the undergrowth and a few small cane huts for cover. From there they poured fire into the advancing Legitimistas, yelling insults at the Nicaraguan conscripts, calling them "dirty low-down greasers"—greasers being a derogatory term applied in the United States to all Central Americans, from Mexican soldiers' habit of using pig grease to clean their muskets.[5] The Americans let out a whoop every time their bullets claimed a target, as if shooting ducks. The noise, flame, and fury created by Hornsby's little command made it appear that there were many more Americans on the hillside than was the case.

But the Legitimistas, heavily outnumbering Hornsby's men, kept coming, given courage by guaro and urged by their officers to come to grips with the Yankees and use their bayonets. The white companies fired as they came, but they lacked training; this, and the alcohol in their veins, combined to produce frequently atrocious aim. By the time the Legitimistas closed to within thirty yards, the cool, dead-eye aim of the Americans and their ability to keep up a rapid reloading rate had a telling effect—the stream of lead stopped the Legitimista advance in its tracks. With more and more of their comrades struck down and with massive .758 caliber Minié rounds zipping by their ears at a thousand feet a second, just as the Legitimistas were near enough to make a bayonet charge, their liquored courage deserted them. They pulled back, leaving a score of dead and wounded on the field.

Walker witnessed all this from where he was stationed with Valle and his men in the center. Here, in the middle of the battle, the Legitimistas pushed forward slowly, dropping to one knee, firing, drizzling powder into their muzzle-loaders, ramming a ball down the barrel with a ramrod, and then advancing a little farther before again going down on one knee and firing. The enlisted men were goaded on by officers, many of whom were still on horseback, who flailed their men with riding whips and the backs of their swords to drive them forward. Soon the Legitimistas in the center were close enough to mount a charge. Yelling as they came forward in several waves, the men of the first line fired on the run before leveling their muskets to use the bayonets projecting a foot from the end of the four-foot-long barrels.

Valle's men held their ground in the face of the charge, firing a coordinated volley. In Doubleday's words, the result was that the Legitimistas "went down as if grass before the scythe."[6] So many men from the first line fell that those behind came to an abrupt halt. The second-line men brought up their muskets; it was their turn to fire a volley. Smoke puffs appeared as if by magic along the entire length of the Legitimista line. Two hundred balls of lead flew on the warm morning air toward William Walker and his waiting defenders.

Doubleday, standing beside Walker, heard the balls hum by his ears. Then, to his horror, he saw Walker sink to his knees, clutching at his chest. "I assisted him to his feet," Doubleday later said, "when he quickly assured his alarmed men that he was alright."[7] One musket ball had grazed Walker on the throat. More seriously, another had hit him in the chest, with such force that it knocked him off his feet. Walker, once he was standing again, felt inside his jacket and was amazed to discover that the ball that entered his jacket had not drawn blood. Instead, letters from Provisional Director Castellon that had been in his pocket had been shredded by the musket ball. The letters absorbed the impact of the round—indirectly, Castellon had saved Walker's life.

The second Legitimista line now charged with bayonets extended. Some of Valle's men had hidden inside several houses beside the road, and without warning, they appeared at windows and doors and opened fire on the flank of the surging Legitimista line. This had a devastating effect on the attack, with musket balls scything along the ranks from one side and randomly plucking the life out of men who didn't even know where the rounds came from. The uncertainty caused by this fusillade, with its accompanying crackle of detonations and subsequent cloud of smoke, caused the Legitimista attack in the center to waver, then give way. Survivors pulled back, to maintain poorly directed musket fire from a distance.

Checking his right flank, Walker could see that Hornsby's men were holding the Legitimistas at bay and were exchanging fire with a stationary enemy. But when Walker looked around to the left, he could see that Valle's men and the Americans under Markham were in danger of being outflanked by superior numbers. Markham's men, stationed behind wooden fences, were sending a steady fire toward the Legitimistas trying to get by them but hadn't been able to prevent a number of attackers from reaching the beach in the rear. So Walker sent Doubleday scurrying to Hornsby with orders to take Americans who could be spared from the right to support Lieutenant Robert Gay and the few Falange members holding the beach.

Once Doubleday delivered this message, he followed Hornsby and the handful of men called away from the hillside and hastened toward the lake. As Doubleday ran, he saw a Legitimista colonel who sat astride a white horse and ignored the fire from the arriving Americans as he urged his men to the charge. The colonel's horse suddenly reared up and then fell down dead with a bullet in the heart, spilling its rider to the ground. The dazed officer was helped to his feet by his men—Doubleday later learned that this was Colonel Manuel Arguello. The arrival of the Hornsby party checked Arguello's men, who withdrew, some firing as they went. Arguello, sword in hand, reluctantly followed them. He would live to fight los Yanquis another day. Just as Doubleday was congratulating himself on helping turn back the Legitimistas on the left, he felt "an exceedingly sharp, stinging sensation in my side."[8] He sank onto the ground, on his rump, with one hand clutching his side.

Dr. Alex Jones, who was just behind him, called out, "Doubleday? Are you all right?"

Doubleday calmly turned and handed his rifle up to Jones, figuring he had no more use for it. "I've got it this time," he told the doctor. "Plumb through me."

Before Jones could respond, he spotted Legitimista movement on the beach close by. "Look out!" he called to Hornsby and the others, pointing to the danger.[9]

As Jones and Hornsby's men ran to take cover at the corner of a house ten yards to the rear, Doubleday attempted to rise to follow them. To his dismay, his legs wouldn't obey him, and he collapsed full length on the ground. Moments later, Legitimista soldiers were running by him, just feet away, as they charged toward the house where Jones and the others were sheltering. Thinking Doubleday dead, the Legitimistas ignored him, standing to fire at the Americans at the house and then reload, all the time with their backs to the prostrate figure. Again Doubleday tried to stand. This time he succeeded. Seeing the white uniforms of the enemy between him and his comrades, Doubleday could only think of reaching his friends. Holding his paining side, he ran through the Legitimista ranks with bullets flying all around him and miraculously reached the others without receiving another wound—from either side.

Years later, Doubleday would encounter Dr. Jones in the streets of San Francisco, when the commissary half-jokingly reprimanded the doctor for "abandoning" him there beside Lake Nicaragua as the Legitimistas charged. "For a man shot 'plumb through,'" Jones would respond with a smile, "you did some creditable running through the enemy's ranks to rejoin your friends."[10]

While Jones, Doubleday, Hornsby, and their handful of Falange comrades were engaged in fighting for their lives beside the narrow beach, another band of Legitimistas advanced along the beach itself, toward the jetty. Lieutenant Robert Gay and five other Americans stationed on the gray sands of the beach knelt in a skirmish line and fired volley after volley at the advancing Legitimistas, but on came the enemy, ignoring their casualties. Gay and his men threw aside their rifles, drew pistols, and, with Gay in the lead, charged along the sand into the attackers with six-guns blazing and yelling like maniacs. This charge stopped the Legitimistas in their tracks, then drove them back.

On the back of Gay's charge, seeing the Legitimistas on the beach in retreat, John Markham called his men to their feet and led an advance toward the woods on the left. In the face of Markham's advance, the Legitimistas on that flank gave way. Theirs was no ordered retreat; these men turned and fled headlong to the woods. On seeing this, Valle called on his men to drive back the enemy still holding firm in the center. The Democratico troops joined their stiff-legged, limping colonel in a steady advance up the slope to the west, following the direction of the Transit Road, forcing the enemy back in front of them as if driving sheep.

Meanwhile, Walker arrived at the beach with several Americans. They came "with the rush of a whirlwind," said Doubleday.[11] Reinforcing Gay and his men, they dislodged the last enemy holding ground along the edge of the lake. Soon there was a loud cheer from the Democratico troops, as the Legitimistas in the center and both flanks were seen to be in wholesale retreat. Attempts by Legitimista officers to reform their units were futile; their soldiers threw away their weapons and ran for their lives.

Most of all, the Americans enjoyed the sight of "Holy Joe" Guardiola beating a hasty retreat—"Holy Joe" because the general's first names translated as "Saint Joseph." General Guardiola galloped from the battlefield trailed by the lancers of his escort, heading north toward Rivas. His officers would lead the survivors, including a large number of wounded, back to Rivas, but many men deserted Legitimista ranks that morning.

The Battle of Virgin Bay was over. The Americans had won. This was William Walker's first military victory in Nicaragua. What was more, as a fighting force, Guardiola's army had, for now, been rendered useless. Nineteenth-century New York newspaper editor and author Richard Harding Davis would later express the opinion that Walker's overwhelming victory at Virgin Bay "shows how fatally effective was the rifle and revolver fire of the Californians." He added: "Indeed, so wonderful was it that when some years ago I visited the towns and cities captured by the filibusters, I found that the marksmanship of Walker's Phalanx was still a tradition."[12]

With the battle over, Dr. Jones took a look at Charles Doubleday's wound. Doubleday was lucky—a musket ball "had struck the broad buckle of my sword-belt."[13] While the bullet had not penetrated Doubleday's body, the force of its impact had driven the belt buckle into his side so violently that it created a painful gouge; the wound would trouble him for months. Overall, Walker's casualties were minimal. Two of Valle's men had been killed, and three wounded. All the Americans survived the battle, and apart from Walker's own minor injuries and Doubleday's wound, Benjamin Williamson and a Private Small received serious though not life-threatening wounds—a bullet had passed right through Small, emerging from his back, miraculously without doing any major damage. Both men would recover fully.

The Legitimistas, on the other hand, had suffered heavily. Close to sixty Legitimista bodies were buried by Transit Company staff in a trench beside the Transit Road. Informed reports put the total number of Legitimista wounded at more than one hundred, many of whom subsequently died from their wounds. Walker issued orders for those enemy wounded found on the battlefield to be carried into La Virgen, where Dr. Jones bandaged them up—to the surprise of the locals and to the Legitimistas themselves. Walker observed: "The poor fellows, who expected to be shot, were exceedingly grateful for the attentions they received."[14]

As enemy casualties were being collected on the battlefield, word reached Walker that one of Valle's officers was busy killing wounded Legitimistas. So he sent Spanish-speaker Doubleday, who refused to let his injury keep him off his feet, to call on the man to stop at once. The officer in question turned out to be none other than Colonel Mariano Mendez, the mad Mexican, who in August had returned to the Democratico north after the fiasco of the Battle of Rivas and volunteered for Valle's expeditionary force.

Doubleday found Mendez using the butt of a captured musket to end the life of a badly wounded Legitimista lying on the battlefield. When Doubleday angrily informed Mendez that Colonel Walker forbade him to do that, the wily old Mexican shrugged, tossed the musket aside, and walked away. But after a few paces, he stooped and took up another discarded Legitimista musket, one with a bayonet affixed, then stood over another seriously wounded Legitimista. Mendez glanced at Doubleday, then proceeded to end the Legitimista's life with a bayonet jab to the throat. Doubleday had to angrily spell out that Mendez must not kill enemy wounded, period. Mendez, disgusted, tossed the weapon aside and slouched away.

Walker's troops also collected Guardiola's heavily laden ammunition carts, while foraging parties scouring the battlefield and the surrounding woods brought in more than 150 discarded Legitimista muskets, with which Walker planned to equip future recruits. Abandoned enemy horses were also rounded up, and using these, Valle, Mendez, and several Falange members scouted the vicinity during the afternoon, reporting back to Walker that

there was no sign of Legitimista troops. At the same time, Walker questioned the enemy wounded, from whom he learned all the details of Guardiola's march from Rivas to do battle with him and of the Honduran general's
hollow threat to throw the Americans back into the sea.

Walker allowed his troops to rest at La Virgen overnight, but the next day, he
marched them back along the Transit Road to San Juan del Sur, which he felt
he could more easily defend than La Virgen. He took with him the wounded
of both sides and the captured arms and ammunition.

Once back at San Juan del Sur, Walker sent a mounted messenger up the
coast road to León, carrying a dispatch for Provisional Director Castellon
telling of the sound defeat he'd inflicted on the Legitimista army at Virgin
Bay and of Walker's occupation of San Juan del Sur. Walker also requested
additional men and supplies for a push north against Rivas. But, Walker
stressed, he did not want conscript soldiers. He had seen the ranks of both
sides in this civil war filled by the unwilling and the unfit and had seen the
results on the battlefield. Any man sent south to join his force, wrote Colonel
Walker to Provisional Director Castellon, had to be a willing volunteer.

The wounded Charles Doubleday, resting up at San Juan del Sur, felt that
Walker had been rash and overconfident in his first assault on Rivas but
seemed to have learned from his mistake; his new policy of consolidation
and reinforcement was, to Doubleday's mind, the prudent course.[15] Little
did Doubleday know that Walker was planning an even more rash operation.

When Walker's messenger reached León, he found the city gripped by a
fresh outbreak of cholera, with Director Castellon one of the many who had
come down with it. Castellon, confined to his bed and very weak, read
Walker's dispatch with considerable difficulty. An hour after learning of
Walker's Democratico victory over Guardiola's Legitimista army at La Virgen, Don Francisco Castellon died.

❦ 7 ❦

WALKER'S SECRET PLAN

A MESSENGER FROM LEÓN BROUGHT WALKER A LETTER FROM DON Nasario Escoto, the new provisional director of the Democraticos, telling of the death of Don Maximo Castellon. Walker was saddened by the news; he had found Castellon to be good-hearted and gentle-natured—not the ideal leader of a revolution, but a genuine man just the same.[1]

Congratulating Walker on his victory at Virgin Bay, Provisional Director Escoto advised the American colonel that while he would like to send him reinforcements, and volunteers as requested, the cholera epidemic was making it difficult to recruit even common laborers for government service, let alone soldiers. He would undertake to send Walker supplies by sea and do his best to find volunteers to join the Falange in the south but couldn't promise anything.

Walker's force, meanwhile, was growing by other means. Daily now, deserters from the Legitimista army at Rivas arrived at San Juan del Sur to volunteer to join Colonel Valle's Democratico unit, telling tales of brutal treatment at the hands of Legitimista officers. These deserters also passed on information about the military situation at Rivas. At the same time, from the village of San Jorge, Democratico sympathizers come flooding west with red ribbons on their hats and broad smiles on their faces to join Valle's unit.

Despite these additions, Walker would not move from San Juan del Sur until he had the promised reinforcements from Provisional Director Escoto. Other reinforcements came from south of the border; as news of the Legitimista defeat at La Virgen spread, Democratico sympathizers who had fled into northern Costa Rica at the beginning of the war arrived in San Juan del

Sur to offer their services to Colonel Walker. Among them was American physician Dr. J. L. Cole, who had married the daughter of a leading Rivas family, the Aguartes.

Then, one day, Walker's first guide in the Meridional Department, old Don Maximo Espinosa, appeared out of the blue. Walker had last seen of Don Maximo back in Tola on June 28, when the Falange had left Espinosa and his nephew watching over the captured Legitimista lancers. Espinosa told Walker that once news reached Tola of the Falange's retreat from Rivas, he had gone into hiding in the countryside near his Santa Ursula plantation, relying on former employees for food and information and hoping to soon hear that Walker had returned. Walker, relieved to see Espinosa alive and well, invited him to take up the appointment Director Castellon had given him back in June, that of Democratico commissioner of taxes for the Meridional Department, based in San Juan del Sur.

Espinosa enthusiastically set about raising money for the Democraticos via port duties and by imposing a tax on all local businesses. Of the two leading bars in San Juan del Sur, one was run by the French consul, the other, the Dime Saloon, by American John Priest, who was also the U.S. consul for the area. When Prefect Espinosa assessed Priest for tax, Priest was furious. He hadn't paid tax to the Legitimistas, and he certainly had no intentions of paying tax to the Democraticos. Not only did he refuse to pay, but Priest also threatened to summon a U.S. warship to protect his right to sell liquor to sailors and soldiers without paying tax, by virtue of the fact that he was the official U.S. representative in the port.

When this was reported to Walker, he didn't bat an eyelid. He simply issued orders for a twenty-four-hour guard to be mounted outside the Dime Saloon by Valle's soldiers, to prevent customers from entering the saloon until the tax had been paid. Not surprisingly, several hours later, Priest turned up at Prefect Espinosa's office and paid his tax in full.

On September 20, the 1,257-ton Nicaragua Line steamer *Sierra Nevada* arrived at San Juan del Sur from San Francisco. Built in New York four years previously, she was considered one of the soundest ships on the Central American run. Passengers streaming ashore were met by Walker's recruiting officers. No longer was William Walker perceived as either a failure or a joke—news of the victory at La Virgen meant that he was able to recruit a handful of Americans from among the steamer's passengers. Young and keen for adventure, they were armed with captured weapons, and, like the rest of Walker's men, would serve in the clothes they wore at the time they joined the Falange. For a uniform, they were given black dye for their shirts and a red Democratico ribbon to wear around their hats. These new men, along with several Americans enlisted locally, including Dr. Cole, brought Walker's little force up to sixty men fit for duty. Colonel Valle's Nicaraguan unit, meanwhile, had grown to be more than two hundred strong.

Word now reached Walker that the Legitimistas' commanding general, Major General Ponciano Corral, had come down from Granada and dismissed General Guardiola from his post, taking personal charge at Rivas and reorganizing the city's defenses. "Butcher" Guardiola had slunk off back to Honduras. While Walker felt that Corral would probably be no better at soldiering than Guardiola, he was told by Valle and others that the affable Corral, popular with all classes when mayor of Granada and a cabinet minister, would be more likely to lift the morale of the Legitimistas at Rivas.

Before long, fresh intelligence arrived—General Corral was marching from Rivas with his main force to do battle with Walker at San Juan del Sur. Walker immediately assembled his men and marched west, planning to ambush Corral on the Transit Road. But Corral unaccountably turned around and returned to Rivas, so Walker abandoned his ambush location and continued on to La Virgen. Shortly after the column arrived there, Walker's scouts intercepted a mounted Legitimista courier from Granada who had expected to find General Corral's army at La Virgen. Among the dispatches carried by the courier was one to Corral from the adjutant general of the Legitimista army, Major General Fernando Chamorro, telling Corral that Chamorro couldn't send reinforcements that Corral had requested. Chamorro revealed that through illness and desertions, the Granada garrison was badly depleted, leaving the city lightly defended, while the morale of troops and civilians alike was drooping. Chamorro also warned that Legitimista party leaders were losing heart and despairing of the ability to keep fighting if the Democraticos actively pressed the war.

Having read these very informative dispatches, Walker returned them to the courier, along with a note from Walker to General Corral, advising him that Walker had taken the liberty of reading them. The astonished courier was given back his horse, told he could find General Corral at Rivas, and sent on his way. Walker had added a comment in his note—with both sides having exhausted themselves in this war, he said, what the country needed was peace.

Later that same day, a response arrived from General Corral, politely acknowledging receipt of the intercepted dispatches. But there was also a slip of paper on which were written what Walker took to be "cabalistic signs."[2] Suspecting they may have been Freemason's signs, Walker showed the piece of paper to Charles Hornsby and Julius De Brissot, both of whom, he knew, were Freemasons. De Brissot, who held high rank in the Masonic Order, said that this was indeed a message using Freemasons' code and that Corral inquired whether he could communicate confidentially with Walker. Walker was well pleased. Not only did he now know the state of enemy defenses and morale at their capital, but he also knew that their field commander was open to a peace parley.

But rather than move toward Rivas, Walker marched back to San Juan del Sur, later explaining that he didn't feel he yet had a large enough force to take on Corral's army of at least twelve hundred men at Rivas if Corral chose to fight. Besides, he would say, intelligence brought to him out of Granada by an escaped prisoner confirmed the state of affairs described in the captured Legitimista dispatches, and his thoughts turned to the plan that had been in his mind for some time—the secret plan that he had revealed to Colonel Valle. But to make that plan work, Walker felt he still needed more men.

On October 3, a few days after Walker's return to San Juan del Sur, the 1,117-ton Pacific Mail Line steamer *Cortes* dropped anchor in the cove. Built in New York in 1852 as the *Saratoga*, 220 feet long, with three decks and two masts, the *Cortes* had been purchased by Cornelius Vanderbilt for his Independent Line in 1853 before going to the Pacific Mail Line the following year in the buyout of Vanderbilt's competitive operation. Now, after the Nicaragua Line lost two of its vessels in shipwrecks on the coast of Mexico, the *Cortes* was under charter to Charles Morgan and Cornelius Garrison of the Accessory Transit Company to help fill the gap left by their loss.

As the hundreds of San Francisco passengers came ashore from the *Cortes*, Walker and his officers stood on the edge of the beach, watching them. Through the surf, Nicaraguan natives carried men, women, and children on their backs and shoulders from small boats to the sandy shore. Now, with a smile, Walker recognized a passenger limping onto the beach and leading a party of thirty-five men armed with rifles and pistols. He was Charles Gilman, one of Walker's followers during the Sonoran expedition, the man whose leg Walker had amputated during that ill-starred episode. In California, Gilman had spent many months recovering before being fitted with a wooden leg. In Walker's opinion, "Gilman was a man of strong mind, with all the sentiments of a soldier," a man possessed of "a good store of military knowledge."[3]

More importantly, in Mexico, Gilman had demonstrated his total loyalty to Walker, and he had done so again by helping recruit the thirty-five men who had accompanied him from San Francisco. Best of all, as far as Walker was concerned, Gilman followed his orders without question. Walker immediately gave him the rank of lieutenant colonel, appointing him deputy to Charles Hornsby, whom he now promoted to full colonel.

Among Gilman's men were George R. Davidson, who had served in the U.S. Army's Kentucky Regiment during the Mexican War, as well as John P. Waters, John M. Baldwin, and A. S. Brewster, all of whom had U.S. Army experience. Walker immediately put Gilman's party to work guarding the latest Treasure Train on its trek across the isthmus to La Virgen and its connection with a lake steamer. On the return of this party to San Juan del Sur, Walker, now with almost a hundred North American soldiers, reorganized the Falange into a battalion of three companies. Hornsby commanded the battalion, with Gilman as his deputy, while John Markham, who had performed so well at Rivas and Virgin Bay, was promoted to captain and given command of a company. Two of the new arrivals, Brewster and Davidson, received captain's commissions and command of the other two companies.

At the same time, Walker divested himself of the services of Mariano Mendez, sending the colorful but wayward Mexican back to León. Walker's excuse was that Valle's men complained that Mendez treated them roughly and had reportedly been rustling the cattle of local landowners. Before the unhappy Mexican departed, he leaned down from the saddle of his horse and cautioned Walker in a low voice: "The Nicaraguans are to be governed only with silver in one hand and the whip in the other."[4]

At this point, too, Walker and Charles Doubleday fell out. Years later, Doubleday would claim that he submitted his resignation after Walker and he had walked alone along the beach at San Juan del Sur and Walker told him in confidence that he planned to become virtual emperor of all of Central America—this, said Doubleday was a "conspiracy against the popular liberty," and he could not support it.[5] In reality, it seems that Doubleday, who had come to think of himself as Walker's chief aide, expressed the opinion that the operation Walker would soon embark on was ill conceived—Walker's latest general order, now that he had added thirty-six more Americans to the Falange, was for preparations to be made for the entire force to march to Lake Nicaragua for an offensive operation.

Walker himself would write that Doubleday "left at this time because having, without invitation, stated to (me) his opinion about certain movements being made." Doubleday made these remarks in front of Walker's other officers, generating a terse response from Walker: "When my commissary's opinion is required it will be asked for!"[6]

Walker would brook no insubordination from his officers, then or later. One of his admirers, the poet Joaquin Miller, a California miner who knew a number of men who fought under Walker, said that Walker "never took advice, but always gave commands, and they must be obeyed."[7] As for Doubleday's unsolicited advice, Walker later wrote, "At the time the remark was made, it was of the first necessity for the force to feel that it had but one head."[8] Doubleday himself admitted, "I was young, which is my excuse for venturing to remonstrate against the course that he (Walker) had determined upon."[9]

Doubleday, whose pride was hurt, immediately resigned. But he asked for and received a character reference from Walker. After Doubleday showed that reference to the representative of the U.S. Mail Line at Panama, he was given a free steamer ticket to New York. Walker lamented the loss of Doubleday, whom he considered "industrious and exact in the performance of his duties."[10] But in Walker's view, no man was irreplaceable, and he would permit no one to contest his decisions.

Charles Doubleday would one day swallow his pride and again serve William Walker, praising Walker "for the example he gave to the world of courage and high purpose."[11] But that was some way off; on October 3, Doubleday immediately departed San Juan del Sur in an open boat and sailed to Costa Rica. From there he took a Peruvian brig to Panama. Within weeks, Doubleday would be back home in Ohio, a long way from tropical Nicaragua, experiencing snow for the first time in years, regaling friends and family with tales of his adventures, and, with feelings of envy and regret, reading the regular U.S. newspaper reports of unfolding events in Nicaragua.

The same day that the *Cortes* arrived and Doubleday left, a boat arrived from Realejo carrying Captain Ubaldo Herrera, originally a native of Legitimista stronghold Granada but now a firm Democratico, bringing with him thirty-five Nicaraguans from the north. These men were the promised reinforcements from Director Escoto. Although few in number, they were all volunteers, as Walker had stipulated. Herrera's little company brought Colonel Valle's battalion strength up to more than 250 men.

Walker was almost ready to implement his secret plan. But there were logistical reasons to delay a little longer. To begin with, Captain Herrera had also proudly brought Walker a small, brass two-pound cannon from León. To augment this, that same day Walker purchased a new six-pound iron naval gun from Captain Reed, skipper of the *Queen of the Pacific*, a square-rigged coal ship chartered by the Nicaragua Line and currently in port to re-fill the *Cortes's* bunkers. Walker ordered gun carriages built for the two guns. With horses and mules at a premium, once the carriages were readied, the guns would have to be dragged by a detachment from Valle's battalion.

That night, as Walker and Charles Gilman dined together, they discussed the Accessory Transit Company. Gilman, fresh from San Francisco, told Walker "that there was a struggle in the company itself, between rival parties aiming to get control of it. The impression made on [me] was that the agents in New York and San Francisco [Morgan and Garrison] were acting together to depress the market price of the stock."[12]

Walker filed this information away in the back of his mind for future reference. Matters involving Vanderbilt, Morgan, and Garrison were not at the top of his list of priorities. For now, Walker was focusing on his next military operation. With a force of 350 men including almost 100 Americans, plus two field pieces, Walker now had enough confidence to attempt an operation so audacious that Julius Caesar would have been proud.

It took a week to build the gun carriages. On October 11, to the tap of kettle drums played by a Nicaraguan drummer boy in Valle's battalion and by Walker's youngest recruit, Norris, an American youth of perhaps fourteen who had come down on the *Cortes* with Gilman's party, Walker's entire force marched briskly out of San Juan del Sur. They marched over the Transit Road to La Virgen, taking the two cannon with them.

The troops were quartered at La Virgen, with orders to keep out of sight. Shortly after, the green-hulled, double-decked lake steamer *La Virgen* hove into view. Brought to Nicaragua by Cornelius Vanderbilt to operate with the *Central America*, the *Director*, and the *Morgan* on the lake, the side-wheel steamboat was making a scheduled run to Virgin Bay from the San Juan River.

When the *La Virgen* arrived, Colonel Charles Hornsby and a detachment of Falange troops waited for her passengers to disembark and then went aboard. Hornsby was known to the skipper, Joseph N. Scott, an American and a veteran of the Transit Company's lake and river operations. Scott's welcoming smile dissolved when Hornsby presented him with written notification from Colonel Walker that his steamboat was being commandeered until further notice. Scott protested vehemently, as did Transit manager Cortlandt Cushing when he found out. Scott and Cushing argued that, as the lake and river steamers were owned by a U.S. company, the U.S. government considered them to be sailing under the U.S. flag.

Walker, a trained attorney among other things, was the last person with whom the pair should have argued points of law. He dismissed their argument by pointing out that the Transit Company's contract with the Nicaraguan government, with which Walker had made himself totally familiar, specifically stated that these vessels were to operate under the Nicaraguan flag, which meant Nicaraguan authorities could requisition them if need be. Walker would later admit that previously, he'd deliberately lied "to disarm Mr. Cushing." He had assured the Transit Company man that he knew of no way in which the steamers could be of use to him, although he did show Cushing the document signed by Provisional Director Castellon authorizing him to act in respect to the Transit Company and its debts to the Nicaraguan government.[13] His lie ensured that the Transit Company took no steps to keep its vessels out of Walker's hands.

Through that night, sentries stood guard over the steamer and around the settlement to prevent word leaking out that Walker had taken control of *La Virgen*. Next day, Thursday, when the steamer was scheduled to sail on, Walker's entire force was crammed aboard, along with the two field guns. Walker even took along a pair of horses, one for Colonel Valle and another for Lieutenant Colonel Gilman.

A little after 4:30 P.M., the overloaded side-wheeler slowly pulled away from the jetty and turned her bow toward San Carlos, on the eastern side of the lake. No one on board except William Walker and Chelon Valle knew where *La Virgen* was heading. On her scheduled run, the steamer would head across the lake to San Carlos and the San Juan River. But once she was on the lake, up in the pilothouse Walker gave Captain Scott a new heading, and the skipper resignedly spun the wheel. The prow gradually came around to port, until it pointed north.

On *La Virgen*'s two crowded decks, Valle's Nicaraguan soldiers looked at each other with surprise. This quickly turned to excitement. Soon, Democraticos were clapping each other on the back, shouting like madmen, and dancing around, cheering with joy. The Falange's Americans looked at them as if they were lunatics, until someone explained that it had dawned on the Nicaraguans just where they were heading—Colonel Walker was bypassing Rivas and taking them to attack Granada. Granada, where the Legitimista leadership sat, protected by a depleted, demoralized garrison. This was Walker's secret plan. Rather than continuing to strike at the body of the enemy in the hope of causing a mortal wound, he was going straight for the head, to remove it with one bold thrust. If he succeeded, the war would be as good as over.

In the late afternoon, with the sun descending in the western sky to its left, the green-hulled lake steamer, its heavy load making her sit low in the water, headed up the lake, taking Walker's little army toward its appointment with destiny.

≈≈ 8 ≈≈

TAKING GRANADA

O N THE MOONLESS NIGHT OF OCTOBER 11, WITH HER PADDLEWHEELS
turning slowly, *La Virgen* eased by the ruined Spanish fort standing
guard at Granada's lakeside jetty. The steamer's two engines barely turned
over. All lights aboard had been doused. The fireboxes were damped, the
side curtains drawn. Everyone on board crouched low. Not a word was uttered. Yawning Legitimista sentries at the fort did not see or hear a thing as
the steamer slipped by.

A little before 10:00 P.M., three miles north of the city, the boat's anchor
was gently slipped over the side. A cable was then attached to the trunk of
large tree on shore, and a single flat-bottomed iron boat was used to ferry
the entire command ashore in a drawn-out shuttle service, with the men on
each run hauling the craft along the cable. On Walker's orders, his troops
only took bedrolls, coats, full ammunition pouches, and their weapons.
When the two horses brought along for the incapacitated colonels went
ashore on the boat, the spooked animals kicked up enough ruckus to seemingly wake the dead. But there was no reaction from the city outskirts away
to their left.

Just short of 3:00 A.M., Walker and his keyed-up men set off overland for
Granada. The Americans marched in front, Valle's battalion in the rear. Having been born in Granada, young Captain Herrera led the way southwest.
Herrera was supremely confident he knew where he was, but the pitch dark
meant that no one could see beyond the man in front, and progress was slow
until sunup.

With the dawn, Walker and his men could see, with relief, the Mombacho Volcano rising behind the city in the distance like a giant signpost that

said, "Here is Granada." Walker later wrote, "In a few minutes the column reached the road running from the city to Los Cocos."[1] As the 350 soldiers picked up the pace, they met women straggling along the road, returning from Granada's early morning market with their empty wicker baskets. According to the startled women, all was quiet in Granada, with no one expecting an attack.

When they were just half a mile from the city, the bells of its six churches began to ring out a rapid peal. Some Americans feared that the alarm was being sounded, but it turned out that this was a peal to celebrate an unexpected Legitimista victory two days before—in northern Nicaragua, a Legitimista army under Colonel Tomás Martinez had driven the Democratico army of the late General Munoz from the town of Pueblo Nuevo.

There was no sign of military activity in Granada as the column pushed on. The Nicaraguan state flag, of horizontal blue stripes separated by white stripes, could be seen hanging from the tall spire of the Parochial Church in the Granadine Plaza. Apart from the massive stone churches, some palatial private homes of wealthy Granadinos, and a few public buildings around the plaza, the city's buildings were all single-storied—because of the danger of collapse during Nicaragua's occasional earthquakes.

The city's white-painted adobe mud walls glowed in the light of day as Colonel Hornsby and the advance guard reached huts on the northern outskirts of Granada. Farther inside the city limits, barricades could be seen in place across the wide, boulevard that led toward the city center. Hornsby ordered his men to throw off their bedrolls and coats, then led them forward at the jog. Soon they were charging the barricade, letting out bloodcurdling yells. Several fired on the run, gunning down sentries where they stood. After quickly taking the barricade, Hornsby and his men doubled on up the street. Behind them, Walker brought up the force's main body.

Granada had been established by the Spanish in 1523. With its lakeside location, long boulevards, vast central plaza, and grand churches and public buildings in a mixture of Moorish and Spanish styles featuring graceful arches and shady arcades, Granada, a city of twenty-five thousand people and national capital of Nicaragua ever since the country left the Central American Federation in 1838, was considered the most beautiful metropolis in all

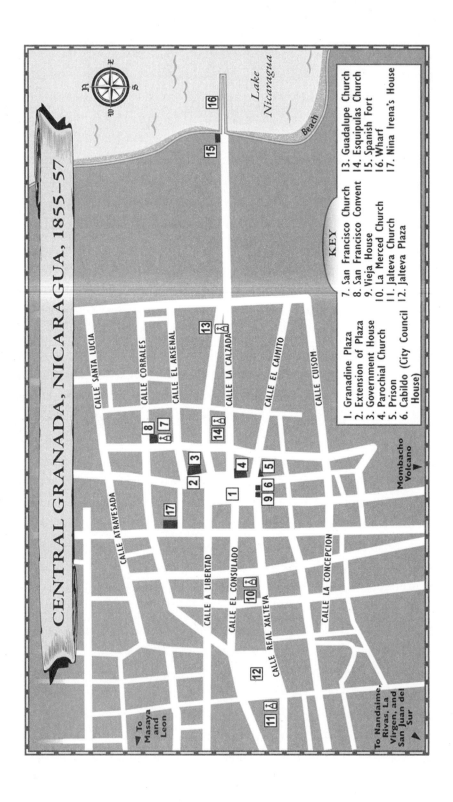

CENTRAL GRANADA, NICARAGUA, 1855–57

CALLE SANTA LUCIA
CALLE CORRALES
CALLE EL ARSENAL
CALLE LA CALZADA
CALLE EL CAIMITO
CALLE CUISOM
CALLE ATRAVESADA
CALLE A LIBERTAD
CALLE EL CONSULADO
CALLE REAL XALTEVA
CALLE LA CONCEPCION

To Masaya and Leon

To Nandaime, Rivas, La Virgen, and San Juan del Sur

Mombacho Volcano

Lake Nicaragua

Beach

KEY

1. Granadine Plaza
2. Extension of Plaza
3. Government House
4. Parochial Church
5. Prison
6. Cabildo (City Council House)
7. San Francisco Church
8. San Francisco Convent
9. Vieja House
10. La Merced Church
11. Jalteva Church
12. Jalteva Plaza
13. Guadalupe Church
14. Esquipulas Church
15. Spanish Fort
16. Wharf
17. Nina Irena's House

of Central America. But Walker's men had no time to admire the scenery or appreciate the architecture as they dashed toward the plaza.

Hornsby's tall, gaunt figure stood out as he led the charge through the suburbs. One barricade after another was rushed, with the Legitimistas manning them fleeing back up the broad street toward the plaza. It was only as some of the invaders diverted a block east to the convent next door to the San Francisco Church, Granada's first house of worship, which was being used as a quartel by the Legitimista garrison, that any resistance was encountered—muskets popped from the convent windows. "But these were few and straggling."[2] The quartel was quickly captured.

A victorious shout up ahead told Walker that the city's main plaza had been gained. As Walker himself, sword in hand, reached the broad Granadine Plaza, he saw puffs of smoke to his left from Legitimista muskets being fired from the gallery of Government House. During Spanish occupation, this had been the house of the captain general of Nicaragua. While Walker was an obvious target for the marksmen at Government House, he wasn't hit. But beside him, Colonel Valle's unarmed drummer boy dropped down dead. Americans returned fire, then rushed Government House. Battering in doors, they thronged inside and roughly made prisoners of the few Legitimista troops defending the building. That was the extent of organized Legitimista resistance in the city.

Walker's troops fanned out through the streets extending from the plaza, looking for Legitimista troops. They found these streets deserted. All the doors and shutters of the city had been rapidly closed when the first shots were heard. Here and there, the flag of one foreign country or another could be seen draped from a window to indicate that the residents were neutral foreign nationals. A few Legitimista prisoners were taken in the suburbs without a fight, but most of the defenders abandoned their capital, leaving behind stockpiles of weapons and ammunition in the city arsenal and gunpowder mill.

The proud city of Granada, which had resisted General Jerez's siege for months in 1854, had fallen to William Walker's small force in minutes. Three Legitimista soldiers were killed in the assault, while Colonel Valle's drummer boy was the only Democratico casualty. The Americans of the

Falange came through unscathed. In the coming weeks, when the story that Colonel William Walker and fewer than one hundred Americans had taken Granada in ten near bloodless minutes on October 12 reached the United States—news transmitted to the East and West Coasts via the Nicaragua Line's ocean steamers—it would be headline news across the country. Editorial writers would praise Walker and his men to the skies. To the press, this was proof of the courage, constancy of purpose, and ingenuity of Americans and their superiority as soldiers. As one U.S. journal put it when discussing the war in Nicaragua eighteen months later, these were "the peculiar forces of character which distinguish us above other nations."[3]

Cornelius Vanderbilt, reading these same reports and editorials in New York, would have had mixed feelings. On the one hand, the long-term future of Transit Company operations was made more secure by this extension of American influence in Nicaragua via Walker and his troops. That would have suited the Commodore, who was intent on covertly regaining control of the Transit Company. At the same time, Walker's actions had the capacity to soothe the fears of potential Transit Route travelers who were worried about being caught in the middle of a civil war, meaning that in the immediate term, Transit business was likely to stabilize and even to pick up. That did not suit the Commodore. While the company's fortunes were seen by the marketplace as waning, more shares would be disposed of by shareholders, further depressing the share price and allowing Vanderbilt to increase his shareholding for a song.

For the moment, Vanderbilt would have been perfectly happy for the Nicaraguan Transit Route to be thought of as a dicey proposition. Vanderbilt would not have thanked Walker for creating a contrary view. But for the moment, too, unaware of Walker's ultimate intentions regarding the Transit Route, Vanderbilt would not have taken the adventurer's actions personally. Vanderbilt's benign view of Walker, like the situation in Nicaragua, was soon to change, dramatically.

Once Grenada was secured, Walker strolled to the American embassy. The U.S. minister—ambassadors at that time were called "ministers" to the host countries—was fifty-three-year-old John Hill Wheeler, a native of North Carolina. A stout, pompous man with thick gray hair and a handlebar mustache, Wheeler had sheltered one hundred American women and children at the embassy while the city was under assault. Once he knew that Americans were in charge in the city, he became one of the first residents to reopen his door. Walker politely presented the ambassador with his compliments and assured the frightened women and children filling Wheeler's house and central courtyard that no harm would come to them.

Returning to the plaza, Walker spotted Democratico soldiers slinking away carrying goods looted in the city. Incensed, Walker drew his sword and arrested them. Colonel Valle subsequently agreed to enforce a looting ban among his troops, but he explained to Walker that this went against the past Legitimista habit of looting captured Democratico cities and towns, and many of Valle's men had felt they were entitled to reciprocate. Valle was overjoyed that Granada had been taken, and taken so easily—after all the sacrifice of the previous year's failed Democratico siege, which had cost Valle both a brother and a leg. He alone had known Walker's secret plan to take the city via the lake, revealed to him at Realejo. He never divulged that secret to anyone, although, as he boarded the *Vesta* at Realejo to accompany Walker on the mission to the south, he had promised his daughters he would bring them back gifts from Granada.

As leading Legitimista politicians presented themselves to Walker at Government House during the morning, Valle, who nursed a bitter hatred for the Legitimistas, demanded that all opposition leaders be shot. But Walker knew that other Legitimista leaders around the country would not come to terms if they believed the American's policy was, like theirs, one of executing any enemy who came into his hands. Walker would not sanction executions. He merely placed some Legitimista leaders under house arrest and put others on parole, accepting their word that they would not attempt to escape.

Meanwhile, Walker freed a hundred political prisoners from Granada's city prison. With some of them under sentence of death, these prisoners had been forced by the Legitimistas to labor in Granada's streets in chains.

Most were Nicaraguans, but one was a U.S. citizen. Every one of them gratefully volunteered to join the fight for the Democraticos and was provided with arms captured from the Granada arsenal. Walker's command had grown to 450 men.

Walker rose early on October 13, the day after his capture of Granada, and immediately went to work, appointing a local resident, Don Fermin Ferrer, as the new prefect of Granada, answerable to him. Wealthy, with a grand townhouse in the city and a large cattle property in the Chontales district in the country's central north, Ferrer had a reputation for being a fair and honest man. Walker also employed the services of another Granada resident, Don Carlos Thomas, a multilingual importer and exporter, to help him write, in Spanish, a proclamations through which Walker would rule Granada for the time being.

The next day, a Sunday, Walker and a number of his officers attended 8:00 A.M. Mass at Granada's Roman Catholic cathedral. This move was as much political in its motivation as it was spiritual. The conservative Legitimistas were known as the Church Party—because they supported and were in turn supported by the Catholic Church in Nicaragua. Not only did the little nation's church leaders have the power to influence the hearts and minds of the people, but they were also among the country's major landowners—large tracts of property were held by the church itself, and individual priests also owned farms and plantations; several even had gold mines in the mountainous east. To Walker, the long-term control of Nicaragua depended on the cooperation of the Catholic Church, so he embarked on a policy of making himself amenable to the church hierarchy.

Despite having been christened a Protestant, Walker quickly won the support of the Catholic curate of Granada, Father Agustin Vijil, who delivered a sermon at the Granada Mass of October 14 in which he pointed out "the necessity to the country of a force strong enough to curb" the civil war.[4] The force, by inference, with the American officers sitting in front of him, was that led by Colonel Walker. What's more, Walker would later reveal, Father Vijil "warmly cooperated" with him in his efforts to bring about peace and "made his counsel valuable to the negotiations which followed."[5]

Walker did not plan to occupy Granada for long. He was already looking at the next step in a campaign mapped out before he even set foot in Nicaragua. Granada played no part in that plan. Unbeknownst to Cornelius Vanderbilt and everyone else connected with the Transit Company at the time, control of the Transit Route was Walker's objective, and always had been, as his second contract with Provisional Director Castellon revealed. Walker later admitted that the Transit Route was "intrinsically more important to the Americans than the occupation of a town forty or fifty miles from" it. He regarded possession of the Legitimista capital "merely as a means of getting good terms from (General) Corral."[6] At this point, the municipal authorities of Granada offered Walker the presidency of the republic. He declined the offer but agreed to accept the post of commander in chief of the Army of the Republic of Nicaragua "to maintain order within the State," should a new government of national unity be formed with representatives from all political persuasions.[7]

The Granada city authorities dispatched two emissaries to Rivas to meet with General Corral and discuss a peace treaty. The emissaries were authorized to say that Colonel Walker proposed that General Corral should play a prominent part in a new government of national unity and that Walker himself only sought the post of commander in chief of the new national army. At the same time, Walker put the lake steamer *La Virgen* at the disposal of the U.S. ambassador, John Wheeler, who volunteered to go also to Corral and urge a peaceful solution to the civil war. Wheeler was subsequently detained by the Legitimistas at Rivas, before escaping back to Granada two days later. Meanwhile, at the town of Nandaime, just to the south of Granada, the city's emissaries met up with General Corral, who was on the march with his troops. The emissaries soon sent a message to Walker at Granada—General Corral refused to negotiate with them.

Next morning, Walker received a note from Corral himself, complaining that Democratico skirmishers had fired on his camp while he was meeting with the emissaries. Walker realized that while Corral was reluctant to deal with the Democraticos, he was trying to keep open the lines of communication with the American colonel. Walker responded with a note saying that as there was no armistice in place, he and his troops would continue to vigorously conduct the war against the Legitimistas. Corral replied, this time stating that no peace was possible based on the principles of the Democraticos. Walker did not respond.

Meanwhile, other Legitimistas were about to murderously disrupt peace negotiations.

THE WALKER WAY

WITH HER IRON PADDLEWHEELS TURNING SLOWLY, THE 1,800-TON SS *Uncle Sam* glided into the bay at San Juan del Sur. The two-year-old steamer was fast, handsome, and so luxurious by ocean steamer standards of the day that San Francisco's *Daily Alta California* called her a "floating palace."[1] Her anchor dropped into the sparkling blue-green water with a splash, and she came to a dead stop. Formerly owned by Edward Mills and briefly part of Cornelius Vanderbilt's Independent Opposition Line before Morgan and Garrison added her to the Transit Company's Nicaragua Steamship Line, the *Uncle Sam* had just completed a scheduled run down from San Francisco in near record time.

It was Wednesday, October 17, five days since William Walker and his little army had captured Granada. News of Colonel Walker's success was relayed to the hundreds of passengers ferried ashore in San Juan del Sur's ubiquitous fleet of flat-bottomed iron boats, and it caused great excitement. There was a feeling of pride in Walker and his American cohorts, and envious and admiring looks were cast at sixty-one men who had come down from California with the other passengers. Led by the one-armed Parker H. French, they were here to join Walker's Americans fighting the Nicaraguan war.

French had promised Walker that he would return with seventy-five recruits for the Falange. He had not quite achieved his target, but the sixty new men he had recruited were not to be sneezed at—they would almost double the strength of Walker's Falange. French's men brought with them a large quantity of ammunition and a shiny brass six-pound field gun. Chief among these new recruits was thirty-three-year-old Birkett D. Fry from Kanawha County, West Virginia. A former U.S. Army lieutenant who had served initially as a private in the Voltigeur Regiment during the Mexican War, Fry had been educated at the Virginia Military Institute and West Point. Failing to graduate from either, he'd received his commission in the field. Fry had been working as a lawyer in California since 1849.

As the waiting fleet of blue and white stagecoaches progressively carried the other steamship passengers away across the Transit Road to La Virgen, French and his newly arrived recruits gathered their baggage and their thoughts. They were informed by Democratico tax collector Don Maximo Espinosa that Colonel Florencio Xatruch's Legitimista troops at Rivas and General Corral at Nandaime with the main army stood between the newly arrived Americans and Colonel Walker at Granada. Inspired by Walker's use of the lake to take Granada, French convinced Fry and the other new men that they could impress Walker and grab some glory by carrying out a daring surprise attack of their own.

On his last visit to Nicaragua, French had come up the San Juan on river and lake steamers. He now authoritatively informed his companions that troops of the Legitimista army held the fort at San Carlos, at the head of the San Juan. And, he said, the lake steamer carrying the latest batch of Transit travelers from California would have to pass right under the San Carlos fort on its way to delivering those passengers to their river steamer connection at El Castillo. Here, said French, was the ideal opportunity for the sixty newly arrived Americans to take the Legitimista garrison at San Carlos by surprise— the same way that Colonel Walker took Granada by surprise. French's companions, thirsting for action, thought it a grand idea.

At French's instigation, he, Fry, and their companions marched to Virgin Bay, boarded the lake steamer *La Virgen*, along with the hundreds of civilian Transit passengers, and set off for the scheduled thirty-mile cruise across the lake. As the steamboat neared San Carlos, the size and scale of the massive old stone fortress on the hilltop daunted the would-be attackers. And then those with good eyes caught sight of uniformed Europeans, not dark-skinned Nicaraguans, manning the defenses up there.

What Parker French did not know was that after the civil war flared, Legitimista troops had been withdrawn from guard duty on the San Juan River to bolster the armies in the west of the country. To protect passengers and gold shipments, in July the Transit Company had brought down from New York a large group of Italians, Germans, French, and Poles with military experience, to replace the 150-man Legitimista garrison at El Castillo. These Transit Company troops, well armed and outfitted in smart uniforms, had shortly after transferred to San Carlos at the request of Don Patricio Rivas, the Legitimista collector of customs there. Most of these men had later gone to serve under General Corral. It was the remnant of this company of European guards that now garrisoned Fort San Carlos.

The Transit Company guards had also refurbished the artillery at the fort. When Peter F. Stout visited San Carlos as one of the first Transit passengers to go up the San Juan in July 1851, he had seen twenty-five local soldiers and seven old Spanish cannon at the fort, although only one of the guns had been mounted at the time—the other six lay in the mud. Now, the snouts of several guns, including a monster twenty-four-pounder, poked out between the fort's battlements, and all were capable of blowing the lake steamer out of the water.

When Parker French's followers realized that the San Carlos garrison would be no pushover, it was unanimously agreed that their ammunition supply was insufficient to sustain an attack. So French ordered master Joseph Scott to turn *La Virgen* around and steer for Granada. French and his party were duly landed at the crumbling stone jetty at Granada. But to the horror of the hundreds of Transit passengers, Captain Scott refused to sail back to San Carlos. Instead, he returned to Virgin Bay, where he made his disconsolate passengers disembark.

At Granada, French reported to William Walker with his recruits. But when French blithely told Walker of his aborted San Carlos mission, Walker was appalled. "It was a most foolish if not criminal act," Walker declared.[2]

French looked at Walker dumbly. It had to be explained to French that to use a boat carrying civilians for a military undertaking meant putting the lives of those civilians at risk. Walker "was not much surprised" by French's role in the ill-conceived enterprise but was disappointed by the fact that Fry, a man with considerable military experience and knowledge of the law, had agreed to be a part of what today would amount to a war crime. Walker would later say that he was forced to overlook the matter because of "the existing circumstances"—he needed every man he could lay his hands on should the Legitimistas attack Granada, which seemed to be their intention.

Birkett Fry had come to Nicaragua with glowing references from Walker's recruiting agents in San Francisco. One was attorney A. Parker Crittenden, a "respectable, honest-looking man," in the judgment of one filibuster recruit.[3] Crittenden had experience with Narciso Lopez, and his failed revolution in Cuba, and had drafted many of the new state of California's laws. Crittenden was also, along with Edmund Randolph, one of Walker's closest friends. The other recruiter was Edward J. C. Kewen, brother of the late Achilles Kewen, who had died beside Charles Doubleday at the Battle of Rivas. In a letter carried by French, Crittenden and Kewen had assured Walker that Fry would be "a valuable accession to the enterprise." The long-faced, bearded Fry himself informed Walker that French had promised him a colonelcy in the Falange. That was why, he said, he had thrown up his good law job and left behind Martha, his wife of two years. Walker would describe Fry as "amiable in manner and honorable in sentiment." Besides, Walker liked the military cut of the man. Despite the Fort San Carlos incident, he gave Fry his colonel's commission.

The new recruits were divided into two companies, with their officers chosen from among them. Using the Winfield Scott model then employed by the U.S. Army, a captain and three lieutenants were appointed to each company. The two new company commanders were Captains S. C. Asten and Charles Turnbull. Walker made another of the *Uncle Sam* recruits, Edward J. Sanders, who, he would later judge, "had much more energy of character" than did Fry, a major. French also asked Walker for a commission, but Walker, unimpressed by the San Carlos incident, gave him Charles Doubleday's old job as Commissary of War, which kept him under Walker's watchful eye at headquarters.

Captain Joseph Scott refused to embark Transit passengers for the trip across Lake Nicaragua. He guessed that the Fort San Carlos garrison must have seen the armed Americans on board the vessel before it suddenly veered away and headed for Granada, and he feared that they might fire on the steamer the next time it approached San Carlos's guns. Scott felt that he could only safely resume the carriage of passengers past San Carlos to El Castillo once hostilities ended. That left the hundreds of stranded eastbound travelers lolling around the La Virgen settlement.

Without warning, a detachment of Legitimista troops from Colonel Xatruch's garrison at Rivas marched into La Virgen. As they entered the settlement, Legitimista soldiers fired indiscriminately into the hundreds of civilians in the streets. Three Transit passengers, American citizens, fell dead, and a number of others were wounded. As panicking civilians ran for their lives or dragged wounded companions into cover, with women and children screaming in terror, the troops advanced on the Accessory Transit Company's headquarters at the double. As they passed up the street, several Legitimistas paused to search the pockets of the dead Americans.

Cortlandt Cushing and his staff just had time to close the headquarters building's doors before the Legitimistas arrived on the front porch. Using the butts of their muskets, the troops broke the door down. Crowding inside, they seized Cushing and looted the building. The Legitimistas then marched out back to Rivas, taking Cushing and their loot with them. Cushing was imprisoned at Rivas by Colonel Xatruch until the Accessory Transit Company paid two thousand dollars in exchange for his release.

Walker quickly seized on the Legitimista outrage at La Virgen, turning it into a propaganda coup. As soon as he had captured Granada, he had closed down *Defender of Order,* the Legitimista newspaper. Using the newspaper's office and printing press, he set up his own journal, *La Nicaraguense,* or the *Nicaraguan.* Walker's paper would be published every Saturday under the editorship of Juan Tabor, a Granadino who spoke fluent Spanish and English. Initially, half the paper's content was in Spanish, half in English; later, it would be two-thirds English. Walker himself would write articles for its pages. The front page of the inaugural edition of the *Nicaraguan,* published on October 20, featured an indignant report of the Virgin Bay incident, decrying the murder of American citizens and the kidnap of another.

When the news of the Legitimistas' La Virgen raid broke in the United States several weeks later, it was under headlines such as "Massacre of Americans at Virgin Bay." From one end of the United States to the other, newspaper editors and their readers were outraged by the story. Not only were they up in arms at the murder of Americans, but the raid also put America's Nicaraguan Transit Route to California under threat. Until now, Transit passengers crossing Nicaragua from coast to coast had been treated as the neutrals they were in this civil war. Now, an American lifeline to and from California was in jeopardy.

With Colonel William Walker portrayed as an enlightened American bringing civilization to the barbarians of Central America, support for him in the United States soared. Conversely, the killings at La Virgen fueled a national distaste for the native people of Nicaragua, no matter what their political persuasion, Legitimista or Democratico. The deprecating nickname of "greaser" from now on took on a more hateful connotation.

The events at Virgin Bay would be compounded by another fatal blunder on the part of Legitimistas the following day.

A Nicaragua Line ocean steamer from New York dropped anchor at Greytown. The town had been totally rebuilt since being leveled by the bombardment from the USS *Cyane* a year back, and it was business as usual in the town. Word of the outrage at La Virgen the previous day had yet to come downriver, so, in ignorance of the danger ahead, the ocean steamer's passengers transferred to waiting Transit Company river steamers to be taken up the San Juan.

Above El Castillo, the passengers joined the largest of the lake steamers, the gleaming, all-white 421-ton *San Carlos*, a product of the Harlan and Hollingsworth yard in Delaware. The crowded paddle-steamer sallied up the river. She was just passing Fort San Carlos and was about to enter the lake with her westbound passengers when a cannon at the fort on the hill boomed. Just as Captain Scott had feared, the men garrisoning Fort San Carlos had been made jittery by the recent strange behavior of the *San Carlos's* sister vessel, *La Virgen*. To be safe rather than sorry, the men from the garrison opened fire on the *San Carlos* with their heavy gun. Their aim was sadly perfect— a twenty-four pound cannon ball slammed into the side of *San Carlos*. In a splintering of wood, the projectile instantly killed an American mother and the infant she was nursing. The foot of another child was taken away by the cannonball. Increasing speed, the steamer escaped onto the lake while the shocked passengers tended to the dead and injured.

The *San Carlos* continued on to Virgin Bay, where she unloaded her shaken passengers and the casualties. These passengers from New York continued on to San Juan del Sur, but there were still hundreds of eastbound passengers sitting at La Virgen, prevented from traveling to New York or New Orleans. When Walker learned of the shelling of the *San Carlos*, he ordered the steamer to bring the stranded Transit eastbound passengers up the lake from La Virgen to Granada, putting them under the protection of his army. The westbound passengers reached San Francisco ten days later, and their stories of Legitimista atrocities against civilians in Nicaragua quickly fueled incensed newspaper editorials. The tales also created a rush on Walker's recruiting agents from vengeful fellow Americans. Walker could not have hoped for better press had he engineered the Legitimista blunders himself.

Just the same, Walker felt it vital to quickly demonstrate that law and order prevailed in Nicaragua, fearing that unless he acted firmly, the Transit Company's board would now consider the Nicaragua route too dangerous and abandon it. The Transit Route was at the heart of Walker's plans for Nicaragua. Now, frustratingly close to gaining control of the Transit, he could not afford to have Charles Morgan and Cornelius Garrison close it down. Little did Walker know that at that very moment in New York City, Cornelius Vanderbilt was also frustratingly close to his objective—that of regaining control of the Transit Company from Morgan and Garrison, in a surprise stock market attack akin to Walker's taking of Granada. And like Walker, the last thing Vanderbilt wanted was the Nicaraguan Transit Route to be shut down. For, once shut down, it might never reopen.

Walker was aware that in the wake of the *Cyane* incident, the U.S. government was in no position to criticize a tough-minded response to the murder of its citizens in Nicaragua. He also believed that, as mad Mariano Mendez had warned him, the locals had to be ruled with an iron hand; only one law was understood in Nicaragua, the law of *fusilado,* the firing squad. So, early on the morning of October 22, Walker ordered the arrest of Granada-based Legitimista cabinet minister Mateo Mayorga—the same minister who had praised Emanuel Mongalo and Nery Fajardo in the

Defender of Order for torching the Espinosa house during the Battle of Rivas. Simultaneously, Walker issued a proclamation declaring that he held Mayorga personally responsible for the unlawful killing of American civilians in Nicaragua. Accordingly, said the proclamation, Colonel Walker ordered that Minister Mayorga be executed by firing squad, at once.

As interior minister, Don Mateo Mayorga, a lawyer by profession, had been the Legitimista minister responsible for law and order, and this was why Walker selected him to be his sacrificial lamb. No trial or legal process was involved. Even avid Walker supporter, author, and newspaper editor Richard Harding Davis would later remark that "this act of Walker's was certainly stretching the theory of responsibility to breaking point."[4] But neither Mayorga nor anyone else had the opportunity to argue the legality of his summary sentence.

That same day, Mayorga, who, like his fellow Legitimista leaders, had been under house arrest at Granada, was led from his residence by Walker's officer of the day, Captain Ubaldo Herrera. A detachment of Colonel Valle's troops formed around the dazed prisoner, who was marched to Granada's main plaza. The detachment halted in front of a wall outside Granada's cathedral, a wall pockmarked by musket balls from numerous executions carried out on this very same spot by the Legitimista authorities in the past.

Mayorga was made to sit on a chair in front of the wall, facing the plaza. As Captain Herrera blindfolded the prisoner, a silent crowd of off-duty soldiers and thousands of Granadinos gathered to watch, standing some way back. The men of Captain Herrera's detachment formed up opposite the seated prisoner. On Herrera's command, they loaded their muskets. Herrera drew his sword. With weapons loaded, Herrera ordered his men to take aim. The muskets came up to the horizontal. The soldiers sighted along the barrels, aiming for Don Mateo Mayorga's heart. Herrera dropped his sword, at the same time calling the command to fire. A dozen muskets detonated. Flame shot out the end of the barrels. When the smoke cleared, Mateo Mayorga, his white shirtfront suddenly crimson with his lifeblood, could be seen slumped on the ground, dead.

As Walker hoped, once the news of the execution of the Legitimista minister for the interior reached the United States, American newspapers would praise the filibuster leader for enacting prompt retribution for the murder of American citizens by Legitimista troops.

It was the middle of the day on October 22. Legitimista commander in chief, General Ponciano Corral, paced up and down, anxiously reading and rereading a letter just received from William Walker. Corral was a dashingly handsome man. Tall, curly-haired, and close to fifty years of age, he was, on his mother's side, the descendant of African slaves. Corral was well liked by his compatriots and had a reputation as a conciliator. But in Walker's view, Corral "lacked decision and was more fertile in perceiving difficulties that in defying or overcoming them."

Corral had marched his army from Nandaime, which he considered too difficult to defend, to the picturesque hill town of Masaya, twenty-five miles to the west of Granada. Here, he built barricades at the sloping approaches to the town, at the same time sending urgent orders to Colonel Tomás Martinez at Managua to bring Legitimista reinforcements from the north. The commander in chief would not entertain an advance against Granada until those reinforcements reached him. Most of the remaining members of the Legitimista hierarchy joined Corral at Masaya, among them the Legitimistas' token president of Nicaragua, the ineffectual José Maria Estrada.

Shortly after the execution of Mateo Mayorga, Pedro Rouhaud, a French resident of Granada, had set off from the capital to find General Corral. It was Rouhaud who brought Corral this letter from Colonel William Walker. In it, Walker informed Corral of the execution of Mayorga and the reasons for it. Most worrying to Corral, Walker's letter also said that "all the Legitimista families of the city (Granada) would be held as hostages for the future good conduct of (President) Estrada's officers toward American women and children."

Corral shared the letter's contents with his officers. As Walker had expected, it immediately caused consternation among Corral's subordinates, many of whom had families at Granada. According to the Nicaraguan version of events—Walker failed to mention it in his memoirs—the letter from

Walker additionally stated that if he did not receive a favorable response to his request for peace talks by 9:00 that night, he would start executing Legitimista officials being held at Granada.[5] The fact that Walker had summarily executed Mayorga sent a chill message—he meant business and was likely to carry out his threat to shoot his Granadine hostages.

Heated discussion now took place among the Legitimistas at Masaya. Some of Corral's officers implored him to enter into peace negotiations to save their family members. Others proposed doing nothing until the expected reinforcements arrived from the north. Some Legitimista soldiers at Masaya were all for continuing the war and even spoke of deposing Corral as commander in chief if he parleyed with Walker, replacing him with the aggressive Colonel Martinez once he arrived with the northern reinforcements.

But as General Corral had just learned from a messenger from the north, Colonel Martinez and his reinforcements might never reach Masaya, certainly not in time to save the hostages. When news that Walker had taken Granada had arrived, Martinez's army had abandoned Pueblo Nueva and fallen back to Managua. Then, just south of Managua, marching to join Corral at Masaya, Martinez had collided with a Democratico column led by General Mateo Pineda and the irrepressible Colonel Mariano Mendez, who were bringing a mixed band of irregulars down from León to link up with Walker at Granada. Those Democratico irregulars now had Martinez's troops pinned down. Neither force was able to move.

There was another ingredient in the mixture—Corral's personal ambition. Walker had stated that Corral should be a leading member of any new government that emerged from a peace agreement between the warring parties. Walker's peace ultimatum presented Corral with the opportunity to step over his party leader, Estrada, to obtain a prominent position in the new government and become the most powerful Legitimista in that new government and, perhaps before long, the new president of Nicaragua.

A little before 9:00 that night, Rouhaud arrived back in Granada and was escorted directly to Walker. As Walker was to put it, Rouhaud bore "gratifying intelligence"—Corral had agreed to personally come to Granada first thing next morning to conduct peace negotiations with Walker.

At dawn on October 23, Colonel Birkett D. Fry and a contingent of mounted American Falange members set off from Granada to meet Corral and escort him into the city. Walker had chosen Fry quite deliberately for this task. With his military bearing and in his U.S. Army uniform, Fry looked suitably martial and official. But more importantly, Walker was sending Fry, a newly arrived senior officer, to meet Corral to give credence to the rumor then abroad that large numbers of new American recruits were reaching Walker with each new arrival of Atlantic and Pacific steamers. And in seeing Fry, Corral would hopefully gain the impression that these new recruits were men of quality.

Colonel Fry and his American escort found Corral and his lancer bodyguard at a property called La Carmen on the Masaya road. The two senior officers exchanged salutes and greetings before the parties combined to ride to Granada. A little after 9:00 A.M., Walker received word that Corral, Fry, and the escort were at the Polvon, the city's gunpowder mill, on the outskirts of the Granada suburb of Jalteva. Walker mounted up and, accompanied by senior Falange and Democratico officers, rode to meet the Legitimista commander in chief.

When the two mounted commanders came face to face, they formally saluted each other, then rode side by side to the Granadine Plaza. With their subordinates coming along behind, they rode through the Jalteva Plaza and passed by the Jalteva Church. Along Calle Real Jalteva the procession trotted, passing the ruined bell tower of another church, La Merced, destroyed the previous December during the Democratico siege of the city. From the doorways and windows of the white-painted adobe brick houses lining the street, the people of Granada watched the horsemen pass. The women in particular looked dazzlingly colorful in their Sunday-best outfits. With smiles on their faces and tears in their eyes, the people waved and cheered the passing parade of generals and colonels, overjoyed at the prospect of peace after seventeen months of brutal civil war.

When the riders reached the Granadine Plaza, Walker's entire Democratico army was there, formed up neatly in ranks. At the front of the assembly stood Walker's 160 Americans in their three companies. At the rear, Valle's 450 Nicaraguans were formed up by company. In between the Falange and the Democratico battalion stood Walker's trump card. Here were hundreds more Americans who had seemingly materialized overnight, all standing to attention with muskets on their shoulders and red ribbons on their hats. Corral said nothing, but he could not hide his surprise at the number of men in Walker's force—close to one thousand, he would have calculated—and the fact that more than half of them were Yankees.

As Corral was ushered into Government House by Walker to commence peace negotiations, he had no idea that the American had employed a ruse learned from Julius Caesar. The Roman general, in his 52 B.C. assault on the rebel Gaul city of Gergovia in France's Auvergne Mountains, had put helmets on his hundreds of mule drivers and put the mule drivers on their pack mules. Then, forming them up like cavalry, he had sent the muleteers off with one of his legions as if he was mounting a combined cavalry-infantry attack. The rebel Gauls, watching from the city walls, were deceived into sending a large force from their camps outside Gergovia to intercept this army. When the Gauls realized that these were not cavalry troopers and this was a feint, they had gone rushing back to Gergovia, but it was too late—Caesar had overrun their camps behind their backs, using his main force of real cavalry and several infantry legions.

Since boyhood, Walker had been versed in Caesar's campaigns in Gaul, having recited every word of Caesar's war memoirs, the *Commentaries*, to college administrators when he was only twelve. The deception at Gergovia must have impressed him in his youth and influenced him now. Overnight, he had sent his officers around the hundreds of American Transit passengers who had arrived from San Francisco aboard the *Cortes* and *Uncle Sam* and who were waiting impatiently in Granada for the Transit Route to the east to reopen. The officers had reminded the travelers that the only way they would get out of this place was if the civil war concluded. And, they said, the only way the civil war could be concluded quickly was if Colonel Walker could convince the Legitimistas that he had many more American troops serving under him than actually was the case. This ruse, the officers had said, would steer the Legitimistas into signing a peace treaty when General Corral came visiting next morning. To end the war and get the hell out of this place, the vast majority of American Transit travelers had gladly collected a musket and a red ribbon from the Granada armory and had fallen into line in the plaza that morning behind the real soldiers of the Falange. All they had to do was stand in place, look fierce, and not drop their muskets.

The ruse worked; Corral genuinely believed that Walker had been reinforced by hundreds of American recruits. Besides, Corral was ready for
peace and was looking for an excuse to do a deal with Walker. Vain and ambitious, he had not forgotten Walker's earlier communication suggesting that
Corral should be a member of any new government of national unity. Other
senior Legitimistas had warned him that Walker's stipulation that he himself
be made commander in chief of the new Army of the Republic of Nicaragua
was full of danger. But Corral was confident he could control Walker. The
meek and mild American, it seemed to Corral, was a tractable little man
with puffed-up ideas about being a soldier. Besides, Walker was an outsider;
Corral was confident that he could soon freeze Walker out of local affairs.
After all, everyone knew that this Yankee newspaper editor could not even
speak Spanish.

Corral sat down at Government House together with his secretary,
Walker, a translator, and Father Vijil, who acted as moderator. On the table,
Corral laid a prepared and detailed agenda. Even Walker seemed surprised
that Corral had come with his peace terms mapped out. Corral also produced his written authority from President Estrada to act on behalf of the
Legitimistas and commit them to peace terms without the need for their
ratification—what Corral and Walker agreed here today would be accepted
by the Legitimista leadership.

On the other hand, Walker made it clear that any treaty agreed between
them would have to be ratified by the Democratico political leadership at
León. Corral had no problem with that, seeing Walker as merely a middle
man, and "treated with him simply as the colonel commanding the forces
occupying Granada." That suited Walker. He allowed Corral to dictate the
course of the meeting, later saying he let Corral "develop freely the terms he
desired." For his part, Walker was mostly silent, "saying little by way either
of objection or amendment." In the end, "the treaty, as signed, was nearly altogether the work of Corral." This way, no one could later accuse Walker of
dictating terms to the Legitimistas. As it happened, Walker found Corral's
terms easy to work with, and easy to work around if necessary.

The treaty drawn up on October 23 provided for a new government, the
Provisional Government of the Republic of Nicaragua until national elections could be held, those elections to take place no later than fourteen

months from the date of the treaty. Corral nominated Don Patricio Rivas to fill the post of provisional president. Rivas, a Legitimista and former head of state of Nicaragua in 1839 and again through 1840–1841, was considered a moderate. Currently, Rivas was the Legitimistas' collector of customs on the San Juan River.

The treaty also placed Walker in command of the Army of the Republic, with the contracts of all foreign troops serving on both sides recognized by the new government. All officers on both sides were to retain their ranks and rates of pay. Corral specified that Legitimista commanders Colonel Martinez and Colonel Xatruch be given charge of the Managua and Rivas garrisons of the new Army of the Republic of Nicaragua (ARN). At Corral's suggestion, too, Walker's Americans were to be absorbed into the new Army of the Republic, with the *Falange Americana* ceasing to exist as a separate entity. The debts of both sides in the civil war would become the debts of the new government. The Legitimista stronghold of Granada would continue to be the Nicaraguan national capital, and the blue and white Nicaraguan state flag used by the Legitimistas would be retained as the flag of the republic, with the Democratico flag consigned to history.

On the face of it, Walker had conceded a great deal to the Legitimistas, to the detriment of the Democraticos. He asked for just one thing—that the clause in the 1838 Nicaraguan Statute, which provided for the naturalization of foreigners to make them citizens of Nicaragua, be recognized and validated by the treaty, and Corral agreed. On behalf of the Legitimistas, Corral signed the treaty at the meeting. Walker immediately sent a copy to Provisional Director Escoto at León for ratification by the Democratico leadership.

That afternoon, with General Corral still in Granada, the alarm was raised when the lake steamer *Central America* came plowing across the lake from the direction of San Carlos. Neither Walker nor Corral was expecting the boat, and both immediately suspected the other of treachery. But it turned out that Captain Joseph Scott was at the steamboat's helm, and he had come on his own initiative to collect the stranded Transit passengers. The news that the Legitimistas had signed the peace treaty had spread fast, with the result that the Legitimista garrisons at San Carlos and El Castillo had simply melted away. The San Juan River was once more open to safe navigation by Transit passengers.

Walker delayed giving approval for the passengers to embark on the *Central America* until Corral departed Granada later that afternoon. Still unaware that he had been deceived by Walker's Caesarian stratagem, Corral set off back to Masaya taking a copy of the treaty with him. He went away delighted with the outcome of the negotiations and fully believing that he'd had the better of Walker. As he departed, the Legitimista general rode past leading Legitimista socialite Dona Irena Ohoran, a close friend, in the street; Walker briefly lived at her house in the first days after the fall of Granada. Grinning, Corral held up the leather case containing the treaty document and, in the language of cock-fighting, Nicaragua's national pastime, said to Dona Irena, "We have beaten them with their own game-cock!" Walker was the cock.

Once Corral left the city, it was no longer necessary to keep up the deception about the additional American "troops," and Walker gave Captain Scott permission to take the Transit passengers on board the *Central America*. After twenty dramatic days in Nicaragua, during which they had seen five of their fellow passengers killed and others injured by the Legitimistas, the travelers gratefully departed. Without incident, the heavily laden *Central America* steamed across the lake, by Fort San Carlos, and down the San Juan. When these passengers reached New York in early November, they would gush their stories to the press. Soon all of America would be reading about the barbarism of the Legitimista troops at Virgin Bay and San Carlos, and of the brilliance of Colonel William Walker, the quiet American who took Granada, fooled the Legitimistas, and forced the warring parties to the peace table to end Nicaragua's civil war.

One of those passengers didn't continue east—C. J. Macdonald, a Scotsman who had been living in California for some years, informed Walker that he was remaining in Nicaragua to act as the business agent of San Francisco's Cornelius K. Garrison. And on the afternoon of the twenty-third, the one-armed Parker French came to Walker to say that Macdonald, on Garrison's behalf, was prepared to loan $20,000 worth of gold to the new Nicaraguan government from the latest California gold shipment, against moneys due to the government by the Transit Company. This proposal took Walker by surprise. He had been under the impression that Garrison and his partner Charles Morgan had been locked in a battle with Cornelius Vanderbilt for the control of the Transit Company's stock. "The advance by Macdonald, however," Walker said later, "indicated another plan on the part of Garrison and Morgan."

Before Walker had set off for Nicaragua in May, he'd approached Garrison in his San Francisco office. "It was generally said that the company was indebted to the Republic by a large amount," Walker had told the banker, before "proposing an advantageous mode of settling this debt." But at that time, Garrison had not been interested in anything Walker, the then failed Sonoran filibuster, had to say, telling his visitor "that his principals had instructed him to have nothing to do with such enterprises as he supposed Walker to contemplate." Now, just five months later, how different both their situations were. And here was Garrison offering to loan the Walker enterprise $20,000.

After viewing Macdonald's written authority from Garrison to act as his agent in Nicaragua, Walker approved the arrangement. French drew up an agreement, which was sent with the remainder of the gold shipment to New York. There, Garrison's partner Charles Morgan would endorse the arrangement and pay restitution to the gold's owners, using the funds of his new New York City bank, Charles Morgan and Company, of which Garrison was the San Francisco agent. The $20,000 in gold went into the coffers of the Commissary of War. At least now Walker could pay his troops and purchase arms and ammunition.

That same day, Walker wrote to his "intimate friend" A. Parker Crittenden in San Francisco, "saying that any arrangements he might make to get five hundred men into the country would be fully approved." He urged Crittenden to approach Cornelius Garrison, for, in the wake of the unsolicited gold offer, Walker believed "that Garrison might be brought to cooperate largely in the policy of introducing the American element into Nicaragua."

On October 29, General Corral marched his Legitimista army into Granada from Masaya to combine them with Walker's men. Although the treaty had yet to be ratified by the Democratico leadership at León, the next day a lake steamer brought the proposed new president, Don Patricio Rivas, from San

Carlos to Granada. Don Patricio, a man of slight build, with thinning brown hair and a pencil-thin mustache, had the air of a bureaucrat. As he disembarked from the steamer at the Granada jetty, he was jointly received by Walker and Corral, who conducted him to the *Cabildo,* the City Council House on the Granadine Plaza. There, Rivas knelt on a cushion in front of a crucifix, and before Father Vijil and the assembled dignitaries, he swore to abide by the treaty of October 23 and to faithfully perform the duties of provisional president of Nicaragua.

Standing behind Rivas, Corral indicated to Walker that the pair of them should next kneel beside the new president and also take an oath, which Corral had prepared. Corral had said nothing of this previously to Walker, who immediately suspected that Corral was trying to embarrass him. Walker had received a report from a Spanish-speaking informant about Corral's comment likening Walker to a Democratico fighting cock. But Walker didn't object. Kneeling on one side of President Rivas, he, like tall, erect Corral, read aloud a short oath that bound them to the treaty.

Later that same day, President Rivas announced the appointment of Corral as both his minister for war and the new government's minister general. The former post made Corral Walker's superior, while the latter gave Corral broad powers in other spheres. In turn, Minister Corral issued a proclamation naming William Walker commander in chief of the Army of the Republic of Nicaragua, with the rank of general of division.

The following day, October 31, Corral invited General Walker to the executive chamber at Government House. Producing a crucifix, Corral advised him, through an interpreter, that for his appointment as commander in chief of the army to be confirmed, it was necessary to take yet another oath. If Corral had been expecting Walker the Protestant to refuse to again kneel before the crucifix, he miscalculated. Without hesitation, Walker dropped to his knees and took the oath.

This same day, General Jerez arrived in Granada from León leading a delegation of seven senior Democraticos and bringing the news that the Democratico cabinet had ratified the peace treaty brokered by Walker. The deal was official. Nicaragua's civil war was at an end.

After briefly living at Dona Irena Ohoran's house, Walker took up residence in Granada with the wealthy Vieja family in their two-story townhouse on the Granadine Plaza. There, on November 1, he received a visit from President Rivas. Don Patricio had moved into Government House across the plaza, but so too had War Minister Corral, and to many observers, it seemed that Corral had Rivas entirely in his power. But overnight, Rivas received warnings from friends that it was not a good idea to be seen to be leaning too far toward the Legitimistas if the peace was to last. So Rivas had come to Walker to ask his advice on the makeup of his new coalition cabinet; he went away with the American's list of recommended ministers.

Corral readily accepted Walker's proposals that Legitimista-leaning Granada moderate Don Fermin Ferrer, whom Walker had appointed prefect of Granada, be minister of public credit, and Parker H. French, as a so-called neutral, be minister of hacienda, or secretary of the treasury. The only sticking point was the appointment of a minister for foreign relations. Walker proposed Democratico general Maximo Jerez for the post. So far, no Democratico had been appointed to the cabinet as the peace treaty required. Corral had to give ground. By the end of the day, Rivas was able to convince him to accept Jerez as foreign minister. But at the first meeting of the cabinet, Corral refused to shake Jerez's hand. It was not an auspicious beginning to the new coalition government.

Benito Lagos was a prisoner in Managua Prison. A Democratico, he had been imprisoned by the Legitimistas after they occupied Managua early in 1855; he was charged with "political crimes." Even after the peace treaty was ratified, Colonel Tomás Martinez, former Legitimista commander in the north and now military governor of Managua, was slow to release political prisoners. On November 3, Benito Lagos found himself hustled to Colonel Martinez's office.

Martinez, a squat man with a mustache and thick beard, lay a small package of letters on his desk in front of the prisoner and made him a proposition. If Lagos would carry those letters north to Honduras, using his status as a leading Democratico to pass through Nicaragua's Democratico north unchallenged, Martinez would give him his freedom. Lagos didn't have to think twice—he immediately agreed to undertake the mission. Martinez gave him a good horse and pointed him toward Honduras.

On November 4, more than fifteen hundred Nicaraguan conscript soldiers gladly handed in their weapons and went home. From Granada, León, Rivas, and Managua, overjoyed barefoot men in white clogged the roads as they tramped back to their towns and villages.

Upward of two hundred Democratico soldiers chose to remain in the new national army, and they formed the ARN's Nicaraguan Battalion, under the command of Colonel Valle. A small number of foreigners, mostly Frenchmen and Germans, serving in the Legitimista army also chose to stay in the army, creating the French Company and the German Company. To a man, the Americans of the former *Falange Americana* also stayed on; Walker formed them into three ARN units—the First Rifle Battalion, the First Light Infantry Battalion, and a small cavalry unit, the Mounted Rangers.

On the morning of November 5, the now General Walker was at his desk in his new office on the second floor of Government House when Colonel Valle came through the doorway with his characteristic stiff-legged limp and a fierce scowl on his face. Valle slapped a package of letters down on the commander in chief's desk.

"General," said Valle, "there is a traitor in our midst!"

$$\approx 10 \approx$$

CLOSING IN
ON THE PRIZE

IT WAS NOT YET WINTER, AND ALREADY SNOW WAS FALLING IN MANHATTAN. Before a crackling fire, Cornelius Vanderbilt and a group of friends played poker at his Washington Square mansion. Vanderbilt had two interests apart from making money, and both were about winning. One was harness horses; he kept a troop of trotters in a large stables complex out the back of 10 Washington Square. He drove the horses himself, hitched up two at a time to the light, single-seat, four-wheel buggies that were all the rage for rich New York City gentlemen. Any given afternoon between three and four o'clock, Vanderbilt would race his dashing bays. In top hat and white cravat and with a cigar jammed between his teeth, he would beat any fellow buggy driver he encountered on Bloomingdale Road—Broadway north of Fifty-ninth Street—a favorite place of competition for rich horse-fanciers like himself. On one such occasion, he would overtake and beat his eldest son, William, or Billy as the Commodore called him. "Them's good horses of yours," Vanderbilt said as his team glided past his son's straining pair. "But you must give them some more oats before you go out racing!"[1]

Cards were Vanderbilt's other passion. He'd played poker and whist in the *North Star*'s saloon all the way to Europe and back in 1853, consistently beating his sons-in-law, his doctor, his chaplain, and the yacht's skipper. On the occasions he bothered to frequent the city's gentlemen's clubs, it was the Manhattan Club, or the Union Club, to play cards. Apart from the card table, the Commodore didn't mix with his fellow rich New Yorkers, and certainly not with his neighbors here on uptown Washington Square, which had only become fashionable since he built beside what had formerly been a parade ground where George Washington had drilled his troops. Those neighbors, bankers and property developers such as the Jays, Schuylers, Rhinelanders, Van Rensselaers, and Lipsenards, weren't invited to the Commodore's card games. Old friends from his early days, such as Jacob Van Pelt, and favored sons-in-law, they were his card-playing companions.

Vanderbilt was a master player. He knew when to hold, and when to fold. And with his cold, stone face and penetrating eyes, he could intimidate opponents and pull off a bluff like no man alive. He played cards the same way he did business—slyly, expertly, and for keeps. But he didn't play cards for high stakes—he wanted his playing partners to come back to play him again. High stakes were reserved for his business dealings, when he'd happily destroy any adversary in the quest for a seven-figure profit. "He strips the street of five millions with the same nonchalance as he would win a hundred dollars at cards," one contemporary commentator would say.[2]

Tonight, as the cards were dealt and he puffed on a cigar, the Commodore was in good spirits. For Vanderbilt was close to pouncing on the men he'd promised to ruin, Charles Morgan and Cornelius Garrison. The war in Nicaragua had been good news to Vanderbilt, because it had depressed the price of Accessory Transit Company stock. Quietly, discreetly, he and friends such as Thomas Lord had bought up floating Transit Company stock, steadily rebuilding the Commodore's shareholding and that of men whose vote he knew he could depend on.

The latest news to reach New York from Nicaragua had been all the more welcome to Vanderbilt. Even as William Walker was settling into his powerful new role in Granada after engineering a peace deal that ended the civil war and put him in command of the entire Nicaraguan army, the ten-day-old news that had just reached New York City told a totally different story—of the Legitimista army's murder of American Transit passengers at La Virgen and on Lake Nicaragua. That news sent the value of Accessory Transit Company stock diving, as investors were gripped by the fear that Nicaragua's bloody civil war would put the company out of business.

It's "fine pickings for insiders," the New York *Herald* remarked of this Transit Company bear market.[3] And so it was—through his proxy buyers,

Vanderbilt happily snapped up more cheap shares in the company. While others bailed out of the Accessory Transit Company, Vanderbilt didn't share their pessimistic outlook for Nicaragua. It was almost as if he knew that within several weeks, the news would be of peace and order in that country through the agency of William Walker, with the Transit Route once more operating safely and securely.

For the moment, the word on Wall Street was wholly negative as far as the Transit Company was concerned, with the company's deteriorating prospects exacerbated that November as its board announced that the decline in the Transit business due to the Nicaraguan civil war would for the first time force the company to borrow money, at the interest rate of 7 percent, to cover current debts. Again stock was dumped, and again the asking price slumped. At the same time, to attract buyers, the company's latest bond issue had to be offered at a discount of 15 percent. The New York *Herald* railed against the company's performance. The company's enemies were not in Nicaragua, the *Herald* said; they were its own inept managers, Morgan and Garrison.[4]

As the month continued, more Transit Company shares would hit the market, and more shares would be snapped up by Vanderbilt. With the Commodore publicly focused on launching a transatlantic ocean steamer service to France the following year, Morgan and Garrison did not see him coming. At the same time, unlike Vanderbilt, they did not have sufficient faith in the future of the Transit business to buy up the cheap shares themselves.

Vanderbilt, enjoying his poker game, was only weeks away from winning the larger game by completing his overthrow of Morgan and Garrison and resuming control of the Accessory Transit Company.

The letters carried by Benito Lagos were addressed to Dona Ana Arbizu and Don Pedro Xatruch in the southern Honduran district of Tegucigalpa, birthplace of General José Santos Guardiola. Dona Ana was a well-known friend of Guardiola. Xatruch was the brother of Colonel Florencio Xatruch, former Legitimista commander at Rivas, a friend of Guardiola and now military governor at Rivas.

William Walker's new ally in Granada, Father Vijil, curate of Granada, had written to his superior, the vicar general of Nicaragua, Father José Hilario Herdocia, in León, assuring him that Walker did not wish to disturb the status quo and that the Catholic Church could count on the general's support. With Walker now controlling the country's military, it was clear to the church leaders that it would pay to court him, and Father Herdocia had quickly written to Walker, congratulating him on bringing peace to the country and assuring him of the church's future cooperation.

So, it was no surprise to Walker when he learned that Father Manuel Loredo at Managua had urged his parishioner Lagos to head south, not north, with the Martinez letters, and take them to Colonel Valle at Granada. These were the letters that Valle slapped down on the desk in front of Walker, who recognized the handwriting on several of them—that of Ponciano Corral. Corral's brief note to Pedro Xatruch in Honduras, said, in Spanish:

Friend Don Pedro
    We are badly, badly off. Remember your friends. They have left me what I have on, and I hope for your aid.
    Your friend,
    P. Corral[5]

The letter addressed by Corral to Senora Arbizu was marked "Private." The contents, hastily written and a little garbled, were actually intended for "Butcher" Guardiola. They read:

Granada, November 1st, 1855
    General Don Santos Guardiola
    My esteemed friend,
    It is necessary that you write to friends to advise them of the danger we are in, and that they work actively. If they.delay two months there will not then be time.
    Think of us and your offers.
    I salute your lady; and commend your friend who truly esteems you and kisses your hand.
    P. Corral

P.S.: Nicaragua is lost; lost Honduras, San Salvador and Guatemala, if they let this get body. Let them come quickly if they would meet auxiliaries.

A third letter, written by Colonel Martinez at Managua to Senora Arbizu, expressed Martinez's concern about what Corral considered the plight of both himself and the Legitimista cause in Nicaragua. The fourth letter, from Colonel Florencio Xatruch at Rivas, told his brother Pedro in Honduras that he had wanted to return home to Honduras after the Nicaraguan peace settlement but had remained at Rivas at the request of Legitimista friends, to be of service to them.

Walker would express his surprise at the content of the letters: "The two from Corral were sufficient to amaze anyone who had heard him a few days before solemnly swear to observe the treaty of the 23rd." From all four letters, Walker deduced that Guardiola and Pedro Xatruch had both previously offered to give the Legitimistas in Nicaragua help to remove Walker and his Americans. The reference to "two months" suggested to Walker that Guardiola had recently communicated to Corral that it would take two months to raise an army in Honduras and Guatemala large enough to march down into Nicaragua to deal with Walker and his troops.

Walker reacted quickly. Ordering the guard at Granada strengthened, and with no one permitted to leave the city, he sent courteous invitations to the president, all cabinet members, including Corral, and Corral's senior Legitimista friends to attend a meeting in Walker's office.

Before long, Corral ambled into Government House with two Legitimista associates, chatting amiably to them, blissfully unaware of the reason for Walker's summons. As Corral and his companions approached the stairs to the second floor, General Walker and several of his officers descended the stairs. There were letters in Walker's hand, but Corral, still none the wiser, greeted Walker with a friendly smile.

In response, Walker thrust the letters at Corral. "Are you the author of these?" the American demanded coldly, in perfect Spanish.

Corral froze in his tracks. His eyes dropped to the letters. He recognized his own handwriting and, with sinking heart, recognized his incriminating correspondence. Now, too, it dawned on him that Walker was fluent in Spanish and that the diminutive American had been playing him for a fool.

And all this time, Corral had thought he had Walker's measure. Realizing that it was pointless denying authorship of the letters, Minister Corral numbly nodded in affirmation. Behind him, American soldiers had materialized. Firm hands gripped Corral's arms.

A little before 2:00 P.M. on November 8, Colonel Charles Gilman, who was mounted, followed a detachment of American riflemen who marched Ponciano Corral from Granada Prison on the southeast corner of the Granadine Plaza. Corral, in chains and dressed in a white shirt and trousers, held the arm of Father Vijil and looked an "unhappy man." He was on his way to his execution.

Under Nicaraguan law, a cabinet member could only face trial for treason in the nation's senate. Because the senate had been dissolved the previous year, and Corral had never officially resigned as a general of the army, Walker had him tried before a military court-martial. Sitting in the meeting chamber of Granada's City Council House, Walker's military court had Colonel Charles Hornsby for its president, Colonel Birkett D. Fry as judge advocate, and Parker H. French as defense counsel. Six American officers sat in judgment. Walker later claimed that Corral had no objections to being tried by Americans, and in fact preferred them to native Nicaraguans.

The trial had been brief. "I am not a traitor," Corral said in his defense as he faced the bench. "These dealings were to save my country. I am solely responsible." The guilty verdict had been inevitable. The court had recommended mercy, but Walker showed none. "Mercy to Corral would have been an invitation to all the Legitimistas to engage in like conspiracies," he later wrote.

Prisoner and escort proceeded through the Granadine Plaza, which was lined with American troops, passing through a vast, silent crowd. There was strong popular sympathy for Corral, and one of his former officers, José Maria Noguera, had tried unsuccessfully to enlist support from other Legitimistas to break Corral out of jail. But, with Walker and the Americans now controlling the armed forces and receiving more Yankee recruits with each steamer arrival, the disarmed Legitimistas were powerless to intervene.

Permitted to visit Corral in his prison cell, Noguera had burst into tears and begged his general's forgiveness for not being able to save him. But Corral, resigned to his fate, had told Noguera not to be distressed. "There is nothing more you could have done."[6]

The previous evening, Corral's daughters Carmen and Sofia and many leading women of Granada had accompanied Father Vijil to the Vieja house on the plaza, to beg clemency from Walker. He had made them one concession, postponing the execution from noon to 2:00 P.M. An American on guard outside the Vieja house, on hearing of the two-hour postponement, had exclaimed, "Oh, my God, how generous!"[7] Not even a personal entreaty from Walker's friend "Little Irena" Ohoran could change Walker's determination to execute Corral.

According to Sofia Corral, one of Walker's officers—possibly De Brissot, but more likely Hornsby—visited Corral in prison shortly before the execution hour. Identifying himself as a fellow Freemason, he offered to render whatever favor he could under the circumstances. Corral penned a hasty note to his mother and daughters, telling them that he went to his death a confirmed Christian and an innocent man. "I forgive my enemies," he added. The American officer duly passed the note to the Corral family.[8]

The execution party halted outside the city's Parochial Church. At the church entrance stood a number of Corral's colleagues, among them Don Enrique Guzman, a friend since childhood. Given permission by Colonel Gilman to approach the condemned man, a tearful Guzman embraced Corral. Corral, in contrast, was composed and dignified.[9] A raised platform stood in front of the stone wall of the Parochial Church's Santisimo Chapel, with a chair placed on it. Colonel Gilman dismounted and asked Corral to climb the platform and be seated, and Corral complied but declined a blindfold. The men of the firing squad loaded their rifles, then Gilman advised that he would wait until Corral signaled he was ready. As Gilman took his place beside the executioners, Father Vijil stepped away from the prisoner, who, with his head bowed, was saying a final prayer.

The crowd, many thousands strong, stood stock still, not uttering a word; all eyes were glued on the condemned man. Watching the proceedings from across the square, from the balcony of the Vieja house, were William Walker, Foreign Minister Jerez, and the man appointed by President Rivas to replace Corral as war minister, Don Buenaventura Selva, the Democratico brother-in-law of the late Provisional Director Castellon. Of President Rivas there was no sign; he had closed himself away inside Government House.

Corral finished mouthing the words of his prayer, then looked up, crossed himself, and, looking directly at Gilman, nodded. "Take aim!" called Gilman, drawing his sword. The rifles of the firing squad came up. The men had been instructed to aim for the heart. Corral looked directly ahead. Gilman didn't protract the affair. Bringing down his sword, he called the instruction to fire in a loud voice. The rifles crackled. The crowd saw Corral sag on the chair. A collective groan went up. Women, and not a few men, began to cry. Corral was pronounced dead, and his corpse handed over to the Corral family, to be buried at once. The people of Granada would mourn the popular Ponciano Corral long after the passing of the novena, the traditional nine nights of prayer that followed a death in Nicaragua.

In his memoirs, Walker devoted one brief paragraph to the execution of Corral. But it was soon to occupy much space in the U.S. press, which generally condemned it. "Walker was bitterly, and I think, unjustly denounced by the press of the United States for Corral's execution," said one of Walker's officers later, "by the same journals that approved the shooting of Mayorga." Support was not widespread locally either. "Public sentiment in Nicaragua, even in the Democratic ranks, was not agreed as to the wisdom or necessity of his death," said the same officer.[10]

The American ambassador to Nicaragua, John H. Wheeler, whose close friend U.S. President Franklin D. Pierce had given him his present diplomatic post, had quickly warmed to William Walker, making him his "invited guest and welcome friend."[11] Wheeler, a lawyer and a Southerner from South Carolina, "admired the character of General Walker" and was all for his planned American colonization of Central America. The bigoted, racist ambassador was convinced that, like him, Walker "had only contempt for the Spaniards and those mongrel races, who occupied with indolence and semi-barbarism one of the finest and most productive regions on the continent."[12]

On November 10, two days after the execution of Ponciano Corral, Ambassador Wheeler announced formal U.S. recognition of the Rivas administration as Nicaragua's legitimate government. He did so without consulting Washington and without the approval of the man who had been U.S. secretary of state since 1853, William Learned Marcy. This recognition was formalized by Wheeler at a function at Government House, where he delivered a flowery speech in which he congratulated Nicaragua on achieving peace.

President Rivas responded, using words with the ring of Walker's authorship about them: "The Republic counts on new and powerful elements of liberty and order which cause us to conceive well-founded hopes that the country will march with a firm step in the path of progress toward the greatness offered it by its free institutions and natural advantages."[13]

In Washington, Secretary of State Marcy was furious when he learned that Wheeler had recognized a nonelected government. Sixty-nine-year-old Marcy, a former senator and onetime governor of New York, was well respected in Washington for his intellect and diplomacy. Among his triumphs had been the Gadsden Purchase, which added a slice of Mexico to the United States during William Walker's Sonoran venture. But an attempt by Marcy to have Ambassador Wheeler recalled was rebuffed by President Pierce and several cabinet members who were also close friends of Wheeler.

This defeat incensed Secretary Marcy. He did not approve of Wheeler's actions; nor did he approve of Rivas or of Walker. From this point forward, Marcy would do everything in his power to make things difficult for both Ambassador Wheeler and the Rivas administration. Most of all, Marcy was determined to frustrate William Walker's ambitions in Nicaragua and to rid Central America of filibusters. "The course of events might have been very different," Walker would later write, "if the federal administration at Washington had frankly approved the conduct of its representative."[14]

ON A
COLLISION COURSE

As December winds swept down from Canada to chill New York City, Cornelius Vanderbilt celebrated. He was not a heavy drinker, but his victory called for a glass of champagne and a Havana cigar, in his office behind the Washington Place house.

Vanderbilt had regained control of the Accessory Transit Company. It had taken him the best part of a year, but by the end of November 1855, he and his friends had acquired a controlling shareholding in the company. At the company's January board meeting, Vanderbilt would be elected a director once more, along with several of his sons-in-law. The directorships of Charles Morgan, Cornelius Garrison, and their associate William C. Ralston would be terminated. Morgan would cease to be the company's New York agent when his contract expired at the end of January. Garrison was likewise on notice that when his contract as the company's agent in San Francisco expired in February, it would not be renewed. Meanwhile, wily attorney Joseph L. White had switched his allegiance and his vote back to Vanderbilt and was continuing as the Transit Company's general counsel.

Morgan and Garrison, overwhelmed by Vanderbilt's covert assault, were out the door, and Vanderbilt was back in control of the company he founded. The Commodore had not yet ruined his enemies as he promised, but there was time enough for that.

On the morning of December 17, 1855, bullying her blunt bow through Pacific waves, the Nicaragua Line's SS *Sierra Nevada* steamed south along the coast of Nicaragua. Word had yet to reach California that Cornelius Vanderbilt was once again master of the Accessory Transit Company, but when it did, the *Sierra Nevada* and the other ships in the Nicaragua Line fleet would again become known as "Vanderbilt steamers." On this run, the *Sierra Nevada* was carrying 750 passengers and millions of dollars in gold. The California gold shipments these days consisted of more than gold dust—a federal mint had opened in San Francisco the previous year, and in its first twelve months, it turned out $4 million in gold bars and in $25, $50, and $100 gold coins. By May 1855, the mint was producing $1.5 million in gold coin a month.[1] There were also several private mints in the city producing thousands of dollars in gold coin every day.

A little before noon on December 17, the *Sierra Nevada* entered the cove at San Juan del Sur after a twelve-day run down from San Francisco. In addition to 610 passengers intending to cross Nicaragua and travel on to the Atlantic seaboard, the steamer carried 140 American "colonists," whose journey would end in Nicaragua. These colonists were part of the flood of mostly American immigrants enticed to Nicaragua in the wake of William Walker's peace settlement. Walker had convinced President Rivas to authorize the creation of the government-owned Nicaraguan Emigration Company to manage the colonization process. To run the program, Walker had Rivas appoint well-connected, Granada-based American businessman Joseph W. Fabens, "a man of high character," in the view of one of Walker's officers, to the newly created government post of director of colonization.[2] Migration agents were appointed in the United States—in San Francisco, it was Walker's lawyer friend and recruiter A. Parker Crittenden; in New Orleans, newspaperman John P. Heiss, a friend of Walker's during his years in the New Orleans newspaper business. An agent had also been appointed in New York.

On November 23, President Rivas had issued a colonization decree that provided for 250 acres of land for every American signing up to the program via these official agents. The decree, which would be published in the United States by the Nicaraguan Emigration Company, also stated that colonists would be free from public service *"except when the public safety shall otherwise demand."*[3] The provisional Nicaraguan government still considered a country in a state of emergency, which conceivably would be relaxed once national elections were held.

In the meantime, new colonists had signed up by the hundreds, fueled by the promise of free land, by poor prospects in the California gold fields, and by high unemployment in New York City and New Orleans. They sailed for Nicaragua knowing full well that, for the moment, anyway, they would be going into military service in General Walker's Army of the Republic of Nicaragua. Yet, they didn't seem to mind. As one early "colonist" noted, "Many of Walker's soldiers, like myself, were drawn to Nicaragua by a desire for adventure in a foreign land."[4] The romance of soldiering for William Walker gave ordinary men newfound status in California. Horace Bell, who gave up his job as a Los Angeles Ranger to join Walker's filibustering army, would remark, "To sympathize with filibustering at the time was popular. An actual filibuster was a hero, a lion!"[5]

Among the men lining the ship's wooden rails as the *Sierra Nevada* crept to her usual anchorage off San Juan del Sur stood one such filibuster, James Carson Jamison. The twenty-five-year-old Missouri native was a strapping six foot one, weighed 170 pounds, and wore a beard in the Abraham Lincoln style, without a mustache. Jamison had failed in his attempt to join the U.S. Army for the Mexican War and then tried his luck panning for gold in California for several years. There, he'd heard about the Americans in Nicaragua. "My blood grew hot at the thought of the stirring adventures that awaited me if I could attach myself to Walker's army," he would later say.[6]

On the voyage down from San Francisco, Jamison had been elected senior lieutenant by the forty-five men of his company of recruits, which was to become Company D of the ARN's First Light Infantry Battalion. But, on the last night of the voyage, several of those men, including a Lieutenant Charles Pierson, had become drunk and caused a riot. Now as the *Sierra Nevada*'s anchors hit the water half a mile offshore, Jamison prepared to be the first man ashore. As soon as the steamer anchored, Jamison was rowed to the beach by a ship's boat, which passed iron rowboats coming the other way to commence ferrying passengers to shore.

Once on dry land, Jamison reported to the ARN's senior officer at the port, thirty-five-year-old Lieutenant Anthony Rudler, commander of Company F of the First Rifle Battalion, which garrisoned the town. Rudler himself had only come down to Nicaragua from San Francisco in October. Born in France and raised in Georgia, he'd served as a captain with the Second Louisiana Infantry during the Mexican War. When the *Sierra Nevada's* passengers came ashore, Rudler's men arrested the recruits who had rioted aboard her—four men pointed out by Jamison were jailed, while Charles Pierson, being an officer, was placed on parole. But when Pierson attempted to parade with the company, Jamison thought fast, taking it on himself to demote Pierson to the ranks and then have him locked up with the other prisoners.

As Jamison and his fellow new recruits were being drilled on the sand, Edward J. C. Kewen, twenty-nine-year-old younger brother of the late Achilles Kewen, the Walker deputy killed at the Battle of Rivas, came ashore from the *Sierra Nevada*, accompanied by two fellow passengers from San Francisco. One was attorney Edmund Randolph, Walker's best friend. The other man, barely in his twenties, was William R. Garrison, son of Cornelius Garrison. They were joined by Captain Frank Anderson; he had promised Walker he would return as he soon as his leg wound had healed, and he'd even brought his own horse down from San Francisco with him— "Brandy," a fine stallion.

Kewen, Garrison, and Randolph, provided with mules by Lieutenant Rudler, set off, escorted by Anderson, for Granada, there to meet with General Walker and talk business.

Earlier in December, Cornelius Garrison, in San Francisco, had learned that Commodore Vanderbilt, in New York, had rebuilt his stake in the Accessory Transit Company and was poised to regain control of the corporation. Garrison was as intractable as a crocodile and as slippery as an eel. Even a friend and admirer declared that Garrison was so tricky his competitors should assign "twenty men to watch him."[7] Not content to sit back and let Cornelius Vanderbilt beat him, Garrison had sent his son down to Nicaragua with Edmund Randolph to see if a deal could be done with Walker over the Transit Route—a deal that would shut out Cornelius Vanderbilt.

Once Kewen, Randolph, and young Garrison arrived in Granada, they went into a meeting with General Walker behind the closed doors of his second-floor Government House office, joined by Garrison's agent in Nicaragua, C. J. Macdonald. Downstairs at Government House, President Rivas was totally unaware that the three men had arrived in the city and was oblivious to the deal being hammered out above his head.

In early November, Walker had instructed Parker H. French, the new coalition government's minister for hacienda, to write to the president of the Accessory Transit Company in New York. The letter required the company to appoint commissioners to settle the outstanding financial matters in dispute between the government and the company, as a clause of the Transit charter provided. The Transit Company's legal counsel, Joseph L. White, whom Walker considered "the leading mind of the corporation," had immediately replied.[8] He said that the company had previously appointed two commissioners to deal with Legitimista Commissioners Lacayo and Tejada, and accordingly, the matter still lay in the hands of those four gentlemen, not with the company. This ignored the fact that French had advised the company in his letter that the powers of Commissioners Lacayo and Tejada were forthwith formally revoked.

Walker was aware that White had subsequently also written to Cortlandt Cushing, the Transit Company's manager in Nicaragua, telling him that the company would make the Nicaraguan government suffer if it did not settle the dispute on the company's terms—a veiled threat to pull out of Nicaragua. In theory, the company (Vanderbilt) had the whip hand in this affair, but slippery Cornelius Garrison was about to tilt the balance of power Walker's way.

Since October, Garrison had been sending American colonists down from San Francisco aboard Nicaragua Line steamers free of charge. As company agent, he'd billed these passages against the moneys owed by the company to the Nicaraguan government. James Jamison's batch of recruits had been among those to come down under Garrison's subsidy scheme. Clearly, Garrison wanted to be friends with Walker. Now, at the Granada meeting, Edmund Randolph told Walker that after being shown the Transit contract by Cornelius Garrison, both he and fellow lawyer Crittenden were "clear and decided in the opinion that it had been forfeited" by the Accessory Transit Company for failure to pay commissions to the Nicaraguan government.[9]

This opened the way for Garrison's son William to present Walker with a Transit Route proposal worked out in San Francisco between his father and

Walker's agent Crittenden. The deal was this: Garrison and his partners would guarantee to operate a shipping line to and from Nicaragua and the United States. Walker, for his part, must guarantee that the Rivas government would revoke the Transit Company's contract with the Nicaraguan government, on the grounds that the company was in breach of its financial obligations and had deliberately avoided arbitration of outstanding claims, in contravention of the contract. The Nicaraguan government would then reassign the charter to a syndicate headed by Edmund Randolph; that syndicate would in turn assign Transit Route rights to Garrison and Morgan.

Young William Garrison proposed to Walker that the Rivas government seize all Transit Company assets in Nicaragua as part payment for the hundreds of thousands of dollars that the Nicaraguans contended were owed them by the Transit Company in unpaid commissions. Those assets included the company's lake and river steamers, lighters, depots, accommodation buildings, employees' houses, jetties, roads and other fixed facilities, and the Transit's stagecoaches, horses, and mules. In Commodore Vanderbilt's own estimation, those assets were worth close to a million dollars.[10] For the time being, the Nicaraguan government would lease the seized Transit assets to Edmund Randolph's syndicate, which would pay the government a $400,000 bond advanced by Morgan and Garrison. Randolph would lease the assets on to Garrison and Morgan.

The proposal was to Walker's liking. He sought no financial consideration from Garrison and Morgan, nor was he offered any. Focused on nation building and political power, he was not interested in monetary gain. Garrison was prepared to help pave Walker's road to power and, as a final carrot, offered to carry all colonists to Nicaragua free of charge once he and Morgan had the Transit contract. It was agreed that Walker and Randolph would draw up a new charter. Ironically, if this deal came off, it would be swift and sweet revenge for Garrison and Morgan, having been so recently outwitted by Cornelius Vanderbilt and losing control of the Transit Company. Vanderbilt had worked so long and so sneakily to regain control, and now, just as he reclaimed the company, William Walker was about to make it worthless. It looked as if the Commodore had been outsmarted by competitors Garrison and Morgan and by a Tennessee adventurer with not the slightest interest in making money.

❧ 12 ❧

BLINDSIDING
VANDERBILT

THE SECRET DRAFT OF THE NEW TRANSIT COMPANY CONTRACT HAD been completed. Taking one copy with him, William Garrison set off to join Transit passengers heading east, to travel to New York and seek Charles Morgan's endorsement. As he set off, young Garrison had company—the one-armed Parker H. French. Once U.S. Ambassador Wheeler recognized the Rivas government, Walker had convinced President Rivas to appoint French as Nicaragua's new ambassador to the United States, replacing the Legitimista incumbent, José de Marcoleta. Filling French's seat in the Nicaraguan cabinet would be the former Democratico war minister, Mariano Salazar.

As Garrison and French went east, Edward Kewen and C. J. Macdonald went west, to take the waiting *Sierra Nevada* up to San Francisco to deliver a copy of the draft Transit contract to Cornelius Garrison. Edward Kewen had also been given another mission by Walker. In San Francisco, Kewen was to make very public inquiries about purchasing an ocean steamer on behalf of the Nicaraguan government, for a passenger service between San Francisco and Nicaragua. Apparently, Walker didn't want Garrison to think he was offering the only option available to the Nicaraguan government.

At Walker's urging, Edmund Randolph had decided to remain in Granada, spending Christmas and New Years with his friend. Randolph took a room in the spacious city house of one of the most beautiful women in Granada, Dona Irena Ohoran. Of mixed Spanish-Irish blood, the diminutive Dona Irena was known locally as *Nina Irena*, or "Little Irena." This was a name that even William Walker used for her.[1] Since

Walker and Little Irena were introduced by Ambassador Wheeler, Walker had become close to the dark-eyed beauty, even briefly living in her house, and it was rumored among Walker's men that their chief and the middle-aged but eye-catching Little Irena were lovers.[2] Randolph planned to wait in Granada until responses to the draft contract were received from Garrison and Morgan. He and Walker hoped that the deal would be finalized by February. Then they would spring their surprise on Commodore Vanderbilt.

Newly arrived Lieutenant James Jamison had been posted to Granada, and now, with Christmas just days away, he and several of his men sat idly on the steps of their quartel on the Granadine Plaza. Jamison spotted a comical figure "swinging with a tremendous stride across the plaza in [his] direction. He wore trousers that were too small and much too short for him, yet his coat was brilliant with braid. A long plume waved above his hat, and his sword clanged on the pavement."[3] He was looking at Captain "Napoleon" Tejada, who was serving on General Walker's staff.

"Where is Jamison?" Tejada demanded loudly.

"Here I am," Jamison replied, so nervous about the news that Tejada might be bringing from General Walker's headquarters, he later admitted, that he forgot to address the captain as "sir."

"You are to present yourself at headquarters at once," said Tejada. "General Walker wishes to speak to you."[4]

Terrified that Walker was going to discipline him for demoting and locking up Lieutenant Pierson, perhaps even dismiss him from the army, Jamison hurried behind Captain Tejada across the plaza to Government House, then mounted the stairs. At the door to the general's office, Tejada knocked, then motioned for Jamison to go on in. As Jamison entered Walker's office, he saw the general, in civilian dress as usual, in conference with a number of officers. Walker looked around, and Jamison came to attention. Taking up a piece of paper from his desk, Walker, blank-faced, crossed the room to Jamison.

"Lieutenant," he said in his soft Tennessee drawl, "here is your commission as lieutenant in the Army of the Republic of Nicaragua."[5]

Jamison, towering six inches above his commander, looked down, accepted the handwritten commission, saluted, then turned on his heel and marched back out the way he had come, a much relieved young man.

The Republic of Nicaragua's new "Ambassador and Plenipotentiary General," Parker H. French, arrived in Washington, D.C., and proceeded to the State Department's offices in the Northeast Executive Building. He planned to explain that he was José de Marcoleta's replacement as Nicaraguan ambassador to the United States and present his credentials from President Patricio Rivas to Secretary of State William L. Marcy.

But for three days running, French and his secretary, Henry Dillingham, were made to spend fruitless hours waiting in the corridor outside Secretary Marcy's office. Then, at the end of the third day, one of Marcy's subordinates came out to French and delivered a blunt message from the secretary. Horace Bell, one of Walker's junior officers, was to describe French's rebuff by the State Department in his own colorful language—the secretary, via his deputy, "in language forcible but politely diplomatique, informed Mr. Envoy that if he did not clear out and vamoose the capital, and take himself to his own country, he would hand him to the authorities as an offender against the laws of the land."[6]

According to Bell, French departed the secretary of state's office and Washington in high dudgeon, threatening to revenge himself on Marcy.[7] French certainly wasted no time in leaving the capital and heading for New York to find a ship bound for Nicaragua, for French had realized that Secretary Marcy had learned a secret from his past. In 1850, French, then just twenty-four years of age, had gone to New York from St. Louis, where he had been working as a builder, and advertised for clients who would join "Captain French's Overland Express Train" to California via Texas, New Mexico, and Arizona. French, an orphan who ran away to sea at fifteen and served as a cabin boy, had absolutely no experience as a wagon train master, but "this enterprising vagabond" was able to convince fifty men to sign up for French's Overland Express to California, paying $250 each.[8] They had sailed for New Orleans on April 26 aboard the SS *Ohio*, arriving at the beginning of May. Just several weeks later, William Walker would sail from New Orleans to Panama aboard the same ship, on his way to his new life in California. It is probable that he heard about French's planned expedition during his last weeks in New Orleans.

French's party spent a week in New Orleans, living the high life at the St. Charles Hotel while French recruited another seventy expeditioners, plus sixty employees who each paid French half price for the privilege of traveling to California while working for him. On May 31, the enlarged party had taken a steamer to Texas, from where they set off overland in a train of wagons. At San Antonio, French had used forged bank drafts to pay for supplies, at the same time claiming he was an agent of the U.S. government. By the time the Overland Express crawled into El Paso (then called Franklin), French's clients had begun to suspect that the young "captain" was a fraud. And when they opened his money chest and found it empty, they knew it for a fact. French then fled the train and crossed the Rio Grande into Mexico, after which the Overland Express split into four groups, two of which headed into Mexico. At Corralitos in the Mexican state of Chihuahua, French had reappeared with a gang of local banditos and attempted to raid one of these groups, only to be beaten off.

There are two versions of what followed. One has French being shot in the side and right arm during this failed holdup of his former clients; with his elbow shattered, he was forced to have the arm amputated to save his life. In the other version, French and several accomplices were captured by Mexican authorities and thrown in Durango Prison. During an escape attempt, his companions were killed; French survived, but with his right arm shattered and requiring amputation. Neither story was flattering to French.

Twenty-three men and boys from the second Overland Express party that had headed into Mexico arrived in San Francisco in late December. They sailed up from Guaymas on an American barque. French himself had turned up in San Francisco some months later, brazenly telling the story that he had lost his arm fighting Mexican bandits.[9]

Secretary Marcy had been made aware of French's Overland Express crimes and misdemeanors by the time the one-armed envoy turned up at his office. Marcy's probable source of information was Transit Company legal counsel Joseph L. White, who was no doubt alerted to French's history after French had been made a minister in Nicaragua's coalition government. White's source may well have been Sylvanus H. Spencer, who was then captain of the Transit Company river steamer *Machuca* operating on the San Juan River and who had been one of French's Overland Express clients from New York.[10]

While French's background made a mockery of his ambassadorial appointment, Secretary Marcy would probably have rejected any envoy sent to Washington by the Rivas government. According to the New York *Herald,* the secretary of state was convinced that President Rivas was nothing more than William Walker's hostage, doing whatever Walker told him to do.[11] Marcy was determined to frustrate Walker's Central American ambitions any way he could.

The secretary of state was aware of widespread unease in Latin America about the presence of William Walker and his American filibusters in Nicaragua. Rivas's foreign minister, Maximo Jerez, had written in late October to the leaders of the neighboring Central American nations advising of the change of government and expressing friendly sentiments. But former Nicaraguan ambassador to Washington José de Marcoleta and the ambassadors of Costa Rica, Honduras, and Chile all lodged complaints with the U.S. State Department, questioning the legitimacy of the nonelected Rivas government. Only El Salvador had failed to complain. On the contrary, its moderate president, José Maria San Martin, an old friend of Patricio Rivas, even wrote a congratulatory letter to the new Nicaraguan president.

In Costa Rica, Nicaragua's southern neighbor, the Legitimista president, Juan Rafael Mora, was convinced that William Walker had plans to extend his influence throughout Central America. This impression was enhanced by a letter that President Rivas was to soon send his fellow Central American presidents, urging them to nominate delegates to a convention at which all the member states of the former Central American Federation, dissolved in 1838, would discuss the possible reformation of that federation. The

Costa Rican press railed against Rivas and the new regime in Granada, and on November 20, President Mora issued a proclamation condemning the Nicaraguan government and warning the people of Costa Rica to prepare to combat what he characterized as the threat from the north posed by the empire-building Yankee, William Walker, and his *filibusteros.*

To Mora's mind, evidence of this threat had been the presence of recently deposed Honduran president, Trinidad Cabanas, as William Walker's invited guest in Nicaragua. Mora was convinced that Cabanas, a Democratico, was in Granada to secure a force of Walker's American riflemen to restore him to power in Honduras. After that, Mora was sure, Walker's Americans would march down into Costa Rica, a country with a population of just 112,000, and impose Walker's control over the little country. The Yankees were coming, he warned, sooner or later, and Costa Rica should be prepared to repulse them.

In Washington, now that he'd sent Walker's one-armed envoy packing, Secretary Marcy set out to stop the flood of American recruits into Nicaragua from the United States. If need be, he would invoke the Neutrality Act of 1818 and have these Nicaragua-bound "colonists" literally dragged from southbound vessels.

On Sunday, December 23, Walker's off-duty men, lazing in the shade of the arcades around the Granadine Plaza, watched the elderly Trinidad Cabanas emerge from the Vieja house, where he had been staying with General Walker, and mount a waiting horse. The wizened Cabanas was joined by several leading Democraticos and an escort of American soldiers of the ARN's Mounted Rangers. With a clatter of hooves on worn cobblestones, the party trooped from the plaza and headed along the Calle Jalteva Real, passing through the Jalteva Plaza, where they swung right and made for the road that led north via Masaya and Managua to León.

There was a sour look on Cabanas's face as he rode away. He had not achieved what he came for. President Mora of Costa Rica had been right—with elections due in Honduras in February, Cabanas had urged Walker to send him back to Honduras with an army of Americans to forcibly restore him to the presidency. That would enable him to run in the February elections as the incumbent. Nicaragua's Democratico foreign minister, the lame doctor and former general Maximo Jerez, had strongly supported the idea, while President Rivas had been adamantly opposed. More importantly, Walker had not been interested; he had other priorities, closer to home. Besides, Walker had come to find Cabanas "a man of narrow mind, strong prejudices, and bitter animosities."[12] So, twenty days after he'd arrived at Granada, a frustrated Cabanas headed north to the Democratico stronghold of León accompanied by Jerez, supposedly to celebrate Christmas with friends.

New York City. It was 2:00 P.M. on Monday, December 24, and with Christmas just a night away, John McKeon, federal attorney for the Southern District of New York, was thinking about anything but chasing criminals, when he was handed a cable from Washington, D.C. McKeon, a forty-seven-year-old Democrat, read an instruction from the Justice Department. At the request of the State Department, the U.S. attorney was to prevent the imminent departure of the Nicaragua Line's SS *Northern Light*. He was to seize any weapons and ammunition being carried as cargo, remove any passengers bound for Nicaragua to join William Walker's army in contravention of the Neutrality Act, and question one particular passenger, Parker H. French, about an expedition he led to Texas five years earlier. McKeon immediately sent a messenger to the U.S. Marshal's office with instructions to seize the ship.

When deputy U.S. marshals Reyer and Cook arrived at Pier Number 3 on the North River, the Nicaragua Line's place of departure, they found the pier crowded with five hundred people who had come to see off friends and loved ones heading for Nicaragua. The *Northern Light* was still at the pier, towering above the crowd. At 2,767 tons, she was the Nicaragua Line's largest steamer. Cornelius Vanderbilt built her in 1851 for $290,000, expressly for the Nicaragua run. She was a pretty ship, with pleasing rounded lines, her dark green oak hull trimmed with red and white lines at the guard streaks. She had steam up, all the passengers were aboard, and with just a single gangplank and one hawser connecting ship to pier, the *Northern Light* was ready to sail at 3:00 P.M. Reyer and Cook went aboard and announced that they had orders to seize the ship in the name of the U.S. government.

With the *Northern Light*'s skipper, Captain Edward Tinklepaugh, ashore at the Custom House, the deputy marshals instructed Chief Engineer Coles not to start the ship's engines. When the engineer demanded to know the reason for the district attorney's action, he was told: "The seizure was ordered on the ground that the people on board are not bona-fide passengers, but adventurers going out to enter Walker's army."[13]

Scanning the passenger list and looking over the steerage passengers thronging the ship's deck, the deputy marshals suspected that at least 350 of the steamer's 670 passengers had no intention of going all the way to California. Reyer and Cook considered them "roughs" and noted that they were "poorly clothed and obviously in destitute circumstances."[14] Some of them were mere children and could not possibly have afforded even the steerage fare to California; they had to be traveling free of charge, courtesy of Cornelius Garrison and Charles Morgan, who, until the next directors meeting in the new year, still controlled the Transit Company and so continued to provide free passage for Walker recruits.

Captain Tinklepaugh then arrived, carrying his customs clearance and accompanied by the Transit Company's general counsel, Joseph L. White, who had been summoned from his office by the ship's officers. The hard-bitten Tinklepaugh, considered one of the most conscientious skippers on the Central America run, shrugged when informed of the deputy marshals' mission and said, "I know nothing about filibustering."[15]

"The *Northern Light* will sail at her appointed hour," attorney White emphatically declared.[16] But when the deputies shook their heads and showed White their warrant, he conceded that the ship would not leave after all. White then took Captain Tinklepaugh ashore with him, to pay a visit to District Attorney McKeon.

As the crowd on the pier continued to mill, a man was pushed into the water. He was just being fished from the harbor, spluttering and shivering, when Captain Tinklepaugh returned, alone. Out of earshot of the two deputies, Tinklepaugh discreetly ordered the ship to get under way. The gangplank came up, the last hawser was slipped, the ship's Morgan Iron

Works engines began to turn over, and the two giant iron paddlewheels on her sides slowly rotated through the water. With the two deputy marshals still aboard and the crowd in a state of delight, the *Northern Light* eased out into the stream.

When word of the ship's attempted escape reached D.A. John McKeon, he dashed to Pier 3. Waving a fist at the departing ship, he ordered her to stop, but the *Northern Light* continued on her merry way. The crowd surged around McKeon, jeering him.

"Throw him overboard!" someone proposed.[17] Several rough voices seconded the motion.

McKeon, "much excited and very pale," according to a New York *Express* reporter who had by that time arrived on the scene, climbed up onto a plank, from where he tried to address the unruly crowd, warning them that they were creating a riot and that if they didn't immediately leave the dock, he'd call the police. In response, "some young urchin" threw an apple at the district attorney's head; it just missed his hat and sailed into the harbor, bringing a derisive cheer from the crowd. Unable to make himself heard above the catcalls, McKeon stepped down and pushed his way clear of the crowd. Determined to stop the steamer, he hurried to a jetty where the armed U.S. revenue cutter *Washington* was tied up. When he ordered the sailing vessel to go after the *Northern Light,* her master pointed out that there was not a drop of wind.[18]

Thinking fast, McKeon commandeered a steam-powered tugboat. With McKeon aboard the cutter, the tug towed the *Washington* down the harbor. A vast crowd quickly swelled at the Battery to watch what transpired, in "a high state of excitement."[19] The *Northern Light* had yet to reach Ellis Island when the tug and her tow overtook her. One of the cutter's cannon boomed a warning to the ship to stop. It was a blank cartridge. The *Northern Light* sailed on. The tug and cutter drew level with the steamer. Again the cannon fired. This time, a cannonball soared over the bow of the *Northern Light,* plopping into the gray water and creating an impressive plume. Now Captain Tinklepaugh gave up the flight and hove to.

On the orders of the cutter's commander, the steamer turned around and returned to the North River, dropping anchor off Pier Number 3. The revenue cutter anchored close by, placing herself between steamer and the sea.

For the moment, no one seemed sure what would happen next, and as darkness fell, all on board the *Northern Light* settled down for a night at anchor. The passengers were ordered to remain on board, but as the steamer lay there overnight, boatmen from the Battery slipped out and took off some passengers. Once it was realized that this was going on, at two o'clock in the morning the pilot boat *Edmund Griffins* came alongside, and the deputy marshals loaded 189 men and boys onto her from the *Northern Light*. The indignant travelers didn't go voluntarily, putting up some resistance and damning the deputies for all they were worth. Some wanted to throw Captain Tinklepaugh into the harbor for allowing this to happen. Others blamed President Franklin Pierce.

"If ever we catch Frank Pierce in New York," one was heard to call, "he should never be allowed to leave before we have tarred and feathered him!"

A boy of no more than eight, who declared that he was among those "who were to do all the fighting" in Nicaragua, exclaimed, "If the boys want to get along, the authorities won't let them. We could all have land of our own, if they would only let us off."

A giant of a fellow responded, "Oh, they want us to make boots at Sing Sing." He was referring to Sing Sing Prison at Ossining, New York.

Said the eight-year-old, "I be damned if I do!"[20]

This group was conveyed to Pier Number 3, where they were released and told to go home. Meanwhile, as another group of forty passengers was arrested and put aboard the revenue cutter *Washington,* there was a scuffle, and two passengers were put in irons. All these men were taken ashore for questioning. Among them was Nicaragua's one-armed ambassador, and with daylight, there followed what a San Francisco newspaper would describe as "an interesting interview between the District Attorney and Parker H. French."[21] In that interview, French apparently claimed diplomatic immunity, producing his credentials as Nicaragua's ambassador, and McKeon, uncertain how to handle the situation, warned French that he would not be permitted to sail from New York under any circumstances, then let him go, pending specific charges. French would soon disappear.

Once Christmas Day dawned, the *Northern Light* was relocated to an anchorage off Bedloe's Island—the island's name would change to Liberty

Island once the Statue of Liberty was erected there forty years later. Fifty U.S. Marines were stationed on the steamer over the next two days to prevent contact between ship and shore. Finally, on December 27, the government gave the ship permission to sail, minus the 239 filibuster recruits removed on the twenty-fifth. Three days behind schedule, the *Northern Light* raised her anchor and steamed out of the harbor, Nicaragua bound. Not every Walker recruit had been removed from the ship, for there were several gentlemen in first and second class, including a fellow from Hungary by the name of Schlessinger, who had avoided the district attorney's net and who had every intention of volunteering his services to Walker once they reached Nicaragua.

For Cornelius Vanderbilt, who would, within weeks, officially exercise control over the Accessory Transit Company once more, this government interference with company ships and Nicaragua-bound passengers was not something he would tolerate, as he would very soon show. How different his attitude would have been had he known that William Walker was at that very moment leading a covert conspiracy to put him out of business.

THE GATHERING STORM

TODAY, THE INTERSECTION OF CLAY AND MONTGOMERY STREETS IS AT the very heart of San Francisco's financial district; there are banks on all four corners. On January 2, 1856, a new business opened its doors on one of those corners. It was a bank—Garrison, Morgan, Fretz, and Ralston. The firm was using the dollars, money-managing talents, and reputations of Cornelius Garrison, Charles Morgan, Ralph Fretz, and William Ralston. Thirty-one-year-old William Ralston was the bank's manager, and as he unlocked the firm's front doors, he had four male employees ready and waiting to serve the public of San Francisco. The bank had been slated to open the previous year, but a run on the city's existing banks in April and May had closed down half a dozen of them, including a branch of the Wells Fargo Bank, after they had been unable to meet customer demand for withdrawals. Now that the market had settled down, the partners in the new bank were confident of success.

That afternoon, as Ralston was dealing with his bank's first customers, and as the Pacific Mail Line's *Golden Gate* steamed sedately across San Francisco Bay toward the heads carrying four hundred Panama-bound passengers, William Walker's representative Edward Kewen was at the offices of the *Daily Alta California*, the city's first and largest daily newspaper, talking with its editors. Kewen, fresh off the *Sierra Nevada* after his visit to Granada, made it known that the Nicaraguan government was interested in purchasing the Accessory Transit Company's five-year-old 1,181-ton *Brother Jonathan*.

Originally built for Edward Mills and operated by him for two years, the *Brother Jonathan* had been purchased by Cornelius Vanderbilt in 1852 for the Nicaragua run. But in March 1854, after leaving San Juan del Sur for San Francisco overcrowded with 1,100 passengers—she was built to carry 750—the strain had proven too much and one of her boilers had given out. Running two days late, the *Brother Jonathan* had limped into San Francisco under sail and with just one paddlewheel working. Although repaired, the steamer had been taken off the Nicaragua run and was doing the occasional charter to Oregon. But Kewen gave the newspaper the impression she was just what the Nicaraguan government was looking for.

Kewen not only boosted a prospective purchase of the steamer but also boosted American migration to Nicaragua from California, and the next day, the *Daily Alta California* reported:

> We understand that the representatives of the Nicaragua Republic have de-cided to make the purchase of the *Brother Jonathon*, provided she will bear the inspection to which she will be submitted by a competent committee upon her arrival from the upper coast whither she went a few days since. We learn from Colonel Kewen that he has had ten thousand applications from persons anxious to join the expedition, but [who] are deterred from going for want of a suitable means of transportation. If the Government can succeed in obtaining a steamer the desires of these applicants can be gratified.[1]

Apart from keeping Cornelius Garrison on his toes, this propaganda ex-ercise would help blindside Commodore Vanderbilt to the secret deal being put together between Walker, Garrison, and Morgan. But it is unlikely that Vanderbilt was impressed when news of Nicaraguan government interest in the steamer reached him in New York at the end of the month. More than anyone else, Vanderbilt knew that after eighteen months of civil war, the Nicaraguan government was as good as bankrupt and could not afford to buy as much as a rowboat.

In the same January 3 issue in which it published Kewen's misinforma-tion, the *Daily Alta California* reported that three young men from San Francisco serving in General Walker's army in Nicaragua had died—not from bullet, bayonet, or sword, but from disease. In the wake of the rainy season, cholera and yellow fever had made their annual reappearance. And this time, the Americans in Nicaragua were not immune. This, said the paper, "will have a tendency to dampen the zeal of those who may be longing for the charms of Central America."[2]

A fire crackled in the grate, for in New York City, it was the dead of winter. Young William Garrison sat across the desk from Charles Morgan in Morgan's Manhattan office in nervous silence, watching as the business magnate read the document that the young man had brought up from Nicaragua. If Morgan did not agree to the Transit charter proposal, then the deal that William Garrison had been sent by his father to seal would fall to dust.

Sixty-year-old Charles Morgan was a large man, with a large appetite. He had a prominent, ugly nose, a wide mouth, and sad eyes. His thin, gray hair was swept over his pate. Like Cornelius Vanderbilt, Morgan was a self-made man. At fourteen, he took himself to New York City from Connecticut and became a clerk, later opening a ship's chandlery store. Expanding into importing, he had established a fleet of sailing ships trading with the West Indies before moving into steamships, becoming a pioneer of steamer services around the Gulf of Mexico in the 1830s. Like Vanderbilt, Morgan had become as much a money man as a steamship man.

Morgan dipped a pen in an inkwell and began to add clauses to the proposed contract. First and foremost, Morgan also wanted Vanderbilt's exclusive rights to build the Nicaragua shipping canal—Vanderbilt had to be shut out of Nicaragua entirely.

Close to noon on January 3, an ocean steamer pulled away from San Francisco's Long Wharf and made for the sea. Though due to depart at 9:00 A.M., the Nicaragua Line's SS *Uncle Sam*, bound for San Juan del Sur, had been delayed by a visit from U.S. deputy marshals. There were 300 "through passengers" aboard, bound for New York City. The remaining 120 would go no further than Nicaragua. Sixty-five of them had signed up in A. Parker Crittenden's San Francisco office as colonists and were sailing free of charge. The remaining 55, the *Daily Alta California* reported on January 6, "went down of their own account."

Secretary of State Marcy's determination to cut off support for William Walker had by this time been communicated to the federal authorities in San Francisco. But there was massive sympathy in California for local hero Walker. So the U.S. marshal in San Francisco did not prevent Crittenden from using his law office as a filibuster recruitment center. And even though the daily press published the details of how many Walker recruits sailed on each Nicaragua Line departure, unlike their counterparts in New York, U.S. deputies in San Francisco made no attempt to take recruits off vessels before they sailed. The U.S. marshal's office did draw a line at artillery, however, and when it became known that a cannon had been loaded aboard the *Uncle Sam*, a warrant was issued, the ship detained and searched, and the weapon removed. The *Daily Alta California* reported that another, smaller piece of ordnance found on the *Uncle Sam* at the same time was subsequently returned to its owner.[3]

Days later, as the *Uncle Sam* steamed south down Mexico's Pacific coast for Nicaragua, no one aboard was aware that the Pacific Mail's *Golden Gate*, which had sailed a day ahead of the *Uncle Sam,* had caught fire off Manzanillo and lay wrecked on the Mexican shore after the loss of the lives of more than two hundred passengers and $1.1 million in gold. It was a curious fact that while Vanderbilt's competitors and partners lost a number of ships in this way, he rarely did. And unlike other steamship operators, Vanderbilt never paid a cent for insurance coverage. Instead, he relied on hands-on management, and luck. Both served him well.

Since the beginning of 1856, Lieutenant James Jamison had been stationed at the hill town of Masaya, twenty-five miles west of Granada. Jamison was enthralled by the sights and sounds of Masaya, a town of twelve thousand mostly Indian residents, which sat on a hilltop five hundred feet above Lake Masaya. The lake was the town's only freshwater source, and Jamison watched in awe as Indian women daily climbed a winding stairway cut in the rocky hillside, carrying a full bucket of water in each hand and expertly balancing a third on their heads, without spilling a drop.

One night, at about two o'clock, several days after Jamison's Company D settled into their barracks at Masaya, the Americans were abruptly awoken by a terrifying rumbling underfoot and the sound of detonations. Thinking the town was under artillery attack, the garrison rushed to arms. It took the local priest and the *alcalde*, or mayor, to assure them that there was nothing to fear—this had only been Mount Masaya, an active volcano, reminding the town that it was there.

There was much about this country that the Americans would have to become accustomed to if they were to make it their home, active volcanoes among them.

Cholera was raging in Granada, and this time, the strain was just as deadly to the Americans as it was to the locals. Granada hospital was overflowing. Dr. Alex Jones, although now the ARN's paymaster general, was among the volunteers helping the army's new surgeon general, James Nott, tend to Americans and Nicaraguans alike. The epidemic soon claimed the lives of increasing numbers of Walker's men. Among the first to go was Lieutenant Colonel Charles Gilman—the one-legged Sonora veteran who had commanded Ponciano Corral's firing squad; Corral's devout family and friends would have said it was God's vengeance.

As the epidemic claimed American lives, Walker gave each victim a military funeral, complete with honor guard. Walker had recently formed a military band from a dozen Germans who had previously served in the Legitimista army, and for each victim, the band solemnly played the "Death March" as the coffin was carried from hospital to cemetery. A rifle volley followed, and fired over the grave. As the death toll mounted, Walker lamented, "The disease seemed to select those officers who were most capable and useful."[4] Even physician James Nott eventually fell victim to the epidemic. The military funerals became so frequent that the morbid tones of the "Death March" ringing through the streets of Granada began to sap morale, and Walker had to order the band to desist, although the military funerals and graveside volleys continued. By early February, shortly after the arrival of a new surgeon general, Israel Moses, the epidemic petered out, and men thanked their lucky stars that they had been spared.

By early February, too, Vanderbilt was again officially in complete control of the Accessory Transit Company. As expected, he had ejected Garrison, Morgan, and Ralston from the company's board, and at the company's January stockholders' meeting, he had himself elected president and his friend Thomas Lord elected vice president. As expected, too, Vanderbilt did not renew the contracts that Garrison and Morgan held as the Nicaragua Line's shipping agents. He appointed himself in their stead.

He also quickly acted on another front. At this point, Vanderbilt saw William Walker as a positive influence in Nicaragua. Walker had brought the country's civil war to an end, and it was Walker and his filibuster army who guaranteed the peace and protected trans-Nicaragua travelers and the treasure trains. All of this meant that travelers could use the Transit Route and Vanderbilt's steamers with confidence. So, to keep Nicaragua in a peaceful state, Vanderbilt honored the arrangement that Cornelius Garrison established with Walker to carry filibuster recruits to Nicaragua free of charge.

To Vanderbilt's mind, an Americanized Nicaragua would be a far safer place than Panama for transiting and canal building. Vanderbilt wanted filibusters in Nicaragua, so he could not have district attorneys and deputy marshals delaying his ships and dragging passengers ashore. The matter had to be sorted out. In January, both Joseph White and Captain Tinklepaugh had been indicted by District Attorney John McKeon for their part in the Christmas Eve *Northern Light* affair. Claiming that the matter had arisen from a misunderstanding, both would subsequently be acquitted. Determined to ensure that government intervention in Nicaragua Line departures did not reoccur, the Commodore wrote to McKeon on February 6:

I have taken the presidency of the Transit Company as well as the agency.

I am desirous to have no difficulty with the ships.

Any mode you may point out to save trouble that may arise I will most cheerfully join you in.

Therefore, if at any time you see or hear of anything wrong, you will always find me ready to make it right so far as it is in my power.

Yours truly,

Cornelius Vanderbilt[5]

Was Vanderbilt prepared to bribe the district attorney to go easy on his steamers? His letter could be read that way. One way or another, the February sailings of Nicaragua Line ships from New York proved to be without interruption or incident.

On February 18, William Garrison arrived back in the Nicaraguan capital after his visit to New York. Charles Morgan had not hurried his response to the new Transit contract draft, making young Garrison wait weeks in Manhattan. To take advantage of the reassigned Transit charter, Morgan had to find funds and vessels for a new Nicaraguan shipping line as well as for the Transit bond and lease payments. In the end, he calculated how he and partner Cornelius Garrison could make the deal work to their best advantage, at the same time providing Nicaragua with a basic shipping service from San Francisco, New York, and New Orleans. Walker had no difficulty accepting the contract clauses added by Morgan. C. J. Macdonald had arrived from San Francisco several days earlier with Garrison's approval of the proposed new Transit charter. Now, Walker would write, "it was decided that the blow should be struck" against Vanderbilt.[6] All Walker had to do was convince President Rivas to revoke the old contract and sign the new one over to Edmund Randolph.

Together with best friend Randolph, who was confined to bed at Nina Irena Ohoran's house by a protracted liver ailment, Walker drafted a revocation decree that stated that the Accessory Transit Company was losing its charter because it had failed to pay the contracted commission on profits, "falsely and fraudulently alleging that no profits were made and no commissions due."[7] And because the Atlantic and Pacific Ship Canal Company, of which Vanderbilt was also once more president, had failed to build either a canal or a railroad across Nicaragua, its charter was also revoked for failing to meet its obligations. Walker's draft decree also provided for a Nicaraguan commission of inquiry to determine the exact amount owed to the government by the companies. Once the amount of that indebtedness was ascertained, the Transit Company's assets in Nicaragua would be offered for sale to Morgan and Garrison in settlement of that debt.

Walker then went to see President Rivas and Minister General Don Fermin Ferrer at Government House, to finally broach the subject of the revocation of the Transit Company's contract. To Walker's relief, both Rivas and Ferrer were strongly in favor of the idea, and the president signed the decree depriving Cornelius Vanderbilt of his charter, "not only without hesitation but with undisguised pleasure," Walker would note.[8] But Walker was surprised to meet angry resistance from Rivas when he presented the president with a second decree, which reassigned the Transit charter to Randolph and his syndicate.

"It is a sale of the country!" the president exclaimed.[9]

The discussion became an argument, but not one in which Walker would raise his voice. The dispute continued into the night, and Walker returned to his quarters at the Vieja house with the matter unresolved. Next morning, a resolute General Walker again crossed the plaza to the president's office and resumed the discussion. Using his powers of reason and considerable eloquence, the unrelenting Walker was able to eventually talk the emotional Don Patricio into seeing his point of view. Still, the president's signature on the reassignment decree was obtained "with much difficulty," and even then only after Walker agreed to remove some of the clauses that Morgan and Garrison had asked for. Finally, on February 19, Walker walked out of the president's office with the signed second decree in his hand. It was done. The Transit contract and Atlantic and Pacific Ship Canal charter had both been taken from Vanderbilt and handed to his archenemies Morgan and Garrison.

Still, Walker and his colleagues agreed, the changeover must be handled with care and discretion, to give Morgan and Garrison as much time as possible to prepare while Vanderbilt was off guard. There was also another reason to delay. An aristocratic young Cuban, F. A. Laine, had recently been in

Granada for discussions with Walker. Laine was the agent of Domingo de Goicuria, a wealthy Cuban involved in Narciso Lopez's failed bid to throw the Spanish out of Cuba. Goicuria, who was living in exile in New Orleans, had proposed to Walker, via Laine, that he would bring 250 men from the United States to serve under Walker. He had also undertaken to use his own money to buy arms, uniforms, and footwear for Walker's troops. In return, Walker would use his men and resources to help Goicuria seize power in Cuba once Walker had consolidated his power in Nicaragua.

Laine had returned to New Orleans with a memorandum of agreement to this effect signed by Walker. Goicuria and his 250 recruits would sail from New Orleans aboard the Nicaragua Line's *Prometheus* when the steamer made its scheduled departure in early March. Walker fully expected that, should word of the loss of the Transit charter reach Cornelius Vanderbilt in New York before the *Prometheus* sailed, Vanderbilt would cancel the present arrangement under which Goicuria and his 250 men would sail to Nicaragua free of charge. There was even a possibility that Vanderbilt would cancel the sailing. A delay in the revocation and reassignment announcement would mean that the *Prometheus* would sail before Vanderbilt could act, bringing Goicuria and his men to Nicaragua at Vanderbilt's expense.

So, Walker waited. The decrees would be published in Nicaragua in the fourth week of February. In the meantime, the new Morgan and Garrison Line, as it would be commonly known, would prepare to take over the Nicaragua run. Morgan would transfer two of his own ships up to New York from the Gulf of Mexico, where they were currently on the New Orleans–Havana–Santa Cruz run, which Morgan dominated. One of these ships, the SS *Orizaba*, would serve the New York–Greytown route, the other, the SS *Tennessee,* would take over the New York–New Orleans–Greytown run currently served by the *Prometheus.*

Morgan and Garrison had no way of immediately servicing the San Francisco–San Juan del Sur route but seemed confident that Vanderbilt's greed, and his obligation to Transit Company stockholders, would cause him to keep ships on the run to Nicaragua from San Francisco, New York, and New Orleans. His competitors probably expected him to offer spirited competition on the route, for there was nothing to stop him from dropping passengers at Greytown and San Juan del Sur, where they would pay the Morgan-Garrison concern the thirty-five dollars it cost to travel across Nicaragua by the river and lake steamers and stagecoaches. The plan was, of course, to shut Vanderbilt out of Nicaragua altogether over time, and Morgan intended to secure another two ships for the Nicaragua service within a few months. Once he was certain of passenger volumes, he could order new ships from Jacob Westervelt, his favorite New York shipbuilder.

Meanwhile, on publication of the decrees, the Rivas government would notify Transit Company manager Cortlandt Cushing that all Transit Company assets in the country were forthwith seized by the government and that he was out of a job. Those assets would be vested in the care of Joseph N. Scott, the company's former ace lake steamer captain, who went to work for the new Morgan and Garrison operation. Most other former company staff would also be retained by Morgan and Garrison.

With the takeover of the Transit Company's operation on track, Walker put Vanderbilt to the back of his mind and turned to political affairs—as he must, for there were ominous rumblings coming from both north and south of the border.

≈ 14 ≈

GOING TO WAR
WITH WALKER

O N FEBRUARY 4, GENERAL WALKER BADE FAREWELL TO A THREE-MAN delegation leaving for Costa Rica. By this stage, Foreign Minister Jerez had resigned from Nicaragua's coalition government because Walker refused to invade Honduras and restore the exiled Trinidad Cabanas to power. Meanwhile, Democratico Buenaventura Selva had resigned as war minister because he resented Legitimistas receiving government appointments. For the moment, apart from President Rivas, the cabinet had just a single member, Minister for Hacienda Fermin Ferrer. But these were the least of Walker's problems. To the north, Legitimista General Guardiola was elected president of Honduras on February 6. El Salvador also soon had a new president, after a cholera outbreak took the life of José Maria San Martin on February 1. For the time being, San Martin's successor, Rafael Campo, who would take office on the twelfth, remained silent on the subject of Nicaragua and the filibusters, but the mood in his country was firmly anti-Walker.

It was Costa Rica in the south that caused William Walker the most concern. Ever since President Juan Rafael Mora had issued his November 30 proclamation condemning Walker and accusing him of having ambitions to control all of Central America, Mora had been using the Costa Rican government newspaper to agitate against President Rivas's toleration of Walker and his Americans. And to provoke the fears of Catholic Costa Ricans, both Mora and the bishop of San José, Anselmo Llorente, had delivered speeches warning the people of Costa Rica against the threat posed by the Protestant filibusters to the north. Not a few Legitimistas had fled from Nicaragua to Costa Rica—most notably, in December, Ramón Rivas, eldest son of the

Nicaraguan president. And they all supported President Mora's view that the Yankees were a threat to all of Central America.

To placate Costa Rican fears, Walker had written to President Mora on January 17: "You are entirely mistaken with respect to my character if you suppose that I shelter hostile thoughts against Central America. I have come to Nicaragua with the intention of maintaining order and good government." He had nothing but good intentions, he said, and "it is certain that my plans and conduct have been interpreted malignantly, and I feel that the Government of Costa Rica has taken heed of the false inculpations of my treasonous enemies. Time and faithful history will in the future vindicate my conduct."[1] President Mora had not replied. So, Walker had decided to send a delegation to both remonstrate against the fact that Costa Rica was harboring Nicaraguan Legitimistas and to dispel Costa Rican fears about his intentions.

To lead his delegation, Walker chose Louis Schlessinger, a recent arrival from New York. Schlessinger had "come to Nicaragua with excellent recommendations from people of repute."[2] He had told Walker he was a Hungarian national who served as a major in the forces of Hungarian revolutionary Lajos Kossuth, who in 1848–1849 had led a failed uprising against Austrian rule of Hungary. Schlessinger had even written about his adventures for the *Atlantic Monthly*, describing himself as one of the military refugees from the surrender of the fortress of Comorn, the last stronghold of the Hungarian revolutionaries.

Kossuth's revolution had been a cause célèbre for romantics and revolutionaries the world over. "I wish to heaven I had my liberty," Irish political prisoner Thomas Meagher had written enviously in 1849 from the British penal colony of Van Diemen's Land—today's Tasmania—in Australia. "I'd be off to join the beggars by the first ship."[3] William Walker had also been an ardent admirer of Kossuth and his revolutionaries, writing editorials in support of them in the New Orleans *Crescent*. Thomas Meagher, who was to gain fame as the commander of the U.S. Army's Irish Brigade during the U.S. Civil War and who would, by 1857, be a vocal supporter of William Walker, had seen the exiled Hungarian revolutionaries as romantic figures: "They walk the world in glory, awakening everywhere the noblest sympathies, renewing amongst men the high-toned sentiments of the old heroic days."[4] Walker, himself schooled on the legends of knights of old, courtesy of the novels of Sir Walker Scott, was of the same mind. To have one of Kossuth's officers serving under him no doubt gave him quite a thrill.

Schlessinger's ambassadorial qualifications included the fact he spoke four languages. Walker also felt that Schlessinger possessed tact and the right bearing for an envoy. To accompany the "special commissioner," Walker selected American ARN officer Captain W. A. Sutter and Colonel Manuel Arguello—the same Colonel Arguello who had fought against Walker at the Battle of Rivas the previous June. Since the end of the war, Arguello had served in a senior Nicaraguan government civil post—his appointment had sponsored Democratico Minister Buenaventura Selva's resignation from the cabinet. Like Julius Caesar, Walker attempted to act magnanimously toward former enemies and welcomed them into his fold. He had found former foe Arguello a conscientious administrator and hoped that since Arguello was a Legitimista, the man might "remove prejudices" when the deputation dealt with Costa Rica's Legitimista government.[5] As he headed south, Schlessinger carried a document from Walker that set out "conciliatory terms for a treaty concerning the proper conventions for the Federation of Central American States."[6]

Nineteen days after leaving Granada, Special Commissioner Schlessinger was sitting with his two colleagues, bored and frustrated, in Costa Rica's Pacific port of Puntarenas. On reaching the Costa Rican town of Liberia, Schlessinger had been forced by local authorities to hand over the Walker proposal. While the document was taken by the Costa Ricans to their capital, San José, together with a letter from Schlessinger asking Foreign Minister Bernado Calvo for a date for a meeting, Schlessinger and his companions had been escorted down to Puntarenas, fifty miles west of San José, to await a response.

Now, a party of grim-faced Costa Rican officials headed by Colonel Rudesindo Guardia, military governor of Puntarenas, strode into the room. As the Walker deputation came to their feet, Colonel Guardia thrust

Walker's document at Schlessinger. The proposals, Guardia told the delegates, were wholly unacceptable. Guardia had orders to expel the Nicaraguan delegation from the country on the first vessel leaving port. But as Schlessinger and Sutter were hustled away, the Legitimista member of the party, Manuel Arguello, departed with Colonel Guardia—Arguello had defected to the Costa Ricans.

On the first day of March, President Juan Rafael Mora stood before the Legislative Assembly of Costa Rica in San José. Mora had celebrated his forty-second birthday only several weeks before. Elected to the Costa Rican presidency in 1849 at the age of just thirty-five, he had been re-elected four years later. Like Walker, Mora was short; the Costa Ricans had nicknamed him "Don Juanito," or "Mr. Little John." Mora and his brothers were rich coffee merchants. The economy of tiny Costa Rica was built on its coffee exports to the world, which had created a ruling class of wealthy coffee barons like Don Juanito. Mora was a popular ruler. During his term in office, he had done much for the country's poorer barefoot farmers, including extending voting rights to many Costa Ricans who had previously been excluded by land ownership provisions. He had erected Costa Rica's parliament building and established its first university, the Universidad de Santo Tomás.

For four days the Legislative Assembly had met in extraordinary session to discuss the situation in Nicaragua, and for four days Mora pushed his countrymen toward a confrontation with William Walker. Apart from the lancers of the Presidential Honor Guard, Costa Rica had no standing army. That situation was about to change. Ever since his November declaration that Walker and his Yankee filibusters must be thrown out of Central America, Mora had been collecting weapons, buying gunpowder, and turning lead into shot. And now, the president convinced the assembly to vote him absolute power and to authorize him to raise a war loan of a hundred thousand pesos to permit him to conscript, arm, and maintain an army of nine thousand men—one in every twelve Costa Ricans. He also received the assembly's authority to lead that army into Nicaragua.

"We do not go to contend for a piece of land," he told his countrymen, "or to acquire ephemeral power. Not to achieve miserable conquest, or much less for sacrilegious purposes. No! We go to struggle for the redemption of our brethren from the most iniquitous tyranny."[7] With dark, intense eyes, the little president looked around the assembly and then stormed dramatically, "To arms! The moment has arrived. We march into Nicaragua to destroy this impious *Falange* which has reduced the people to oppressive slavery. We march to fight for the liberty of every man!"[8]

As the members of the assembly burst into riotous applause and cheers, the president called for a vote on a final motion. On Saturday, March 1, 1856, the parliament of Costa Rica voted to declare war on President Patricio Rivas of Nicaragua and on William Walker and his Yankee filibusters.

Before Secretary of State William Marcy could come to his feet, Cornelius Vanderbilt strode into the his office.

On March 12, the news reached New York City that the Nicaraguan government of Patricio Rivas had canceled the charters of both the Accessory Transit Company and the Atlantic and Pacific Ship Canal Company. Vanderbilt had exploded with rage and indignation. Dropping everything, he had immediately set off for the federal capital. Now Vanderbilt slammed a copy of the revocation decree down on the desk in front of the secretary of state. "One William Walker has interfered with my *American* property, Marcy!" he roared, before demanding redress by the U.S. government.[9]

Secretary Marcy, calm and deliberate, conducted the Commodore to a seat, then invited Vanderbilt to explain the cause of his concern. And in language full of expletives, Vanderbilt detailed how the filibuster Walker had conspired with Vanderbilt's commercial enemies Morgan and Garrison to deprive him of his lawful rights in Nicaragua. Locking his fingers, Marcy sat back and listened as the magnate raged. Marcy, like the *New York Times*, was acquainted with the "well-known abuses and shortcomings" in the way the Transit Company had dealt with the Nicaraguan government in the past. And perhaps also like the *Times,* Secretary Marcy believed that the

Nicaraguan authorities had previously displayed a "want of proper spirit" and should have long ago "visited with forfeiture" the assets of the Transit Company as retribution for those abuses and shortcomings.[10]

In fact, Marcy saw Vanderbilt's reaction as hypocritical. "I can see no valid claim to haste on the part of you Transit people," he said, once the Commodore had vented his anger, "as you only recently interfered with the action of the Administration against the young filibuster."[11]

As Vanderbilt knew, Marcy was talking about the *Northern Light* incident the previous December. Vanderbilt replied that he had not been president of the Transit Company at that time so could not answer for what the company's officials did then.

Marcy nodded slowly. He knew that although Vanderbilt did not have the title of president of the company at that time, he had been in control of the company in December and was merely waiting for the January stockholders' meeting to formally vote him back into the president's chair before he took a public role. It was laughable that Vanderbilt expected Marcy to believe otherwise. It was also laughable that in December, Vanderbilt was all for allowing filibuster recruits to sail on his ships to join Walker in Nicaragua, in opposition to the secretary of state's stance, and was still of that view as recently as February, when he wrote to District Attorney McKeon seeking his cooperation. And yet, here was Vanderbilt now, demanding that the government act against Walker—only after Walker's actions had hurt him financially.

Despite being riled by Vanderbilt's sudden and mercenary change of tune, Marcy could not deny that he himself would like nothing better than to see Walker removed from Central America. So, the secretary of state promised the Commodore that he would look into the matter. Despite that promise, Vanderbilt left the State Department dissatisfied and determined to ramp up the pressure on William Walker.

The next day, Vanderbilt met with British ambassador John Crampton and urged the British government to prevent Morgan and Garrison from unloading ocean steamer passengers at Greytown, effectively snuffing out their Transit Company trade. Vanderbilt was aware that Walker was a thorn in the side of the British government, which was particularly worried that he would use his filibuster troops to occupy Greytown and return it and the Mosquito Coast to Nicaraguan control. The ambassador was sympathetic to

Vanderbilt's approach, agreeing that Her Majesty's officers at Greytown could "materially contribute, by protecting American property."[12] Crampton also agreed to ask his government to permanently station a warship at Greytown and informed Vanderbilt that a representative of the Transit Company duly authorized by Vanderbilt could "ask for the assistance of the commander of any man-of-war in Her Britannic Majesty's navy in the port."[13] Now Vanderbilt was getting somewhere.

In quick succession, the Commodore also met with the Washington ambassadors of the Central American states of Costa Rica, El Salvador, Guatemala, and Honduras and the ambassador of Colombia (known as New Granada until 1886)—which then included Panama. He also met with the ambassadors of the South American nations Chile, Peru, and Brazil. The Costa Rican ambassador, Don Felipe Molina, would later write a detailed report of his meeting with Vanderbilt, for President Mora. As Vanderbilt did with each ambassador, he urged the Costa Rican envoy to motivate his government to act against Walker in Nicaragua.

Vanderbilt had clearly received information direct from Nicaragua, for, during his meeting with the Costa Rican ambassador, he informed Molina that Walker had recently introduced a new Nicaraguan flag of his own design. That flag, the Commodore said, featured five horizontal blue stripes on a white background, with a five-pointed red star in the center. This star, apparently designed in emulation of the lone star on the flag of Texas, had, according to Vanderbilt, spawned a motto of Walker's creation: "Five or none." This motto, said Vanderbilt, represented Walker's militant ambitions for Central America—he planned to conquer all five nations and make himself their emperor. Five nations, or none.[14]

When Vanderbilt set off back to New York, it was still "with some misgivings."[15] While he had received assurances from the Latin American diplomats that their governments would take a hostile view of Walker and his filibusters, and while they had been warm to his offer of assistance to those governments that took action against Walker, there was no guarantee that any of them would have the gumption to act.

15

THE BATTLE
OF SANTA ROSA

To the welcoming peal of church bells and the cheers of the local people, on the afternoon of Wednesday, March 12, 1856, a Costa Rican advance guard marched into the dusty northern Costa Rican town of Liberia, in the province of Guanacaste. Five hundred strong, the force was made up of newly recruited infantry, some in sandals, others marching barefoot, wearing the typical uniform of the Central American soldier—white trousers, shirt, and jackets. Their straw hats were circled by red bands—President Mora hoped that, by wearing red ribbons, his troops would conciliate the Democraticos of Nicaragua once his army entered their country.

Leading this advance guard was General José Joaquin Mora, brother of the president. Riding beside him was his deputy, Colonel Manuel Arguello, who had so recently defected from William Walker's service. Behind them came their junior officers. Mounted on superb horses, smiling and waving to the cheering women and children of Liberia, these excited young men such as staff officer Manuel Quiros, Lieutenant Justo Castro, and Captain Manuel Roja wore tailored black uniforms and black, broad-brimmed Spanish-style felt hats with red bands. Expensive Toledo steel swords hung at their sides; these young gentlemen knew how to use them, too, after years of training in swordsmanship. But apart from Colonel Arguello, a veteran of the Nicaraguan civil war who had faced Walker's *filibusteros* before now, not one officer had any experience in battle. The sons of Costa Rican coffee barons, the young officers were typically educated in Europe. Horsemanship came naturally to them; in Central America, the sons of good families grew up in the saddle. Their chief pastimes were racing each other on horseback and

179

riding up to the balconies of beautiful senoritas, with a guitar and a song.[1] Now, they were riding north to kill *Yanquis*.

This column had left San José on March 4, just three days after the declaration of war, to the sound of tapping drums, tooting bugles, and the cheers of the population. A second force, of 250 men, had departed San José the same day. Led by General Florentino Alfaro, it headed northeast, via Alajuela, toward the Sarapiqui River. While General Mora was under orders to advance as far as Liberia and then wait for the main expeditionary army of 3,000 men to join him, General Alfaro's orders were to reach the San Juan River via the jungle, following the Sarapiqui River, which flowed into the San Juan below El Castillo. Alfaro was then to make his way up the San Juan to launch surprise attacks on the filibuster garrisons at El Castillo and San Carlos, seize them, and close off the river to steamer traffic. This would prevent supplies from reaching Walker from America's Atlantic states. President Mora himself would meanwhile lead the main push into southwestern Nicaragua, to seize the steamer port of San Juan del Sur, cutting Walker's supply route from California.

President Mora was a shrewd tactician. Like Walker, he appreciated the strategic significance of the Transit Route and the tactical advantage of denying Walker his supply routes before the Costa Ricans actually did battle with Walker's main force. The Costa Rican army's western drive up through Guanacaste province to San Juan del Sur was the least complex of the two offensive operations. Traversing easy terrain, it would involve a force that would outnumber the filibusters by three to one. But Mora knew that his would also be the most obvious attack and likely to draw a spirited response from Walker's troops. General Alfaro's force had the more difficult task, for his men had to literally hack their way to the San Juan River through thick, mosquito-ridden jungle and around alligator-infested swampland along the Sarapiqui. But Alfaro had surprise on his side.

As the advance guard dispersed to quarters in Liberia to await the arrival of President Mora and the remainder of the army, force commander General Mora sent scouts north toward the Nicaraguan frontier. That same day, seventy miles to the south, President Mora arrived at Puntarenas from San José, having left Vice President Francisco Oreamuno in charge at the national capital. Mora rode into the seaport trailed by a wave of lancers of the

Presidential Honor Guard, who clattered over the cobblestones on pampered steeds. The president was accompanied, too, by a flock of newly commissioned officers, men who would lead the recruits then assembling in Puntarenas. Among them was Ramón Rivas, the son of the president of Nicaragua. Greeting the president in Puntarenas was his brother-in-law, forty-six-year-old José Maria Canas. A Salvadoran, the tough-minded Canas had battle experience in various conflicts in his homeland, and Mora had made him one of his generals for this campaign.

As President Mora made his preparations in Puntarenas and his brother enjoyed the hospitality of the people of Liberia, neither was aware that William Walker's filibusters were at that moment advancing into Costa Rica from the north.

Late in the evening of Wednesday, March 19, Louis Schlessinger and 240 weary men of the ARN Corps of Observation arrived at a Costa Rican cattle ranch called the Santa Rosa. They had been marching for six days. After Walker learned of the Costa Rican declaration of war on March 11, he had immediately drawn up a decree, which was unhesitatingly signed by President Rivas, proclaiming war against Costa Rica. In Walker's words, "to guard against any surprise on the line of American travel across the Isthmus," the Corps of Observation had promptly been formed and sent south into Costa Rica.[2]

Because Schlessinger had recently been in the area, and despite Walker's belief that Schlessinger had a "timid nature," he'd been commissioned a colonel and put in charge of the newly formed Corps of Observation. Days before, Domingo de Goicuria's promised 250 new recruits had arrived from New Orleans, and the men of four of the new corps' five companies were Goicuria recruits.[3] One company was made up entirely of Germans, another of Frenchman, with few in either company able to speak English. The corps' fifth unit was the recently promoted Captain Anthony Rudler's Company F of the First Rifles, which had been taken from garrison duty at San Juan del Sur.

As Schlessinger's command marched south, Walker had also sent two companies across Lake Nicaragua by lake steamer to the San Juan River.

One company garrisoned the old Spanish fortress at El Castillo; the other had orders to continue farther east down the river to a place the Americans called Hipp's Point—where the Sarapiqui River joined the San Juan. There, the company was to establish an outpost and prevent any Costa Rican attempt to come down the Sarapiqui and seize the San Juan. It was as if Walker had second sight, for, with this maneuver and Schlessinger's advance, he had correctly anticipated and moved to counter both of President Mora's lines of attack.

Now, in darkness and with their rifles on their shoulders, the men of the Corps of Observation, most dressed in black-dyed shirts and with the blue ribbon of the ARN around their black hats, arrived at the Santa Rosa ranch. Fifty miles inside Costa Rica, the Santa Rosa was owned by a Nicaraguan Democratico, Dr. Manuel Barrios. To get here, Schlessinger had force-marched his men well into the night. Once they arrived, exhausted filibusters gratefully found quarters in the sprawling, deserted Santa Rosa hacienda. Built by a Spanish grandee in 1661, the stone house featured a two-story central building that was built on a stone platform ten feet high and contained three large first-floor reception rooms. Accommodation and service wings extended either side of the main building at ground level. All the buildings were surrounded by shading verandas. As Schlessinger and his sixteen officers occupied the main hacienda building, the enlisted men made themselves at home in the wings.

Schlessinger's path south had been a troubled one. At Rivas, he had argued with Walker's commandant there, Major A. S. Brewster, over "numerous irregularities" on Schlessinger's part, the nature of which was unclear.[4] Then, near the town of Salina in Costa Rica, the only surgeon attached to the Corps of Observation, an unnamed new arrival in Central America, became so irritated by Schlessinger's irregularities—which included the failure to post pickets at night or to send patrols ahead during the day—that he pulled out of the column, volunteering to take letters from Schlessinger back to Walker in Granada. And Schlessinger had let him go.

Posting sentries and leaving orders that the men could do as they pleased the next morning as long as they presented themselves for arms inspection at 2:00 P.M., Schlessinger went to bed. As his troops also bedded down, they

"Commodore" Cornelius Vanderbilt in the 1840s.
LIBRARY OF CONGRESS

William Walker, San Francisco, 1854, at the time of the
failed Sonora expedition. LIBRARY OF CONGRESS

The beach at San Juan del Sur, 1850s.
LIBRARY OF CONGRESS

The American-owned hotel known as the Half Way House on the Transit Road between San Juan del Sur and La Virgen.
LIBRARY OF CONGRESS

San Juan del Sur, from the sea, today; the panorama that Vanderbilt steamer passengers had as they arrived from California.
COURTESY OF STEPHEN DANDO-COLLINS

American Falange and Nicaraguan Democratico soldiers landing at San Juan del Sur from the brig *Vesta* and a Costa Rican ketch, 1855, prior to advancing inland to attack Legitimista forces. NEW YORK PUBLIC LIBRARY

The First Battle of Rivas, 1855. This drawing shows Walker and his American volunteers, at left, charging the Legitimista field gun during the battle. LIBRARY OF CONGRESS

General Juan Santos "The Butcher" Guardiola, president of Honduras, who personally fought Walker in 1855, and lost. LIBRARY OF CONGRESS

American Falange and Nicaraguan Democratico troops aboard the lake steamer *La Virgen* at Virgin Bay, as Walker sets off to capture Granada, 1855. LIBRARY OF CONGRESS

San Francisco Church, Granada, today. The church and the convent, to left, were used as military barracks by all sides between 1854 and 1857 and were the scene of bloody fighting. COURTESY OF STEPHEN DANDO-COLLINS

John Hill Wheeler, c.1844. American ambassador to Nicaragua and a Walker supporter 1855–1857, by which time he was stout and gray-haired. LIBRARY OF CONGRESS

U.S. president Franklin Pierce, who recognized the Rivas government established by Walker in Nicaragua. LIBRARY OF CONGRESS

The southeastern corner of the Granadine Plaza, Granada, Nicaragua, today. The building in the center was Granada's prison in the 1850s. It was from here that General Ponciano Corral was led to his death in 1855. COURTESY OF STEPHEN DANDO-COLLINS

The 1855 execution by firing squad in Granada of Corral, by Walker's troops. The former commander of Legitimista forces had conspired against the Nicaraguan coalition government initiated by Walker. LIBRARY OF CONGRESS

Filibusters relaxing on their way to Granada. LIBRARY OF CONGRESS

Juan Mora, president of Costa Rica, who personally led his armed forces against Walker's army in Nicaragua between 1855 and 1857, unwittingly supported by Cornelius Vanderbilt.

Sick Costa Rican troops stagger into their capital, San Jose, following the 1856 Second Battle of Rivas. They claimed the battle as a victory over Walker but brought cholera back to their country; the epidemic would claim ten thousand Costa Rican lives.

La Merced Church, Granada, where Nashville-born William Walker took the oath to become president of Nicaragua in 1856. COURTESY OF ED MANFUTT

The reception room at Government House, Granada, 1856, when Walker was president of Nicaragua. An unidentified secretary deals with visitors waiting to see Walker. LIBRARY OF CONGRESS

The Vieja House in Granada where Walker lived while commander in chief of the Nicaraguan army and where guests including Edmund Randolph stayed when Walker became president. LIBRARY OF CONGRESS

The smoking twin volcanoes on Ometepe Island, Lake Nicaragua, today, from Virgin Bay.
COURTESY OF STEPHEN DANDO-COLLINS

American troops of Walker's Army of the Republic of Nicaragua landing at Virgin Bay from a lake steamer, 1856. LIBRARY OF CONGRESS

American recruits in Walker's army being drilled after arriving in Nicaragua, 1856.
LIBRARY OF CONGRESS

Walker troops land from a lake steamer at Granada pier on Lake Nicaragua, 1856. It was from this pier that Walker evacuated American civilians and survivors of Henningsen's garrison in late 1856.
LIBRARY OF CONGRESS

Cornelius Vanderbilt in the 1850s, at the time of his war with William Walker. LIBRARY OF CONGRESS

Walker A.R.N. troops at El Castillo, 1856, with the Spanish castle on the hill above that would be central to attempts to retake the river in 1857.
LIBRARY OF CONGRESS

Today a Costa Rican national monument, Hacienda Santa Rosa in Costa Rica was the site of the 1856 Costa Rican victory over Walker troops led by Louis Schlessinger.
COURTESY OF AARON QUIROS MONTIEL

Hacienda San Jacinto, Nicaragua, site of the 1856 Nicaraguan victory over Walker troops led by Byron Cole, and today a Nicaraguan national monument.
COURTESY OF ED MANFUTT

Slaughter of American civilians and burning of the lake steamer pier at La Virgen, 1856, as Costa Rican forces invade Nicaragua for the second time. The murder of the Americans made headlines across the United States. LIBRARY OF CONGRESS

New York steamship operator and Vanderbilt competitor "Live Oak" George Law, who actively supported Walker against Vanderbilt. LIBRARY OF CONGRESS

General George Henningsen, Walker's English-born deputy, seen here, c. 1861, as a brigadier general of the army of the Confederate States of America.
LIBRARY OF CONGRESS

The sixteenth-century Spanish entrance to Government House, Granada, all that remains of the original building after Henningsen put Granada to the torch on Walker's orders.
COURTESY OF STEPHEN DANDO-COLLINS

The Guadalupe Church, Granada, today, scene of bitter battles over three weeks in late 1856 between Walker troops under George Henningsen and the Allied Army surrounding the city. COURTESY OF STEPHEN DANDO-COLLINS

The lake wharf at Granada and Spanish fort site, today. Fighting took place here between Walker troops and the Vanderbilt-supported Allied army in late 1856.
COURTESY OF STEPHEN DANDO-COLLINS

Hipp's Point on Nicaragua's San Juan River, scene of bloody 1856–1857 battles between Walker troops and Costa Rican forces led by Vanderbilt mercenaries.

El Castillo, 1857. Costa Rican troops led by Vanderbilt mercenary Sylvanus Spencer holding prisoner American passengers off a California steamer.

U.S. Secretary of State Lewis Cass, who supported Vanderbilt's campaign against Walker. LIBRARY OF CONGRESS

"Colonel" Henry Titus, who attempted to retake the San Juan River for Walker after Costa Rican forces supported by Vanderbilt had seized it in 1857. COURTESY OF THE NORTH BREVARD HISTORICAL SOCIETY

"General" William Walker, photographed by Matthew Brady in New York or Washington, summer of 1857, looking gaunt after surviving the Allied siege of Rivas, but by this time famous and feted in the United States. LIBRARY OF CONGRESS

Cornelius Vanderbilt's massive Mausoleum on Staten Island, built with a sweeping view over the island where he was born to New York harbor and the sea, where he made his first fortune. Only male members of the Vanderbilt clan may be interred here.
COURTESY OF STEPHEN DANDO-COLLINS

Vanderbilt University, Nashville, Tennessee, c.1901, built in William Walker's hometown as a result of Cornelius Vanderbilt's million-dollar munificence. LIBRARY OF CONGRESS

were blissfully unaware that the advance guard of the Costa Rican army was just thirty miles away at Liberia.

The morning passed quietly at the Santa Rosa ranch. Schlessinger sent several horsemen out to try to find a guide before he ventured further south. The ordered arms inspection was postponed from two to three o'clock. Men, in shirtsleeves and with their rifles stacked here and there, lounged about the hacienda grounds. Some butchered several head of Santa Rosa beef, and everyone was looking forward to steak for supper. Sentries stood on the elevated veranda of the main building, but no defensive positions had been prepared.

Sitting on the hacienda veranda with a notepad on his knee as he sketched the scene before him was a young man from New York, George Forrester Williams. A pioneer of a new breed, the war correspondent, Williams had been sent to Nicaragua by Frank Leslie, publisher of America's first illustrated magazine, *Frank Leslie's Illustrated*, whose inaugural edition only hit the nation's newsstands the previous December. Williams's accounts of the exploits of General Walker and his army of Americans in Central America had already fueled phenomenal sales for the magazine. Published alongside Williams's stories were his pen-and-ink illustrations. To support his accounts of the Battle of Rivas and the massacre of Americans at La Virgen, Williams had drawn imagined scenes based on interviews with men who had been present. Williams had been permitted by General Walker to accompany the Corps of Observation on active duty, and he was hoping to see some real fighting close hand. He would soon see more than enough action.

A little before 3:00 P.M., a rifleman sent out scouting came galloping up to the hacienda as if the Devil himself were on his tail. "Here they come!" he bellowed.[5] Schlessinger's adjutant, nineteen-year-old Major Cal O'Neal, one of Walker's "Originals" and a veteran of the Battles of Rivas and La Virgen and of the storming of Granada, looked out from the veranda to see waves of white-clad Costa Rican troops appearing from the trees to the south. They were running toward the hacienda, urged on by officers on horseback. O'Neal turned and dashed inside the hacienda to find Schlessinger. But the unit's commander had disappeared.

The attack was being mounted by General Mora's five hundred men of the Costa Rican army's advance guard. Early that morning, Mora, at Liberia, had received intelligence from his scouts that an estimated three hundred filibusters were encamped at the Santa Rosa hacienda. Another Costa Rican commander might have sent south for orders from President Mora or may have even withdrawn in fright. Not José Mora. He'd ordered his troops to arms, and by 9:00 A.M., the advance guard was on the march to Santa Rosa. The Costa Ricans went into action after marching thirty miles through the heat of the day.

Without a commander, individual filibuster officers were left to make their own decisions. Intent on preventing the enemy from outflanking the hacienda, Captain Rudler led his forty men to the limited cover provided by a corral a little way from the house. There, with some men kneeling, others lying flat, Rudler's company fired concentrated volleys against the steadily advancing enemy. Several Costa Rican officers were seen to fall from their horses, but the hundreds of Costa Rican foot soldiers kept pushing forward, firing from the shoulder, pausing to reload, then advancing again. Few had ever fired a gun before their brief weapons training in San José, but their lack of accuracy was compensated for by their massed firepower. Several of Anthony Rudler's men fell around him. With the rapid Costa Rican advance cutting him off from the house, Rudler ordered his unit to fall back toward distant trees before their position was overrun.

To the left of the house, Captain Creighton's company stood in ranks facing the enemy, with the men on the right hard up against the building. Adjutant Major O'Neal joined Creighton just as his men fired a volley. A dozen Costa Ricans went down, dead or wounded. The enemy advance wavered, then resumed. Frantically, Creighton's men reloaded. O'Neal, sword in one hand, pistol in the other, looked around to see that the company of Captain Prange had broken; most of its Germans and Prussians were running for their lives. Captain Thorpe's company was in slow retreat. The French company of Captain Legeay had attempted to occupy the hilly, broken ground to one side of the hacienda, but the Costa Ricans were driving them off the rise, killing a number in their rush.

Creighton's company loosed off another volley. But fewer Costa Ricans fell this time—with the enemy drawing ever closer, the aim of Creighton's inexperienced recruits was no longer steady. The Costa Ricans replied—a hundred musket balls scythed toward Creighton's men; a dozen Americans fell. That was enough for many survivors; they turned and ran. American officers tried to stop them. "But the panic was such that they found few willing to listen or to follow," Cal O'Neal later reported.[6]

The battle swiftly became a rout. The Costa Ricans would record that the fighting lasted fourteen minutes. To O'Neal and other survivors, it seemed to have been all over in a matter of five minutes.[7] As the Corps of Observation disintegrated, most of its men fled. With his troops giving chase, General Mora rode up to the hacienda and saw dead and wounded lying everywhere—more wearing black than white. A number of wounded filibusters were taken captive. Before long, more prisoners, captured while trying to escape, were brought to the house. In all, eighteen filibusters were made prisoners. Fifty-nine dead filibusters littered the Santa Rosa grounds. The Costa Ricans lost nineteen men killed in action; another man would die in hospital at Liberia. Mora's dead included his best young officers—Quiros, Gutierrez, Roja, and Castro, the flower of the Costa Rican elite, who, only days before, had reveled in the welcome at Liberia.

In the late afternoon, as the dead of both sides were buried in Santa Rosa grounds, with the corpses of the filibusters tossed unceremoniously into a single, unmarked grave, the eighteen dejected filibuster prisoners were bundled none too gently into an outbuilding with their hands bound behind their backs. Not a single prisoner was an officer. One of them protested that he was a newspaper correspondent and a noncombatant, but the Costa Rican soldiers contemptuously ignored reporter Williams as they thudded the door shut.

The word would soon flow across the country, then across Central America and to the United States and rest of the world: Suffering three times more fatalities than the Costa Ricans, William Walker's vaunted Yankee filibusters had been defeated at Santa Rosa by an army of peasants.

$$\approx 16 \approx$$

COURTS-MARTIAL
AND FIRING SQUADS

T O MEET THE COSTA RICAN THREAT, WALKER HAD ORDERED HIS TROOPS in the north to withdraw to Granada, and with the sun sinking below the hills, the First Rifle Battalion marched into Granada from León. General Walker heard them arrive. He was at the Vieja house on the plaza, lying in his bed, bathed in sweat. The sound of tramping feet wafted in through the open window, whose shutters had been thrown back to admit the cooling evening breeze off Lake Nicaragua. Walker was burning up. He couldn't move. He had to ask his doctor what day it was. Saturday, March 22, said Surgeon General Israel Moses. The doctor looked worried, for the general, who seemingly had been immune to the epidemics claiming the lives of so many of his men, had suddenly come down with yellow fever. And yellow fever has a 50 percent mortality rate—it was even odds whether Walker would survive.

That same day, one of the lake steamers reached Granada, and fifty new recruits came ashore, scrambling over the new jetty being built beside the ruined old fort and forming up in front of their company commander. They had come from New Orleans on the last sailing of the *Prometheus* before word reached the United States that the Transit Company's charter had been annulled. And with the new arrivals came Parker H. French, the inimitable one-armed ambassador rejected by Secretary of State Marcy. After leaving his secretary Dillingham in Manhattan, French had made his way to New Orleans, where, apparently using a false name, he'd managed to find a berth on the *Prometheus*.

French brazenly proceeded to Government House, planning to report to General Walker. With Walker gravely ill across the plaza, one of the general's senior officers dealt with French. Word of French's ejection from Washington had preceded him to Granada—as had, finally, the story of the Overland Express debacle of 1850. One of Walker's men, Horace Bell, would say that when French presented himself at the "National Palace," as Bell called Government House in Granada, he was roughly taken by the shoulders, faced about, and kicked out of the country.[1]

By the evening of the next day, Sunday, Walker, shaking, pale, and weak, his aching head feeling as if it was being crushed, willed himself to sit up. His aides, Captain Dewitt Clinton and the Cuban F. A. Laine, then helped him to the dining table. A note was put in the general's hands. From Major Brewster at Rivas, it delivered to Walker the first gut-wrenching news of the disaster at Santa Rosa. The news had been conveyed by a mounted survivor of the brief battle, who had ridden hard for three days to reach Rivas. Other survivors from the Corps of Observation would straggle into Rivas for days and weeks to come, many in tattered clothing, some without boots, a few without weapons.

Against Dr. Moses' advice, an agitated Walker decided to take one of the lake steamers down to La Virgen to seek more information from Santa Rosa survivors at Rivas. In the night, the steamer plowed south, taking Walker and members of his staff down the lake. By Monday's dawn, the steamboat was tying up to the long jetty that now extended well out into Virgin Bay, and Walker went ashore and headed for Rivas.

Dr. Moses' prescribed treatment for yellow fever was a series of cold baths to reduce the general's temperature. "The news of the stragglers from Santa Rosa was a better tonic than a cold bath," Walker would later note. "The necessity for mental and moral action has a wonderful effect in driving the reluctant body to perform."[2] Though still suffering from the fever, Walker issued fresh orders. The majority of his army was to concentrate at Rivas. President Rivas was to transfer the seat of government northwest to

León. There, Walker hoped, Democratico leaders such as Maximo Jerez would rejoin the Rivas government now that the country was under attack by a Legitimista army. Before Rivas departed Granada, he signed a proclamation drawn up by Walker declaring martial law in the southern and eastern provinces, making General Walker's word law there.

As Walker was establishing his new headquarters in a building on the plaza in Rivas, Louis Schlessinger walked in. Overcoming their surprise, Walker's staff officers closed around him. Schlessinger was full of excuses for the Santa Rosa debacle, blaming the inexperience of the men under him and accusing them of lacking "disciplined courage." And he boldly proposed to organize a new force for the occupation of Guanacaste.[3]

By this time, several of Schlessinger's officers had also returned to Rivas, and all, particularly Cal O'Neal, whom Walker trusted implicitly, were scathing in their criticism of Schlessinger. Some even implied he had taken money from the Costa Ricans, feeling certain that the enemy knew of the filibuster column's advance and had been lying in wait for the filibusters. Walker couldn't believe it of Schlessinger. "Such conduct was not suited to his timid nature," he would later say. "Had he sold his men, he would never have returned to Nicaragua."[4] Despite this, Walker ordered his arrest; Schlessinger was charged with neglect of duty, ignorance of his duties as a commanding officer, and cowardice in the face of the enemy. Until the court met, Walker set him free on his parole.

Within days, Schlessinger slipped out of Rivas and disappeared. The *New York Times* reported on his desertion, commenting, "It is supposed that he went over to the Costa Ricans, having sold himself to them before the battle."[5] Schlessinger was tried in his absence. The court-martial found him guilty on all charges, including an additional charge of desertion, sentencing him to death by firing squad. A subsequent standing order issued by Walker called for Schlessinger to be shot on sight.

Louis Schlessinger's story appeared in the press around the world, and in September, French journalist Alfred Assolant revealed that Schlessinger had never been an officer in Lajos Kossuth's revolutionary army. In fact, Schlessinger was not even Hungarian. An Austrian, he had been a corporal serving in the Austrian army in Hungary at the time of the Kossuth uprising, having started out as a drummer boy. To escape punishment for an infringement, Corporal Schlessinger had deserted from the Austrian army and joined Kossuth's rank and file.

On the afternoon of Tuesday, March 25, five days after the Battle of Santa Rosa, fifteen of the eighteen filibuster prisoners were herded into a sun-scorched courtyard in the Costa Rican town of Liberia. General Mora had withdrawn to Liberia with his wounded and his prisoners, and there he had been joined by his brother, the president, and the three thousand men of the main body of the Costa Rican army.

During the morning, there was a court-martial in the town, at which all eighteen prisoners had been tried for invading Costa Rica under arms. All were found guilty, with fifteen sentenced to death. Two filibusters, Phillip Toohey, an American, and Theodore Heinung, a Prussian, had their sentences commuted by President Mora. Shortly after the Costa Rican declaration of war on March 1, the president had issued a decree proclaiming that any man found bearing arms against the Costa Rican government would face the death penalty. It appears that Toohey and Heinung may have been unarmed when captured; they were carted off to prison in San José. A third man was also spared—with the aid of his pad of pen-and-ink sketches, George Forrester Williams was able to convince the court that he was an unarmed newspaper correspondent. Williams would be taken north with the advancing Costa Rican army and released on Nicaraguan soil—President Mora wanted newspaperman Williams to tell America all about how the Yankee filibusters had been routed at Santa Rosa by the Costa Ricans.[6]

As 4:00 P.M. approached, the fifteen condemned men were lined up against a long, bleak adobe wall. All were unwashed; their clothes were grimy and smelly. Several wore rough, bloodied bandages. A company of Costa Rican riflemen formed up in front of them and busily loaded their weapons. The chaplain of the Costa Rican army, Father Calvo Francisco, conversed briefly with several Irish Catholics in the line of haggard prisoners, then withdrew. Father Francisco spoke a little English, and he had earlier conversed with the prisoners and learned their names and where they were from. While they were all branded *filibusteros Yanquis*, only three of the condemned men were actually citizens of the United States—Isaac Rosey, John Guillin, and Theodore Lindecker.[7]

The remainder had migrated to the United States to make new lives for themselves, only to be attracted to Nicaragua by visions of adventure. Five of them were Irish; when questioned by the priest, these sons of Erin had declared that they were members of the green Erin brigade. The Costa Ricans subsequently came to believe that the "Green Erin Brigade" was a unit in Walker's army. Of the other condemned men, two were Greek, one German, one Prussian, one French, one Romanian, and one Panamanian.[8] Most had only arrived in Granada on March 9 as part of the Goicuria enlistment. Meeting with a firing squad just three weeks later was certainly not what they had in mind when they signed up in New Orleans to colonize Nicaragua.

Precisely at 4:00 P.M., an officer called out a command. The men of the firing squad raised their weapons to their shoulders and took aim at preselected targets. The condemned filibusters, staring at the business end of scores of muskets, called out final farewells to each other. The officer barked another command. The muskets boomed as one. Blood splattered the adobe. And the ill-fated filibusters crumpled to the ground.

News of the defeat at Santa Rosa was a blow to the morale of Walker's men. It led to heavy drinking and arguments about matters of honor. At the northern town of Matagalpa, where the company of Captain Jack Dunnigan was garrisoned, Lieutenant Kelley and Private Murphy had both fallen in love with the same beautiful *chica*, a local girl, and fueled by liquor, they fought a duel over her in the town's main plaza.

With their comrades and the townspeople watching from the sidelines, Kelley and Murphy faced off. Murphy held a six-shot dragoon pistol at his side, Kelley, a five-shooter. As Captain Dunnigan was giving the pair instructions, Kelley, the younger of the two, raised his pistol and drew a bead on Murphy.

"Hold on now, Lieutenant Kelley," called Private Murphy, an Irishman, "till the captain says the word, me boy!"[9]

On Dunnigan's command, both men raised their pistols and fired. Kelley was struck in the foot and limped from the field of battle.

In Granada, Lieutenant James Jamison saw another duel take place. One of Walker's aides, Captain Dewitt Clinton, took exception to some comment from Captain McArdle, a native of Albany, New York, and issued a challenge. On March 28, they met to satisfy honor. Sixty paces from the combatants, Jamison was among the numerous onlookers as Clinton and McArdle stood back to back and then took fifteen paces prior to turning. On the command from the referee to fire, Clinton fired harmlessly into the air. In the same spirit, McArdle casually pointed his pistol to one side and fired. McArdle's bullet thumped into the ground at Jamison's feet.

In another duel at Granada witnessed by Jamison, two lieutenants faced each other on the lake beach on the city's eastern fringe. Both had taken the agreed number of paces and waited, with pistols at their sides, for the referee's word to fire. Just then, a horseman, Lieutenant Morgan, who was another aide to General Walker, galloped up. It was no secret that Walker opposed dueling among his officers—it only robbed him of good men.

"Gentlemen," called Lieutenant Morgan, "General Walker's compliments, and he directs me to say that the duel may continue, but that he wishes to inform you that the survivor will be shot." On that basis, the two lieutenants put up their pistols, shook hands, and walked away.[10]

On the night of March 28, drinking by the troops in the capital was excessive, and a number of Walker's men became very drunk. Brandy was the favorite filibuster tipple, or wine when the brandy ran out. When neither was available, the Americans resorted to the local guaro, which was more potent than either brandy or wine and could be had from Nicaraguan farmers for a few American dimes per bottle. In a Granada billiard hall that evening, the usually reserved Lieutenant Colonel Edward Sanders and the tetchy Major John Markham, infected by the prevailing gloom, drank more than usual. Both were intoxicated when they exchanged cross words, and before anyone could intervene, they were exchanging bullets with Colt six-shooters across billiard tables. Remarkably, neither they nor any bystanders were injured. The same could not be said for the billiard tables.

At morning parade the next day, many men were worse for wear as they attempted to form neat ranks in front of their general. Walker, who was still so ill from yellow fever he could barely sit astride his horse to take parade, was furious to see that his own brother, Captain Norvell Walker, was blind drunk. To make an example of him and to show that he had no favorites, Walker summarily withdrew Norvell's commission and dismissed him from the Army of the Republic of Nicaragua.

❧ 17 ❧

A KILLING OR TWO

TWO DAYS LATER, LIEUTENANT JAMISON AND HIS COMPANY D comrades were among 620 ARN troops who paraded in the plaza at Rivas. From the back of his horse, Walker surveyed his soldiers. Like the popular young major, Cal O'Neal, most of Walker's "men" were no more than boys, in their teens and early twenties. Typical of many was Private Francis W. Carter, who had run away from home in Franklin, Tennessee, to join General Walker's army. He was not yet fourteen. It wasn't only impressionable Southern youths who marched for William Walker—twenty-two-year-old William L. Birney from Harrison City, Ohio, was working as a schoolteacher in Arkansas when the lure of adventure caused him to throw in his job and head for Nicaragua after reading about Walker's exploits in the newspapers.

Walker addressed the rows of black-clad troops. "The words were few and simple," Walker would himself later note. "[I] endeavored to place before them the moral grandeur of the position they occupied." He bluntly told his men that they were on their own, without the support of a single friendly government, and betrayed by those they had helped. Now, they had to choose between yielding their rights, or nobly dying for them.[1] James Jamison, for one, was uplifted by the speech: "I have never forgotten his closing sentence—'A name is great only as the principle it represents makes it great.'"[2]

To the sounds of beating drums and bugle calls, the companies then passed their general in review order, the men looking inspired and determined as they marched by. Walker could see that his speech "had the desired effect and created a new spirit among the men."³ His troops went to quarters chattering among themselves.

Lieutenant Jamison made his way to a private house in the city—all Walker's officers were billeted with local families; in Jamison's case, it was with the family of Don Francisco Ugarte, a wealthy merchant of Spanish Castilian stock. Speaking a little English, Don Francisco had told Jamison that he was a Democratico supporter. Ugarte and his family had immediately made Jamison welcome. Don Francisco's daughter was married to Dr. Cole, the American resident of Rivas who had been serving with Walker since the previous September. This made Jamison feel all the more at home, as did Don Francisco's two beautiful, unmarried nieces, who lived with the family.

The SS *Cortes* eased into the cove at San Juan del Sur at the completion of her scheduled run down from San Francisco. Those on shore expecting the usual rush of passengers quickly realized that something was awry. The steamer didn't drop anchor, and the lighters that left the beach to make their way out to the ship were waved away. A ship's boat brought a single passenger ashore. William Garrison, son of Cornelius Garrison, stepped onto the beach and then hurried up the sand and into the town. Told that General Walker was at Rivas, Garrison went looking for transport inland.

Out on the bay, the *Cortes* maneuvered close to the anchored Transit Company coal hulk sitting in the cove. Soon, the *Cortes* was steaming away, towing the coal ship behind her. Once out to sea, the *Cortes* turned south, for Panama, where she would deposit her U.S.-bound passengers. It was April 1, but this was no April Fools' joke. No more Transit Company steamers would be calling at San Juan del Sur; Cornelius Vanderbilt had struck a first blow in his war against William Walker. All Transit Company services to Nicaragua had been terminated.

On arriving at Rivas, William Garrison informed Walker that when the *Cortes* was approaching San Juan del Sur, she had been passed by a steamer of the Pacific Mail Line that was heading north from Panama, bound for San Francisco. The northbound steamer, said Garrison, had sent the *Cortes* a signal by flags, conveying a message to her master, Captain Collens, from Cornelius Vanderbilt in New York. That message had instructed Collens to remove the coal ship from San Juan del Sur and to disembark his passengers in Panama.

Unbeknownst to young Garrison, one of Vanderbilt's sons-in-law and former Transit Company agent in New York, James Cross, was aboard the Pacific Mail ship. After Vanderbilt returned to New York from his diplomatic mission to Washington, D.C., he had dispatched Cross to the Pacific, via Panama, to terminate the Nicaragua Line service to Nicaragua from San Francisco and to tie up all four ships of the line operating out of the bay city. Cross had been behind the message sent to Captain Collens of the *Cortes*. A sheepish Garrison confessed to Walker that this sudden movement by the Transit Company "had not been provided for."[4]

Walker, seated on a chair and still recovering from his tussle with yellow fever, scowled up at Garrison in disbelief as he realized that Morgan and Garrison had expected Vanderbilt to keep Transit Company ships on the Nicaragua run until they could put their own ships on the route. Morgan and Garrison, it turned out, did not yet have a single ship to allocate to the Pacific route. Walker, through Morgan and Garrison's lack of foresight, was now cut off from supply from San Francisco. "How long before another steamer will come from San Francisco?" Walker asked.

Garrison blanched with embarrassment. "It might be several weeks," he replied. His father had a strategy in mind, he hurried to add, one that would enable Garrison to lay his hands on one of Vanderbilt's own West Coast steamers. But it would take a few weeks to work out.

Walker impatiently demanded to know precisely how many weeks it would be before his communications with California were restored by Garrison's father.

Garrison cast his eyes to the floor. "At least six," he guiltily replied.[5]

Walker, disgusted, dismissed the young man from his presence. "At the very outset," he would later say, "the new contractors, Morgan and Garrison, by their timidity—to use no harsher word—jeopardized the welfare of those who had acted on the faith of their capacity and willingness to fulfil their agreements." Garrison's agent in Granada, C. J. Macdonald, was equally disgusted with the "hesitation and weakness" of Morgan and Garrison; he quit Garrison's employ. Macdonald later served as a volunteer in Walker's army.[6]

While Walker was scathing in his criticism of Morgan and Garrison, it was clear that the pair had simply not been ready to take up the Transit charter as quickly as Walker had wanted. Their focus was different from Walker's—it was on making money. Over the past winter, once they had realized that Vanderbilt had outsmarted them and regained control of the Transit Company, the pair had set out to rise phoenixlike from the ashes of their defeat and to make a stock-market killing. Once the market knew that the Commodore was back in charge of the Transit Company, the price of company stock had begun to rise. At that point, Morgan had dumped his entire Transit Company holding and that of his partner Garrison. The duo, remarked the *New York Times*, "lately in the administration of the company, is selling the stock much as Vanderbilt had done after the latter lost control."[7]

In a bid to prevent the share price from dropping as a result of this, Vanderbilt and his friends had bought every dumped share. Then, Morgan had invested heavily in selling Transit Company shares "short." In this stock market practice, investors actually bet on a stock's price going down, rather than up. They in effect borrow the shares from brokers at one price, hoping that it will sink much lower, promising to pay the market price at some time in the future. If the share price rises by the time they have to pay up and "cover" their investment, they lose money. But if the price goes down, as they hope, they make the difference between the initial price and the covering price.

Despite Vanderbilt's best efforts to keep the Transit Company share price up by buying the dumped stock, his determination to keep his fleet of ocean steamers tied up and so deprive Walker of his seaway lifeline only served to panic the market. Many disenchanted shareholders sold their Transit Company shares for whatever they could get, in the belief that the now charterless company was done for. When Morgan sold his shareholding in February and went short, Transit Company shares were trading at $23. Vanderbilt and his friends had kept buying stock, supporting the price, and on March 12, the shares had only dropped to $22. But when the news hit New York the next day that the Nicaraguan government had annulled the Transit Company's charter, the bottom fell out of its share price. By the time Morgan covered his "short" investment some months later, Transit Company shares had dropped to $13. Morgan made $10 a share, walking away with a profit of millions of dollars.[8]

Walker knew nothing of this. Nor did he care. All he was interested in was maintaining his lines of supply. With the arrival of the next steamer from California at least six weeks away, he reasoned that "one motive for holding fast to the Transit was, for the moment, taken away."[9] Almost petulantly, Walker gave orders for his troops at Rivas to prepare to depart the city and abandon the Transit.

As day broke over La Virgen on Monday, April 7, an American employee of the Morgan and Garrison Transit operation walked out onto the veranda of his barrack house and stretched. Suddenly he saw movement to the south. Armed men in white were swarming into the settlement. The alarmed American ran to the Transit headquarters building, yelling a warning. As he and eight other Americans gathered on the veranda, locking the doors behind them and standing there defiantly with folded arms, the building was surrounded by Costa Rican troops with bayonets fitted to their muskets. The Costa Rican officer in charge ordered his men to open fire. Musket balls filled the air. All nine unarmed Americans were cut down by the hail of lead. Some were killed instantly. The others were finished off with bayonet and sword.

While some Costa Ricans battered down the locked doors, others rifled the pockets of the dead Americans. Inside the building, the Costas forced open stored trunks, looking for more valuables. A detachment trotted to the lake jetty, which they set alight. As these troops took over La Virgen, another, larger Costa Rican detachment was marching west along Cornelius Vanderbilt's macadamized Transit Road, to San Juan del Sur and the sea. At the same time, in the near distance, the vanguard of the Costa Rican expeditionary army could be seen tramping up the road from the frontier with drums rattling and flags flying. Trundling along in the rear came a long train of supply wagons and field guns. As the smaller force headed west, the main column of more than three thousand men continued by La Virgen, where the jetty burned, and marched up the road toward Rivas, just nine miles north.

Mounted scouts had informed President Mora that the city of Rivas had been all but deserted by Walker, who left behind a garrison of just two companies of native Nicaraguans under the command of a Cuban officer. Locals soon told Mora that two days back, Walker put most of his men aboard the largest lake steamer, the *San Carlos*, at La Virgen and steamed away, heading east. No one had any idea what Walker was up to or where he was going.

Mora's informants had been right—Walker did steam away across the lake with his army. First he went to San Carlos, where he had taken on board the ARN company stationed there. Then he'd proceeded down the San Juan River to the first set of rapids, from where a company under Captain Baldwin and Lieutenants Green and Rakestraw was disembarked to continue downriver to relieve the company stationed at El Castillo and Hipp's Point. Once the relieved company had boarded the *San Carlos*, Walker turned around and made for Granada.

Lieutenant James Jamison, one of the hundreds of men aboard the overcrowded *San Carlos*, later attempted to excuse this strange bout of lake and river steaming by claiming that Walker had done it to "observe the movements of the enemy."[10] Others would say that it was ineptitude that sent Walker on a roundabout excursion that took him and his army from Granada to Rivas to the San Juan River and back to Granada over a period of ten days. Walker himself would later brush over this strange episode, not even bothering to offer his recent fight with yellow fever as the cause.

By April 8, Walker, back in the Nicaraguan capital, received word that Mora's army had occupied Rivas, La Virgen, and San Juan del Sur. Now, Mora controlled the Transit Road.

In New York City on April 8, the SS *Orizaba* prepared to sail for Nicaragua. Finally, a month after the *Northern Light* made her last run to Greytown for the Vanderbilt-controlled Accessory Transit Company, Morgan and Garrison had their act together sufficiently to start one ship on the Atlantic route to Nicaragua.

A journalist from the *New York Times* had come to the North River wharf to watch the Morgan and Garrison steamer make her maiden departure for Greytown. He was not alone. "An immense crowd was on the wharf," he reported in next day's paper, "it having been intimated that some arrests would, doubtless, take place, and that fun might be safely looked for."[11]

Cornelius Vanderbilt had tied up every one of the eight steamers he previously had running to Nicaragua. On March 17, he had announced in the press: "The Nicaragua Line is withdrawn for the present, in consequence of the difficulties in that country growing out of the extraordinary conduct of General Walker, in seizing or taking by force the property of American citizens. I deem it a duty I owe the public, to the country, and to the Transit Company, to remain quiet, by letting the ships of the company lay at their wharves, until our government has sufficient time to examine and look into the outrage committed upon their property."[12]

That same day, Vanderbilt had written a letter to Secretary of State Marcy, demanding that the U.S. government step in to restore Transit Company property in Nicaragua to its rightful owner. The New York press failed to accept the Commodore's argument, and neither did William L. Marcy. For, as various newspapers pointed out, the Transit Company was a Nicaraguan corporation—a fact, they reminded their readers, that Vanderbilt and the Transit Company had trickily used to their advantage in the past. The press suggested, none too sympathetically, that Vanderbilt apply to the Nicaraguan government for financial compensation.

Despite failing to receive support from either the press or the U.S. government, Vanderbilt did not shift from his obstinate resolve—his steamers sat idle at their New York and San Francisco wharves with their crews out of work and out of pocket while Morgan and Garrison scrambled to find vessels to replace them. Experienced Nicaragua hands had been grabbed by Charles Morgan, who made former *Northern Light* skipper Edward Tinklepaugh master of the two-year-old *Orizaba*.

Promptly at noon, Captain Tinklepaugh, on the *Orizaba*'s bridge, called down to the deck crew, giving the order for the gangplank to be hauled in and lines to be cast off fore and aft. At that moment, Assistant District Attorney Joachimssen appeared on the dockside. Sent by District Attorney McKeon, he was accompanied by six deputy U.S. marshals.

"I arrest this vessel," bellowed the elderly assistant D.A. before striding up the *Orizaba*'s gangplank just as crew members were about to withdraw it.

One deputy marshal scurried up the gangway behind Joachimssen; the other five held back, remaining on the dock. Bells clanged on the bridge, as Tinklepaugh, ignoring the D.A.'s pronouncement, telegraphed "slow ahead" to the engine room. The mooring lines were dropped with a splash, and the giant iron wheels on the 1,450-ton steamer's sides began to slowly rotate. As the ship moved away from the dock, the gangplank fell into the water. Joachimssen and the deputy were stranded on board, and the watching crowd was delighted.

"That's right, take the old cud to Nicaragua," someone shouted close by the *New York Times* reporter.

"Pitch him overboard," another member of the crowd suggested to the steamer's crew.

"General Walker will hang the devil if he ever gets hold of him in Nicaragua," said someone else, "and it would be a pity to waste the hemp on him."[13]

The crowd roared with laughter. The *Times* reporter would note that there were more remarks in a similar vein, "accompanied by occasional oaths and cheers for Captain Tinklepaugh particularly, and General Walker and Nicaragua generally." But the pleasure of the onlookers dissolved when the *Orizaba* came to a stop several hundred yards out in the stream. A ship's boat was lowered, and it rowed back to the dock to collect the five remaining deputy marshals and a mysterious sixth man.

Joachimssen had brought the ship to a halt by showing Captain Tinklepaugh warrants for the arrest of nine of his passengers who "proposed to join General Walker's army and aid in carrying on the war against a Government with which the United States is at peace." He also pointed out that an armed U.S. revenue cutter was waiting outside the Narrows, with orders to detain the *Orizaba* if her master could not produce a pass from the assistant district attorney. Realizing he'd been outwitted, "Captain Tinklepaugh expressed his willingness to have the parties arrested if they were on board."

The ship was searched by the marshals, who were accompanied by Frank H. Savage, the mystery man. Even with the help of Savage, a paid informant, the marshals could only find four of the men on their list. At the top of that list was C. Carrol Hicks. "Captain Hicks belongs to Alabama," the *Times* would report, "and has just returned by the last steamer from Nicaragua, where he holds a commission in General Walker's army." Hicks and the other three were landed at Pier 4, away from the supportive crowd. But as the prisoners were marched away up West Street, one managed to escape. Hicks and two companions were immediately brought before a judge, who set bail at twenty-five hundred dollars each. None of the prisoners had the remotest chance of raising that sort of money, and all three were lodged in Eldridge Street Prison pending a Neutrality Act trial.

Joachimssen gave Captain Tinklepaugh his pass, and at 2:30, the *Orizaba* got under way again, to the "loud huzzas" of the passengers lining her rails. "The *Orizaba* had some 500 passengers," the *Times* would report. "Of these over 300 are questionably bound for General Walker's army. Mr. Dillingham, Secretary to Colonel French, was among the passengers." As the steamer moved down the harbor, the *Times* reporter was deafened by the cheers of the crowd around him.

Later in the afternoon, a man was spotted in the street not far from the U.S. Marshal's office, selling maps of Nicaragua, "evidently to induce persons to emigrate to that country. He was promptly arrested by Marshal Dayton." Once night fell, informant Frank Savage, who had apparently pretended to sign up to go to Nicaragua to learn the identities of Hicks and the others, was tracked down by filibuster sympathizers and severely beaten up. A bulletin posted on the notice board of the Charles Street Saloon on Broadway—"the headquarters of the filibusters" in New York, according to the *Times*—reported the fate of betrayer Savage: "His health is precarious, and dispatches will be received announcing his situation every two hours."

Meanwhile, the *Orizaba* was steaming south down the Atlantic coast in the April dark, bound for Greytown. After dinner, the passengers who hadn't succumbed to seasickness strolled the swaying decks and enjoyed the sea air as the massive paddlewheels churned the ocean. Among those passengers was Colonel Charles Hornsby, one of Walker's most senior officers. After being on leave in the United States, Hornsby was returning to Nicaragua, apparently having used an assumed name to avoid the district attorney's attention at New York.

Hornsby perambulated in the company of six boisterous young men from Nashville. The Tennesseeans were all good friends who had signed up together to join the fight in Nicaragua. One of their number was James Walker, youngest brother of William Walker. Like his big brother, twenty-seven-year-old James was a qualified doctor, but he was going to Nicaragua determined to use a sword rather than a scalpel in his brother's service. According to one of Walker's hometown papers, the *Nashville Gazette*, James was "a gallant young man" who possessed qualities "both of head and heart which eminently fitted him for command."[14]

Without knowing it, as they walked the steamer's decks, Hornsby, James Walker, and their companions passed a man traveling to Nicaragua as Cornelius Vanderbilt's secret agent, a man charged with the task of wrecking William Walker's little empire. Receiving no adequate response from the U.S. government, Vanderbilt had decided to thwart Walker in a more covert way. Hosea Birdsall was employed by the Commodore to take control of former Transit Company property at Punta Arenas, across the bay from Greytown, including river steamers based there. Birdsall also had orders to prevent the *Orizaba's* passengers from going up the San Juan River once the steamer dropped anchor off Greytown. If Birdsall was successful, the Commodore would choke the Transit at its Greytown neck, putting Garrison, Morgan, and Walker out of business.

On April 9, a day after William Walker and his troops arrived back at Granada on the lake steamer, Walker issued orders for all but two companies of his bemused troops to march again. With Walker at their head, 550 men of the Army of the Republic of Nicaragua tramped down the road toward Rivas. They were returning to the city, which was seventy miles away and now occupied by the bulk of the Costa Rican expeditionary army and which Walker had vacated just five days earlier. But now, Walker, feeling physically and mentally strong again, was planning to fight.

When the troops camped for the night beside the Ochomogo River, they were joined by Cuban officer Colonel Muchado and his one hundred Nicaraguan troops, who had withdrawn from Rivas as Mora's Costa Rican army drew near. Muchado's Nicaraguan deputy, Captain José Bermudez, had stayed behind at Rivas, defecting to the Costa Ricans.

At the Hipp's Point outpost on the San Juan River, Captain John Baldwin received a troubling report from a scouting party—some miles up the Sarapiqui River, they'd heard the sounds of a road being cut through the jungle from the Costa Rican side of the border. So, on April 10, Baldwin, "a vigilant and intelligent officer," in William Walker's estimation, sent sixteen Americans led by Lieutenant Tom Green from Texas to investigate.[15]

Green's party struggled up the soupy green Sarapiqui, paddling against the current in a bungo. These local dugout canoes typically accommodated eighteen to twenty men. By the middle of the day, eighteen miles from the junction of the San Juan and Sarapiqui Rivers, they heard sounds of slashing machetes ahead. Coming ashore, Green and his men slowly, carefully crept toward the road makers. Spotting toiling Costa Rican soldiers through the thick foliage, the Americans took up firing positions, selecting targets among scores of Costa Ricans sweating to cut a path wide enough for horses and mules to pass along.

On Lieutenant Green's word, the Americans opened fire. This volley from nowhere cut a swath through the Costa Ricans. There was consternation and panic in the road-building ranks. The Americans quickly reloaded. Again Green and his men fired a withering fusillade, knocking more white-uniformed figures from their feet. Only when General Florentino Alfaro and many more Costa Ricans began arriving from the rear, summoned by the firing, did Green and his men realize they had taken on a force of more than two hundred men.[16] The clouds of smoke and muzzle flashes from American rifles gave away their position, and some Costas began to return fire. In his enthusiasm, Green's deputy, Lieutenant Rakestraw, jumped to his feet, firing his pistol and yelling encouragement to his men. A Costa Rican musket ball found him, and he went down. Keeping low, Tom Green and his other men maintained a steady rate of fire.

A number of the men of General Alfaro's command had been claimed by illness during their horrific month-long struggle through the jungle. The remainder were exhausted and close to starvation by the time they blundered into Lieutenant Green's ambush just eighteen miles short of their objective. Convinced, from the enemy firepower, that there were hundreds of Yankees lurking in the trees, General Alfaro's conscripts wanted no more of this impossible mission and soon withdrew in disorder. "The routed Costa Ricans did not stop in their flight until they had fallen back to San José," Walker would observe.[17] Abandoned by most of his men, General Alfaro had no choice but to abandon his mission.

When Lieutenant Green and his men cautiously broke cover and inspected the enemy dead, they counted twenty-seven Costa Rican bodies. Lieutenant Rakestraw was the only American fatality, while two of Green's men had been wounded.[18] Just sixteen Americans had terminated President Mora's attempt to catch Walker by surprise via the back door. Now it was up to Walker to close the front door on Mora himself, at the Transit.

18

THE SECOND
BATTLE OF RIVAS

A T SEVEN O'CLOCK IN THE MORNING OF APRIL 10, 1856, HUNDREDS of men in black were running to the attack as the sun rose over Rivas. Panting, gripping tightly on to heavy rifle, musket, pistol, and sword, they were tense as they ran, dreading the moment that bullets might start flying their way, and praying that they'd taken the Costa Ricans by surprise.

Walker's army of 650 men had spent much of the previous night resting on the south bank of the Gil Gonzales River. Lieutenant James Jamison had fallen fast asleep there beside the river after marching for two days since leaving Granada and dreamed of home in Missouri.[1] At midnight, Walker had briefed his officers on how he wanted the attack carried out, and at 3:00 A.M., the troops were roused from their slumbers.

Rivas had a single central plaza. Two streets led through the suburbs to the plaza from the north and the south. Similarly, two parallel streets tracked from east and west to the plaza. All the streets, which, like the plaza, were paved with mud brick, were narrow and lined unevenly with single-story adobe brick buildings that fronted directly onto the raised side-walks. According to an enemy agent caught spying on Walker's encamped army the previous evening and left hanging, dead, from a bough of a tree by the river, President Mora had made his headquarters in a large, private house in one of the streets on the western side of the plaza, opposite the city's powder magazine.

Walker's objective was to capture Mora and force him to take Costa Rica out of the war. The filibuster general was sending his troops into Rivas from the north, south, and east, so that they could clean out resistance on their

way to converging on Mora's headquarters in the west of the city. The energetic Lieutenant Colonel Edward Sanders led four rifle companies, entering
Rivas from the east along Calle San Francisco and Calle San Pedro. Sanders
encountered several Costa Rican sentries on the outer edge of the suburbs;
they ran off without putting up a fight. At the trot, Sanders and his two hundred men then pounded along the two deserted streets, reaching the plaza
without encountering resistance.

The Rivas plaza was a cobbled square one hundred yards across. Occupying the entire eastern side of the plaza, the tall, roofless stone walls of the
Cathedral of San Pedro and its adjoining convent stood stark and derelict.
Seriously damaged by an earthquake twelve years earlier, the church buildings were no longer used. Commercial buildings with shading verandas extended along the northern and southern perimeters of the plaza, while an
inn and a warehouse occupied the western side.

Sanders and his men quickly swung right and entered the Calle de
Polvon, the northernmost of the two streets running west. This street led to
the gunpowder magazine and, directly opposite it, the house where, according to the executed spy, President Mora was in residence. With their final
objective eighty yards from the plaza, Sander and his men bunched together
in the slim avenue and hurried on. Forty yards down the street, they came
on two small brass cannon standing facing east; ammunition carts sat a little farther on. Whooping like men who had won a lottery, Sanders's troops
stopped to secure the cannon, then dragged them back to the square.[2]

By the time Sanders was able to convince his men to leave their trophies
and recommence the advance toward the magazine, puffs of smoke began to
appear all along the western street. Bullets whined around the Americans,
and Sanders's men begin to fall all around him as he pushed forward. Mora
had billeted his troops in houses throughout Rivas's western quarter, the
most built-up part of the city, and on his orders, loopholes had been
punched through adobe house walls that faced the streets. As Sanders discovered, the entire street ahead of him was lined with holed walls, from
which hundreds of now alerted Costa Ricans began to open fire with musket and rifle. Caught in the open and facing a now withering fire that cut
down his exposed men, Sanders had no option but to order a retreat to the

plaza. His men gladly retreated, carrying their wounded with them as bullets kicked up dust all around.

Meanwhile, Major A. S. Brewster had brought three rifle companies up the streets from the east, and they cleared the southern side of the plaza without incident. Seeing Sanders's men in trouble on the street leading to the magazine, Brewster brought his men across the plaza to the second west-running street, hoping to move along it and swing around and attack the enemy headquarters from the west. But as soon as Brewster and his command entered this second western street, they came under intense rifle fire from French and German marksmen in Costa Rican pay who occupied a tower of the San Francisco Church, four blocks along this street. Fine shots and equipped with Minié rifles, they soon took a heavy toll on Brewster's men. The street was a death trap, and like Sanders, Brewster was forced to pull his men back to the plaza in search of cover.

Colonel Bruno Natzmer, an Austrian who had previously served as chief of staff to Chelon Valle, Walker's loyal Nicaraguan colonel, now arrived at the plaza from the south with two hundred men of the Second Rifles. With progress down both western streets blocked, Natzmer's men occupied the buildings on the southern side of the plaza, from where they tried to bring fire to bear on loopholes along the western streets.

The hundred native Nicaraguan troops under Colonel Machado had been advancing cautiously toward the plaza down the road from the north, passing the burned-out ruin of the Espinosa hacienda on the Santa Ursula Hill, scene of the first Battle of Rivas. The heavy fire ahead had awoken Costas occupying houses along the western side of the road, and they began firing at the Nicaraguans through loopholes. Colonel Machado was riding a horse, waving his sword, and urging his troops forward in fiery Spanish when he stopped in midsentence and toppled from his horse, struck down by several musket balls. As Muchado's terrified horse bolted back down the road, his troops looked at the colonel lying dead in the dust at their feet, then followed the horse's example. Beating a hasty retreat, they headed for woodland north of the city. They would play no further part in the battle.

General Walker now came riding up one of the eastern streets, with Colonel Birkett D. Fry and the reserve troops of the First Light Infantry

Battalion right behind him. On reaching the plaza, Walker found that his attack had bogged down, with the men of the advance elements now occupying the buildings on all sides of the plaza. There was sporadic American rifle
fire from those plaza buildings that had a line of sight to the western streets,
and from the one tower of the San Pedro Cathedral still standing, a steady
popping of American rifles could be heard—Major John Waters and his dismounted Rangers had taken possession of the tower and were using it as a
sniping position. In streets leading up to the plaza, men sat with backs to
the walls, with no intention of going any further while three thousand Costa
Rican muskets lay in wait for them in the streets west of the plaza.

Walker, still on horseback, ordered Colonel Fry to lead the First Light Infantry in a frontal attack across the plaza and down the western street leading to the magazine, to fulfill Sanders's original mission. But Fry could see
that this was suicidal.

"General, it is utterly impracticable," Fry protested.

"Then, if you will not lead the men, I will," Walker declared, urging his
horse out into the street, sword in hand, presenting an inviting target to
Costa Rican marksmen.[3]

Lieutenant Jamison, farther up this street with his reserve company,
watched Walker in amazement. "Bullets were flying thick all around him,
and his clothing and his horse were covered with the debris from the walls
of the buildings. He sat on his horse seemingly the least excited of all the
belligerents."[4] Edward Kewen, who had been serving as a civil administrator
with the government, had come along on this mission as a volunteer. He and
several other men now dashed out into the open, grabbed Walker's mount,
and dragged horse and rider back into cover.

Walker's intelligence had been correct—the Costa Rican president was indeed in a house across the street from the powder magazine. President
Mora had made his quarters in the house of Dona Francesca Carrasco, a
well-to-do widow whose husband, Pancho, had been a victim of the civil war.
Dona Francesca was also an ardent Legitimista. Highly intelligent and well
educated, she not only played hostess to Don Juanito but had also acted as

his secretary while he was in the city, penning his letters as he dictated them. Since the filibuster attack began, Mora had been astonished to see Dona Francesca produce a musket and join his officers and men shooting at the Yankees from her house's windows and loopholes.

Now that there was a lull in the battle, with just the occasional potshot from both sides, Mora called for volunteers from those with him in the Carrasco house to go out and spike the two cannon captured by the filibusters, before Walker could turn the guns against the Costa Ricans. Half a dozen men put up their hands. Two of Mora's staff officers, José Maria Rojas and Francisco Rodriguez, soon equipped themselves with iron spikes and hammers. The other volunteers stood ready with loaded rifles. At the word from Mora, the door was flung open, and Rojas and Rodriguez hurled themselves out into the street, with the riflemen close behind. Then, to the astonishment of everyone, Senora Carrasco dashed after them, musket in hand.

The Costa Rican sabotage party, including its female member, ran down the Street of the Magazine toward the plaza and the two brass cannon standing at the plaza entrance, where Sanders's men had left them. Hundreds of Costa Ricans at loopholes all the way along the street commenced covering fire, forcing filibusters around the plaza to keep their heads down, and permitting the party to reach the guns. As Dona Francesca and others stood guard, firing at any filibuster they saw trying to take aim at them, the two officers hammered their spikes into the cannon's touchholes. In seconds, the spikes were driven home.[5] And then the members of the party scurried back the way they came, with every one of them, including Dona Francesca, making it back to the Carrasco house alive, their mission a complete success. "The enemy had made the cannon useless," James Jamison would later lament.[6]

The gall of the Costas in making this successful sally against the cannon infuriated quick-tempered Major John Markham. One of Walker's "Originals" and a survivor of the last Battle of Rivas, Markham called for volunteers to accompany him on a charge across the plaza and down the street to take the enemy headquarters. In response, Captain Linton, Lieutenant Jamison, and twenty-eight enlisted men, twelve of them from Jamison's Company D, answered the call.

With the major in the lead, brandishing his sword and yelling like a man possessed, the thirty-one volunteers sprinted across the plaza and plunged down the street that led to the magazine. Once they entered the narrow street, the Americans came under sustained fire. The "mad excitement" of the charge carried the volunteers as far as the two ammunition carts, fifty yards along the street from the plaza, and just ninety feet from their objective, the Carrasco house.[7] But by that point, as many as a thousand enemy muskets and rifles were being brought to bear on them.

"The bullets ripped and stung," Jamison would say, "and reddened the pavements with blood."[8] Captain Linton spun a pirouette on the sidewalk and fell dead with a bullet to the heart. In the lead, Major Markham went down with one knee almost blown away. James Jamison's right leg was taken from under him. Falling flat on his face, he lay in the middle of the street; he could see that he'd been hit in the lower part of the right leg. Through searing pain, Jamison saw two men from his company fall dead close by. Half of the thirty-one men who entered the street had by this time been killed or wounded.

"Retire to the plaza," gasped the wounded Major Markham, gripping his wounded leg.[9]

Hauling the ammunition carts with them as portable cover, and with enemy bullets continually splintering the wood, the assault party made a painful retreat, leaving their dead where they lay. Jamison, unable to walk, was half dragged to the plaza by his men. Troops of the First Rifles who'd taken part in Colonel Sanders's initial charge down this deadly street were sheltering on the elevated veranda of a building on the northern side of the plaza. As bullets zipped and chipped all around them, Jamison and other wounded were roughly pushed up onto the veranda to join them before the remaining members of the assault party hurriedly dispersed to cover.

On the veranda, Jamison found himself in the company of a number of Sanders's wounded. The building fronted by this veranda was a dry goods store, and some enterprising members of the First Rifles had dragged huge blocks of cheese out from the store and used them to create a protective breastwork along the edge of the veranda. The cheese was near rock hard and, as Jamison witnessed, could stop a bullet. Colonel Sanders placed his best shots along this breastwork. To Jamison's amusement, when not taking aim at Costa Rican heads, these riflemen burrowed into the barricade with their jackknives and snacked on chunks of cheese.

One of these marksman in particular took Jamison's eye. Known merely as "Arkansas," he was a tall, angular backwoodsman, and he had found a spot at the western end of the veranda where there was a recess in the wall beside one of the thick wooden veranda posts. From this protected position, Arkansas was able to fire at several houses along the street leading to the magazine. Arkansas and a buddy had come to Nicaragua with their long Missouri rifles, and he soon proved that he could use the weapon. Looking for a target at a loophole down the street, he took aim and fired. With a spray of white paint and orange dust, his bullet bit the adobe brick wall beside the loophole. It took Arkansas several more rounds to find his range, but once he did, he became lethal.

"By Gum, I fetched him!" he exclaimed as a Costa Rican at a loophole threw up his arms and collapsed with a large-caliber bullet in the brain.[10]

Replying rounds thudded into the wooden pillar beside Arkansas, but none reached him. After each shot, he slid his Missouri rifle to his friend, who, lying nearby, reloaded it while Arkansas used the friend's weapon. In this way, the sniper team from Arkansas maintained a rapid rate of fire. Jamison would later hear that Arkansas kept up his sniping for hours, wounding or killing as many as fifty Costa Ricans and forcing the Costas to abandon the nearest house. This was, Jamison would say, "the most spectacular sharpshooting I saw in Nicaragua."[11]

From up in the cathedral tower, Major John Waters and his Mounted Rangers were shooting at anything that moved in the western quarter of the city. One of Waters's deputies, the "impetuous" Lieutenant Gillis, had recklessly exposed himself to enemy fire early on and paid with his life.[12] Now Waters's men kept their heads down and made every shot count.

From his vantage point, Waters could see that Colonel Sanders had managed to get men up onto the red tile rooftops of the inn and warehouse on the western side of the plaza. Sheltering behind the hip of the roofs, these men popped up from time to time to fire down into the western quarter, before dropping down into cover again to reload.

There was movement on the steps behind Waters. He glanced around, to see General Walker's brother, Norvell Walker, clambering up into the tower with a bottle in his hand. Even though Walker had dismissed him, Norvell had trailed the army down to Rivas. Now, he found a cozy corner in the tower with a view of the action below, and there he sat, to the annoyance of Waters and his men, drinking and talking, talking and drinking.

James Jamison and more than twenty other wounded were carried off the veranda and into the dry goods store, where bales of cotton were used as temporary hospital beds. Around noon, Jamison was lying on a bale, waiting for medical attention, when General Walker arrived on the scene. Looking calm and collected, Walker moved around the room, talking with each wounded man, treating officers and enlisted men alike. Reaching Jamison, he sat on the bale beside him and uttered a few "kind and hopeful" words before moving on to the next man.[13] His brief visit was enough to lift Jamison's sagging spirits.

A little after midday, there were shouts of alarm from several quarters. Costa Rican reinforcements had been seen arriving in the western sector during the late morning—these were the garrisons from La Virgen and San Juan del Sur, summoned by President Mora. Now, from the second street leading into the city's western quarter, a hundred Costas came charging into the plaza.

Assaulting a large building on the northwestern side of the plaza, the Costas crashed in through the doors and windows, driving out men from Bruno Natzmer's command who had been occupying it, and taking control of the building. From here, the Costa Ricans could pour a deadly fire across the plaza at Walker's men. Realizing that he must recapture this building, and quickly, Walker called for volunteers. Lieutenant Robert Gay, an "Original" who'd gained renown on the Virgin Bay beach during the Battle of La Virgen, was the first to come forward. He was joined by Major William Kissane Rogers of the Commissary Department and eleven others, including Walker aide Captain Huston and James Jamison's latest company commander, Captain N. C. Breckenridge. Agreeing that this would involve close-quarter fighting indoors, all thirteen men armed themselves with pistols. Keeping low, Gay and his comrades scuttled to the building next door to that occupied by the Costas. Then, on Gay's word, they charged along the veranda to the attack.

Gay and Huston were both gunned down at the doors to the building. Moments later, Breckenridge reeled away clutching his head. But those behind the officers crashed in through doors and window shutters, just as the Costas had done not long before. Inside, in desperate face-to-face combat, another four Americans died, but more than thirty Costa Ricans were killed; the remainder fled out the back. Walker would reconcile the death of Gay and half the men who accompanied him with the fact that the building was retaken. "The gallantry of those who went with Gay was, in its spirit," Walker the romantic would later say, "more like that of the knights of feudal times."[14]

A bid to keep up the momentum and capture the house next door proved less successful. New Yorker Captain McArdle, who had been fighting a duel with one of Walker's aides not many days ago, led this attack. It was kept up, on and off, for several hours, but only resulted in more American dead. At one point, McArdle was at a door, which the Costa Ricans had left partly open so they could fire out through the opening. McArdle thrust his pistol in through the gap and fired several shots to the left and right, bringing cries of pain from within. Then, from inside, a bayonet was plunged into McArdle's wrist, pinning his arm. Seconds later, another Costa put a musket to McArdle's gun hand and fired, blowing off his hand. With a yelp, McArdle withdrew his arm, then looked in disbelief at the bloody stump where his hand had been. "The damned rascal got my pistol!" he exclaimed.[15]

McArdle would live, unlike his dueling partner of several days before, Captain Dewitt Clinton, who lay dead not many yards away. As McArdle was helped away and the attack continued, a Costa Rican soldier, shot dead, tumbled out a doorway. A Private Soule scurried to the body, knelt beside it, and, ignoring enemy bullets kicking up dust all around him, calmly ransacked the dead man's pockets for souvenirs, then scampered back into cover, unharmed.

General Canas, President Mora's brother-in-law and third-ranking among the Costa Rican commanders, was inside a house on the Street of the Magazine, not far from the Carrasco house. As the afternoon wore on, and with sunset not long off, Canas decided that something drastic had to be done to force the filibusters from the buildings on the plaza. Remembering the story of the Nicaraguan pair, Mongola and Fajardo, who had set fire to the Espinosa hacienda in Rivas the previous year, Canas sent for Sergeant Luis Pacheco.

Twenty-three-year-old Pacheco, a slight man with a long face and a thin mustache, was a mixed-race native of the Costa Rican town of Cartago. Just before this war had broken out, Pacheco had been convicted of rape, but President Mora had pardoned him—in the expectation that in his gratitude Pacheco would make a good soldier. Now it was time for Pacheco to repay the favor and to prove himself. Canas pointed out to Pacheco that at the top of the street, at the western end of the plaza, was an inn owned by Roberto Guerra. Canas ordered Pacheco to set fire to it, hoping the fire would spread to other buildings around the plaza and drive the Yankees out.

A torch was prepared, lit, and handed to Pacheco. The door was then flung open, and Sergeant Pacheco was pushed out into the street. Praying that he would somehow be spared, Pacheco dashed up the street toward the plaza. American marksmen opened up on him, and like angry bees, bullets hummed by his ear. To his own amazement, Pacheco reached the wall of Guerra's Inn unscathed. With a grunt, he heaved his burning torch up under the eaves of the roof.

Without waiting to see if the fire would take, Pacheco, still under fire from the filibusters, turned and sprinted back the way he'd come. As he ran, he felt the impact of slugs hitting him, but his legs continued to drive him back to where he'd started from. Again he was hit. Pacheco staggered, then stumbled and sprawled facedown on the sidewalk outside the thick wooden door that offered salvation. The door swung open. Private Ramon Montoya reached out and dragged the sergeant in from the pavement. As Yankee bullets thudded into the wall around the doorway, the door was slammed shut. Pacheco had survived. Sitting propped against a wall, he studied with some fascination the sources of the blood discoloring his white clothes; he had, he discovered, received five separate bullet wounds. Two other soldiers in the room, Privates Venancio Lascarez and Remigio Garro, gave Pacheco little chance of seeing another day and would be amazed to find him still alive the next day in a field hospital.[16]

For long minutes, General Canas waited to see smoke rising from Guerra's Inn. But the general was disappointed; Pacheco's torch didn't ignite a fire. So Canas called for volunteers for a second attempt. Two youths came forward. One was a Nicaraguan private, a local Legitimista. The other was Juan Santamaria, a Costa Rican drummer boy from Alajuela whose nickname was *el Erizo*—the hedgehog. The wounded Sergeant Pacheco, sitting against a wall, ripped the bottom from his own grimy, bloodied shirt, dipped it in paraffin, and tied it around the top of a chair-leg size piece of timber produced by another soldier. Pacheco handed this to young Santamaria and prayed that God would go with him. The Nicaraguan boy was also provided with a torch, and both torches were lit. General Canas wished the pair good luck and then ordered the door opened.

The Nicaraguan youth was the first to emerge into the street. Santamaria the drummer boy was right behind him. Sprinting down the pavement with their burning torches, they kept close to the buildings as Costa Ricans all along the street strove to provide covering fire from windows and loopholes. The Americans, anticipating this second sally, sent a fusillade of bullets hurtling toward the pair. The Nicaraguan, peppered with bullets, spun and fell. His torch tumbled uselessly into the dust. Santamaria continued on.

Reaching the inn's nearest corner, Santamaria thrust his torch up under the eaves as bullets kicked up dust all around him. As, Costa Ricans at loopholes watched with bated breath, the drummer boy turned to make his return run. They saw the boy hit by several rounds at once, then crumple to the ground at the entrance to the plaza. There he lay, on his back, eyes wide, as if studying the blue Nicaraguan sky. His comrades prayed he would get to his feet again, but Juan Santamaria was dead. Yet his mission had not been in vain—smoke was oozing out from beneath the eaves of Guerra's Inn.

Lieutenant James Jamison dragged himself out onto the veranda of the dry goods store. The men there told him that the Costas had set fire to the city. Peeking over the wall of cheese, Jamison could see smoke rising from the roof of the inn on the western side of the plaza.

Beside Jamison, Captain Jack Dunnigan sat taking a swig from a bottle of patent bitters. As Dunnigan drank, a bullet from nowhere suddenly hit him in the throat, damaging the thyroid. Dunnigan clapped a hand over his bleeding throat and, in a hoarse whisper, remarked, "Never before has my drinking been cut short in so discourteous a manner."[17]

As Dunnigan crawled away to have his wound attended to, Jamison again took a peak over the wall of cheese. Not only was the inn burning, but smoke was also rising on the northwestern side of the plaza from fires set by the Costas in the west of the city.

The ARN officers in the northern buildings decided that once night fell, they would evacuate their wounded around the plaza to the San Pedro Convent, and Lieutenant George Winters was ordered to make his way to the convent to have preparations made to receive the wounded.[18] Winters was a young man who believed his life was charmed, and instead of threading his way through the buildings skirting the plaza, he decided to take a short cut—across the middle of the plaza. With a valuable pearl-handled revolver in his hand, Winters leaped from a northern veranda and, in a crouching run, headed across the plaza toward the cathedral and convent.

By this time, Costa Rican marksmen had occupied rooftops in the western sector. They saw Winters's running figure; so too did the snipers in the San Francisco Church tower. Winters had crossed thirty yards of plaza when a .758 Minié round smacked into his right thigh, shattered it, then continued on to shatter his left thigh. Winters dropped to his knees as if forced down by some invisible power. Unable to believe he'd been wounded, Winters tried to rise again but couldn't. With bullets hitting the pavement all around him, he could only kneel there, waiting for the bullet that would end it all.

From a spot near Jamison on the veranda of the dry goods store, Captain Myron Veeder suddenly hurdled the wall of cheese, dropped down into the plaza, then dashed toward the downed man. "Bullets came like hail in an Atlantic storm," the watching Jamison would recall.[19] As Veeder reached Winters, so many rounds ripped into the brick paving around the pair that the men were momentarily obscured from view by a cloud of red dust raised by the fusillade. Out of the dust came Veeder, with Winters over his shoulder. Winters was still holding his pearl-handled revolver. Miraculously, the pair reached cover. Somehow, Veeder emerged from the rescue unscathed, although his jacket was riddled with bullet holes.

By 11:30 P.M. Guerra's Inn was a gutted, smoldering ruin, and buildings in the northwest were burning strongly. Occasional shots punctuated the night, but otherwise, there was not a sound. Remarkably, as this seventeen-hour battle was fought out, a population of eighteen thousand people had been sheltering in back rooms throughout the city, praying for the killing to end and the soldiers to leave.

Once the sun went down, Walker had his units quietly evacuate the buildings on the western, northern, and southern sides of the plaza, one by one. A few rooftop marksmen on the northern and southern sides kept up a steady rate of fire to make the Costas think Walker's men were still hunkered down around the plaza, and Major Waters and his Rangers remained in the cathedral bell tower, from where they shot at anything moving in the western sector.

Sixty American wounded lay in the ruined, roofless convent; Jamison was one of fourteen officers among them. In the moonlight, Jamison recognized several: his own company commander, Captain Breckenridge, a bloodied bandage around his head; Lieutenant Theodore E. Potter, a tall, slim man from Minnesota with neat beard and mustache whose wound was not life-threatening; and Willie Gould, a young private from Jamison's company. Slight, fair-haired, blue-eyed, his boyish face drained of blood, Gould lay unconscious; the doctors, Moses, Cole, and Jones, held little hope for him. Jamison spotted General Walker moving among the wounded, talking with them, checking their bandages. Walker's face gave nothing away; despite the desperate situation, he was "as inscrutable as a sphinx."[20]

A survey of his troops told Walker he had four hundred men fit to fight, with, on average, just three rounds per man remaining. With so little ammunition, it was pointless continuing the assault. Walker ordered his army to prepare to withdraw. The operation had to be carried out silently, discreetly, so that the enemy didn't come charging down on top of them. Major Brewster would command a small rear guard. The horses of officers and Mounted Rangers were brought to the convent, and all wounded who could ride were put in the saddle. Walking wounded would go with them, in the middle of the column, as it retreated. The critically injured were a different matter.

Walker went to where George Winters lay and spoke quietly with him. The ashen-faced Winters nodded slowly. After speaking with the other seriously wounded men who remained conscious, the little general addressed the wounded as a group. He told them that the army must withdraw, but critically injured men would only jeopardize the chances of the others and would have a better chance if they stayed behind, with the hope that the Costa Rican surgeons would take over their care.

These men knew it was highly unlikely the enemy would spare them, but not one objected. On the contrary. "Save the army, general," one man called, "and take no thought of us."[21] The critically wounded were carried to the raised altar platform in the ruined cathedral—perhaps on that once-sanctified spot, they would attract the sympathy of the Catholic Costa Ricans.

Jamison, watching this take place, was red hot with a fever brought on by his wound; his right leg had blown up to twice its size. Desperate to catch the cooling night breeze coming off the lake, he crawled across the convent floor and into the adjoining cathedral. In a corner where the breeze found its way in through the broken walls, Jamison sagged against a mound of rubble and gratefully closed his eyes.

Jamison awoke with a start. In the moonlight, he checked his pocket-watch—4:00 A.M. Above his head, a Costa Rican bullet hit a bell in the cathedral bell tower with a resonating clang. The Costas were shooting at the Rangers' sniping position. But when there was no return fire, it dawned on Jamison that the Rangers had gone. The army must have withdrawn, and Jamison had been overlooked! His comrades had probably seen him sleeping, and thought him dead. "For a moment [I] was appalled at my predicament," he would later say. "I knew that capture meant death."[22]

Overcoming his panic, Jamison crawled toward the cathedral's rear door, armed with sword and pistol and dragging his swollen leg behind him. Pulling himself up over the pile of rubble blocking the door, he slipped down the other side, came to his feet, and looked around. With no idea what direction to follow and using his sword as a crutch, he hobbled through the Rivas suburbs. Behind him, the Costas continued to fire into the deserted American positions. At the city outskirts, hearing horses approach, Jamison dived over a wall of cactus plants. A troop of Costa Rican lancers cantered by in the darkness.

Jamison continued his awkward flight, following a main road, until he realized he was going south, toward Costa Rica. Glumly, he turned around and limped back the other way, toward Rivas and Granada beyond it, certain he would be caught and put before a firing squad. But fortune favored him; Jamison stumbled onto a pony standing abandoned in the road. Catching and mounting it, he circled around Rivas and then rode north to link up with Walker and his bloodied army as it withdrew toward Granada.

As dawn broke over Rivas on the morning of April 11, Norvell Walker awoke from a drunken sleep in the cathedral's bell tower. When he'd dropped off to sleep the night before, he had been accompanied by Rangers. Now he was alone. To his horror, Norvell realized that the army had gone and he had been left behind. Slithering down the steps to the ground below, he fled the ruined cathedral and scampered after his brother's long-gone army.

After several hours of daylight, it dawned on President Mora that the filibusters had pulled out. With bayonets fixed, his troops moved through
the city, looking for remnants of William Walker's army. At the San Pedro
Cathedral, Costas crashed through the thick doors that faced onto the
plaza. At the altar platform, the crippled Lieutenant George Winters and
his wounded comrades sat or lay. Winters, with back to the altar, raised his
pearl-handled revolver and fired, cutting down the first Costa Rican to take
a step toward him. He fired again, as with angry yells, the soldiers in white
charged the altar. Winters and the other American wounded were bayoneted
to death. The story would later be told by Americans who fought at Rivas—
more legend than fact, in all probability—that George Winters emptied all
six barrels of his revolver before the Costas got him.[23]

Elsewhere in the city, Don Francisco Ugarte, the man who had billeted
Lieutenant Jamison, emerged from his home and sought out President
Mora. Ugarte proceeded to point out houses where five wounded Americans
had taken refuge with friendly locals. Costa Rican troops dragged the five
filibusters out into the street, then shot them dead on the spot.

President Mora sent out lancers to round up filibuster stragglers, but his
army was in no shape to give chase to Walker's main body. Walker himself
estimated that the Costa Ricans suffered six hundred killed or wounded in
the battle, a figure repeated in the American press. Actual Costa Rican casualties, revealed much later by Costa Rican sources, numbered over eight
hundred.[24] As the exhausted survivors took stock of their situation, their
president issued a proclamation, telling the people of Costa Rica that on
April 11, the nation's army had won a great victory against the Yankee army
of the filibuster Walker at Rivas.

The Second Battle of Rivas was over, and William Walker was in full retreat.

❦ 19 ❦

PRESIDENT WALKER

I N RIVAS, THE VICTORIOUS COSTA RICANS CONTEMPTUOUSLY THREW the American dead down city wells. Within days of the battle, a cholera epidemic broke out and steamrolled through the ranks of the Costa Rican army occupying Rivas, La Virgen, and San Juan del Sur. In fear of catching the disease, President Mora and his brother General Mora rode for Costa Rica on April 26, leaving General Canas to bring the shattered army home. Prominent Rivas Legitimistas, including Dona Francesca Carrasco, rode with the president's party. Once back in Costa Rica, President Mora would present Dona Francesca with a medal for her bravery during the Second Battle of Rivas.

Remnants of the Costa Rican army traipsed to San Juan del Sur. Five hundred died there before they could board vessels for home and were buried on the beach. On April 29, the last contingent of Costa Rican troops left the Jocote ranch on the Transit Road and, under Colonel Lorenzo Salazar, marched south for the border at the La Flor River. At Rivas and San Juan del Sur, General Canas left behind his dead and dying, together with a note for William Walker, asking him to take care of the sick Costa Ricans abandoned by him. "I expect your generosity will treat them with all the attention and care their situation requires," Canas wrote. "I invoke the laws of humanity in favor of these unfortunate victims of an awful calamity."[1]

Canas proposed the later exchange of Costa Ricans who survived with "more than twenty prisoners who are in our power, and whose names I will send you, in a detailed list."[2] No such list was ever received, and there was no evidence the Costa Ricans spared any American prisoners. When the

ARN reoccupied La Virgen and San Jan del Sur in early May, Walker instructed his doctors to do what they could for the Costa Rican cholera sufferers. For the time being, Walker wisely kept out of Rivas, the center of the outbreak. When he later reoccupied the city, he had Don Francesco Ugarte tracked down and arrested for betraying the wounded American soldiers on April 11. Found hiding in the village of Obraje, Ugarte was in short order tried, convicted, and hanged.

In Walker's estimation, only 500 of the 3500 Costa Rican troops who invaded Nicaragua returned home alive; combat and cholera between them took 3000 lives.[3] But the Costa Rican calamity hadn't ended there. The survivors took cholera back to Costa Rica with them, and it swiftly spread through the little nation, killing men, women, and children. By the time the epidemic had run its course, 10,000 Costa Ricans had perished, out of a population of just 112,000. The epidemic even claimed the life of Juan Rafael Mora's vice president, Francisco Oreamuno.

In the United States, news of Walker's military reverse at Rivas briefly dented his reputation as the unstoppable "gray-eyed man of destiny"—as Walker's own newspaper, *El Nicaraguense*, called him. The astonishing news that the Costa Ricans had been driven out of Nicaragua within weeks by a disastrous cholera epidemic was greeted in the United States with both astonishment and joy. Walker was given credit by many for luring the Costa Ricans into Nicaragua so they could be destroyed by the disease. Some of his supporters now considered him a genius. His opponents, like President Mora and Cornelius Vanderbilt, would have considered him merely lucky.

Meanwhile, Walker's army had grown—two hundred recruits had escaped the D.A.'s attention on April 8 and come down from New York on the *Orizaba*'s maiden voyage. The new arrivals more than canceled out Walker's losses at Rivas—fifty-eight killed, sixty-two wounded, and thirteen missing.[4] But the three hundred through passengers on that same *Orizaba* sailing were stranded in Nicaragua for a month, for Morgan and Garrison had yet to organize a steamer between San Juan del Sur and San Francisco. And a number of those passengers, forced to sit at La Virgen for four weeks, came down with cholera; some died there. To the relief of the frustrated surviving passengers, a Morgan and Garrison steamer, the *Sierra Nevada*, dropped anchor on May 19 and took them on board for the last leg of their trip to California. Understandably, those passengers were far from pleased about their enforced stay in cholera-ridden Nicaragua. Neither was William Walker. After all the promises from Morgan and Garrison, the businessmen had failed to keep up their end of the bargain.

It turned out that Morgan and Garrison had been banking on acquiring the Transit Company's San Francisco–based *Sierra Nevada* from Cornelius Vanderbilt. Garrison had put up the loan for Vanderbilt to build the ship back in 1851. And when the mortgage came due at the end of March 1856, Garrison had foreclosed. This had forced the auction of the ship, and Garrison had put in the winning bid, outwitting Vanderbilt's son-in-law James Cross, who had been sent to San Francisco to prevent this very sort of thing from happening. This maneuver had cheaply secured the *Sierra Nevada* for the Morgan and Garrison Line, and she was now sailing under their colors. But the means of acquiring her, while clever, had cost time, and lives. Even worse for Walker, when these passengers arrived in San Francisco and told their harrowing tale, ARN enlistment inquiries at Parker Crittenden's office, not surprisingly, dried up for months.

With the Costa Ricans knocked out of the short war, other opponents seized Walker's attention—most important, Cornelius Vanderbilt. Walker had belatedly realized that Vanderbilt, until recently his tacit supporter, was now out to destroy him for taking away his Transit charter. When the *Orizaba* arrived at Greytown on April 17, Vanderbilt's agent Hosea Birdsall slipped ashore while the ship was waiting for the river steamers to arrive and take off her passengers. As British Ambassador Crampton had promised Vanderbilt, a British warship, the *Eurydice*, was stationed at Greytown. Birdsall informed her commander, Captain John W. Tarleton, that there were five hundred filibuster recruits aboard the *Orizaba* and showed him an April 8 letter from Thomas Lord, vice president of the Accessory Transit Company in New York, authorizing Birdsall to seek the aid of the British navy in the recovery of Transit Company assets in Nicaragua.

Captain Tarleton subsequently sent the *Orizaba*'s Captain Tinklepaugh a note, announcing that he would not permit his passengers to go up the San Juan River and telling him to off-load them at some other port. The tough-as-nails Tinklepaugh, supported by Colonel Hornsby and James Walker, who were among his passengers, sent a written reply to the British officer containing an implied threat that the U.S. Navy would again be asked to bring its guns to Greytown if the British navy interfered with the Transit. Rattled by this and not wanting to damage his career by causing another *Prometheus* incident, Captain Tarleton looked over the *Orizaba*'s waybill and questioned Tinklepaugh's passengers. After two Americans vowed and declared that they were genuine migrants to Nicaragua, Tarleton backed down, giving Tinklepaugh permission to land his passengers, to the frustration of Vanderbilt's agent Birdsall.[5]

This victory for Walker was soon followed by another. Birdsall proceeded to attempt to secure the assets on Punta Arenas, the point across the bay from Greytown, and gave his letter of authorization from Thomas Lord to Joseph N. Scott, Morgan and Garrison's manager in Nicaragua. Scott not only ignored Birdsall but also sent the Lord letter to William Walker, who would later quote verbatim from it.[6] Birdsall, a very ineffective secret agent, was forced to return to New York without having done the slightest good for Vanderbilt in Nicaragua. The Commodore would have to devise another way to foil Walker.

Walker, meanwhile, turned his eye to the political sphere. During May, a supposedly national election for the Nicaraguan parliament and presidency had been held. With the war being prosecuted in the south against the Costa Ricans, the election had involved just the north of the country, with the presidential vote evenly spread among Maximo Jerez, Patricio Rivas, and Mariano Salazar. Following the election, Walker advised that "the irregularity in the voting" and the fact that "the Republic was so disturbed" meant that he "considered the election as invalid," a view that, according to Walker, all parties endorsed.[7]

On May 30, after receiving reports that all was not right with President Rivas and his colleagues at León, Walker rode there accompanied by two hundred riflemen and forty Mounted Rangers. At León, Walker received an enthusiastic welcome from both the common people and President Rivas. That night, there was a lively public reception, where local musicians strummed guitars and sang songs in praise of American valor. But Walker sensed discord among members of the government. Maximo Jerez, who had rejoined Rivas's cabinet, had a cloud over his face, while another minister, Mariano Salazar, made Walker feel uneasy. When Walker shared his concern with Rivas, the president put his colleagues' odd behavior down to rumors that Guatemala and El Salvador were raising armies to invade Nicaragua. But something more suspicious seemed afoot; just what, Walker could not deduce.

News then arrived that Father Vijil, who, at Walker's urging, had been sent to Washington, D.C., to replace the disgraced Parker French as Nicaraguan ambassador to the United States, had received a cordial welcome from Secretary of State Marcy and had been presented to President Franklin Pierce on May 14. When Walker began to discuss the possibility of Vijil coming home, with Jerez replacing him, Jerez became agitated. Then, on June 10, when Walker proposed that the cabinet authorize a new general election, Rivas and Jerez opposed the idea. After Walker insisted, the cabinet endorsed the new election, setting an election date for later that month.

On his way back to the capital, Walker made a halt at the hill town of Masaya. And there, silently, reverently, he stood beside a grave at the Campo Seco, Masaya's cemetery. It was the grave of his youngest brother, James. After James's arrival in Nicaragua in April, Walker had commissioned him a lieutenant and sent him to Company A of the ARN's newly formed Second Light Infantry Battalion, then stationed in Masaya. Once in Nicaragua, James had conciliated his elder brothers, convincing William to reconcile with black sheep, Norvell, and give him back his commission and his command. Intelligent and energetic, young James had proven such a success he was soon promoted to captain and given command of Company A. But in May, James had come down with cholera; he died on May 15. "Had his life been spared," the *Nashville Gazette* was to lament when it published news of James Walker's death, "he would doubtless have been of essential service in the great struggle for the republican liberty in Nicaragua."[8]

As Walker lingered sadly there in Masaya, a dispatch from the north caught up with him. Colonel Natzmer, his military commander at León, warned that President Rivas and Minister Jerez had suddenly withdrawn farther north to Chinandega and that Jerez, as war minister, had ordered Natzmer to remove his troops from parts of León. Suspecting that Rivas and Jerez were about to move against him, Walker promptly ordered all his troops to withdraw into the southern half of the country. Once back in Granada, Walker published a decree dissolving President Rivas's provisional government and appointing Fermin Ferrer acting president. As leading

Nicaraguans who supported Walker, including Don José Maria "Chelon" Valle and Don Mateo Pineda, hurried south to join him, Walker added his own name to the ballot paper for the upcoming election.

The three-day election began on Sunday, June 29, but only in the southern provinces occupied by Walker's troops—who, as nominal Nicaraguan citizens, were also entitled to vote. In response, Rivas canceled the election in the northern provinces, declaring William Walker an enemy of the Nicaraguan people. The election in the south went forward, involving 23,000 of the nation's 35,000 eligible male middle-class voters.[9] According to results published in El Nicaraguense, Rivas received 867 votes; Salazar, 2,087; Ferrer, 4,447; and Walker, 15,835.[10] A clear winner, William Walker had emulated fellow Tennesseean Sam Houston; he was president of his own country.

On election day, Legitimista leader and former president of Nicaragua, José Maria Estrada, had slipped back across the border from Honduras, where he had been given sanctuary by President "Butcher" Guardiola. At the town of Somotillo in the northern mountains, Estrada established an alternative Nicaraguan government, in opposition to both Walker and the Democraticos under Rivas. He also set about raising an army, appointing as his general Tomás Martinez, the former Nicaraguan Legitimista colonel and governor of Rivas who had fled to Costa Rica after being linked with Ponciano Corral's treason. Within a day of Walker's election as president of Nicaragua, former President Rivas, at Chinandega, called on all Nicaraguan men aged between fifteen and sixty to take up arms and drive the Americans from Nicaragua. At the same time, Rivas wrote to the governments of El Salvador and Guatemala, urging them to speedily send the troops they had previously promised for the overthrow of William Walker.

June proved to be a promising month for Walker—not only was he elected president of Nicaragua, but the Morgan and Garrison Transit operation was at last looking professional. Earlier in the month, the New York Daily Times had described it as "neither as permanent nor extensive as it is desirable it should be."[11] But in late June, three Morgan and Garrison steamers had set sail for Nicaragua. On July 6, all three arrived at the same time and landed hundreds of American recruits to bolster Walker's army— the Sierra Nevada from San Francisco, and, arriving the same day at Greytown, a ship each from New York and New Orleans. With the Orizaba sent around Cape Horn to join the *Sierra Nevada* on the Pacific route, two Morgan steamers taken from Mexican Gulf service, the *Tennessee* and the *Calhoun,* had commenced the New York run, while Morgan's SS *Texas* would sail from New Orleans once a month.[12]

When Major Waters and one hundred Rangers reconnoitered as far as León on July 8, they found the city barricaded and occupied by General Mariano Paredes and the five-hundred-man advance guard of a Guatemalan army sent in answer to Rivas's call for help. Five hundred Salvadoran troops led by General Ramon Belloso landed from the sea on Nicaragua's northwest coast that same day. They quickly marched south to link up with the Guatemalans in León.

Even as foreign troops occupied parts of northern Nicaragua, on Saturday, July 12, in the La Merced Church in Granada, thirty-three-year-old William Walker knelt on a cushion in front of a crucifix and took the oath of office as president and chief executive of the Independent Republic of Nicaragua, an oath administered by Fermin Ferrer. Invited guests filled the church, while outside, Walker's army and the people of Granada waited. As Walker emerged into the sunlight and made his way to Government House, thousands of enthusiastic Granadinos and people from as far away as Masaya erupted in applause and cheers. They wore their Sunday best. The women's dresses were all the colors of the rainbow. Children waved the lone-star flag.

"*Viva el Presidente!*" yelled Nicaraguans.

"Death to the enemies of order!" called American soldiers.[13]

Dressed simply in his black campaign coat, baggy trousers, and black felt hat as he celebrated his inauguration, Walker was described by a New York *Tribune* correspondent in the crowd as looking like "a grocery keeper from one of the poorer localities of the Sixth Ward."[14]

Walker had previously assigned fifty Cubans who had arrived with Domingo de Goicuria to serve as the Presidential Guard of President Rivas. Now reconstituted as the Cuban Guard and wearing Spanish-style uniforms and shako headwear provided by Goicuria, the Cubans formed a phalanx around the new president as he addressed the crowd.

Some of Walker's critics expected him to announce that Nicaragua would now be annexed to the United States of America, to become the next U.S.

state, in the same way that Texas had been incorporated into the United States in 1845. The British certainly believed something of this nature was on the agenda, and that the U.S. government was conspiring with Walker to achieve it. British prime minister and former foreign minister Lord Palmerston would write to his foreign minister, Lord Clarendon, that the Americans were "such rogues, and such disagreeable rogues," he feared that "by the indirect agency of such men as Walker and his followers some independent North American State would now be established in Central America, in alliance with the United States if not in Union with them; in short Texas over again."[15]

But when Walker made his inaugural address, he surprised his critics and some of his supporters. "Nicaragua," he declared, as his lone-star flag fluttered from the spire of Granada's Parochial Church behind him, "will control her own destiny at any cost, and will deny the rights of other powers, either neighboring or distant, to occupy or dispose of any part of her territory."[16]

Walker's military band played, his artillery boomed out a twenty-one-gun presidential salute. The people cheered. His soldiers gave him three deep-throated huzzahs. The bells of the city's six churches rang out. Skyrockets screamed into the azure sky. But now, the new ruler of Nicaragua had to cement his rocky throne.

That evening, there was an inauguration banquet at Government House. Among the fifty guests were U.S. Ambassador John Wheeler, foreign consuls, and Catholic clergy. Walker's senior officers, including three generals, were present. Now that he was president, he had made himself a major general, which allowed him to reward Charles Hornsby, Edward Sanders, and Domingo de Goicuria with the rank of brigadier general. His senior Nicaraguan supporters were there—among them loyal old Chelon Valle and the three men whose cabinet appointments Walker would announce within two days—Fermin Ferrer as minister for foreign relations, Mateo Pineda as minister for war, and Manuel Carrascosa as minister of hacienda and public credit.

Walker was not a drinker, so the wines used for the numerous toasts that evening were all light. Walker himself proposed a toast to President Pierce of the United States. And then, as the night became merrier, one of Walker's officers stood, raised his glass, and, with a broad grin, proposed: "To Uncle Billy."

For a moment, Walker looked at him, mystified. And then it dawned on him—*he* was "Uncle Billy." To the astonishment of some observers, who had never seen the new president as much as smile, Walker threw back his head and roared with laughter.[17]

On July 18, the remaining units of General Paredes's Guatemalan army marched into León from the north. That same day, senior military representatives from Guatemala, Honduras, and El Salvador met at the council house on León's plaza with Patricio Rivas and other Nicaraguan Democratico leaders. In that meeting, the generals and colonels signed a concordant in which all parties recognized Rivas as the legitimate president of Nicaragua and which pledged their countries to an alliance that would not rest until Walker and his Yankees had been ejected from Central America.

From now on, the Central American states and parties participating in the coalition against Walker would be known to friend and foe alike as "the Allies." It was the first time in two decades that the countries of Central America had stopped fighting each other and come together in a joint cause. Thanks to William Walker. Thanks also to Cornelius Vanderbilt, for it had been his money that helped arm the troops from Guatemala and El Salvador—money received by those countries' ambassadors in Washington. Not only had the Allies gone to war with Walker, but more important, Vanderbilt, who had more money than all the Central American governments put together, had gone to war with Walker. For Vanderbilt, this was not business; this was personal.

A week after Walker's inauguration, there was another function at Granada's Government House. This gala evening was attended by Granada's elite. The centers of attraction were two American guests of the new president. Elderly General William F. Cazneau was a former general with the army of the Republic of Texas who had participated in the defeat of Santa Anna's Mexican army in 1836. He'd also had the grim task of burying the moldering American dead—legendary Davy Crockett and Jim Bowie among them—after Santa Anna's siege of the Alamo. Cazneau had also been present at the inauguration of Sam Houston as president of Texas. The general was now American commissioner to the Dominican Republic and was associated with Nicaragua's director of migration, Joseph Fabens, in various business ventures in the Caribbean.

Cazneau was accompanied by his equally renowned wife, Jane. Under the pseudonym Cora Montgomery, she had been one of the most influential U.S. journalists for decades. In an article in the *United States Democratic Review* some years earlier, she had proposed the concept of Manifest Destiny—that it was U.S. destiny to expand its borders to the Pacific and elsewhere, a position later adopted by U.S. politicians on both sides of the aisle. Fifty-one-year-old Jane was all for U.S. annexation of Cuba and the Central American states, and over the past year, she had written articles in various American journals, praising William Walker to the skies. Now she had come to deliver the praise personally—and to offer the new president of Nicaragua policy advice.

Walker was able to tell his guests that he was introducing new measures that would enable the rapid Americanization of Nicaragua. Already, he had decreed that English was now a language of equal value to Spanish in Nicaraguan courts of law. And he was moving to set the republic's government on a sound financial footing by issuing millions of dollars' worth of government bonds in the United States, backed by Nicaraguan land. He was abolishing existing high tariffs on imported goods such as cloth, tools, farm implements, and wine—a move designed to encourage American colonists—and in their place would levy a licensing tax on retailers and manufacturers.

More important, Walker had ordered the confiscation of property owned by "enemies of the Republic" and of people who assisted those enemies, appointing William Rogers to the posts of undersecretary of property and commissioner for confiscations. Already, Walker was drafting a list that would before long contain the names of thirty-two leading Nicaraguan families and cover fifty-six ranches and twenty-one town houses. Confiscations would begin in August, followed by property auctions to be advertised in the press in New York, New Orleans, and San Francisco. When put under the hammer in September, the properties would be valued at $753,000.[18] Another fifty-seven families would be added to the list after the initial confiscations.

The highlight of the July 19 gala at Government House was a speech by Ambassador Wheeler, who read the gathering a letter from Secretary Marcy in Washington: "I am directed by the President of the United States to notify you that I am instructed to establish relations with this State."[19] After applause resounded around Government House's executive chamber, the stout ambassador continued. "The government of the United States hopes to unite cordially with you in the fixed purpose of preventing any foreign power that may attempt to impede Nicaragua's progress by any interference whatever. The great voice of my nation has spoken. Its words must not be unheeded."[20]

As President Walker shook the hand of the ambassador and received the congratulations of his guests, he knew that Wheeler had deliberately misinterpreted Marcy's instructions. Once President Rivas had moved to León, away from Walker's direct influence, Marcy had intended that the Rivas government be recognized, not Walker's new regime—of which he would not learn for some weeks yet. But Marcy had made the mistake of not defining in his letter which Nicaraguan government the United States was recognizing, and Wheeler capitalized on that error to make it appear that Walker had U.S. backing.

Marcy would be livid when he learned of this and would again urge President Pierce to authorize Wheeler's recall. But "Wheeler had a warm friend in the President," a colleague of Wheeler's would later write. "And his earnest and long tried friend, the Hon James C. Dobbin, was Secretary of the Navy." With friends like these, "he was in no danger of being recalled."[21]

Now, Walker hoped, with the impression abroad that his presidency had U.S. endorsement, the other states of Central America would lose their enthusiasm for war with him, in the mistaken belief that the United States would come to his aid.

A vast crowd had gathered in the Granadine Plaza. It was Sunday, August 3, and the city was to witness another execution by firing squad. This time, the victim was to be Democratico leader Mariano Salazar, a minister in Patricio Rivas's opposition government in the north

Salazar had been captured at sea, ironically by a vessel he had previously part-owned. That vessel was the schooner *San José*, the same vessel used by Walker and the Originals to escape from San Juan del Sur the previous year after the First Battle of Rivas. Walker had confiscated the *San Jose,* renamed her the *Granada,* armed her with two cannon, and appointed Lieutenant Callender Irvine Fayssoux to be her commander. Thirty-six-year-old Fayssoux, a dashingly handsome, bearded native of Missouri, had served in the navy of the Republic of Texas and had been with Lopez in 1850 during his failed Cuban revolution. Only arriving in Nicaragua recently, Fayssoux had worked briefly but efficiently as Walker's secretary.

The crowd watched as the white-shirted Democratico minister was placed on a chair in front of a church wall and his firing squad lined up in front of him. According to Walker, the Granadinos had no love for Salazar, regarding him as "the author of most of the misfortunes they had undergone during the civil war."[22] Salazar had personally put up money to equip Democratico units that had subsequently looted the shops of Granada and burned the Jalteva Church during the siege of 1854. Walker would say that the Granadinos "regarded it as a special providence that he should be taken by a schooner he had once owned."[23] Salazar's fate had been sealed after he'd been found carrying Allied dispatches when captured en route to Guatemala by Fayssoux.

Once Patricio Rivas learned of Salazar's capture, he had arrested Dr. Joseph Livingston, an American resident of León and former U.S. consul who had aided Walker when he'd first arrived in Nicaragua. Rivas had announced that if Salazar was released, Livingston would also be set free. In response, Ambassador Wheeler had sent a strongly worded letter to General

Belloso, Allied commander in chief at León, warning that if as much as a hair on Livingston's head was harmed, a severe reaction could be expected from the U.S. government. As for Salazar, Wheeler had said, he was a general of an illegal faction opposed to the legitimate government of Nicaragua. Rivas, bluffed by Wheeler and fearful of U.S. government retribution, spared his American hostage and deported him.

In the Granadine Plaza, a fusillade rang out. The bullet-riddled body of Mariano Salazar slumped to the ground. Granadinos cheered. A doctor moved forward to certify death. With the day's entertainment concluded, the crowd began to disperse. In that crowd were two men, an American and an Englishman, whom circumstance had thrown together. Tall, dark-haired, with a long face and a jutting jaw, Sylvanus H. Spencer was a New Yorker of around thirty years of age who until recently had been an employee of the Accessory Transit Company as master of the San Juan River steamer *Machuca*.[24] But Spencer had fallen out with the new Morgan and Garrison management and was out of a job. His colleague, and the elder of the pair, was Englishman William Robert Clifford Webster. In May, Webster had set up in business at Granada as a migration agent, hoping to profit from the wave of immigrants coming to Nicaragua from the United States. But he hadn't found favor with either President Walker or Ambassador Wheeler. It is unclear whether Walker and Wheeler were aware that to this point in his career, Webster had left "a trail of forgery, swindling and defrauding," using a variety of names, including Clifford, Waters, Brown, and Simpson.[25] But either way, their lack of patronage meant that Webster's latest business venture had failed.

Both Spencer and Webster were running out of money, and both were very interested in the news that the Allies had assembled an army at León, an army that could march on Granada any day. Spencer and Webster had been discussing a way they might profit from their local knowledge. Neither man had any love for William Walker—after all, both were out of work because of him. They believed they had a way to bring about the downfall of President Walker. The trick was finding someone prepared to pay them to turn that idea into reality, and pay them well.

The pair would have thought about going to the Allies with their idea. But they knew that the Central Americans didn't like gringos; besides, they didn't have any money. Spencer and Webster would have thought about talking to the British government. It was common knowledge, reinforced for both men during visits to Greytown, that the British wanted Walker out of Nicaragua. If the British weren't interested in their plan, there was always the U.S. government. But the pair knew better than to approach U.S. ambassador Wheeler—he was clearly in William Walker's corner. Spencer and Webster would have to go to the United States.

Of course, there was always the possibility that before long, the Allied armies would attack Granada, defeat the filibusters, and put Walker in front of a firing squad here in this very plaza. In which case Spencer and Webster's idea would be worthless. But few people in Granada believed that the Central Americans could defeat Walker's Yankee soldiers. By this time, Allied troops had been in León for four weeks. Perhaps they would never garner the courage to advance south; that seemed to be the belief of the Granadinos. It was possible that the Allies would just sit there in the north, posturing and arguing among themselves, until Walker had enough fresh American recruits to take the offensive and drive the invaders back across the northern frontier. As Spencer and Webster ambled away from the execution scene, they discussed their options. If, after a few more weeks had passed, the Allies had not made a move, Spencer and Webster would make their own.

Before the month was out, Spencer and Webster would be on a Morgan and Garrison steamer departing Greytown, bound for New York City.

Within days of Salazar's execution, the Morgan and Garrison steamer *Texas* arrived at Greytown after leaving New Orleans at the end of July. Because of April's Nicaraguan cholera scare, there were only a few recruits for Walker aboard, but one particular passenger was about to change the complexion of Walker's administration.

Pierre Soule had represented Louisiana in the U.S. Senate and been U.S. ambassador to Spain. A handsome and charismatic man, he'd been born in France and spoke many languages, including Castilian, the language of

Spanish nobility. "His fine head and noble air made a deep impression on the people of the country," Walker would say.[26] James Jamison, promoted to captain and company commander since the retreat from Rivas and the death of Captain Breckenridge from his Rivas wound, met the former senator in Granada and was greatly impressed by him. Soule was, said Jamison, "the most fascinating person I ever saw."[27]

Soule also charmed the Granadinos. They called him "Your Excellency" and listened to him "with mingled delight and reverence."[28] But sitting across the desk from President Walker in his Granada office, Soule, an impressively large man of fifty-five, clean-shaven and square-faced, with thick silver hair, held no punches. Officially, he had come to Nicaragua to discuss the raising of five hundred thousand dollars in the United States via the sale of Nicaraguan government bonds. As a result of an agreement Soule reached with Walker, a presidential decree would set up a commission to oversee the issue and sale of the bonds. But that was only part of Soule's mission.

Soule, although French-born, was very much a Southerner in mind-set and a firm advocate of slavery. He fervently counseled Walker to introduce slavery into Nicaragua. Under the constitution of the federated states of Central America, dating back to 1826, slavery had been abolished. When Nicaragua left the federation in 1838, its Constituent Assembly had endorsed the slavery ban. But, said Soule, the slave-owning elite of America's South would only invest in Nicaragua if they could use slave labor to cheaply work their properties. Soule himself would buy La Merced, one of the largest confiscated rural properties on offer at the September auction, with plans to plant it with cotton. But, he now warned Walker, he would only invest further in Nicaragua if Walker legalized slavery once more, allowing Soule to bring in slaves. Other Southerners thought the same way, said Soule. And without Southern investment, he assured the new Nicaraguan head of state, the Walker presidency was doomed.

Walker, who all his life had been against the spread of slavery and who had campaigned for the eventual abolition of it in the United States when he ran the *Daily Crescent* in New Orleans, told Soule he would think on the matter.

BATTLES ON ALL FRONTS

CORNELIUS VANDERBILT COULD NOT BELIEVE CORNELIUS GARRISON'S gall. Here, as bold as brass, was Garrison, in Vanderbilt's Manhattan office on West Fourth Street, offering to make the Commodore a partner in Morgan and Garrison's Nicaragua Line.

As the summer of 1856 was panning out, Garrison had come to New York to consult with partner Charles Morgan. They were feeling pretty smug. After a slow start, their Nicaragua Line was doing good business. By dropping the through fare to $175, they had taken customers away from competitors using the Panama route and filled their own steamers. Business was so good, in fact, that after their New York confab, Morgan and Garrison placed an order for a brand new ocean steamer for the West Coast run. This would bring their Nicaragua fleet up to six ships, with three on each coast. To be called the SS *Queen of the Pacific*, the new ship would be built in New York by Jacob A. Westervelt and Sons and be ready for handing over to her new owners the following April.

But even as Garrison and Morgan had been raising glasses and lighting cigars, Vanderbilt had struck his latest blow. With Garrison in New York City, the Commodore had him hauled into court. No doubt at house counsel Joseph L. White's instigation, the Vanderbilt-controlled Transit Company sued Garrison for five hundred thousand dollars, accusing him of making false financial statements to that same amount while he was acting as West Coast agent for the company. In court, the attorney representing the Transit Company, Charles A. Rapallo, had detailed various allegations against Garrison, including a charge that he had billed thirty-five dollars a ton for coal for the company's steamers, using a fictitious coal dealer and forged documents—coal that had only cost twenty-five a ton—with Garrison pocketing the difference.[1]

And now, with that court case only midway through, the forty-six-year-old Garrison was standing across the long, wide table that served as Vanderbilt's desk. And he was offering Vanderbilt a partnership with Morgan and himself, if the Commodore walked away from the Transit Company, whose shares were now worth just three dollars, down from twenty-three on March 12.[2] This way, by making Vanderbilt their partner in the Nicaraguan operations, and by default also making him a partner with President William Walker of Nicaragua, Morgan and Garrison would make an enemy an ally and would no longer have to watch their backs in dread of Vanderbilt's next assault.

"We could make a good business of it," said Garrison, smiling broadly, "to the exclusion of the Transit Company."[3]

Vanderbilt, sitting the other side of the table, didn't even have to think it over. He shook his head. He'd been fighting Garrison and his crony Morgan tooth and nail for years. Garrison may have outwitted him to snare the *Sierra Nevada* in the spring, but as recently as June, Vanderbilt had extracted his revenge. The mortgages on the Transit Company steamships *Northern Light* and *Star of the West*, both of which were tied up in New York on Vanderbilt's orders, had fallen due on May 31. A total of $124,000 had been owing on the pair of steamers, which had cost $380,000 each to build five years back. Vanderbilt had chaired a meeting of Transit Company directors, at which the steamers, "two of the best boats of the old line" in the opinion of the *New York Times,* had been voted to the Commodore personally, for the sum of the mortgage.[4] This had given the ships to Vanderbilt at a bargain price; they were worth three times as much, in the estimation of the *Times.*

But the mortgagees had other ideas—one lender was financier George A. Hoyt, while the other was none other than Charles Morgan. They foreclosed on the two mortgages, seized the steamers, and put them up for auction. Vanderbilt had been certain that Morgan and Garrison wanted the two ships for their Nicaragua run, so, determined to keep the steamers out of their hands, he had been sure to make the winning bids. He had paid over the odds, but at least he had made sure Morgan and Garrison could not add the *Northern Light* and the *Star of the West* to their fleet, forcing Morgan to take the *Tennessee*, the *Calhoun*, and the *Texas* away from the profitable Gulf routes to serve Nicaragua.

In the past, Vanderbilt had gone into partnership with steamship rivals. But that had been different—he had made a fortune then. Garrison was not offering him more than the mere promise of a profit. "I am working for the stockholders of the Transit Company," Vanderbilt now informed Garrison, adding a few expletives, "and I will not betray them."[5] He called to long-serving clerk Lambert Wardell, who worked beyond double doors in the adjoining office, and instructed him to see Mr. Garrison from the premises.

Once the disappointed Garrison departed, Vanderbilt called in Wardell again and dictated a statement in which he detailed the offer just made to him by Garrison. The magnate then sent the statement to attorney Charles Rapallo, so that the attorney might use it in the court case against Garrison.

Even though the price of Transit Company shares had reached an all-time low, the remaining shareholders had recently given the Commodore a vote of support, expressing their "utmost confidence in the ability and energy of Cornelius Vanderbilt, esq., our President."[6] They had little choice—without the Commodore, whose record suggested he might well restore the company's fortunes, their shares were worthless. So the shareholders had supported his policy of keeping Transit Company steamers tied up, even though the vessels could be making money on other routes—to Panama, for instance. The press hadn't been so obliging. The *Times* had been scathing in its criticism of Vanderbilt's bloody-minded strategy: "Commodore Vanderbilt should consent to alight from his high horse," it had railed, "and resume the practical business temper and good sense which characterize his management of steamboat jobs."[7]

But "Mr. Vanderbilt would have his own way," the *Times* had conceded, and the Transit Company's steamers had continued to lay idle for months. Yet, in his own inimitable fashion, Vanderbilt himself had been secretly making a vast profit from his idle steamships—because they had been tied up. Back in March, as soon as he had returned from Washington and ordered the eight ships off the Nicaragua run, the Commodore had paid a visit to competitor William Aspinwall, head of the Pacific Mail Line, and made a deal with him. For two months, Aspinwall had paid him forty thousand dollars a month on the condition that he would not put his steamers on the Panama run in competition with Aspinwall's own vessels. The money had gone to Vanderbilt personally, not to the Transit Company. Other shareholders knew nothing of the deal.[8]

In June, Aspinwall had balked at the payments, so in July, Vanderbilt had negotiated a new secret deal, giving Aspinwall more for his money. This time, in return for forty thousand dollars a month—the amount would later increase to fifty-six thousand a month—with most of the bribe money coming from the Pacific Mail Line and some now also from the U.S. Mail Line, Vanderbilt pledged not to compete on the Panama line, swore to destroy the Morgan-Garrison Nicaragua Line, and undertook to run his steamers to the Gulf of Mexico in competition with Morgan to put even more pressure on his adversary. Vanderbilt in fact established the Vanderbilt Gulf Line, operating out of Galveston and New Orleans, commissioning the construction of two purpose-built steamers for the gulf trade: the SS *Opelousa* and the SS *Magnolia*.[9] When Garrison came to see Vanderbilt, he had been blissfully unaware of this covert deal. Only years later would the deal be uncovered, becoming the subject of court action against the Commodore by Transit Company shareholders, when it would be labeled "immoral and in restraint of trade and commerce."[10]

Over the next two years, this deal would net Vanderbilt personally close to a million dollars. He would not pass on a cent to the Transit Company.[11] Vanderbilt kept his end of the bargain, but his deal with the Pacific Mail and U.S. Mail Lines was not why he was still determined to destroy William Walker, "that tin-sojer in Nicaraguey," as he called the new president of Nicaragua.[12] Walker had taken his property—Transit charter and Transit Company assets in Nicaragua—and then went and climbed into bed with Vanderbilt's competitors. This was why Vanderbilt had marked Walker for destruction.

The New York *Herald* had recently declared that most Americans were in sympathy with the Walker government in Nicaragua. But despite this, and, believing that the Commodore would at any moment launch his steamers on the Panama route, the *Herald* sagely warned that the new American-led government of Nicaragua was playing with fire, and "its gallant head has periled its hitherto bright prospects. It will be seen that it is in Mr. Vanderbilt's power to kill off the new government by opening another route and thus cutting off Walker's communications with San Francisco and New York."[13]

Vanderbilt's tactics were not as the *Herald* predicted, but they were still aimed at killing off the new Nicaraguan government. Quietly and covertly, the Commodore had "poured money into the capitals of the small countries adjoining Nicaragua."[14] It was Vanderbilt who had armed the conscript soldiers of the Allied armies that had blossomed from nothing in the north and now sat at León. He had sent the Allied governments money; he had purchased weapons and ammunition and shipped it all to Central America. The invasion of Nicaragua by the Allied armies had been motivated, financed, and equipped by Vanderbilt. Yet, for all his expenditure in support of the war-making efforts of the Allied governments, no doubt financed, in part, by the Aspinwall bribe payments, Vanderbilt had poured money down the drain if the Allied armies continued to sit on their rumps, like matrons at a church picnic, and failed to engage Walker's filibusters. As far as the Commodore was concerned, there had to be another way to beat William Walker, and by hook or by crook, he would find it.

Colonel José Dolores Estrada watched with paternal pride as the men of his little army filed past his horse toward the San Jacinto ranch house. Sixty-four-year-old Estrada sat tall and straight in the saddle. With thick, gray hair and a noble bearing, he looked every inch the aristocrat. Yet he'd started out in Nicaragua's army back in 1827 as a humble private and worked his way up through the ranks to become a colonel in the Legitimista army during the civil war. After the peace, he had gone north to Honduras rather than accept filibuster-sponsored rule in his country. In July, Estrada had returned to Nicaragua with the Legitimistas' former president, José Maria Estrada (no relation).

But in August, the former president had been assassinated at Somotillo. Yet, instead of dividing the Legitimistas and Democraticos even further, the assassination had thrown them together. General Tomás Martinez, General Fernando Chamorro, and other senior Nicaraguan Legitimista officers vowed loyalty to Patricio Rivas. Soon, General Martinez would march south toward Walker-held territory from Matagalpa with the bulk of what he called the Army of the Septentrion. As Martinez prepared, he had given Colonel Estrada an advance guard of three companies and ordered him to pass down east of Lake Managua toward Granada, gathering recruits as he went.

Colonel Estrada's advance guard numbered just 17 officers and 140 enlisted men. Of the enlisted men, 120 were Matagalpa Indians, tough, brave, and fiercely independent Nicaraguan natives.[15] They marched barefoot, dressed in tattered white shirts and straw hats, and with ancient flintlock muskets on their shoulders. As they moved south into the Chontales district in late August, Estrada's forward scouts had surprised a filibuster detachment herding cattle to feed Walker's troops, on the Los Llanos cattle ranch near Tipitapa. Estrada's scouts had shot the detachment's commander, Captain Ubaldo Herrera, from the saddle.

Now, in the first days of September, Colonel Estrada's column arrived at the San Jacinto ranch of Miguel Bolanos, almost twenty miles to the northeast of Tipitapa—where, Estrada knew, there was a Walker garrison. Here at the San Jacinto ranch, Estrada would wait for General Martinez to join him with the rest of the Army of the Septentrion. Estrada's men were tired and hungry, but before he let them rest, the colonel made them fortify the ranch house, for he expected the filibusters to send out patrols looking for those responsible for the death of Captain Herrera, and he wanted to be prepared. The San Jacinto hacienda was a single-story adobe structure with two wings fronted by porticos, all set on a low rise, with cattle corrals on either side. Estrada's men built adobe barricades at the corrals, and a trench all the way around the house linked to the corrals. Only once these defenses were created did the colonel allow his men to rest.

The rain pelted down. It was the night of September 4, and in the inky darkness, Lieutenant Colonel McDonald and forty men of Walker's Second Rifles Battalion, led by a Captain Jarvis, found what cover they could beneath the trees and pulled their capes up around their necks. The hacienda of the San Jacinto estate was less than a mile away.

Walker—who continued to use the title of General rather than that of President—had been distressed by the death of Captain Herrera. The young captain had joined Walker for the second campaign in the south the previous summer, bravely leading his Democratico company at the Battle of La Virgen and acting as a guide for the taking of Granada. And it had been Herrera who commanded the firing squad that executed Mateo Mayorga. Immediately after Walker had heard that the loyal Nicaraguan captain had been shot from his horse while herding cattle, he sent orders to McDonald, his post commander at Tipitapa, to cross the Tipitapa River and make a reconnaissance in force north toward Los Llanos in search of Herrera's killers.

On the march, McDonald had learned that a hostile force of unknown size had occupied the hacienda of the San Jacinto ranch. He assumed it to be the small force that killed Captain Herrera. Now, as his men hunched their shoulders in the rain, McDonald decided to wait until daybreak before approaching the hacienda.

As dawn broke on September 5, McDonald and his black-clad riflemen approached the hacienda at the double-quick march. The rain had abated, but the ground was soggy underfoot. By the time he was a hundred yards from the hacienda, McDonald could see, in the new day's golden light, the adobe barricades at the corrals and straw-hatted heads lining a trench to the front. On the command of an elderly officer on the hacienda veranda, a ragged line of smoke appeared, stretching the length of the hacienda. Colonel Estrada's untrained Indians were not good shots; not a single bullet claimed its target. But the sight and sound of the volley by 140 muskets staggered the Americans, who had been expecting to face perhaps a dozen natives.

The filibuster attack faltered, then stopped. Running out in front of his men, Captain Jarvis loudly urged them to keep going. Ahead, several of Colonel Estrada's men came out from cover for a clear shot. One of them, Private Exacto Rocha, drew a bead on Jarvis, who raised his pistol and took rapid aim at Rocha. Both fired at the same moment, and both fell. Rocha was killed instantly. Jarvis, mortally wounded, was dragged away by his men, but before an hour had passed, he, too, would die from his wound.

Estrada's men fired another volley. There were no more American fatalities, but the ARN attack was a shambles. Surprised and demoralized, McDonald and his men beat a hasty and disorderly withdrawal and hurried back toward Tipitapa. In their wake, Estrada's dusky recruits let out a victorious cheer.

First Sergeant Andres Castro was, like his comrades, eating a light predawn breakfast. It was five o'clock on the morning of Sunday, September 14, nine days since McDonald's filibusters fled San Jacinto. Twenty-four-year-old Castro was short, slim, and olive-skinned. A native of Managua, he'd served in Tomás Martinez's Legitimista army during the civil war and had considerable combat experience. At the sound of a galloping horse, Castro looked up. Corporal Faustino Salmeron, a scout, came hurtling up to the San Jacinto hacienda in the predawn darkness.

"The enemy are coming!" Salmeron yelled excitedly.[16]

Colonel Estrada emerged from the house and calmly asked Salmeron how many enemy were coming, and from where. The scout estimated that three hundred Yankees were approaching the hacienda from the direction of Tipitapa. Seeming unconcerned by the number, Estrada summoned his officers and instructed them to take up their prearranged defensive positions with their men. As the officers ran to obey, Sergeant Castro grabbed his musket and hurried to join Lieutenant Miguel Velez's platoon at the front of the house.

As the sun began to rise, Lieutenant Colonel Byron Cole halted his mounted contingent with a raised hand. This was the same Byron Cole who'd employed William Walker at his Sacramento newspaper and later arranged the first contract with Provisional Director Castellon that brought Walker and his "Originals" to Nicaragua. Only recently given a senior ARN commission by Walker, Cole had just led an expedition to the mountainous northeast, extending Walker's rule, rounding up deserters, making a study of the territory with a view to future North American colonization, and dispensing Walker government cattle supply quotas to local ranchers. At Tipitapa, on his way back to Granada, Cole had bumped into an ARN column heading for San Jacinto to eject Colonel Estrada and his men. Cole had eagerly taken over its command.

Cole's party was not three hundred strong as Estrada's scout had estimated. It numbered just seventy men, all mounted. Most were volunteers, ARN officers, and former officers serving with Walker's civil administration, who'd been disgusted by the poor performance of McDonald and his men. "Seeing the enthusiasm of some officers and citizens," Walker later wrote, "and desirous of ascertaining more exactly the strength of the enemy beyond Tipitapa," the president had consented to the volunteers' reconnoitering San Jacinto and assigned a company of Mounted Rangers to accompany them.[17]

One of the volunteers, Charles Callahan, only in his twenties, had recently been appointed Walker's collector of customs at Granada. He was also the Nicaragua correspondent for the *New Orleans Daily Picayune* newspaper. Walker permitted Callahan to join the others because the young man had, in Walker's words, "a thirst for action."[18] Such was the enthusiasm of the party; they had ridden through the night to get here. Despite the hard ride, they'd brought along the ARN's mascot, "Warrior," a shaggy dog who lined up with the troops on parade and trotted at the front of marching columns.

Colonel Cole's party dismounted. As horses and mascot were taken to the rear, Cole divided his small command into three sections, appointing Major Cal O'Neal, Major Watkins, and Robert Milligan, a former lieutenant, to lead them. Cole told his officers that, as they were likely to be outnumbered, they must get their men in among the enemy quickly and dispose of them hand to hand. The Americans fanned out, formed three lines, and then, with Cole at the forefront, advanced at the walk for a frontal attack on the hacienda.

In the early morning light, Colonel Estrada, sitting on a battered leather stool on the hacienda's veranda, could see filibusters in their black coats and hats, at a distance of two thousand yards, approaching in three parallel lines and at a steady march. With a yell, the filibusters broke into a trot. One of their lines continued toward the house. The other two swung left and right to tackle the fortified corrals on the flanks.

Estrada ordered his men to hold their fire. He waited and waited, as the charge brought the filibusters closer at a nerve-wracking pace. At a range of a hundred yards, Estrada gave the order. His troops let off a devastating volley. Unlike the skirmish on the fifth, this time Estrada's men displayed much improved accuracy; a victory under the belt had steadied nerves and aim. From one side of the battlefield to the other, Americans were felled. The filibuster charge faltered. Then, as the Nicaraguans reloaded, the Yankees renewed the charge. The Americans reached the trench line, only to be driven back. Again, after a pause to lick their wounds and to count their diminishing numbers, they charged into the jaws of death. Again they were repulsed.

For a third time, the Americans charged. All over the battlefield, there were displays of desperate courage. On the Nicaraguan right, an unidentified filibuster in a U.S. Army uniform made a flying leap and hurdled the trench, only to be shot dead on the other side by Lieutenant Adam Soli. In the center, another Yankee officer crossed the trench. Finding he'd emptied his smoking pistol, the American threw it away and, using his sword, cut down several Nicaraguans who came at him with fixed bayonets.

Sergeant Andres Castro reached to the leather ammunition box on his belt, only to find it empty. Casting aside his musket, he grabbed a large stone from the hacienda's foundations and ran at the American swordsman, crashing the stone into the Yankee's head, killing him. Moments later, an American bullet from the other side of the trench slammed into Castro's leg, and he went down grasping his shattered limb.

Once again, the filibusters were driven back and had to regroup. After this repulse, Cole called a council of war. Since they had criticized McDonald's men for giving up the fight three weeks earlier, the proud Americans weren't willing to acknowledge defeat. It was now agreed to launch a concentrated attack on the corral to the right. A little before 10:00 A.M., with their revolvers reloaded, the Americans went forward at the run, yelling, "Hurrah, Walker!"[19]

The young Nicaraguan officer at the corral, Ignacio Jarquin, had joined General Martinez's army so recently he had yet to receive his lieutenant's commission. Colonel Estrada had told him to sacrifice his life rather then let the filibusters take his position, and Jarquin was faithful to his orders, dying while fighting the Yankees chest to chest. Around him, several of his men also fought to the last. The Americans took the corral, but at high cost. Former ARN officer Robert Milligan was among those killed. Byron Cole took a bullet in the torso, although he tried to shrug off the wound. Cal O'Neal was wounded in the arm but was still full of fight. Major Watkins had a bullet in the hip and was sitting with his back against a barricade, hardly able to move. As the surviving Americans took up defensive positions at the corral, finding cover for the first time during the battle, the Nicaraguans at the other corral and in the trench line poured fire into their position.

Gun smoke clouded the air, and the noise of battle was so great that Colonel Estrada had to shout to be heard. From his veranda stool, he called newly promoted Captain Liberato Cisne to him. Yelling and pointing, Estrada told Cisne to take the platoons of Lieutenants José Ciero and Juan Fonseca, circle around behind the hacienda, and bayonet-charge the Yankees from the rear. Cisne saluted and hurried away. Gathering the seventeen surviving men of the Ciero and Fonseca platoons, Cisne led them to the rear of the house, where they jumped the trench. Then, in a crouch, they moved undetected around behind the corral. On the young captain's command, they all fired at once, then, with fixed bayonets, rose up. With Cisne, Ciero, and Fonseca wielding their swords, they charged into the rear of the filibusters, yelling: "*Viva* Martinez! *Viva* Nicaragua!"[20]

The heads of Cole and his men jerked around. The Nicaraguan charge took the Americans completely by surprise. Totally unnerved and thinking many more Nicaraguans were charging them than was the case, the filibusters broke and scattered in all directions. This time, there was no thought of regrouping. Carrying wounded with them, the Americans fled to their horses, mounted up, and galloped away, after a battle that had lasted much of the morning.[21]

Captain Bartholomew Sandoval received Colonel Estrada's permission to give chase. Estrada himself mounted Corporal Salmeron's horse, but, after going a short distance, left the pursuit to the younger men and returned to the hacienda. The filibusters had abandoned twenty horses, which the

Nicaraguans used for the chase. On the road to Tipitapa, they overtook nine Yankees, killing them all. They tracked another eighteen to the nearby San Ildefonso ranch. Searching the ranch buildings, Corporal Salmeron discovered Byron Cole, sitting, badly wounded and armed with two pistols and a rifle. Cole was too weak to resist; his weapons were knocked aside. The pale lieutenant colonel was dragged outside. The other seventeen hiding filibusters, several of them badly wounded, were also captured. One identified himself as a doctor.

The filibuster prisoners were brought back to the San Jacinto hacienda. Colonel Estrada had found the bodies of eighteen Americans in the grounds; with the nine killed on the road to Tipitapa, the Yankees had lost twenty-seven men. Estrada's losses were twenty-eight men, plus a number wounded. Around the battle site, his soldiers collected thirty-two enemy rifles, some of them the prized new breech-loading Sharps variety, plus twenty-five revolvers, as well as numerous discarded hats, caps, and capes. A number of letters were also found on American bodies, and these were brought to Estrada in case they contained valuable intelligence.[22]

As the American prisoners were locked away in an outbuilding, Estrada scribbled a note to General Martinez, telling of the victory at San Jacinto and asking what he should to with his prisoners. Bearing the note and captured letters, a mounted courier galloped north to Martinez at Matagalpa.

That afternoon, American survivors began to stream into Tipitapa. Bloodied and exhausted, they brought tales of woe from San Jacinto. One of them, Wiley Marshall, died shortly after reaching the town. Garrison commander McDonald promptly hacked down the wooden bridge over the Tipitapa River to slow an enemy advance. *New Orleans Picayune* correspondent Charles Callahan escaped the San Jacinto battlefield only to be captured by local Indians near Segovia. They stripped the young American, administered five hundred lashes, then killed him slowly, agonizingly, by cutting him in pieces.[23]

When twenty-five San Jacinto survivors rode back into the capital, they were accompanied by Warrior the dog, "with his head lowered and his tail between his legs."[24] Once Walker learned the details of the disaster at San Jacinto, he abandoned Tipitapa, withdrawing McDonald's garrison to Managua.

On the afternoon of Tuesday, September 16, Byron Cole and his seventeen fellow prisoners were released from the hut where they'd been kept for two days. Colonel Estrada's troops herded them into a courtyard behind the San Jacinto hacienda. Here, a magnificent old ceiba tree spread.

That morning, Colonel Estrada had received instructions from General Martinez—the prisoners were to be executed, at once. And Estrada was told to save bullets; no firing squad for them. The Yankees were to be hanged. No trial. No time to reflect. No ceremony. No exceptions. Eighteen rope nooses were swiftly prepared.

And there, from the limbs of the courtyard ceiba, one after the other, Byron Cole and his fellow adventure-seekers were strung up and left dangling like decorations on a Christmas tree.

General Ramon Belloso paced the floor. Since 1854, he had been El Salvador's most senior general. Now, surrounded by generals and colonels from four countries, the forty-six-year-old was in a quandary. Should they attack William Walker, or should they continue to wait for Walker to attack them in their strongly fortified position at León?

In 1833, Belloso, then a newly commissioned captain, had ruthlessly put down an insurrection of native Indians in El Salvador. He'd gone on to command Salvador's 150-man Presidential Honor Guard. Now, resplendent in a uniform emblazoned with a fruit salad of gold braid, he looked like a caricature of a Napoleonic general. In June, Patricio Rivas had named Belloso commander of all Allied forces in Nicaragua, much to the displeasure of the generals from Guatemala and Honduras and Rivas's own chief general, Maximo Jerez. Somehow, despite personal rivalries and old cross-border feuds, the Allied armies had operated as one.

But Belloso's reputation had been made many years before, and the younger officers at León suspected that he had lost his courage. They wanted to come to grips with the "buccaneer of the north," as they called Walker, and his pirate crew. And, after sitting at León for two idle months, the electrifying news of Colonel Estrada's comprehensive defeat of Walker's filibusters at San Jacinto signaled to them that it was time the main army went on the offensive. Previously, General Paredes, the Guatemalan commander, had agreed with Belloso when he counseled caution. But Paredes was seriously ill and unable to leave his bed. In his stead, Paredes's zealous young chief of staff, Colonel José Zavala, pushed for action, and other officers agreed with him.

Zavala reminded Belloso word had come that General Martinez was on the march from Matagalpa with four hundred Nicaraguan troops. Planning to link up with Colonel Estrada's advance guard at San Jacinto, Martinez expected to be in a position to threaten Granada before the week was out. The Allies had come to fight Walker, said Zavala and his colleagues. Were they merely to lounge around camp while Martinez did all the fighting and reaped all the glory? Belloso, realizing that the Nicaraguans, Guatemalans, and Hondurans were likely to march on Granada without him, gave in. He ordered the entire Allied army to prepare to march south.

NEW BATTLEGROUNDS

CORNELIUS VANDERBILT'S CLERK LAMBERT WARDELL INFORMED HIM that a Hispanic gentleman was in the outer office to see him. The gentleman's name, said Wardell, was Domingo de Goicuria, and he claimed to have something of advantage to propose to Mr. Vanderbilt.

A frustrated Vanderbilt was in quest of a new weapon in his Nicaraguan war. Despite the money and weapons the Commodore had heaped on the Central American governments, their Allied army was, the last he heard, still sitting in León, which, to his mind, made it about as useful as a ship in a desert. The Transit Company's legal action against Cornelius Garrison had fallen through—Judge Joseph S. Bosworth of the New York Superior Court had thrown out the case on the grounds that without the records relating to Vanderbilt's charges against Garrison, which were all in California, Vanderbilt's claims were nothing more than hearsay. The case had done nothing to advance the Commodore's campaign against Garrison, Morgan, and William Walker.

Now, recognizing his visitor's name and knowing that he was a general in Walker's army, Vanderbilt called for Senor Goicuria to be shown in. When the Cuban walked in, gushing compliments and small talk in heavily accented English, the circumspect Vanderbilt directed him to one of the armchairs across the room, easing himself into another.

Goicuria had come to the United States as President Walker's special ambassador, first to promote the sale of Nicaraguan government bonds. He was then under instructions to sail to Europe to convince the British and the French to invest in Nicaragua. He carried letters from Walker for the

European governments, and in the letter to the British, the American president of Nicaragua decried American interest in annexing Central America and declared that despite U.S. public opinion that favored American annexation of Cuba, this would not happen, either.

In his letter to the French, Walker made an intriguing proposal, one that directly affected Vanderbilt. Mindful of Pierre Soule's warnings about the essential need of slave labor, but clearly not comfortable with slavery on the pattern applied in the American South, Walker proposed an African slave "apprenticeship" program. According to Walker's proposal, the French would ship African "apprentices" to Nicaragua from their African colonies. In return, Walker would grant France the right to build the contemplated Nicaraguan canal—the right he had stripped from Cornelius Vanderbilt. Details of Walker's apprenticeship scheme were not spelled out, but, as apprenticeship involves a prescribed period of indentured labor, Walker apparently intended that African slaves shipped in by the French would be given their freedom after some years of unpaid labor.

To facilitate this program and to satisfy Soule and other potential Southern investors, Walker, on September 22, had issued a decree annulling the 1838 Act of the Constituent Assembly, which had ratified the previous Federal Constitution. This soon became universally known as the Slavery Decree, because it set aside the abolition of slavery in Nicaragua. Walker's stated intent was to "bind the Southern States to Nicaragua" and "to make it appear that the American movement in Nicaragua did not contemplate annexation" to the United States—as the Northern states were antislavery.[1]

Walker still had an ideological problem with slavery and consoled himself that he had not actually reinstated it in Nicaragua with his decree. He would write: "It was generally supposed that the latter reestablished slavery in Nicaragua. Whether this be a strictly legal deduction may be doubted; but the repeal of the prohibition certainly prepared the way for the introduction of slavery."[2] But Walker outsmarted himself. While he had merely created the appearance of slavery's reintroduction, his opponents, especially those in surrounding countries, seized on the Slavery Decree as proof that William Walker had come to enslave the peoples of Central America.

Despite this apparent concession by Walker to supporters in the United States, Domingo de Goicuria had found, in talks with financiers in both New Orleans and New York about the purchase of Nicaraguan bonds, that the money men failed to see either Nicaragua or the government of William Walker as secure investments. Time and again, Goicuria had been politely shown the door. So, not wishing to fail Walker, Goicuria had conceived a grand plan, one that would make his president and Cornelius Vanderbilt partners. It was a plan conceived in naïve ignorance of the fact that Vanderbilt was intent on destroying Walker as a matter of principle.

Without consulting his president back in Granada, the Cuban had come to West Fourth Street to propose that Commodore Vanderbilt loan William Walker's government a quarter of a million dollars. This would reduce the government bond sales target by half and would encourage other investors to follow the Commodore's lead. The idea made good business sense to Goicuria, because, in return for the loan, Vanderbilt would have his Transit Route rights across Nicaragua restored by Walker. Under Goicuria's plan, the day that Vanderbilt resumed shipping services to Nicaragua, he would pay $100,000 to Walker's government, with the remaining $150,000 payable within twelve months.[3]

Vanderbilt nodded. Oh, yes, indeedy, he could be quite amenable to Goicuria's very interesting proposition. Then, to see how far he could manipulate the gullible Cuban, Vanderbilt told Goicuria he'd heard that a New York businessman by the name of George Law had recently purchased thousands of obsolete muskets from the U.S. Army, employing an English arms expert, Charles Frederick Henningsen, to rebore them to take the Minié rifle round, before selling them at a handsome profit. Vanderbilt didn't tell Goicuria that he'd learned this while buying arms for the opponents of Walker or that Law was "Live Oak George," one of the Commodore's greatest competitors. Vanderbilt proposed that if Goicuria approached Law, without mentioning the Commodore, and purchased the weapons for Walker, Vanderbilt would put up the money for the acquisition—supposedly to prove to Walker that he was genuinely interested in Goicuria's loan scheme. In reality, Vanderbilt was using Goicuria. Were Goicuria to obtain Law's weapons, Vanderbilt would send them to the Allies.

Unaware that Vanderbilt was playing him for a fool, Goicuria rushed away to write immediately to Walker, seeking approval of his Vanderbilt loan scheme, at the same time planning to surprise Walker by later sending him thousands of free Minié rifles, courtesy of the nice Mr. Vanderbilt.

William Walker looked around the Jalteva Plaza outside the gutted remains of Granada's Jalteva Church, a burned-out relic of the civil war, as his troops industriously filled ammunition pouches and checked their weapons in preparation for the march against the Allied army. The enemy was near, having advanced to occupy Masaya, just twenty-five miles to the west of Granada. It was a little before midday on Saturday, October 11, and Walker was finally going on the offensive.

As General Belloso's combined army advanced south in late September and early October, Walker's troops had pulled out of one town after another ahead of them. The Allies had briefly occupied Managua on September 24, pausing just long enough to put Walker-appointed Prefect Herrera, brother of the late Captain Herrera, in front of a firing squad and to lodge Colonel Estrada's San Jacinto wounded, including Sergeant Andres Castro, in a hospital.[4] As the Allies advanced, Walker's garrison at Masaya had left in such a hurry it had abandoned a field gun in the middle of the road, allowing the Allies to add it to their arsenal. At Nindiri, three miles from Masaya, Belloso's main force had linked up with General Martinez's Army of the Septentrion. As many as twenty-three hundred Allied troops now occupied Masaya.

With the Morgan and Garrison line now operating efficiently, Walker had received numerous new recruits over the past few months. During the same period, he'd suffered his first large-scale desertions. In July, twenty-three men who had arrived from New Orleans with their own weapons and saddles turned from Rangers to outlaws, raiding French gold mines in the rugged east, until, on August 8, Legitimistas under Captain Damaso Calo shot down twenty-one of them on a mountain road. Then there was the case of the two hundred German recruits from New York—within two weeks of their arrival in Nicaragua, only a handful were still marching for Walker; the rest, finding the soldiering life not to their liking, had slipped away in the night. Despite the desertions, Walker had 1,200 men fit for duty, 135 of them officers. With 200 men at Rivas and San Juan del Sur guarding the Transit and leaving another 200 to garrison Granada under General Birkett D. Fry, 800 men were available for an assault on Masaya.[5]

Amid the preparations in the crowded plaza, Walker, spying a youth barely in his teens whose rifle was bigger than he was, suggested the youngster become a drummer boy.

"No thanks, General," said the boy. "I've never seen a picture of a battle yet that the first thing in it wasn't a dead drummer boy with a busted drum."[6]

At noon, as Walker's army marched out of Granada past waving Granadinos, pride of place in the column was taken by two twelve-pound mountain howitzers recently received from New York along with four hundred Minié rifles, courtesy of a surprise benefactor—"Live Oak" George Law, Cornelius Vanderbilt's fierce competitor. After Law had been approached by Domingo de Goicuria with an offer to buy his Minié rifles, Law had agreed and Goicuria had arranged to send them to Central America aboard the *El Dorado*. At the last minute, Law had discovered that Goicuria intended paying with Vanderbilt's money. Law had not only backed out of the deal but also sent some of his rifles to Walker, as a gift, to spite the Commodore.[7]

Law had additionally given twenty-five thousand dollars to arms expert Charles Henningsen to purchase heavy ordnance for Walker.[8] The howitzers were a product of that largesse. To avoid the attention of New York authorities, they'd been sent to Granada disguised, without their gun carriages. Walker himself was unaware of the extent of the problems his agents in New York were having with the district attorney's office and had blamed the lack of carriages on bungling by his Manhattan representatives. It took carpenters in Granada a week to fashion carriages of a sort for the two guns, but now Walker was ready to blast the Allies out of Masaya.

The lumbering guns and an inclining mountain road turned the march into a crawl. It was 9:00 P.M. before Walker's eight hundred men completed the trek to Masaya. In darkness, the Americans occupied high ground on either side of the road to the east of the town. Ahead, the Allies had built adobe barricades across all roads leading into the town. Pickets exchanged the occasional shot with Allied cavalry scouts, but otherwise, the night passed without incident.

As the sun edged over the horizon behind them, Captain James Jamison and the men of two light infantry companies were dug in around the pair of howitzers, which were primed and loaded. As soon as the light improved, artillery commander Captain Schwartz commenced firing. With impressive detonations, the two big guns let fly, and twelve-pound shells lobbed over the outskirts of the town and then plummeted earthward to explode in the Plazuela San Sebastian, a small square on the eastern side of Masaya, scattering startled Allied troops.

Several more rounds were pumped into the little plaza before Captain Thomas Dolan and fifty black-shirted riflemen rose up and charged the nearest barricade on the city outskirts. Dolan's men only saw the bare heels of withdrawing soldiers in white. Hurdling the barricade, the Americans pounded along the street toward the San Sebastian square. Reaching the plaza, Dolan's men found that Allied troops had left behind a hearty uneaten breakfast, which the Americans happily gulped down.

General Belloso pulled all his troops back to Masaya's main plaza, with the streets leading to it having been barricaded. So Walker called for Captain Hesse. A civil engineer in private life, Hesse had formed a small unit of miners and sappers, and as Walker's troops occupied buildings in the eastern part of town, Hesse's sappers attacked the adobe walls of houses on both sides of the main street with picks and crowbars. Slowly, laboriously, they burrowed through the walls, allowing riflemen to pour through the openings to the next houses, where digging began all over again. It is probable that Hesse or another of Walker's senior officers had been in General Zachary Taylor's forces ten years earlier, when the U.S. Army had used the same technique of bombard and burrow to take the town of Monterey from the Mexican Army during the Mexican War. Schwartz's howitzers again lobbed shells into the main plaza, but this time, the artillery captain's fuses were too short and most shells exploded spectacularly but uselessly in the air. After several hours, one of his howitzers fell off its temporary carriage and was rendered useless.

With the streets leading up to the main plaza absolute death traps and best avoided, Captain Jamison carefully moved his company into the town and assigned his best shots to sniping positions. In the early afternoon, Colonel Markham ordered Jamison's men to fall back to less exposed positions. When Jamison patted one of his marksmen on the back and told him to withdraw, the kneeling American rifleman, who had rested his weapon on a portico railing and was sighting along the rifle's barrel, did not move. Looking closer, Jamison saw a neat bullet hole in the man's forehead; the American sniper was dead.

With the steeples of the churches of Granada in the distance, Colonel José Zavala ordered the seven hundred troops strung out along the Rivas road behind him to move to the attack. Colonel Zavala had been in charge of his country's troops in Nicaragua ever since General Paredes fell ill. With Paredes still in his sickbed back at León, Zavala had camped with five hundred of his Guatemalans and four hundred Nicaraguan Legitimista troops at the village of Diriomo, halfway between Masaya and Nandaime, on the road leading from Granada to Rivas. General Belloso had placed Zavala's troops there to prevent Walker from escaping south and to prevent filibuster reinforcements from reaching Walker from Rivas and San Juan del Sur. But Zavala, who had been arguing with Belloso for months, had other ideas.

There was an American named Harper serving with Zavala as a scout. In April, Harper had come to Nicaragua from San Francisco expecting a commission from Walker, but Walker had recognized him as a man with a criminal record in California and had rejected him. In response, Harper had switched sides. He had been urging Zavala to make a surprise attack on Granada while Walker was occupied at Masaya, and without consulting General Belloso at Masaya, Zavala had ordered seven hundred of his troops to march, leaving a two-hundred-man rear guard to follow along later.

In Granada, just as the Granadinos and Walker's garrison were sitting down to lunch, Zavala's troops reached the southern outskirts of the city and surged toward the Granadine Plaza. Cries of alarm rang throughout the city, and General Fry's troops and civil officials rushed to take up defensive positions. John B. Lawless, an Irish-born U.S. citizen, had a hide-exporting business in the southern suburbs. A longtime resident of the city, he had been on friendly terms with the Legitimistas for years and had several times interceded with General Walker on their behalf. Lawless was certain he would not be harmed by the Allied troops and refused to leave his premises. He was standing in his doorway unfolding a U.S. flag when Allied troops dashed up, grabbed him, and hauled him away. Lawless was taken to the ruined Jalteva Church, stood against a wall, and executed by firing squad. For good measure, his body was repeatedly bayoneted.

Elsewhere, the Reverend William Ferguson, a Methodist minister, and the American Bible Society's Reverend D. H. Wheeler were dragged from their wives and children and hustled to the Jalteva. They, too, were put against a wall and shot. The bodies of all three Americans were then stripped naked and tossed into the Jalteva Plaza. The message was clear—the Central American troops hated Yankees. At the home of Father Rossiter, chaplain to the ARN, an Englishman whose family had recently arrived in Granada from New York was just sitting down to lunch with his wife and young children. Guatemalan soldiers appeared at the open window; one put his musket through the window and fired. The ball missed the Englishman but instantly killed his six-year-old son.

At Granada's hospital, which was filled with Americans and Granadinos wasting away with yellow fellow, Dr. Douglas Wilkins and his medical attendants, the twelve Germans of the ARN band, took up arms and defended the building from doors and windows. Father Rossiter was also at the hospital, and he astonished everybody by grabbing up a rifle and joining the defense.

A detachment sent by General Fry to protect the American embassy had just taken up positions when Zavala's troops arrived and occupied houses across the street. The Guatemalans poured fire into the embassy, taking particular pleasure in riddling the Stars and Stripes fluttering outside.

"Come out, come out, *Ministerio Filibustero!*" the attackers yelled. Ambassador Wheeler declined to accept the invitation.[9]

Government House was defended by Walker's senior civil servants, including Paymaster General Jones, Judge Thomas Bayse, and Acting

Recorder Major Angus Gillis—the latter being the father of the Rangers' Lieutenant Gillis killed during the Second Battle of Rivas; the elder Gillis came to Nicaragua to join Walker's army after hearing of his son's death. Meanwhile, as editor Juan Tabor and his staff defended the office of the *El Nicaraguense,* Tabor, while firing from a window, was hit and collapsed with a shattered thigh. Elsewhere, Major Theodore Potter, now serving with the ordnance department after being wounded at Second Rivas, dived from building to building to direct the defense, then took charge at the Principal, the guardhouse on the plaza, near the cathedral. Meanwhile, Captain Swingle of the artillery seemed to be everywhere.

As the battle for Granada raged, the Americans were determined to hold the main plaza, just as, twenty-five miles away, the Allies were determined to hold the main plaza at Masaya.

By nightfall, Walker's sappers had pushed to within a line of houses surrounding Masaya's main plaza. But those houses were occupied by General Belloso and fourteen hundred Salvadoran and Nicaraguan troops. A courier from Granada now reached Walker, bringing news of Colonel Zavala's attempt to take his capital behind his back. Walker promptly dispatched his chief aide, Lieutenant Colonel F. A. Laine, together with Colonel Thomas Fisher and a company of Mounted Rangers, to provide Fry with what immediate help they could. As for the remainder of the force laying siege to Masaya, Walker ordered it to prepare to withdraw at dawn and march back to Granada to relieve their comrades.

Dew was forming on the ground as Laine, Fisher, and the Rangers set off. Taking a shortcut, they ran into a large enemy detachment in the darkness. Turning aside, they slid down a lane toward Diriomo and barreled straight into more Allied troops—Colonel Zavala's two-hundred-man rear guard marching to join the attack on Granada. Again the Americans evaded the enemy, only to ride into another, smaller party of foot soldiers blocking their way. This time, Fisher decided to fight his way through.

Fisher's Rangers were equipped with the new Sharps rifle—designed by Christian Sharps, it was the first breech-loading rifle to see service in Central America. Sharps' rifle was nine inches shorter than a musket and six inches shorter than other rifles, making it much easier to handle. But the real innovation of the Sharps rifle was the powder cartridge made of paper that was inserted into a chamber in the weapon's breech. After the cartridge was loaded, the breech block was pulled back. This clipped the end off the cartridge, exposing the powder to a Maynard Tape Primer. The hammer was then dragged back and cocked. The trigger, when pulled, released the hammer, which set off the primer, which ignited the powder.

No one had told Fisher's Rangers that they should keep their paper cartridges dry. All their cartridges had been made damp by the night's dew, and when the Americans attempted to fire at the enemy in their path, they merely heard dull, embarrassing clicks. It was suddenly every man for himself. Horsemen dived off in all directions. A desperate hand-to-hand struggle ensued. Most of the Americans made good their escape, but Walker's aide Laine, in his flashy Cuban Guard uniform, attracted more attention than the others—surrounded, he was savagely dragged from his horse.

A little after 9:00 A.M. the next day, having marched since dawn to reach Granada, James Jamison and his men flattened themselves against the ground on the city's western outskirts. Solid shot whooshed overhead, fired by an enemy field gun at a hastily erected barricade ahead. In the far distance, Jamison could see the lone-star flag of William Walker's republic still flying from the steeple of the Parochial Church, the highest point in Granada, indicating that General Fry and his defenders had held out through the night.

A boom from the rear signaled that Captain Schwartz's one effective howitzer, sited on the road, had been brought into action. Its very first shell dropped squarely onto the enemy gun emplacement. In a burst of orange flame, black smoke, and lethal shrapnel, the direct hit shattered the barricade and killed many of the men manning the cannon, bringing a cheer from the waiting ARN troops. Colonel Markham, sword in hand, jumped up and called his troops to charge. With a roar, Jamison and the men of the First Infantry rose up and followed Markham at the run, swiftly capturing the gun position. Now General Walker, astride his horse as usual, ordered the rest of the army to hurry to Birkett Fry's aid.

Colonel Markham yelled to Jamison to secure the San Francisco Convent north of the plaza. Built in 1778 for the Franciscan Order, next door to the San Francisco Church, the building was the ARN's principal quartel in the city. It had been captured from Fry's troops by the Guatemalans during the night, but when Jamison and his light infantrymen swarmed in through one of the convent's side doors, they surprised scores of resting Guatemalan troops inside. Thirty Guatemalans were shot dead as they attempted to escape through a breach in the convent's rear wall caused by a past earthquake; their bodies littered the rubble at the breach. Other Guatemalans threw up their hands to surrender.

Among the captives were Colonel Valderraman, Colonel Zavala's deputy, and his adjutant, Captain Allende. Jamison accepted their surrender; they were luckier than other Guatemalans and Nicaraguan Legitimistas who came out of buildings elsewhere in the city with hands raised—many were gunned down by Americans whose blood had been boiling ever since seeing the bodies of the murdered American clergymen lying in the Jalteva Plaza.

Even though Colonel Zavala was reinforced by his rear guard, his augmented force of nine hundred men was routed by the unexpected return of Walker's eight hundred men from Masaya. The fighting was over within fifteen minutes. Zavala and the bulk of his force escaped, fleeing west to join General Belloso at Masaya, but they left more than two hundred of their comrades behind in Granada, dead or captured. Walker had lost twenty-five dead and eighty-five wounded, some in the aborted attack on Masaya but most in the defense of Granada.

Now Walker allowed himself a brief respite. Jamison and several other officers, including Markham, were just making themselves comfortable in a house on the plaza when Walker strolled in. Without a word, the general clambered into a hammock and fell fast asleep. Like their general, Walker's men could breathe easily, for the moment. They had secured their capital. But the Allies still held Masaya in force.

Word reached Granada that Walker's aide, Laine the Cuban, had been executed by Allied firing squad. In reprisal, Walker ordered the execution of the captured Guatemalan officers, Colonel Valderraman and Captain Allende. For a week, they'd been treated as the honored guests of Walker's officers at Granada. Jamison described them as "men of wealth, superior education, and polished manners." Valderraman and Allende had nightly joined the Americans to feast, drink, laugh, and dance the hours away, even paying their own way, gaining "the friendship and affection of the American officers."[10]

The two Guatemalan officers were marched under escort through the Granadine Plaza to the bullet-scarred wall outside the cathedral. In the watching crowd, Jamison looked sadly at "the dauntless men who had been such delightful companions" as they were placed side by side in front of the wall.[11] Valderraman and Allende declined to be seated and refused blindfolds. Allende calmly smoked a cigarette. When a line of rifles came up, both men looked with a steady gaze down the barrels. At the command the rifles barked. The lifeless bodies of Valderraman and Allende crumpled to the ground. No one cheered their deaths.

Feeling numb, Jamison walked away. "In all my life I recall nothing that impressed upon me more vividly than did this incident, the sorrow and bitterness of war."[12] After the deaths of the two likable prisoners of war, Jamison's enthusiasm for the war clearly waned. In his memoirs, he would not mention any further Nicaragua actions in which he was personally involved; it is likely that, disillusioned, Jamison deserted Walker after the execution of Valderraman and Allende.

With the odds mounting against Walker, Jamison would not be the last of his previously faithful followers to doubt the future prospects of their general's enterprise and give up the fight. But it would take more than a few desertions to defeat Walker. While new recruits continued to arrive in their hundreds, Walker was a long way from beaten, as his chief adversary, Cornelius Vanderbilt, in New York, was well aware.

❧ 22 ❧

WHEELING
AND DEALING

MANHATTAN, OCTOBER 21, 1856, A BUSY FALL TUESDAY. AS HORSE-drawn vehicles clattered by, two men dressed in inexpensive suits paused outside the two-story West Fourth Street office building. There was a brownstone building next door, separated from the office building by a lane that led to massive double doors—home to Cornelius Vanderbilt's stables, where he kept some of the finest harness horses in the country. No sign outside signified the purpose of the office building. From the array of hats visible through second-floor windows, an observer could see that a milliner's workshop occupied the upper floor.

The two men climbed the steps to an entrance hall. Across the hall, a door bore a simple sign: "Office." Removing their hats, the pair passed through the door and entered an anteroom. The walls were bare but for a few paintings of steamships. For furniture, there was a table, hard wooden chairs, and a high desk where a middle-aged clerk stood working, as clerks were wont to do in 1856. The two men introduced themselves. The younger of the two was Sylvanus H. Spencer. The older man was William R. C. Webster.

The clerk disappeared through the double doors leading to an inner office. Returning shortly after, he invited them to follow him into the next room. The inner room was more elaborately furnished than the first. There were more steamship paintings and, on the mantle over the fire, scale models of several more, including the *North Star*, Commodore Vanderbilt's favorite among all the ships he had built over the years. In one corner was a rolltop desk, on top of which sat a large, stuffed tabby cat that "seemed to impart an air of comfort to the place."[1]

Easy chairs were set before the fire, and directly in front of the visitors, there was a long table, at which Cornelius Vanderbilt sat writing. Vanderbilt kept just two things in the table's single drawer, a box of cigars and a checkbook.[2] Wardell the clerk withdrew, closing the doors and leaving Spencer and Webster standing in front of the table with hats in hand, like schoolboys hauled before the principal. Vanderbilt didn't acknowledge them. "He [was] writing, and his eyes [were] fixed on the paper. . . . In a few minutes the countenance [rose], and you [met] its expansive and penetrating glance." Then, to the relief of the pair, "he smile[d] in a pleasant and whole-souled manner."[3]

The Commodore conducted his guests to the easy chairs. He knew of Spencer, a New Yorker who skippered the *Machuca* when the Transit Company ran the Nicaraguan Transit Route. Spencer was a son of John Canfield Spencer, a one-time U.S. secretary of war who'd died only the previous year, and younger brother of Midshipman Philip Spencer, who was hanged without trial for mutiny aboard the USS *Somers* in 1849.[4] Raised in a well-to-do family and provided with a good education, Spencer was the black sheep of the family who went in search of adventure in his early twenties. He'd been one of the adventurers who sailed from New York in 1850 with Parker H. French to take part in the ill-fated Overland Express expedition, before going on to work for the Transit Company in Nicaragua.

Spencer had inherited a parcel of Transit Company stock from his late father, and, as he now informed Vanderbilt, he hated William Walker desperately for what he had done to the company and its stock market value.[5] Spencer's companion, William Webster, was more of an unknown. The Englishman presented himself as a gentleman and claimed to be from a good family and to be well-connected in Britain and Germany. It seems that not even his new partner Spencer knew that Webster had a history as a fraudster.

Telling Vanderbilt that he and Webster had conceived a surefire way to destroy Walker's government in Nicaragua, Spencer said that if the Transit Route could be shut off, Walker could be starved into submission. Vanderbilt was well aware of that. It had been tried before, he said; he himself had used Hosea Birdsall in a failed bid to close off the San Juan River, while the Costa Ricans had tried it with 250 troops and similarly failed. Spencer was undaunted, explaining that securing the Transit Route at La Virgen and San Juan del Sur should be easy enough, if the Costa Ricans could be encouraged to return to the war and again invade southwestern Nicaragua. The San Juan River, however, was a trickier proposition, but even more important because it was Walker's door to the Atlantic states.

This was not new to Vanderbilt, and seeing the Commodore shift impatiently in his chair, Spencer went on to say that the Costa Ricans had the right idea when they attempted to come down the Sarapiqui River behind Walker. But they'd been too clumsy in the way they had gone about it. Spencer had a better idea. After five years working river steamers on the San Juan, Spencer could speak Spanish and knew the region like the back of his hand. He would personally guide a Costa Rican military expedition along the San Carlos River, which entered the San Juan farther west than the Sarapiqui did, above Hipp's Point, for a surprise attack that seized the river and its steamers—if only Vanderbilt would provide the Costa Ricans with money and arms for the operation. And, Webster piped up, the Costa Ricans also lacked professional, experienced officers. But he was acquainted with an Englishman, a former senior officer with the British army in India and a man with years of experience leading native troops, who was perfect for the job and prepared to join them in the venture.

Vanderbilt quickly appreciated that if this latest scheme worked, Walker would be done for and Vanderbilt would come out of their war victorious. The Commodore had never met Walker. Some would say he actually admired what Walker did in taking charge in Nicaragua.[6] Walker's mistake was messing with Vanderbilt's property. How different the two men were. When Walker was twelve years old, he was a child prodigy just beginning college in Nashville. When Vanderbilt was twelve, his father won a contract to salvage the cargo of a vessel aground near Sandy Hook, and young Cornelius had been given three wagons and their drivers and told to get the job done. The transfer at Sandy Hook went well enough, as did the homeward journey over the Jersey sands. But when the wagons reached South Amboy, where the ferry left for home on Staten Island, Cornelius had spent all the money his father gave him and didn't have the six-dollar ferry fare. Cornelius had thought fast. Borrowing six dollars from the local innkeeper, he left one of his six horses behind as security. The next day, Cornelius returned with the six dollars and retrieved the horse.

Vanderbilt was such a wheeler-dealer that at age fifteen, when he wanted to buy his first trading vessel, a hundred-dollar flat-bottomed sailing barge, he did a deal with his mother, Phebe Hand Vanderbilt. If he plowed an eight-acre lot on the family farm at Staten Island that was so stony it had never been plowed before, and in time for his sixteenth birthday twenty-six days later, Phebe would pay him one hundred dollars. Vanderbilt had brought in all the boys of the neighborhood on the promise of free rides on his new boat. They helped him plow the lot, with time to spare.[7]

In the same way he'd wheeled-and-dealed since he was a twelve-year-old, Vanderbilt would look twice at any scheme that made him a winner in his war with Walker. His secret negotiations with Domingo de Goicuria had fallen in a heap. A month after approaching Vanderbilt with his loan proposal, the Cuban had received President William Walker's response: "You will please not trouble yourself further about the Transit Company," Walker had told Goicuria, revoking the Cuban's commission as a brigadier general in his army and terminating his mission to the United States and Europe.[8] As a consequence, Walker's proposal for "African apprentices" was never delivered to the French.

A bitter Goicuria was pressed by New York newspapers to explain his claims of influence with Walker. Soon, parts of Walker's correspondence with Goicuria were published in the press. Edmund Randolph, who was then in New York, had in response published a notice in the *Herald*: "In the Transit business Don Domingo de Goicuria is an intruder, with a dishonest and treacherous intent."[9] Randolph had even offered to fight Goicuria in a duel, specifying pistols at six paces. Goicuria, who protested that he had not betrayed Walker, had agreed to the duel, only to call it off—because, he said, it was impossible to agree on "distance and mode."[10] In the end, combat between the pair had been restricted to the newspaper pages. It is possible that Goicuria did not release the Walker correspondence to the press. Goicuria had shown his letters from Walker to Vanderbilt. It is likely that Vanderbilt had his clerk copy them and then Vanderbilt passed the letters on to the newspapers.

Now, Spencer and Webster were offering Vanderbilt his next-best option, perhaps his last option. So the Commodore made Spencer and Webster a counterproposition. He would authorize them to recover Transit Company steamers on the San Juan River and its tributaries and to close the river to communication by Walker. To facilitate that recovery, he would provide them with arms and ammunition for the Costa Rican army. However, he would not give Spencer or Webster a penny. If they succeeded in engineering Walker's removal, then, once Walker and his filibusters had left Nicaragua, Spencer and Webster could come back to Vanderbilt in this very office, and each receive fifty thousand dollars in cold, hard cash. Without hesitation, Spencer and Webster agreed, and the three men shook hands on the deal.

November 2 is known in Catholic Central America as the Day of the Dead. It was on this day that General José Canas chose to cross the La Flor and invade Nicaragua with a new Costa Rican force. Sylvanus Spencer and William Webster were still on their way to Costa Rica when the invasion began. When they arrived in San José, they would find that despite the previous year's devastating cholera epidemic, President Mora not only had ambitions to kick Walker and his filibusters out of Nicaragua but also wanted to annex southern Nicaragua for Costa Rica to control the Transit Route and the planned Nicaragua canal. Mora was raising more troops in San José, but, fearful that his Central American allies would occupy the Transit Route before he could, he sent Canas's force to seize and hold the Transit west of Lake Nicaragua.

For more than a year, General Canas had trained his battalion in Guanacaste. Of his four hundred men, three hundred were barefoot Costa Ricans. The balance were mounted Nicaraguan Legitimista volunteers, many the sons of well-to-do Rivas families. Canas named this unit the Vanguard Division of Costa Rica, hoping to make the filibusters think it much larger than it was. He needed every advantage, for most of his troops had no combat experience and his officers were painfully young—battalion commander Tomás Guardia was just twenty-four, while Guardia's younger brother and adjutant, Faustino, was nineteen. Both were the sons of the governor of Puntarenas, Rudesindo Guardia.

Canas, marching for San Juan del Sur, had orders from Mora to cut the Transit Route, the "highway of filibusterism," as the Allies called it, and then take Rivas.[11] With the main Allied army now at Masaya, Walker, at Granada, would then be sandwiched between the two forces.

In the late afternoon of November 11, Walker surveyed the enemy positions. Near the Half Way House, General Canas had barricaded the Transit Road ahead of the Puente Grande, a bridge over a ravine, and dug in hundreds of men on high ground. The previous day, General Hornsby, with 250 men and a howitzer, had failed to dislodge Canas. Disgusted by Hornsby's temerity, Walker had suggested that his subordinate take extended leave in the United States, and then Walker himself set off on a lake steamer with 250 men to augment Hornsby's force and expel Canas from the Transit. Overnight, the Costa Ricans, after beating off Hornsby's attack, had been reinforced by 300 Nicaraguans from the Allied army at Masaya, men led by none other than "Madregil"—Colonel Felix Ramirez, the Democratico officer who deserted Walker at the First Battle of Rivas the previous year.

Walker watched his new artillery commander, Charles Frederick Henningsen, supervise the loading of a howitzer. Henningsen was the arms expert employed by George Law in New York City, and he had recently arrived with more rifles and the missing gun carriages for the howitzers. Walker had promptly made Henningsen a brigadier general and put him in charge of ordnance and training.

Forty-one-year-old Henningsen, born in England of Swedish parents, was a vastly experienced professional soldier. Tall, slim, with a neat mustache and complementary beard, he'd fought with the Carlist forces in Spain, rising to the rank of colonel. He had served in the Russian army and, in the Hungarian Revolution, commanded Kossuth's last stronghold, Comorn, where the mendacious Louis Schlessinger had claimed to have also fought for Kossuth. Arriving in the United States, Henningsen had married a rich Southern widow. After his years in Spain, Henningsen spoke fluent Spanish. He knew how to lead and was a weapons expert. How Walker must have wished he'd had Henningsen's services much earlier. Already, in the month that Henningsen had been in Nicaragua, he had vastly improved the shooting of Walker's gunners, showing them how to accurately gauge their fall of shot.

At Puente Grande, having boldly brought a howitzer to within musket range, Henningsen proceeded to rain death onto the enemy lines along the hillside. Accurate enemy rifle fire eventually forced the crew to pull the howitzer back, but it had done its job, distracting the enemy to allow several of Walker's units to outflank Canas undetected. Captain Ewbanks was then sent forward with infantry that quickly took the barricade in front of the bridge, wiping out its defenders. Meanwhile, troops under Colonel Natzmer were cutting through thick undergrowth behind the enemy on the hillside. That undergrowth was so thick that the company of Captain Tom Green, recently promoted commander of the Sarapiqui River episode in February, became lost for a time. But the noise made by Natzmer's men alerted Canas, who ordered a general retreat toward the coast before he was surrounded.

Mounted Rangers led by General Henningsen gave chase. A Costa Rican rear guard made several stands, but Henningsen led a mounted charge that eventually scattered them. *Putnam's Monthly* would remark that "Henningsen is the only man of Walker's crew who has shown any military ability."[12] Canas's force was divided by Henningsen's fierce pursuit. Ramirez's Nicaraguans fled south to Costa Rica, throwing away weapons and knapsacks as they went, to speed their flight. Most of Canas's better-disciplined troops headed north, up the coastal track, with their general. Canas, far from daunted, planned to occupy Rivas.

The Transit Road was once again in Walker's hands, and he now hurried to La Virgen to head back to Granada aboard a lake steamer. As soon as he reached his capital, he prepared to stage a new attack on Masaya.

On the morning of November 15, General Sanders's advance guard launched Walker's second attempt to take Masaya. They ran straight into eight hundred men of the Second Guatemalan Division led by Lieutenant Colonel Joaquim Cabrera, who had reached Masaya from Guatemala in darkness at 12:30 that morning. The Allies were ready and waiting for the filibusters, for unbeknownst to Walker, General Belloso had a spy in the filibuster camp and knew that the Americans were coming. Cabrera's division arrived just in time for the battle.

The Guatemalans were positioned in huts in a plantain plantation beside the Granada road, and it was only by using a howitzer at close quarters that Sanders was able to force them to withdraw. When Walker arrived with the main ARN force after dark, he found Sanders's men encamped and drinking heavily. Before long, all Walker's men were drinking. Moving around his camp in the night, he discovered officers who were exhausted, dispirited, and uncaring; the prospect of another grinding, bloody, and probably pointless street battle in Masaya was not popular. Many of Walker's men were soon blind drunk. Walker himself did not sleep a wink that night, personally doing the rounds of the sentries. Never in his entire time in Nicaragua, he would later write, did he "find it so difficult as on that night to have (my) orders executed."[13]

Twenty-two-year-old Jack Harris from Connecticut was marched out into the Plazuela San Sebastian by Allied soldiers and pushed up against a wall. Captured amid the plantain trees outside Masaya the previous afternoon during General Sanders's assault, Harris had been locked up overnight. Just after dawn, he and his captors had been amazed to hear martial music coming from the filibuster lines—General Walker had brought his army band with him and ordered them to play stirring tunes to put some spirit back into his hungover troops.

Harris, seeing a firing squad form up in front of him, was convinced that he had just minutes left to live. But then there was a terrifying screech, and a nearby house on the square exploded. Seconds later, there was another screech, as a howitzer shell looped in from south of the town. With a spray of adobe and red roof tiles, another building was shattered by a direct hit. Panicking Allied soldiers ran for their lives; the firing squad dissolved before Jack Harris's eyes. Amazed to be still alive, he crouched down, as shells continued to bombard the little square. The Allied troops quickly withdrew

toward the center of town, and as quickly as it began, the bombardment
lifted. As Harris picked himself up, Major Caycee and hundreds of men of
the ARN's Second Rifles poured into the square from outside the town.
Harris then spotted General Walker himself, riding into the town with his
staff. Harris was among friends again. He would live for many more years to
tell the tale of how General Walker saved him from a Central American firing squad with only moments to spare.[14]

In the light of a candle, Colonel Zavala, the Guatemalan commander at
Masaya, sat writing a battle report to General Mariano Paredes at León. All
was quiet in Masaya. At 7:00 P.M., Walker's troops had ceased firing. At one
point during the day, General Belloso had sent one hundred men from his
own bodyguard with Colonel Cabrera and three hundred other Guatemalans
in an attempt to assault the San Sebastian square from the rear, but accurate Yankee rifle fire had forced them to retire. As had happened during the
first battle for Masaya the previous month, the struggle for the city had become stalemated. Neither side could dislodge the other.

Zavala wrote that the Allies controlled eight city blocks around the plaza,
and he reported that Guatemalan units had suffered twelve dead and
twenty-five wounded, while General Martinez's Nicaraguans had similar
losses. Zavala could not speak for the Salvadorans—he wasn't talking to
them. An estimated eight hundred Yankees were burrowing toward the
plaza, and to protect his rear, Walker had set fire to many houses in the town's
Monimbo district. Zavala expected that under cover of night, Walker would
dig trenches toward Allied lines.[15]

At five o'clock in the afternoon of November 19, General Paredes was riding to Masaya with his aide Colonel Serapio Cruz and a detachment of
lancers. Anxious to get into the fight after receiving Colonel Zavala's battle
report, Paredes had dragged himself from his sickbed. Three miles short of
Masaya, he was met by a dispatch rider bearing a message from Zavala that

informed him that the second battle for Masaya was over. Again, Walker had withdrawn in darkness after realizing that victory was impossible.

When Paredes reached Masaya, he surveyed the ruined Monimbo district; 150 houses had been destroyed by fires set by the filibusters. The San Sebastian Church, where Walker had housed his wounded, had been looted and badly damaged. Paredes was shown thirty filibuster graves dug in the earthen floors of several houses.

Meanwhile, Allied commander in chief General Belloso was writing to his war minister back in El Salvador, claiming a great victory. He reported total Allied casualties in the Second Battle of Masaya of 43 killed and 82 wounded, while he estimated that Walker had suffered 150 casualties— the actual number was 100. He also reported that, according to his spy in Granada, Colonel Fisher and Captain Green were among Walker's dead, along with Walker's judge advocate and a surgeon, and that Colonel Natzmer had been seriously wounded.[16] None of this was true—the spy was either poorly placed or sending Belloso misinformation.

Late in the afternoon of November 23, Walker's armed schooner *Granada* cleared the harbor at San Juan del Sur and made for an approaching brig. As soon as the *Granada*'s captain, Lieutenant Fayssoux, who had been expecting the Costa Ricans to attempt to land reinforcements from the sea in a fresh attempt to take the Transit Route, saw the brig raise Costa Rican colors, he ordered his twenty-six crewmen to clear the deck for action.

The brig was the *Once de Abril*—the *Eleventh of April*—named for the Second Battle of Rivas, which the Costa Ricans considered a great victory. Her four nine-pound cannon commenced firing when the *Granada* was at several hundred yards' range, and numerous infantrymen on board opened up with their muskets. By 6:00 P.M., Fayssoux had dropped anchor four hundred yards from the brig, close enough for his two six-pound carronades to be within range but too far distant for enemy small arms to be a threat. Several enemy rounds hit the *Granada*, but despite the hits the casualties, and the fading light, Fayssoux kept up a steady, accurate bombardment, causing numerous casualties on the brig's crowded decks and starting a fire.

At 8:00 P.M., the *Granada* fired a round that pierced the *Once de Abril's* magazine. With a deafening roar, the brig blew up, sending a sheet of flame high into the night sky. The ship sank within minutes. Fayssoux lowered a boat, and by 10:00 P.M., its crew had pulled forty-eight Costa Ricans from the water, including the brig's master, Captain Antonio Valle Riestra, who, like many of the survivors, was badly burned. Sixty-six Costa Ricans had been killed. On the *Granada*, one crewman had been killed and eight wounded. Walker rewarded Fayssoux for this unlikely naval victory by promoting him to captain and giving him the grand Hacienda Rosario at Rivas.

Another twelve of the horribly burned men would die from their burns, taking the Costa Rican death toll from the battle to seventy-eight. Lieutenant Fayssoux later allowed the survivors to return home. The story would quickly spread throughout Central America that the *Granada* sank the *Once de Abril* using a rocket-powered secret weapon.

The same day that William Walker's little navy sank the Costa Rican warship, Sylvanus Spencer and William Webster met with President Mora in San José, passing over a letter of introduction from the Costa Rican ambassador in Washington, Dr. Felipe Molina. Webster had told Molina that he was a wealthy English businessman with influential contacts in the United States and Britain who wanted to acquire the contract to build the Nicaragua canal. No mention was made of Cornelius Vanderbilt. Ambassador Molina enthusiastically recommended Webster and his partner Spencer to his president.

After Don Juanito Mora—dark-haired, with thick sideburns, a high forehead, small mouth and chin, and intense eyes—greeted the pair coolly, Webster informed him that he and Spencer had a plan to help Costa Rica destroy William Walker and annex southern Nicaragua. In return, they and their partners in the Land Transport Company, a new entity they would register in Costa Rica, desired the rights to the trans-Nicaragua canal.

Mora had already received advice from a variety of quarters on how to deal with Walker—from his own people, from the governments of the other

Central American states, and even from a general sent to him by the Spanish government in the summer of 1856. General Morales de Rada had fought and defeated Lopez and his filibusters in Cuba, and for that reason, President Mora had given him a hearing. But in the end, General Rada had not appreciated the situation in Nicaragua, had not appreciated the importance of the Transit Route, and had not offered anything new. Webster and Spencer, on the other hand, sounded as if they were thinking along the same lines as Mora; he asked them to elaborate.

Spencer said that, if given a small force of Costa Rican soldiers, he would personally guide them down the San Carlos River to the San Juan, to launch a surprise attack in the filibusters' rear. When Mora impatiently responded by saying this had been tried before, on the Sarapiqui, without success, Spencer said that the Sarapiqui operation failed because General Alfaro's men had exhausted themselves cutting a path through the jungle and made so much noise that the filibusters had heard them coming. Spencer proposed to float down the San Carlos and then down the San Juan on log rafts carrying the men, equipment, and stores of the expedition, propelled by the natural flow of the two waterways toward the sea. All that the men on the rafts would have to do was go along for the ride. On hearing this, Mora became much more attentive.

Webster said that as a gesture of the pair's goodwill, a colleague would shortly arrive in San José with a shipment of Minié rifles and ammunition to equip the San Carlos River expedition. That colleague was another Englishman, George F. Cauty, who had served as an officer with the army of the East India Company in India. The world's largest private army, its thousands of native Indian soldiers were commanded by British officers who attended the East India Company's officer training college in England prior to taking up their commands on the Indian subcontinent. Like his father before him, Cauty had spent years soldiering in India. He had seen action in a bloody war with the fearsome Sikhs, which had resulted in the British capture of the Punjab in 1849, and in an 1852 campaign in Burma, where the company's troops had defeated the Burmese.

Mora was a man who made rapid decisions. This pair was offering him what he wanted, even supplying weapons for the venture. With nothing to lose and everything to gain, the president sealed an agreement with Webster and Spencer and issued orders for preparations to be made to ensure that the San Carlos River expedition was launched prior to Christmas. Mora was quite unaware that in doing so, he was acting as a pawn of Cornelius Vanderbilt. Thanks to the Costa Rican president, Vanderbilt's latest offensive against William Walker quickly took shape.

HERE WAS GRANADA

A T 3:00 P.M. ON NOVEMBER 24, THE DAY AFTER THE *GRANADA* SANK the *Once de Abril*, the Allied army launched three simultaneous attacks on the city of Granada, from three different directions. General Belloso, the Allied commander in chief, had learned that William Walker had left Granada on the twentieth, taking most of his army with him on a lake steamer to La Virgen. Walker, determined to keep the Transit Route open, intended to attack Rivas with 650 men, to drive out General Canas's Costa Ricans and the several hundred Nicaraguans under old General Maximo Jerez, who had joined him there to hold the city. According to Allied intelligence, Walker had left General Henningsen at Granada with just 440 troops, and Belloso had seized his chance to take Walker's capital, marching the Allied army east from Masaya during the morning of November 24. Spreading around the perimeter of the city, the Allies cut off all escape routes other than the lake.

The Allies knew that Henningsen had his headquarters at the Granadine Plaza. A mile-long avenue, the Calzada, led from the plaza to the lake. Churches dominated the avenue—the vast La Parroquia Church at the entrance to the Calzada, its massive towers soaring into the sky; the Esquipulas Church a little way down the avenue; then the Guadalupe Church, halfway between plaza and lake. To reach the lakeside wharf and escape via steamer, Henningsen's men would have to use this avenue. Belloso's plan of attack called for his troops to cut the Calzada and seal off Henningsen in the center of the city. General Tomás Martinez and his Nicaraguans attacked in the direction of the Jalteva Plaza to the west. General Paredes's

Guatemalans advanced toward the San Francisco Convent north of the Granadine Plaza. Belloso's own Salvadorans pushed toward the Guadalupe Church. The attack on the Guadalupe was the one that mattered most.

At the Jalteva, Martinez's attacking troops melted away in the face of heavy fire from Major Schwartz's artillery. As five hundred Guatemalans attacked the San Francisco Convent, Major Cal O'Neal's younger brother, a lieutenant, was killed in the defense. A distraught Cal O'Neal, barefoot, bareheaded, and in shirtsleeves, mounted his horse and led thirty-two picked men in a mad charge that took the regrouping Guatemalans by surprise and drove them back in confusion. When Henningsen finally succeeded in recalling O'Neal's men, they returned through streets piled with Guatemalan dead. The convent remained in ARN hands.

At the Guadalupe Church, it was a different story; engineer Captain Hesse and twenty-two Americans were overrun and killed by hundreds of Salavadorans. Belloso achieved his objective—in seizing the Guadalupe, he sealed the Calzada and trapped Henningsen inside the city. For good measure, the Salvadorans advanced up the Calzada and also occupied the undefended Esquipulas Church, tightening the net around Henningsen. Meanwhile, Captain Grier, the Granada police chief, who occupied the tumbled-down Spanish fort at the dockside with twenty-seven policemen, was cut off.

With Henningsen at the plaza were more than three hundred able-bodied fighting men, a score of Guatemalan prisoners of war, a dozen black Jamaican crew members from a lake steamer who had been stranded in the city, plus seventy wounded and seventy American women and children. Many of the women were the wives of American officers, ladies such as Edward Kewen's wife, who was nursing the wounded. Another nurse was the attractive actress wife of Edward Bingham, an actor and producer whose American theatrical company was unlucky enough to be performing in Granada at the time of the Allied attack. Bingham and the other actors joined the defense.

From the lake steamer *San Carlos,* Walker peered through the darkness, trying to make out what was happening in Granada a mile away. It was the
night of November 25. For two days, Henningsen had fought off every Allied attack. Intending to break out of the city via the lake, he had driven the
enemy from the Esquipulas Church in his path down the lake avenue, burning buildings behind him as he went—for Walker had instructed him to destroy Granada.

According to Walker, the Legitimistas loved Granada as they would love
a woman.[1] And since he could not hold her himself, Walker planned to deprive the Legitimistas of the belle of Nicaragua. Yet, Walker had come to
love Granada, too. Although originally never intending to spend time there,
he'd been seduced by the city and made it his capital. He even named his
lone warship after the city. And now, in the same way that Cornelius Vanderbilt had sacrificed his beloved *North Star* to achieve his ends, Walker
would sacrifice Granada.

The sky glowed red above the northern and western suburbs from Henningsen's fires. The air was thick with smoke. Walker could make out his
lone-star flag still flying above the Parochial Church, but apart from that,
there was little to be seen. Walker was unaware that Henningsen was fighting on two fronts; apart from dealing with everything the Allies threw at him,
Henningsen had to deal with his own men's despondency. Surrounded,
they'd lost heart and were drinking heavily; Henningsen had to drive them
mercilessly. Using his Allied prisoners of war and the stranded lake-steamer
crewmen as his laborers, he'd transferred the wounded, the women and
children, and his dwindling stores from building to building down the avenue while his lethargic riflemen fought off the Allies. Without his artillery,
he would have been overrun.

A small boat bumped alongside the lake steamer, and one of Walker's
officers boarded the *San Carlos* and urgently reported to his general. He'd
contacted Captain Grier at the lakeside fort, taking him food and ammunition. Grier was in good spirits, although one of his men, a Venezuelan, had
deserted and could reveal to the other side just how few men held the fort.
Even as the officer delivered this report, firing broke out at the fort. Guatemalans launched a frontal attack while another Allied party landed from a
boat in Grier's rear. The shooting at the fort was intense, but brief. After

several minutes, all was quiet. Before long, the sole survivor from Grier's garrison took his chances in the water, which was reputedly inhabited by freshwater sharks, and swam out to the steamer. Grier and twenty-five of his men were dead, and the fort was in Allied hands.

Deeply depressed, Walker steamed back to La Virgen. Night after night over the coming days, Walker returned in the steamer, to hover off the burning city like a worried mother hen, hoping that Henningsen had reached the lake and could be evacuated.

Three days after the fort at the wharf fell, Henningsen managed to relocate his ever-diminishing band to the Guadalupe Church, halfway to the lake. In a prelude to an assault on the church, he'd poured dozens of artillery rounds into it. Sixty of his men then charged the church, to find that the enemy occupiers had fled. The previous day, after the Americans abandoned their last positions on the plaza, leaving every building burning, Allied troops had rushed triumphantly into the famous square. Henningsen had then set off gunpowder under one of the towers of the Parochial Church. The tower had been blown into the air intact, before crashing lethally down onto the Allied soldiers below, crushing many.

Now, in the early afternoon, two men ventured to the Guadalupe Church under a flag of truce. One was an aide to Colonel Zavala. The other was an American. The pair was brought to Henningsen, who stood, tall, spare, and haughty, with folded arms. The Guatemalan officer offered Henningsen surrender terms, which the American, Price, a deserter from Henningsen's force, urged Henningsen's men to accept, telling them they were surrounded by three thousand Allied troops. Henningsen responded by arresting Price and then informed the Guatemalan there could be no question of surrender, inviting the officer to take a good look at his eleven artillery pieces and his determined troops. In abandoning the plaza, Henningsen's men had to leave behind the liquor supplies; morale had since improved dramatically. The Guatemalan also saw Henningsen's prisoners and scores of wounded tended by resolute American women. In a sheltered corner huddled the children, pale but calm. The officer returned to his own lines.

At 3:00 P.M., the Allies launched an all-out assault on the Guadalupe. It was met by canister and grape from Henningsen's artillery. The brave, white-clad ranks were mercilessly mowed down. The assault failed. Another, at 8:00, after dark, met the same bloody and useless end. Henningsen estimated the enemy lost one hundred men in the two unsuccessful attacks.[2] That night, heavy rain fell. Soon, men, women, and children in the Guadalupe began to fall ill.

December 3 saw a force of two hundred men march out of the Costa Rican capital. Armed with Minié rifles, but unaware they'd been supplied by Yankee shipping magnate Cornelius Vanderbilt, these troops were led by Colonel Pedro Barillier, with Major Maximo Blanco as his chief of staff. Riding behind Barillier as the column headed north toward the San Carlos River was Sylvanus Spencer, bearing the rank of captain in the Costa Rican army. Beside Spencer rode George Cauty, the English soldier of fortune recruited by William Webster. Just thirty years of age, this native of Westminster, London, had accompanied the Vanderbilt arms shipment to Costa Rica; Webster himself remained behind in San José. Because of Cauty's military record, President Mora had made him a colonel. Once the column reached the San Carlos, Spencer and Cauty would take charge.

A larger column of six hundred troops would follow in twelve days' time, under the command of General José Joaquim Mora, the president's brother, bringing stores, ammunition, and artillery. A rear guard of three hundred men would follow shortly after. President Mora was backing Spencer and Webster's plan to the hilt and, unwittingly, backing Vanderbilt's ambition to regain control of the Nicaraguan Transit.

Henningsen's band still held out at Granada's Guadalupe Church, surviving on horse meat and rainwater. Cholera and typhus now claimed more lives than did enemy action. Mrs. Bingham, the actor's wife, was among the victims, dying within hours of displaying the first symptoms. Cholera was also

rampant in the surrounding Allied army. One of the first to die had been
Guatemalan commander General Paredes. Colonel Zavala replaced Paredes;
his government promoted him to general.

On December 8, under a white flag, Zavala sent a message to Henningsen, calling on him to enter into surrender negotiations and telling him
that American steamers lately arriving in Nicaragua had brought not a single
recruit for Walker's lost cause. Henningsen sent back a brief reply—he was,
he said, only prepared to parley "at the cannon's mouth."[3]

Zavala had been lying. On the third, 78 recruits had reached Walker at La
Virgen after coming down from San Francisco aboard the *Orizaba*. Two days
later, the lake steamer *San Carlos* brought another 280 recruits to Walker—
30 off the *Tennessee* from New York, and 250 aboard the *Texas* from New
Orleans with Samuel A. Lockridge. A former Texas Ranger, Lockridge had
been sent to New Orleans by Walker expressly to raise more recruits. Those
recruits were in for a tough baptism of fire.

December 11. With Henningsen still holding the Guadalupe Church, General Belloso decided on another massed Allied attack. In the morning, the
first contingent of long-awaited Honduran troops joined the Granada
encirclement—two hundred men under General Florencio Xatruch, the
former Legitimista colonel who'd commanded at Rivas at the end of the civil
war. General Xatruch, whose friend President Guardiola had made him
commander of the Honduran expeditionary army, was anxious to show
General Belloso what his men could do. Belloso sent them against the
Guadalupe Church.

The Allies were unaware that in the night, Henningsen had slipped most
of his people into entrenchments closer to the lake. Thirty handpicked men
under Lieutenant Sumpter Williamson held the church. Armed with
breech-loading Sharps rifles, they took careful aim at Hondurans forming up
for the attack several hundred yards away. The Hondurans thought they
were out of range, but the Sharps rifle had a range of two thousand yards.
When Williamson's men opened up, Honduran farm boy conscripts fell
like flies.

Honduran officers on horseback urged their men to charge. One of those officers was thirty-year-old Captain Juan Canas. The holder of a degree in philosophy, Canas had panned for gold in California before returning home to Honduras in 1851 penniless. Canas had also trained as a doctor; he needed all his medical skills this day. Around him, his men were slaughtered before they could even engage the Americans. It was estimated that half of the two hundred Hondurans were slain before the attack was called off.[4] Captain Canas was among the survivors. In minutes, General Xatruch's proud little Honduran command had been devastated before it could even go into action.

The lake steamer *La Virgen* had been anchored off the burning city since before dawn. It was December 12. The previous day, General Sanders, sent with the steamer to rescue Henningsen and his survivors from Granada, had returned to say that rescue was impossible. Walker had come to suspect that both Sanders and Hornsby were jealous of newcomer Henningsen's appointment as a brigadier general.[5] First Hornsby had let him down at Puente Grande, and then Sanders had failed in his mission. So Walker had come to conduct the rescue himself.

Throughout the day, Walker watched the city from the lake while 160 handpicked men aboard the *La Virgen* kept out of sight. The enemy moved troops onto the lake beach to discourage a landing, but Walker gave no sign of aggressive intent. At nine o'clock, with all lights doused, the steamer slipped away up the lake. Three miles from the city, at exactly the same point where he had landed in 1855 to take Granada, Walker sent the rescue force ashore in small boats. Walker then steamed back down the lake, to anchor again at the same spot he'd occupied previously. When the sun rose, it was as if the *La Virgen* had never gone away. Shortly after, a dark-skinned man swam out from shore. It was Kanaka John, one of Walker's Originals, who'd been with Henningsen. He brought a message, telling Walker that Henningsen could not last much longer and asking that, if a rescue was contemplated, a set of lights be displayed, so that preparations could be made for a breakout. Walker immediately had the lights shown from the steamer.

But the signal was invisible to Henningsen because of the pall of smoke hugging the burning city.

A little before midnight, when Major John Waters led the 160-man rescue force against an enemy barricade north of Granada, the enemy fired first. Impressively built Captain Samuel Leslie, known as "Cherokee Sam" because of his Native American blood, and a popular figure in ARN ranks, led his company in outflanking and storming the barricade. Moving on, the rescuers encountered another heavily defended barricade. Captain Higley's company took this in bloody hand-to-hand fighting in the darkness, losing several men.

Following the Tipitapa road, Waters entered the Granada suburbs at sunup the next day, still clueless as to Henningsen's precise whereabouts. The rescuers charged and overran another barricade, as Waters's casualties mounted to thirteen killed and thirty wounded. When a prisoner revealed that Henningsen was dug in at the Guadalupe Church, Waters sent Captain Leslie ahead to warn Henningsen's men not to fire on their rescuers when they arrived. As Waters carefully picked his way through the back streets, with flames all around, Leslie returned—he had reached the church and found Henningsen. Following the same route, Leslie led Waters and his men to the church. They met no resistance. Unbeknownst to Walker and his officers, General Belloso, believing that Walker's entire army was attacking after the ferocious way the northern barricades had been stormed, ordered his army to pull out of the city and withdraw toward Masaya.

As Henningsen's ragged, pallid survivors were welcoming their rescuers, Cherokee Sam Leslie suddenly threw up his hands and fell down dead—shot in the head by an enemy sniper. Crouching low, Waters and Henningsen conferred. During the three-week siege, Henningsen had lost 110 men killed or wounded in action and 120 to cholera and typhus. Forty men had deserted, 2 were taken prisoner. His survivors included 200 sick and wounded men, plus women and children—whose numbers had been much reduced by disease.[6]

As the two officers were talking, there was a loud explosion at the wharf, and smoke billowed into the air—before Allied troops pulled out, they blew up storage sheds they'd recently built there. Progressively, Waters' men carried the wounded and shepherded the women and children down the avenue to the lake. At Henningsen's insistence, his exhausted men dragged six of their artillery pieces with them. Walker, seeing the refugees coming, brought *La Virgen* into the wharf, and by two o'clock, rescuers and rescued were all aboard, along with Henningsen's precious field guns.

Charles Henningsen stood by the wharf. *Putnam's Monthly,* which generally had no time for Walker, would commend Henningsen: "Surrounded by the enemy, he fought with spirit and skill."[7] Seeing a discarded enemy lance lying nearby, the Englishman took it up and stabbed it into the ground, then jabbed a piece of leather onto the end of the lance. With a piece of charcoal from the wreckage of the burnt-out wharf sheds, he wrote: "*Aqui fue Granada*"—"Here was Granada."[8] As the steamer pulled away from the dock, Henningsen stepped over onto her deck, to be greeted by Walker.

Smoke blanketed the city as the boat churned out into the lake and then turned south for La Virgen. The rescue of the trapped Americans at Granada was complete. As was the destruction of one of the most beautiful cities in the world.

24

CLOSING NICARAGUA'S BACK DOOR

T HE ARN OUTPOST AT HIPP'S POINT, OR POINT TRINIDAD, AS THE Costa Ricans called it, was one of the loneliest in Nicaragua. Located on the western point where the Sarapiqui River joined the San Juan River, it was there to guard against a Costa Rican sally down the Sarapiqui. Its value had been demonstrated back in February, when, from there, Tom Green had destroyed General Alfaro's expedition. Apart from alligators and tropical birds, the current garrison commander, Captain Thompson, and his company of forty Americans had only themselves for company. That situation was about to change, dramatically. Come the middle of the day on December 22, Sylvanus Spencer was standing at the base of a tree from which a Costa Rican with good eyesight surveyed the filibuster post on Hipp's Point. The soldier could see Captain Thompson and his men sitting down to lunch. No sentries were posted, and the Americans' rifles were all in neat stands around the post.

Over the past nineteen days, Spencer and the 200 Costa Rican pathfinders had marched overland to the head of the San Carlos River, chopped down trees and built their rafts, then drifted down the San Carlos to the San Juan, just as Spencer had planned. At the confluence of the two rivers, Englishman George Cauty and 80 men had landed to build a fort. Spencer had continued down the San Juan with Colonel Barillier, Major Blanco, and the remaining 120 troops. Just short of Hipp's Point, they had landed. Now, aware that Thompson's garrison was off guard, Spencer's Costa Ricans moved into position and then launched an attack on the fort.

Although Thompson's men were caught totally by surprise, they reacted quickly and put up do-or-die resistance. But they were outnumbered three to one. When Spencer led the Costa Ricans over the ramparts and into the fort with bayonets fixed, most of the Yankees were killed in the hand-to-hand fighting. Among the few wounded prisoners taken was Captain Thompson. Having gained control of Hipp's Point, Spencer took Major Blanco, forty-five men, and their prisoners and continued the steady floating progress down the San Juan, leaving Colonel Barillier and the remaining Costa Ricans in occupation of the former ARN fort.

It took Vanderbilt's man Spencer a day and a half to complete the navigation of the San Juan on his rafts. On the evening of December 23, Spencer and his troops reached San Juan Bay and paddled to Punta de Castilla—Castle Point. Here stood the ruins of an old Spanish castle, Castillo Viejo, and here Captain Joseph N. Scott, who was Morgan and Garrison's manager in Nicaragua, had recently made a home for his family and himself and set up a depot for the Transit's river steamers.

As Spencer and his men came ashore, they passed four idle river steamers awaiting the next ocean steamer arrival—the stern-wheeler *Sir Henry Bulwer* and side-wheelers *Clayton*, *Wheeler*, and *Machuca*—Spencer's former vessel. Scott was roused from his bed by Spencer and his forty-five Costa Rican riflemen and advised that the four steamers were now confiscated.

At dawn, a furious Scott rowed across the bay to Greytown, passing a large British man-o-war lying at anchor. A steady rotation of armed British vessels had occupied the bay ever since Ambassador Crampton had promised Vanderbilt there would always be a British warship at Greytown. Now it was the turn of the 3,281-ton HMS *Orion*. An impressive-looking two-year-old screw-driven steamship of ninety-one guns, she was one of the largest vessels ever to have visited San Juan Bay.

After Captain Scott tracked down the U.S. government's commercial agent in the port and protested the seizure of his river steamers, the agent went out to HMS *Orion* and demanded that her skipper, Captain John E. Erskine, intervene and protect Captain Scott and his family from Costa

Rican aggression and forcibly restore control of the four little steamers to Morgan and Garrison's manager. Captain Erskine, unhappy that Costa Rican troops were active on his doorstep, landed on Punta de Castilla with a party of marines and announced to Sylvanus Spencer that he'd come to protect American lives and property. In response, Spencer declared that his men had no intention of harming Captain Scott or his family. As for American property, Spencer told the British officer that ownership of the river steamers was in dispute. Spencer then produced a letter from Cornelius Vanderbilt authorizing him to act on behalf of the vessels' original owners, the Accessory Transit Company, to recover its property.

After reading Vanderbilt's letter, and ignoring Captain Scott's protests, the Royal Navy officer then backed off, but not before securing the release of the American prisoners who had been taken at Hipp's Point and who agreed to return to the United States on the next ocean steamer. Captain Erskine also insisted that the Costa Rican army cease to occupy Punta de Castillo, which Britain and the United States both considered Nicaraguan territory. In response, Spencer relocated three of the four captured river steamers to Costa Rican waters, then set off back up the San Juan River in the fourth vessel, the *Machuca,* his own former command.

Steaming up the river, Spencer passed the new Costa Rican garrison at Hipp's Point with a toot and a wave. Plowing on up the San Juan, he continued to the mouth of the San Carlos River. Here, Colonel Cauty had placed his rafts out in the river, stationing a number of men on them to fire on any filibuster steamer attempting to come up or down the river. Spencer planned to steam up the San Carlos River to link up with General Mora's main force, which by then had begun its rafting journey to the San Juan.

Without reducing speed, Spencer gaily turned into the San Carlos from the San Juan. The wash from the *Machuca* swamped Cauty's rafts, knocking occupants into the water, and several Costa Rican soldiers drowned. After stopping to pull men from the water, Spencer decided to take Cauty and his command with him up the San Carlos for the linkup with General Mora.

Oblivious to the fact that the Costa Ricans had taken the river steamers at Greytown and were now on the San Juan River, hundreds of eastbound passengers from the latest *Orizaba* arrival from San Francisco were aboard the *La Virgen,* crossing Lake Nicaragua, as she headed for the town of San Carlos and the San Juan River.

Among these passengers were several of Walker's officers, most heading for the United States. Even during the darkest days of the Nicaraguan conflict, Walker allowed many of his officers to return home on furlough. For some, this was after they had been wounded in action; others went on business for Walker's government. One of the civil officers on the *La Virgen* was Samuel Lockridge, heading back to New Orleans on a fresh recruitment drive. Another was Undersecretary William Rogers, who only intended going as far as Greytown to collect paper for Walker's printing press, which was now located in his new capital, Rivas. Generals Canas and Martinez, who'd occupied Rivas for the Allies, had pulled out after Walker completed the evacuation of Granada, and on December 16, Walker's army had marched into Rivas.

The *La Virgen* entered the San Juan River and steamed east. At El Castillo, the *La Virgen's* passengers disembarked to spend the night at the Hotel El Castillo. In the morning, the passengers would board the river steamer *Joseph N. Scott*—named in honor of Morgan and Garrison's manager in Nicaragua—which waited at the jetty below the El Castillo rapids. The *La Virgen* then turned around and headed back up the San Juan toward Lake Nicaragua.

The Hotel El Castillo, also known as the American Hotel, was owned by a young American couple, twenty-six-year-old John Hollenbeck from Hudson, Ohio, and his German-born wife, Elizabeth Hatsfeldt Hollenbeck. John had been working on Vanderbilt's river steamers when he bought the hotel from a former British seaman in 1852. He had found Elizabeth, who had grown up in New Orleans, managing the hotel. Hollenbeck had given her a 50 percent salary raise on the spot. In March the following year, he'd married her. The industrious couple opened a merchandise store in the town and expanded the hotel, with John hauling rock down from the ruined castle on the hill for the foundations of a new wing—until the Nicaraguan authorities stopped him. The Hollenbecks offered a hammock and a roof over the head for a dollar a night, plus cheap but wholesome American-style food, and were doing great business. But while they were prepared to face the uncertainties of war, they had sent their two-year-old son, John Jr., to stay with Elizabeth's family in Illinois.

The next morning, Lockridge, Rogers, and the Transit passengers departed Hollenbecks' hotel. Boarding the *Scott*, they set off down the river for a rendezvous with an ocean steamer at Greytown.

After Spencer and Cauty met up with General Mora on the San Carlos River, the *Machuca* returned to the San Juan carrying reinforcements. Pulling into the wharf below the El Castillo rapids, she disgorged Costa Rican troops, sending many of El Castillo's two hundred inhabitants fleeing into the jungle. When Spencer, Cauty, and senior Costa Rican officers came ashore, hotel proprietors John and Elizabeth Hollenbeck were hauled before them. Colonel Barillier ordered the couple locked away until further notice. Hollenbeck and his wife would spend the next two weeks in their own woodshed, before being transferred to a dungeon cell for four months.[1]

With just thirty men, Colonel Cauty occupied *El Castillo de la Immaculada Concepcion*—the Castle of the Immaculate Conception—on the grassy hill above El Castillo. Built by the Spanish in 1673, it had been badly degraded by the passage of time and by a 1780 attack by Horatio Nelson, then a young Royal Navy lieutenant. Despite that, the massive stone emplacement still possessed great strategic value. Spencer, meanwhile, had the *Machuca* hauled over the rapids by the Costa Ricon troops, then took the remaining men with him when he and Colonel Barillier steamed away upriver with the *Machuca*.

North of El Castillo, Spencer came across the lake steamer *La Virgen* tied up at the riverbank at the mouth of the Zavalos River—one of the hundreds of small tributaries draining into the San Juan. With the *La Virgen*'s crew busy loading firewood from one of a number of stockpiles maintained along the San Juan by the Transit operators, Spencer was able to capture the larger craft without a fight. She came complete with a small cannon installed by Walker. Sending the *Machuca* back to Cauty at El Castillo, Spencer continued upstream with the *La Virgen*.

When the town of San Carlos and her lofty hilltop fort came in sight, Spencer kept his troops out of view, and with Walker's lone-star flag still fluttering from the vessel's staff, he eased the steamer into the town jetty. The fort's seven cannon were capable of blowing the steamer out of the water, but Walker's garrison commander, Captain Kruger, assumed that the *La Virgen* was on her scheduled return after taking the through passengers to El Castillo and paid her little heed. When Spencer sent a messenger up to Kruger to say there was a message on board for him from General Walker, the unsuspecting captain came down at once. As Kruger stepped on board the *La Virgen*, he found a gun to his head. Spencer warned Kruger he would be shot if he didn't send a note to the fort's garrison ordering immediate surrender. Kruger complied. The order was conveyed up the hill, and Kruger's troops emerged from the fort with hands raised.

Within a matter of days, Sylvanus Spencer had captured Hipp's Point, El Castillo, and Fort San Carlos, plus four river steamers and a lake steamer, all but closing the back door to Nicaragua. Just three lake steamers remained available to Walker, and Spencer had a plan for seizing them, too. Deprived of vessels, Walker would be like a man without legs. And Cornelius Vanderbilt would be one critical step closer to winning his war.

When President Mora learned of Spencer's swift success, he issued a proclamation to his army: "The main artery of filibusterism has been cut forever. The sword of Costa Rica has severed it."[2] Time would tell whether that proclamation was premature.

In New York, although Cornelius Vanderbilt had yet to receive the news of Spencer's successes, he had heard from Webster that Spencer and Cauty had set off from San José with the Costa Rican expeditionary force. Vanderbilt was so confident of Spencer's ultimate success that he published a notice in the New York *Herald* on Christmas Day, for the attention of all Accessory

Transit Company stockholders: "Present appearances indicate a realization of my hopes that the company will be speedily restored to their rights, franchises and property upon the isthmus of Nicaragua."[3]

More than ever, Vanderbilt was counting on winning his war in Nicaragua. His Gulf line was locked in cutthroat competition with Charles Morgan's ships, with neither magnate now making money in the Gulf. Meanwhile, the Commodore's transatlantic steamship venture was not faring well. Using his pet ship, the *North Star*, bought back from the U.S. Mail Line, and the newly built SS *Ariel*, Vanderbilt was losing money on the run from New York to Le Havre. The Cunard Line and the Collins Line were in profit because of their government mail subsidies. Determined to make a success of the European run, Vanderbilt had placed an order for his largest ocean steamer yet, the 4,500-ton *Vanderbilt*. Yet, it could turn out to be a case of pouring good money after bad.

Unlike his fellow Transit Company shareholders, Vanderbilt was at least making money from the Transit business—via the bribes being paid to keep his ships idle. But this Nicaragua business had become more than just a matter of money to the Commodore. This had become all about winning. Vanderbilt was not prepared to let the "tin sojer" and his mercantile friends beat him. In Spencer, Webster, and Cauty, the Commodore had the instruments of war, and Walker's destruction. And everything pointed to their ultimate success. But the drama involving Walker's vital San Juan River corridor was still far from over.

Samuel Absalom of the Mounted Rangers had arrived in Nicaragua from California in December. By the beginning of January 1857, Trooper Absalom was quartered at Rivas. The war-ravaged city didn't impress him. Its once grand plaza, where Private Hughes and other American wounded had been burned to death by Colonel Bosque in 1855, was now weed-infested. The cathedral where George Winters had made his last stand was still a desolate ruin. Guerra's Inn, where Juan Santamaria the drummer boy gave his life to burn out the Americans, was a blackened shell. General Walker had his headquarters on the northern side of the plaza, in the line of low, red-tiled buildings where, the previous April, Robert Gay had died trying to drive out the Costa Ricans. Eight of General Henningsen's prized field guns now lined the veranda on that side of the plaza.

Sitting in the shade of the guardhouse porch on the plaza's western side with his Mounted Ranger comrades, Absalom watched companies of freshly arrived recruits drilling out on the sunbaked plaza. They wore new ARN uniforms brought down from San Francisco on the last steamer run—blue tunics, with a number and letter in white on the breast to signify the wearer's battalion and company, plus canvas leggings and black felt hats. It was unlikely that uniforms would have any influence on the outcome of the war, but General Walker wanted his men to feel like soldiers, and act like them. Absalom estimated that Walker had a thousand fighting men in Rivas, a third of them yellowed and wasted by disease. The new Ranger regretted waiting so long to sign up with Parker Crittenden in San Francisco for twenty-five dollars a month plus 250 acres of Nicaraguan land once the war was won. Several of his friends had come down three months earlier, and all had won officers' commissions, with the few privileges that entailed.[4]

Absalom had been sleeping rough in the streets of San Francisco after failing as a gold prospector. Nicaragua had become his best, if not his only, option. He had arrived with enthusiasm, and with admiration for Walker, but the sickness all around him here, the limited and unchanging diet of beef, tortillas, green fruit, and numbing guaro, and the gloom he felt from his fellow filibusters soon sapped his morale and that of many of his colleagues. The depressed mood that set in after the loss of Granada had been exacerbated since by the disappearance of the *La Virgen.* An armed rowboat had been sent across the lake to San Carlos to find out what had happened to the steamer, but it had failed to return. There was a nagging fear in everyone's mind that the Costas had taken the San Juan River.

General Walker, very much aware of sagging spirits among his men, called for his military band to play some foot-tapping music. Once the drilling ended, the band struck up. Walker and his senior officers brought chairs out onto the veranda to listen. According to poet Joaquin Miller, Walker was partial to a sea shanty.[5] Absalom observed that Walker had a wistful look on his face as the band played. Perhaps, in his mind, Walker was harking back to more peaceful days, listening to a brass band playing on a bandstand in Nashville, or attending an opera in New Orleans with his beloved Ellen. Around him, men who had very little to be cheery about began tapping their feet and whistling along to the music. But Walker himself was more worried than his inscrutable visage let on. The lack of information from the San Juan River was deeply troubling.

The largest steamer on the lake, the all-white *San Carlos*, made her way across Lake Nicaragua from La Virgen, bound for El Castillo on the San Juan River. The *Sierra Nevada* had landed Californian passengers at San Juan del Sur on January 2, and the *San Carlos* was taking them on the next leg of their Transit journey. Several of Walker's most experienced officers had joined the steamer at La Virgen—Lieutenant Colonel Anthony Rudler, and Captain Julius De Brissot, as well as General Walker's brother, Captain Norvell Walker. The three were intending to travel to the United States.

All on board the steamer were unaware that the Costa Rican military had seized control of the San Juan River. When the *San Carlos* passed the town of San Carlos, everything seemed normal there; the Costa Rican troops now manning the fort kept out of sight. A little time later, no one aboard the steamer spotted her green sister vessel, the *La Virgen*, sitting up a stream farther downriver. Once the *San Carlos* had passed, the *La Virgen* emerged into the San Juan, then overtook the larger vessel. There was a cannon on her forward deck, loaded, and aimed at the *San Carlos*. Scores of Costa Rican riflemen also lined her decks, with their weapons pointed at the leading steamer's passengers. From the *La Virgen*, Sylvanus Spencer called on the *San Carlos* to heave to.

The master of the *San Carlos*, Captain Ericsson, a plucky Dane, was all for turning about and running for the lake. The *San Carlos* could outrun Spencer's boat, but Ericsson was overruled—by a passenger by the name of Harris, a son-in-law and employee of Cornelius Garrison, an owner of the *San Carlos*. Harris, aware of the 1855 incident when the Costa Ricans fired on this very same steamer from Fort San Carlos, ordered Ericsson to heave to. After Spencer and scores of Costa Rican soldiers boarded her, the *San Carlos* continued to El Castillo. There, the Transit passengers and Walker's officers were put aboard the waiting *Joseph N. Scott*, then taken to San Juan Bay and landed at Punta de Castilla, where Samuel Lockridge had been sitting in a quandary ever since discovering that the Costa Ricans had seized four river steamers.

As Spencer and his troops headed back up the San Juan River aboard the *Scott*, Lockridge and the Walker officers from the *San Carlos* conferred. Lockridge was aware that any day now, several hundred new filibuster recruits were due to arrive at Greytown from New Orleans and New York, along with weapons and ammunition. He proposed to Harris, Rudler, De Brissot, and Norvell Walker that they wait here for those men to arrive, then lead them to regain the San Juan River from the Costa Ricans. When all agreed, Harris appointed Lockridge to command that operation—because Lockridge was Walker's recruiting commissioner to New Orleans and the others were officially on leave. Rudler, the senior ARN officer present, was unhappy with Lockridge's appointment and declared he would continue to the United States. When Walker later heard of this, he criticized Rudler for not tearing up his leave papers and throwing himself into regaining the San Juan. De Brissot sided with Rudler. Meanwhile, Norvell Walker decided to return to Rivas, via Panama. The earnest but unpopular Lockridge was left to lead the San Juan campaign on his own.

The thirty men of Trooper Absalom's Mounted Rangers company had transferred to La Virgen from Rivas, and during the night, they'd seen a light from a steamer on the lake. In the morning, Absalom and his comrades could see the white-hulled *San Carlos* docked at the lake island of Omeotepe. Shortly after, the *La Virgen* also arrived at the island.

When the *La Virgen* approached Virgin Bay from the island, a company of ARN infantry took up positions on the recently repaired jetty stretching 150 yards into the lake. While on the beach, Absalom's Rangers also prepared for a fight. A quarter of a mile out, the cannon on the steamer's deck commenced a feeble bombardment of La Virgen. Despite the gun's inaccuracy, with balls merely splintering rowboats tethered to the wharf, several young Americans on the long jetty lost their nerve and went to run back toward land, only to be slung back by older, cooler comrades. The troops on the jetty then let off a rifle volley at the steamer, and Ranger Sam Absalom watched with amusement as startled Costa Ricans aboard the *La Virgen* scampered for cover. The boat promptly veered away, then returned to the island. But questions about the fate of the lake steamers and the San Juan River had been answered. The *Central America* and *Morgan*, too, fell into Costa Rican hands at this time; now all the operating lake and river steamers had been captured.

Walker knew from the last mail from the United States that hundreds of new recruits were due to soon leave New Orleans and New York to join him. He could only hope now that those reinforcements would somehow retake the river and the steamers for him.

At the Punta de Castilla Transit depot, an elderly, out-of-service river steamer, her hull damaged and long ago stripped of paint by the elements, her steam engine rusty, her paddlewheels creaky, was up on temporary stocks with workmen swarming over her. The old single-deck paddle-steamer was the *Orus*, which had stuck fast on the Machuca Rapids in 1851. Finally retrieved from the rapids, she had lain disused at the point, but, Captain Joseph Scott assured Sam Lockridge, she could be restored to life. With this one precious steamer, Walker's new recruits could be ferried up the San Juan when they arrived from the United States, to wrestle the river back from the Costa Ricans. To reflect the task she was being prepared for, the old steamer was renamed—the *Rescue*. She was William Walker's last hope.

OPERATION SAN JUAN

THE LATEST BRITISH WARSHIP TO TAKE UP STATION OFF GREYTOWN, the twenty-gun steam corvette HMS *Cossack*, sat off Punta de Castilla with guns trained on the point.

For more than a week, while work continued on the repair of the *Rescue*, 240 new recruits for William Walker's army had been training on the point. Two hundred of them had come off the SS *Texas* from New Orleans. When it became clear to the *Texas*'s master that there were no longer boats to conduct his California-bound passengers up the San Juan and across Nicaragua on their way to California, he had set sail again, taking his paying passengers to Panama. Days later, on January 9, the SS *James Adger* had arrived from New York. To compete with the Vanderbilt Gulf line, Charles Morgan had redirected one of his larger, better-appointed Nicaragua steamers to the Gulf of Mexico, putting the *James Adger* in its place. Until recently laying telegraph cable in Canadian waters, the 1,364-ton *Adger* was neither large nor glamorous. She, too, had been forced to sail on with her passengers to Panama after landing forty more Walker recruits at Punta de Castilla.

Among these latest arrivals were two returning officers—Colonel Frank Anderson, recovered from his last battle wound, and Charles Doubleday, the captain and commissary who fell out with Walker in 1855 and went home to Ohio. Doubleday was returning with an offer of a colonelcy from Walker. A valuable new addition was thirty-year-old Chatham Roberdeau Wheat. From Virginia, "Bob" Wheat was an man of Herculean frame and flashing, dark eyes. A U.S. Army captain in the Mexican War, he'd later gained renown under Lopez in Cuba and been elected to the Louisiana state legislature at the age of twenty-six. Walker had promised him a brigadier general's commission.

On January 16, Captain George Cockburn, commander of HMS *Cossack*, landed at Punta de Castilla and demanded to see whoever was in charge. Sam Lockridge stepped forward. The Walker officers had all agreed to obey Lockridge's commands, but Doubleday, for one, was unimpressed with the Texan, considering him merely "a master of transportation for recruits in Walker's army."[1]

Captain Cockburn commanded Lockridge to parade his men, and under threat of bombardment, Lockridge begrudgingly assembled the recruits. Cockburn informed them that they faced annihilation by a vast force of Costa Ricans on the San Juan River, then read them a letter from his squadron commander, Captain Erskine of HMS *Orion*, offering protection to every British citizen in the filibuster ranks. Should the officer commanding the filibusters refuse to allow Britons to leave, Cockburn had orders to prevent any filibuster from going up the San Juan River. Cockburn then called on all British citizens present to step forward. Twenty men did so.[2] Among them was twenty-six-year-old Laurence Oliphant, son of Sir Anthony Oliphant, and onetime secretary to several British governors general of Canada. Oliphant had signed up to join Walker, in his own words, "for the fun of the thing."[3] Now, facing apparently impossible odds on the San Juan, filibustering didn't sound like fun to Oliphant after all.

Bob Wheat was so infuriated by the pirating of Walker recruits he offered to fight Cockburn in a duel there on the sand. Ignoring the challenge, Cockburn transferred Oliphant and the other Britons to the *Cossack*.

The rejuvenated *Rescue* steamed slowly toward the mouth of the Sarapiqui River, her deck crowded with Sam Lockridge's 220 men. The old steamer had ferried them up the San Juan to land them, their equipment, and several tons of ammunition at the Petako orange orchard, two hours' steaming time below the junction of the San Juan and Sarapiqui Rivers. From that base camp, Lockridge was launching his first assault of the campaign to recapture the river.

The Costa Ricans had fortified Hipp's Point and established another emplacement at Cody's Point, on the opposite bank. As the *Rescue* dawdled toward the Cody's Point fortification, she was greeted by a fusillade of rifle rounds. "Whistling about us," Charles Doubleday observed, "[they] notified us not only of the intention of the garrison, but, by the peculiar sound that Vanderbilt's cargoes of Minie rifles had reached their destination."[4] The *Rescue* quickly retreated out of range, before sliding into the northern bank and landing the filibusters. The cautious Lockridge then had his men fell trees and build a log stockade. Urged on by Doubleday and Anderson, he subsequently agreed to an attack on Cody's Point.

When the attack went forward, it met stubborn resistance from the enemy dug in behind earthworks. At the same time, two cannon at the Hipp's Point fortification shelled Lockridge's men, although with little accuracy. Lockridge's force, far outnumbering the Costa Ricans, swept over the walls and captured Cody's Point and two small brass cannon located there, wiping out the defenders while suffering only "trifling" casualties themselves.[5]

Flushed with victory, Lockridge's officers convinced him to press on against Hipp's Point that night. Anderson, Doubleday, and most of the troops left Lockridge and Wheat at Cody's Point with the cannon, and just before midnight, the *Rescue* deposited them on the southern bank of the river, below the mouth of the Sarapiqui. Opposite Hipp's Point, they took up positions in trees recently felled by the Costa Ricans.

At Hipp's Point, Major Maximo Blanco prepared to defend his position. Sylvanus Spencer had left two hundred Costa Ricans here in December; already, Blanco had lost half his force to disease and desertion. The morale of Blanco's remaining men was at rock bottom after seeing what happened to their comrades at Cody's Point. Now, as the Costa Ricans waited for the inevitable Yankee assault, Blanco prayed that his outnumbered men would put up spirited resistance. Costa Rica was counting on them. So, too, was Cornelius Vanderbilt.

The first rays of the new day signaled the start of the battle for Hipp's Point. From Cody's Point to the north, Wheat's cannon lobbed canister shot across the river, doing little damage but keeping Costa Rican heads down. From across the Sarapiqui to the east, two hundred American riflemen opened fire. For over an hour, Blanco's men returned fire, causing frequent American casualties on the other side of the Sarapiqui. When, eventually, Costa Rican fire slackened, Doubleday led a group of Americans up the Sarapiqui and found a fording place.

Doubleday was surprised that when he and his men emerged from the jungle and charged the Hipp's Point fort, they met no resistance. Mounting the walls, they dropped down inside. Apart from enemy dead, the fort was deserted. After eighteen of his men had been killed and many more wounded, Major Blanco had led the Costa Rican survivors out the back way and into the jungle.

When Lockridge arrived at the captured fort, he contemptuously ordered the enemy dead thrown into the San Juan, knowing the bodies would be carried on the current to San Juan Bay and float by HMS *Cossack*, providing the British with gory proof that William Walker's men had annihilated Costa Ricans on the San Juan, despite their "overwhelming force."

At Rivas, Walker acted as if relief was imminent. On January 3, Adjutant General Phil Thompson's morning report listed 919 men, able-bodied and on the sick list at Rivas. This, Walker knew, compared with 4,000 men in the Allied armies camped at Masaya and Granada, including recent Honduran reinforcements.[6] Despite this, Walker appeared calm and self-contained, as always.

Trooper Sam Absalom had been sent to deliver a message to the general. Waiting his turn at the door to Walker's Rivas office, Absalom saw a captain ahead of him—a big man, with a dark, bushy beard.

Walker was not happy with something the captain had done; precisely what, Absalom never learned. "Captain," Walker said, in a controlled voice, "if this is the way you are going to do business, Nicaragua has no further use for you. We want nothing of this sort done here, sir."[7]

The acutely embarrassed captain departed without a word and was never heard of again. Even though he was surrounded, Walker was prepared to let officers go if they broke his rules.

On February 4, the *Rescue* returned to Hipp's Point after a trip downriver to Greytown to meet the *Texas*. The steamer from New Orleans brought 180 more men, equipped with their own rifles, ammunition, and field guns. The latest arrivals were above the usual cut of boys and romantics attracted to Walker's cause. In Doubleday's opinion, they were "a fine-looking company of men."[8] Another member of Lockridge's party said of them, "I never saw a finer set of filibusters."[9]

The new arrivals were led by forty-two-year-old Henry T. Titus, infamous as one of the "Border Ruffians." The previous year, they had fought a nasty little civil war in Kansas over the issue of slavery. Called Bleeding Kansas, it had pitted slavery advocates such as Titus against abolitionists such as John Brown. Titus, a huge, bearded man wearing a double-breasted frock coat and a black slouch hat with the left side pinned up, had not long stepped ashore before he generated dislike among Lockridge's officers and conflict with Lockridge. Although only offered a captain's commission, in Kansas he'd styled himself "Colonel" Titus and would not be addressed in any other fashion here. As for his men, they would not serve any commander other than Titus, so Lockridge allowed Titus to retain the command of his party, with Colonel Anderson commanding the original group.

As an attack on El Castillo was discussed, Lockridge said that Anderson, as the most senior officer, should lead it. But Titus balked at this. "I'll capture the damned place with my company alone!" he declared.[10]

In Doubleday's opinion, Titus was "blown full of pride by the cheap reputation he had acquired in burning defenseless houses on the Missouri-Kansas frontier."[11] In fact, before leaving New Orleans, Titus had boasted that once he and his men arrived in Nicaragua, they would set things right within a matter of days.[12]

Despite opposition from Anderson and others, Lockridge gave in to Titus. While Anderson's men remained at Hipp's Point, the Kansas men would take the *Rescue* upriver to conquer El Castillo.

With one thousand troops, Generals Canas and Jerez had occupied San Jorge, three miles from Rivas, from where they threatened the Transit Route. So Walker had sent Henningsen and Sanders to throw them out. But when Henningsen began the attack, Sanders held back. Henningsen was now a major general, promoted above Sanders, and he felt certain Sanders was jealous of him and wanted his attack to fail.[13] Fail it did—with Sanders's troops sitting outside the town, Henningsen had insufficient men and his advance stalled after bitter street fighting, losing eighty men killed and wounded for no gain. On February 1, forty new recruits had arrived at San Juan del Sur from San Francisco aboard the *Orizaba*. These new men were thrown straight into the firing line, when Walker personally led the next attack on San Jorge, taking several hundred men with him while leaving the majority of his army to hold Rivas.

Now, at 4:00 A.M. on February 4, the same day that Titus joined Lockridge on the San Juan, Walker and his troops infiltrated San Jorge from the east. The advance guard had reached a breast-high barricade at the entrance to the town plaza before the enemy was called to arms. Allied troops tumbled from their beds and straight into the fighting at the plaza. A senior Nicaraguan officer with a limp was shot in the face and had to be helped to the rear by his men—it was Walker's old Democratico adversary, General Maximo Jerez.

But as had been the case in most of the urban battles Walker fought in Nicaragua, he did not have enough men to sustain the attack and had to order a withdrawal. Young Cal O'Neal, recently promoted to colonel, was brought down by one of the last shots of the battle and was carried away, severely injured.

Two days later, in the Hacienda Maleano, Walker's crowded hospital at Rivas, as Walker stayed at the young man's bedside and "watched over his last agonies," Cal O'Neal died. He had survived both Battles of Rivas, the disasters at Santa Rosa and San Jacinto, and the two failed sieges of Masaya. But in the end, O'Neal's luck ran out. He was not yet twenty-one years of age.

The muster list on February 6 recorded that an officer and nineteen Mounted Rangers deserted en masse the previous day, with their horses and equipment. Last seen riding hard and fast for Costa Rica, the deserters were Sam Absalom and most of his company. At the beginning of February, pamphlets had begun turning up in Rivas, containing a proclamation from Costa Rican President Juan Rafael Mora. Now, Mora promised, Americans who came over to the Allies would not be shot; they would be given protection and free passage back to the United States. Disillusion and desertion would now become Walker's greatest enemies. If Lockridge's bid to reopen the San Juan River did not soon succeed, there would be no Army of the Republic of Nicaragua left to relieve.

This same day, the U.S. Navy's 958-ton sloop-of-war *St. Mary's* dropped anchor at San Juan del Sur, a little distance from Walker's armed schooner *Granada* and the Morgan and Garrison coal ship *Narragansett*. Commander Charles H. Davis had recently taken over command of the *St. Mary's* at Panama. He'd come to Nicaragua with express orders from Washington. Officially, he was to "take such steps as circumstances required for the protection of American citizens" in Nicaragua.[14] In reality, the navy secretary, at the request of the secretary of state and the urging of Cornelius Vanderbilt, had given Davis the job of ending this war by removing William Walker from Nicaragua. While Vanderbilt had been confident of Spencer's ultimate success on the San Juan River, by involving the U.S. Navy, he was writing himself a little insurance. One way or the other, the Commodore was determined to get Walker.

From the castle battlements, thirty-year-old Colonel George Cauty studied the little steamer making toward El Castillo. It was the middle of the morning on Wednesday, February 16, and for Cauty, the unexpected appearance of the steamer was cause for alarm. As were the sight of William Walker's lone-star Nicaraguan Republic flag being flown by the vessel and the scores of dark-clad armed figures she carried. Up to this time, Cauty had been unaware that Lockridge's filibusters were on the river or that Cody's Point and Hipp's Point had fallen to them. Cauty had his drummer sound the call to arms.

Trenches dug by Cauty below the hill were occupied by a captain and thirteen men. Cauty's remaining sixteen Costa Ricans manned the castle ramparts with him. Cauty now calmly instructed his deputy, Colonel Faustino Montes de Oca, to hurry a message down to the trenches ordering the men there to destroy the two river steamers at the town's wharves and to fire the town, starting with the Hollenbecks' hotel. As Costa Rican soldiers soon ran through the town with lighted torches in hand, sending the towns-people fleeing, several Costas clambered onto the *Joseph N. Scott*, which was moored at the wharf below the rapids, and began to smash her machinery. At the wharf on the high side of the rapids, other soldiers attacked the *Machuca*.

As the *Rescue* slid into the river bank below the town, 140 filibusters leaped to the shore and ran to the attack, firing as they came. The *Rescue* immediately reversed into the stream and headed back down the river out of range. The Costa Rican destruction party deserted the *Scott*, their work unfinished. But flames were shooting up from buildings in the town, and the *Machuca* was also burning. When filibusters reached the *Scott*, a quick-thinking American cut the steamer's mooring lines and set her adrift. Driven by the current from the tumbling rapids, the *Scott* drifted east downriver and out of Costa Rican hands.

After the captain and a corporal defending the trenches were killed by the filibusters, the dozen remaining Costas ran up the hill to the castle a hundred feet above.

From the trench line, Henry Titus surveyed the scene. The Hollenbecks' hotel had been razed; their nearby store was also a charred ruin. The *Machuca*, burned to the waterline, had sunk beside the wharf. Now, a little after midday, as an officer came down the hill from the castle under a flag of truce, Titus, grunting with satisfaction, clambered from the trench and began climbing the slope to meet him.

The Castle of the Immaculate Conception had never been taken by storm. The rectangular castle was 195 by 93 feet. Its stone walls were 4 feet thick and 14 feet high, and within those walls, there was a 50-foot central keep. At each corner were bastions equipped with loopholes. The Spanish had originally built the castle to prevent pirates from the Caribbean sacking Granada, as Henry Morgan had done. In 1780, with Britain at war with Spain, the castle had been attacked by twenty-five hundred British sailors and soldiers with orders to capture Granada, León, and Realejo. Horatio Nelson, then a twenty-one-year-old Royal Navy lieutenant, had brought four 4-pound naval cannon and a howitzer up the river and bombarded the castle for a week, sending more than four hundred cannonballs into its walls. The two hundred Spanish defenders had surrendered after running out of food and water, but so many of the attackers, including Nelson, had fallen ill with yellow fever and dysentery that the British withdrew.[15]

Henry Titus could only guess at the size of the castle's Costa Rican garrison. In a letter from General Mora to Major Blanco found at Hipp's Point, Mora had spoken of sending men from the San Juan across the lake to join an Allied attack on Rivas. By this time, Costa Rica's General Cañas was the Allies' new commander in chief. After allowing Henningsen to escape Granada, then retreating meekly to Masaya, Guatemala's General Belloso had received intense criticism throughout Central America and resigned. Cañas, elected Belloso's successor by the other Allied commanders, had urged his compatriot to send him men for a final push against Walker— Mora did in fact send him five hundred of his eleven hundred men.

Mora's letter had suggested to Lockridge and Titus that the castle may have been lightly defended, although they could not be sure. Told by Lockridge that a long siege of the castle was out of the question if General Walker was to be relieved in time, Titus had sent a message up to the castle's commander, demanding his surrender. Now, Titus reached the officer coming down to him—it was George Cauty, who wanted to hear what the American had to say in person. Producing a flask of brandy, "Colonel" Titus shared it with the English officer and, with false bonhomie, offered to accept the unconditional surrender of the castle garrison. The alternative, said Titus, hoping to bluff his opponent, would not be pleasant for Cauty or his men.

Cauty later related Titus's comments to the Costa Rican ambassador to London, Pedro Perez: "He told me he had a large battery of cannon of great caliber mounted for the attack and that his force consisted of 1,000 men. This appeared so 'gassy' that I paid no attention to it."[16] Titus, a man prone to half-truths and exaggerations, had been half right—counting Anderson's men, there were close to five hundred filibusters on the San Juan, and downriver, Lockridge had six field guns, although none were of any great caliber.

The English mercenary, given confidence by the knowledge that not even fellow countryman Lord Nelson had been able to blast his way into the castle, could have simply told Titus to do his worst and then bade him good day. But Cauty had fought more real battles than Titus had ever dreamed of, and quickly sized up the big man as an oaf and a fool. Playing along with Titus, Cauty agreed that his situation was indeed hopeless. He would dearly love to surrender, he said, but to do that, he would need the permission of his superior, General Mora, at Fort San Carlos. Cauty asked Titus to give him twenty-four hours to obtain that permission. And—Titus agreed.

One of Cauty's men was subsequently permitted by Titus to leave the castle, get into a bungo above the rapids, and paddle off to the west. Titus and his men then withdrew to the other side of the river and made camp above the rapids. Here, they settled down to await an enemy capitulation next day.

The lake steamer *Morgan* eased into the riverbank west of El Castillo. Sixty Costa Rican soldiers jumped ashore, then made their way east through the trees, led by Captains Joaquin Ortiz, Jesus Alvardo, and Luis Pacheco; this was the same Luis Pacheco who, as a sergeant in Rivas on April 10 the previous year, made the first unsuccessful attempt to set fire to Guerra's Inn.

These troops had come in response to Colonel Cauty's note. Rather than asking General Mora for permission to surrender, Cauty had sought reinforcements to help him throw back Titus's filibusters. General Mora sent 60 percent of his 100-man Fort San Carlos garrison, hoping the element of surprise would compensate for lack of numbers, and these troops progressively worked their way down the riverbank, until, by 10:00 A.M., they were behind Titus's 140 unsuspecting men. Once in position, the Costas rose up from the undergrowth, yelling their battle cries, and launched a bayonet charge.[17]

At the castle, George Cauty, who'd been expecting this attack since sunrise, broke into a relieved smile. "We heard firing in the hills," he later said, "and loud shouts and 'Vivas for Costa Rica,' which we answered." Within thirty minutes, the fighting was all over. "The filibusters fled, throwing away their arms, ammunition and provisions," Cauty recounted, "so that the road for two miles down the river was strewn with them. Fortunately for Colonel Titus a steamboat arrived at the wharf just in time to take them off." The Costa Ricans would estimate that seventy of Titus's men were killed or wounded.[18] The attempt to retake the San Juan for Walker had faltered, badly. Vanderbilt's noose tightened a little more.

The *Rescue* had arrived in time to help Titus and his surviving Border Ruffians escape. She landed them twenty miles downriver, at San Carlos Island, which sat in the middle of the San Juan River. There, Lockridge and forty of Titus's men had built a log emplacement, calling it Fort Slatter. Lockridge's officers considered Titus an idiot for allowing Cauty to hoodwink him. Titus's courage was questioned, as were his motives. The New York *Tribune,* when it reported the El Castillo fiasco, would say: "Some attribute Titus's conduct to sheer cowardice, while others affirm that he sold the battle." The *Tribune* added: "His officers swore that they would no longer serve under such a poltroon, and his men vowed that they would shoot him for his cowardice."[19]

Titus, humiliated, declared his intent to travel via Panama to join Walker, and departed on the *Rescue.* His bungled attack did have one plus—the *Rescue* had taken the drifting *Scott* in tow and brought her down to San Carlos

Island, and there Lockridge's men set to work repairing her damaged ma-chinery. When Titus arrived at Greytown on the *Rescue*, he argued with a British naval officer, who arrested him and detained the old steamer. But, shortly after, the U.S. sloop-of-war *Saratoga* arrived in the bay, and her pres-ence inspired the release of both Titus and the *Rescue*.

Before long, the SS *Tennessee* arrived from New York, carrying not a single Walker recruit. Largely because of bad publicity stemming from the Slavery Decree and its suspension of the ban on slavery in Nicaragua, the flow of recruits from the Northern states had dried up, even though the press was still generally supportive. "Again and again we have called Walker a hero," declared the new illustrated journal *Harper's Weekly* in its January 31, 1857, issue. "We shall not take it back."

Morgan and Garrison were also suffering. Now that it was known in the United States that the San Juan River had been closed by the Costa Ricans, no through passengers were signing up for the Nicaraguan Transit. The Morgan and Garrison Line was keeping its commitment to Walker by deliv-ering his recruits, supplies, and mail to Greytown and San Juan del Sur, but had resorted to selling through passages via Panama. On this latest voyage, the *Tennessee* sailed on to Panama. And Henry Titus sailed with her.

As rain bucketed down, Lockridge and his men huddled in temporary shel-ters at Fort Slatter and Hipp's Point, wet, hungry, and downhearted. Every rainy season, northeasterly winds off the Caribbean deposited two hundred inches of rain on eastern Nicaragua.[20] Old hands in Nicaragua knew that this downpour could continue for weeks.

At El Castillo, Colonel Cauty and his reinforced garrison enjoyed the pro-tection of the old castle keep. There, Cauty, who felt certain the filibusters would be back, conceived a novel plan. His men procured pieces of firewood from the Hollenbecks' woodshed, and in a dry castle workshop, the center of each small log was bored out. Gunpowder was packed into the cavity, and wooden plugs hammered into place at the ends. As soon as there was a break in the rain, the wood was loaded into a long, narrow bungo and covered with a tarpaulin. Steered by Captain Luis Pacheco, who had volunteered for this mission, the canoe was carried down the San Juan by the current.

Dotted along the river there were Transit wood depots. Here, firewood periodically felled in the jungle by subcontractors such as John Hollenbeck and cut to size for the steamers' fireboxes stood piled in readiness for steamer use. At two of these depots, between El Castillo and San Carlos Island, Pacheco infiltrated his doctored wood into the stockpiles. Abandoning the bungo, which he would have struggled to paddle on his own back up the San Juan against the current, Pacheco set off overland with a compass loaned to him by Colonel Cauty, and he made his way back to El Castillo. "Captain Pacheco fulfilled my instructions exactly," Cauty later told Ambassador Perez.[21]

In the middle of the day on February 18, fifty-year-old Commander Charles Davis, captain of the USS *St. Mary's*, walked into Walker's bleak Rivas headquarters. He was a tall, slim man with longish gray hair and handlebar mustache. Politely addressing Walker as "Mr. President," Davis saluted.[22] He had been permitted by both sides to enter Rivas to meet with Walker.

In the discussions that followed, Davis said that the captain of the coal ship *Narragansett* at San Juan del Sur would like his small boats back. Walker, who had confiscated the boats for an ultimately aborted mission against the captured steamers on Lake Nicaragua, responded that the coal ship had been chartered by Morgan and Garrison, so the ship's boats were technically theirs, not the master's. What's more, said Walker, Mr. Morgan and Mr. Garrison would like their other boats back—the lake and river steamers seized by the Allies. If Davis asked for the former, said Walker, wearing his lawyer's hat, then the commander must also ask the Allies for the latter. Davis said he would go to San Jorge and talk to the Allied generals on the subject. He would also ask, he said, if American crews on the lake and river steamers were being made to operate them against their will. Davis had clearly come to Walker, with the approval of the Allies, in the hope of convincing him to surrender. But Walker would not even contemplate the idea. After staying in Rivas overnight as Walker's guest, Davis traveled to the Allied field headquarters at San Jorge next morning.

As soon as Walker heard that the U.S. Navy officer had left San Jorge, he personally led an attack on the town. It was important for him, Walker was to write, "while waiting the result of Lockridge's effort to open the Transit, to let [my] troops see that they were not thrown entirely on the defensive."[23] Walker's attack succeeded in driving the Allies from San Jorge, but General Canas managed to regroup his units and wheel them around behind Walker. Just in time, Walker realized he was about to be cut off from Rivas and fought his way back there. Rivas, the center of his shrinking dominion, was his only refuge. He prepared to hold it at all costs.

For Walker, everything now hinged on Lockridge's retaking the San Juan River and bringing his five hundred men to join his general. With those fresh men, Walker could launch a counterattack from Rivas and drive the Allies off.

TO THE VICTOR,
THE SPOILS

THE *RESCUE* ARRIVED AT SAN CARLOS ISLAND WITH 140 NEW MEN LED by Captains Marcellus French and W. C. Capers, fresh off the *Texas* from New Orleans. Some were youths from Mobile, Alabama, but most were "old Texans, of the right stripe for settling and civilizing," in the opinion of one of Lockridge's men, Orderly Sergeant George W. Sites from Philadelphia, who was thrilled to see them. These men were, said Sites, "determined to help in whipping the Costa Ricans on the river."[1] According to Charles Doubleday, they were former Texas Rangers: "These men were of the kind equal to anything requiring courage and skill in action."[2]

They were sorely needed, for after the departure of Henry Titus, his Kansas ruffians had lost interest in Nicaragua. In the incessant rain, their depression spread to Lockridge's other men, many of whom had come down sick. Over several days, a number of men, including sentries, slipped off the island at night, to float down the river on rough rafts to San Juan Bay and passage home. Lockridge's command, reduced to 250 men by casualties and desertion, was brought up to close to 400 by the latest arrivals, and when the rain lifted, so, too, did spirits. Lockridge's officers pressed for a new attack on El Castillo.

One of Walker's staff officers had arrived with the New Orleans recruits. Major John Baldwin had come from Rivas via Panama, bringing a letter in which Walker confirmed Lockridge's command on the San Juan and commanded that if Lockridge was unable to get by the enemy on the river, he and his men were to make their way to Rivas overland, through the jungle, to reinforce Walker. The arrival of the new men "gave us hope of forcing the

passage of the river," said Doubleday, and Lockridge agreed to another attempt to take El Castillo.[3] This time, every man would take part. All were
loaded onto the *Scott* and *Rescue* together with their rifles, ammunition, and
two tons of gunpowder, and the boats set off west.[4]

Late on March 29, the *Rescue* eased into the riverbank a mile east of El
Castillo, around a bend in the river and out of sight of the Costa Rican garrison. Twelve miles below El Castillo, the *Scott* had proven too heavy to
manhandle over the Machuca Rapids. After getting the lighter boat over,
Lockridge had continued west with the *Rescue*, loading her with men and
equipment and leaving the *Scott* behind with a small guard.

Lockridge now landed his men, then took a party with him as he scaled a
steep rise known as Nelson's Hill—because, legend had it, Horatio Nelson
had bombarded El Castillo from there. From the summit, the castle was visible on the next hill. But a deep ravine separated the two hills. Lockridge observed that to reach the castle overland, attackers would have to run down
one hill, cross the ravine, and then run up the next hill—in range of the defenders' guns every step of the way. As the sun set, Lockridge and his party
slithered back down the slope to the men at the steamer. They all camped
on the riverbank overnight.

When the new day dawned, Lockridge called an officers' conference,
then announced that the odds against them were too great. Titus and his
men, in excusing their inglorious flight from El Castillo, had put the number of the Costa Rican reinforcements in the hundreds. Against such
numbers, holding such a strong emplacement, Lockridge estimated that a
hundred Americans would die in taking the castle, whether attacking by
land or by water.

As the others voiced their opinions, Lockridge added that a note had
come down on the *Texas* from Walker's New Orleans agent, informing him
that no more Morgan and Garrison steamers would sail for Nicaragua; no
more reinforcements or supplies could be expected.[5] This news staggered
Lockridge's men, and depression spread through the ranks. No one suggested a night attack or trying to bluff the Costas the way that the Costas

had bluffed Titus. Instead, Lockridge's officers unanimously voted to call off the operation.

Then, with Lockridge failing to reveal that he had orders from Walker to attempt to reach him overland if all else failed, Anderson, Doubleday, French, and Capers decided to go back down the river to Greytown to catch the next steamer bound for Panama, via which they would join Walker at Rivas, a ten-day journey. A hundred men, including most of the newly arrived Texans, joined them. The other three hundred, Lockridge included, voted to go home. In guilty silence, they all reboarded the *Rescue.*

Once the *Rescue* reached the Machuca Rapids, Anderson and those planning to go to Panama loaded up the *Scott,* which waited below the rapids, then steamed away, leaving Lockridge and the others who planned returning to the United States struggling to drag the *Rescue* down over the rocks.

It was 9:00 A.M. on April 2. Julius De Brissot, captaining the *Scott,* had nosed the river steamer's prow into a sandbank just above Hipp's Point.

Pausing only to take on wood from the riverbank en route, the *Scott* had hurried on ahead of the *Rescue.* When the steamer reached the mouth of the Sarapiqui River, Frank Anderson, wanting to be sure the Costas had not occupied Hipp's Point behind their backs, landed a patrol on the riverbank to check out the abandoned fort while most of his men waited on board the *Scott.*

Charles Doubleday was in the steamer's wheelhouse on the upper deck, leaning on the sill of the wheelhouse window as he watched the members of the patrol wend their way through the trees toward the point. Behind him, the steamer's boiler hissed steam and stokers loaded wood into her firebox. "Suddenly I felt myself hurled into the air with terrific force," Doubleday would recall.[6]

The steamer was rent by a massive explosion that ripped off her bow, blew the upper deck and wheelhouse to smithereens, and threw men high into the air. Moments later, Doubleday lay in wreckage amid scalding boiler water. Flames leaped up all around him. Men on the upper deck had been blown into the water; others onto land. Orderly Sergeant Sites was one of those who, like Doubleday, found himself in the wreckage on the lower deck, surrounded by blackened bodies. "The groans of the wounded were heart piercing," Sites later told the New York *Herald*. Some of the injured, Sites said, ran around the boat "with the skin of their arms and hands hanging in strips, shrieking and groaning and begging to be put out of misery."[7]

"The powder!" someone yelled.[8]

There were two tons of gunpowder on the lower deck, protected against the rain by canvas tarpaulins. Those tarpaulins were on fire. If the gunpowder went up, all the survivors from the first explosion would be blown up. "I could only gaze at it," the badly scalded Doubleday recalled, "and wonder how soon the second and final act would come."[9] Frank Anderson and Bob Wheat, who were leading the shore patrol, ran to the boat. Scrambling up the *Scott*'s side, they dragged the burning canvas away and tossed it into the river, saving the day.

Sixty men were killed in the blast, and twenty-five injured—most of those severely. When the *Rescue* arrived on the scene a little later, the *Scott* survivors were taken on board. She carried them down to Greytown, from where they were repatriated to the United States, with all thoughts of joining Walker having evaporated.

Various theories as to why the *Scott* blew up abounded in the coming weeks and months. Walker put it down to "ill luck."[10] Some blamed poor repair work after the *Scott* was retrieved from El Castillo with her machinery damaged. Doubleday, who slowly recovered from his burns, felt that "the engineer had pumped cold water into the superheated cylinder, and the boiler had burst."[11] Sites told the New York *Herald*, "Several eyewitnesses believed that it was caused by some miscreant, who threw a flask of powder into the furnace. It is not known who it was. We know it must have been powder, from the fact of the faces of the wounded being a great deal blackened with powder. We had at least two tons of powder on board the *Scott*, but not a bit of it was disturbed by the explosion."[12]

It was indeed powder that caused the explosion, as George Cauty and Luis Pacheco immediately realized once the news of the event reached them. As Cauty told the Costa Rican ambassador to England, years later, when the *Scott* stopped to refuel, she must have taken on board pieces of the gunpowder-filled firewood that Pacheco had planted at the riverbank depots weeks before the disaster.

And so it was that Cauty, a wily mercenary in the employ of Cornelius Vanderbilt, finally sealed the fate of the San Juan River filibusters with an improvised explosive device and brought to a close the last attempt to reclaim the river and send hundreds of desperately needed men through to Walker at Rivas. Walker was now irretrievably cut off from the Atlantic and Gulf states.

The Allied generals and colonels clustered around a table in a forward headquarters tent at Cuatro Esquinas, or Four Corners, a crossroads a mile from Rivas. It was April 10, and General José Maria Mora, the latest Allied commander in chief, proposed one final all-out assault on Rivas.

Arriving at San Jorge on March 18 by lake steamer, General Mora had brought 560 much-needed reinforcements from the Third Costa Rican Division. Attempts on March 6 and 16 by General Canas to take Rivas by storm had been repulsed by Walker, at a cost of more than 1,000 Allied casualties. General Mora, impatient for final victory, had then personally taken charge of all Allied forces. Canas had, however, been able to claim some success—on March 6, General Sanders and 160 men sent by Walker to clear the Transit Road had been met by 150 Costa Ricans under Major Juan Estrada near the Jocote cattle ranch. Sanders's force had retreated in disorder, allowing Estrada, soon promoted to colonel, to occupy San Juan del Sur. Despite the fact that Walker's little warship *Granada* still sat in the cove, Estrada had succeeded in cutting Walker's supply line from California. Now, both ends of the Transit were closed. Walker was completely cut off at Rivas.

Although the Battle of the Jocote, as Estrada's encounter with Sanders came to be called, was trumpeted throughout Central America as a great Allied victory, General Mora knew that as long as Walker continued to occupy Rivas, the war was not won. Mora himself had subsequently launched an attack on Rivas just before daybreak on March 23. The assault, involving eighteen hundred Allied troops and launched at three locations, had been bloodily thrown back by Walker's men, costing the Allies hundreds of casualties for no gain. Another Allied attack on Rivas on March 24 had the same result. Then, on the twenty-sixth, Mora occupied the Rivas suburbs of Puebla and Apaaco and closed off all roads into the city. An entire company of filibusters was soon captured while trying to sneak out to forage for food. The noose was squeezing even tighter around Walker and his dwindling army.

Yet, like Walker, the Allies had major supply problems. Worse than that, cholera was rife, the soldiers' pay was months in arrears, and faced by Yankee filibusters who seemed unbeatable, morale was poor, with desertions constantly draining the ranks. A lengthy siege could not be sustained. Having received 250 fresh Nicaraguan conscripts from the north under General Tomás Martinez on April 3 and 500 Guatemalan reinforcements on April 7, General Mora detailed a new plan at the Four Corners meeting: An attack would take place the next day, April 11, the first anniversary of Walker's reverse at Rivas, and consequently a symbolic date for Central Americans. Mora asked for 1,000 fresh men from all four Allied armies. And to lead them, he chose a Nicaraguan general—this was, after all, a war to liberate Nicaragua. The general was limping Maximo Jerez, who had recovered from his San Jorge wound. The assault would commence at dawn.

As Mora conducted his council of war, Walker was in conference with his senior officers at Rivas. Walker had noted that the enemy was unusually quiet. For weeks, the Allies had regularly shelled the city. Two twenty-four-pounder cannon sited on rises twelve hundred yards outside the city proved particularly annoying, and occasionally lethal, although their spent balls were collected by General Henningsen's men and melted down into six-pound balls that were fired back at the enemy. Even the guns were silent, and Walker, aware of the significance of the April 11 anniversary to the Allies, sensed that an attack was imminent. He instructed his officers to concentrate their men around Rivas's plaza and prepare to repel an early-morning assault.

As dawn approached, every able-bodied American waited at barricades, loopholes, and field pieces around the plaza. Ammunition was piled ready.

There was no shortage of rifle rounds—tens of thousands had been received from supporters such as George Law in the United States. And hundreds of artillery shells had arrived in recent months from San Francisco. Church bells had been collected from surrounding villages and melted down to create cannonballs, and scrap metal had been gathered and turned into grape and canister shot in Henningsen's artillery workshop.

To oppose four thousand Allied troops, casualties and desertion had left Walker with five hundred Americans, with only half of them fit to fight. On March 7, seventy Californian recruits had reached him via the *Orizaba,* wearing the cheap red flannel shirts then popular on the California gold fields; with neither uniforms nor black dye to give them, Walker had called them the Red Star Guard and sent them into battle in their red shirts. Within a month, less than half the Red Star Guard remained. On March 19, the *Orizaba* had delivered twenty more Californians. These would prove to be Walker's last recruits. With the San Juan River lost and the Allies now controlling San Juan del Sur, Walker had to fight to the end with the men he had.

American deserters had told General Mora that a house on the southern side of Rivas's plaza was occupied by two American ladies and undefended. Just before dawn on April 11, 250 Costa Ricans burst into the house from the rear. The screams of the terrified women alerted Lieutenant Sevier, whose twelve-pound howitzer stood in the middle of the plaza. Sevier hurriedly aimed the weapon at the house and depressed the short barrel. When the door opened and Costa Ricans poured out, Sevier fired. Twelve pounds of shrapnel blanketed the doorway. Costas fell like hay before the scythe. Stunned survivors stumbled back into the house.

Walker's loyal Nicaraguan officer, Mateo Pineda, recently promoted to brigadier general, led the forty native Nicaraguans who remained in Walker's army plus a company of Rangers to seal off the rear of the house, trapping the Costa Ricans inside. General Henningsen then fired six-pound balls into the front of the house, peppering the walls with holes. When Pineda called in Spanish for the Costas to surrender, more than two hundred crawled from the house and raised their hands. Of the ladies, we hear nothing.

Across town, General Zavala led five hundred newly arrived Guatemalan Indian farm boys through the northern suburbs toward the plaza. To give these recent draftees the courage to go against the filibusters, Zavala had filled them with guaro. Reaching barricades manned by the companies of Captains McEachin and McMichael, the liquored Guatemalan farmers were shot down "like so many cattle," in Walker's words. "The Guatemalan officers cared no more for their men than if they were sheep."[13] Few came any closer than sixty yards of the American positions before the assault was called off.

At the same time, 250 sober Nicaraguan recruits led by General Martinez advanced along the road from the west. As they broached the Santa Ursula Hill, they came under heavy fire from an American rifle company in the ruins of the Santa Ursula hacienda. Martinez's men were driven back with heavy loss; the survivors refused to launch a fresh assault.

General Mora's offensive ended not long after it began, with 700 of the 1000 Allied troops involved killed, wounded, or captured.[14] Walker lost three killed and nine wounded. His troops took 220 prisoners and collected 250 discarded Minié rifles. Unable to feed many prisoners, Walker sent 150 wounded Allied soldiers back to their own lines. The remaining prisoners were made to bury their own dead.[15] April 11, 1857, was not a day to be remembered as the Allies had hoped. Such losses could not be sustained, and Mora suspended further large-scale military operations.

On April 14, one of Walker's officers, John S. Hankins from Arkansas, slipped back into Rivas after a dangerous mission through enemy lines. He'd succeeded in meeting the *Orizaba*, which put into San Juan del Sur from Panama, and returned with mail.

In a letter from Samuel Lockridge, Walker learned that the attempt to recapture the San Juan had ended in failure. There was another letter, containing another shock for Walker. From Edmund Randolph, who was still in

New York, this letter notified Walker that, due to Walker's failure to retrieve the lake and river steamers and his inability to provide security for Transit passengers, the Garrison and Morgan Line had suspended all sailings to Nicaragua. In March, Parker Crittenden in San Francisco had written to warn Walker that Cornelius Garrison was acting strangely, hinting that the arrangement with Morgan and Garrison was under threat. Walker had dismissed that warning. With total confidence in his own ability to overcome the Allies, he had expected the pair to share that confidence, not to act like the businessmen they were. The news of Morgan and Garrison's decision shook Walker to the core. "Their conduct was the result of weakness and timidity," he said of them, describing their action as "treachery." "[I] expected them to show more nerve and commercial sagacity." In his opinion, in dumping him "they jeoparded their reputation of skilful merchants fully as much as it damaged their character for honesty and integrity."[16]

Walker, surrounded by the Allies, thwarted by Vanderbilt, let down by Lockridge, and abandoned by Morgan and Garrison, was looking defeat squarely in the face. But he would not give in.

General Charles Henningsen and Colonel John Waters dismounted amid a sea of tents at Cuatro Esquinas. Allied soldiers watched them with unconcealed hate as Lieutenant Thomas T. Houston of the U.S. Navy met them with a salute. Seven days earlier, on April 23, Houston had escorted all American women and children from Rivas to safety at San Juan del Sur, under an American flag and guarded by U.S. Marines from the *St. Mary's*.

Houston led Henningsen and Waters into a nearby tent, where Commander Charles Davis was waiting. The pair had lost weight since Davis had last seen them, in Rivas. The filibusters had been surviving on a small ration of mule meat. "A little more of this," Henningsen had said with a laconic smile when his ration had been put in front of him a few days before, "and we'll have to start eating the prisoners."[17] Yet, the courtly Henningsen continued to carry himself with the dignity of a European royal.

Commander Davis had sought this meeting. General Zavala provided safe conducts to allow Walker's representatives to pass through Allied lines, and Walker begrudgingly allowed them to come.

"General," said Davis to Henningsen, "I am in possession of information which, in my opinion, renders President Walker's position at Rivas untenable." He suggested that the only way to end pointless bloodletting was for Walker to evacuate Rivas.[18] In other words, Walker must agree to surrender and leave the country.

Davis had conducted strenuous behind-the-scenes negotiations with the Allied generals. Their commander in chief, General Mora, was prepared to let Walker's men leave the country but had wanted to keep Walker in Nicaragua, to try him, and then execute him. Davis insisted that Walker must be allowed to leave and guaranteed to remove him to the United States. Only after Davis made Mora concede that the Allied army was in no fit state to continue the siege of Rivas beyond another twenty days, had Mora given in—Davis could remove Walker, if Walker could be convinced to surrender.[19]

But Henningsen failed to agree with Davis that Walker's situation was untenable, so Davis explained that Lockridge had ceased his efforts to reopen the San Juan River. This was news to Henningsen and Waters, and at first, they refused to believe it. Walker had known this for weeks, ever since receiving the letter from Lockridge. But he had kept the knowledge of Lockridge's failure to himself, allowing his followers to continue to hope for the impossibility of salvation from the east. Meanwhile, Walker hoped that in the west, the Allies, exhausted by their failure to take Rivas and notoriously arguing among themselves and regularly changing commanders, would fold up their tents and go home, leaving Nicaragua to him.

Davis next announced that Morgan and Garrison intended to send no more steamers to Nicaragua. Again, Walker knew this but had not shared it with his officers. And finally, Davis revealed that he knew that Walker's army only had enough rations for a few more days. Davis then proposed surrender terms that would see Walker and his men returned to the United States by the U.S. Navy and asked Henningsen to relay those terms to Walker at once. It had by that time dawned on Henningsen and Waters that their situation was far more desperate than Walker was prepared to admit; they had to talk sense into their commander in chief.

In the midevening darkness of May 1, William Walker slowly climbed the side of the *St. Mary's.* Ahead of him, his sixteen most senior officers and aides had already boarded the U.S. warship. Wistfully he looked across the bay toward the *Granada*, his brave little ship of war. The Allies had tried to bribe Callender Fayssoux into giving her up; James Mullen, who'd come down from Nashville with Walker's brother James and who later deserted, had offered Fayssoux five thousand dollars from Ramón Rivas to hand over the *Granada*, but Fayssoux had remained loyal to his general and held on to his ship.[20]

Walker's intent had been to escape aboard the *Granada* and use her for a return to Nicaragua once he had rebuilt his forces and his resources. But Commander Davis insisted that she also be handed over to the Allies, along with all Walker's rifles, cannon, and ammunition. The *St. Mary's* lay anchored with all the guns of her broadside aimed at the *Granada*, and Davis had made it clear he would sink the schooner if Walker did not instruct Fayssoux to hand her over. Walker would quibble but surrender the schooner he would.

As part of the May 1 surrender terms, Walker's 407 remaining Americans—148 soldiers fit for duty, 86 armed citizens of his civil service, and 173 at the hospital (including the sick, wounded, and doctors and medical attendants)—would be ferried across Nicaragua with the American women and children aboard the lake and river steamers and put aboard the sloop-of-war USS *Saratoga* and the new steam frigate USS *Wabash* at Greytown, to be transported to New York and New Orleans. Walker and his officers would be taken by the *St. Mary's* to Panama, from where they would be conveyed to New Orleans.[21] At 5:00 P.M., Walker had addressed the last assembly of the Army of the Republic of Nicaragua in Rivas. "You have written a page of American history which it is impossible to forget or erase," he had told the last hungry, exhausted remnants of his army.[22] And then, after thanking his officers and other men for serving him, he had stepped aside to allow Henningsen to read the surrender terms aloud.

With a sigh now, Walker continued up the gangway from the captain's gig. As he stepped onto the warship's deck, a U.S. Navy officer looked up from the list of surrendering officers he had compiled and brusquely asked the name of the last man to board.

"William Walker," was the proud reply, "President of Nicaragua."

By November 23, not quite thirty weeks since Walker's surrender, the USS *Saratoga* had been swinging at anchor off Greytown for months. Since taking one Walker party to New York, she had been stationed here in San Juan Bay with orders to prevent filibusters from returning to Nicaragua.

Through the summer of 1857, "General" William Walker had been received as a hero in the United States and mobbed and cheered wherever he appeared. He'd had a private meeting at the White House with the new U.S. president, James Buchanan—"Secretly he possessed a penchant for freebooters," the *Atlantic Monthly* said of Buchanan.[23] Walker was spoken of warmly in the U.S. Senate by his idol, Sam Houston. Walker's photographic portrait had been taken by Matthew Brady, the leading photographer of the day; the portrait showed a gaunt Walker still recovering from yellow fever and a starvation diet in Rivas. In speeches before large and enthusiastic gatherings in several cities, Walker had blamed Secretary of State Marcy, the British government, and Cornelius Vanderbilt for his removal from Nicaragua and made it clear he intended to reclaim his lost Nicaraguan presidency, and soon. Many, including Cornelius Vanderbilt, would have considered this an empty boast.

At 7:00 A.M. on November 23, the *Saratoga*'s captain, Commander Frederick K. Chatard, was called on deck—a steamer was entering the bay. Chatard, who'd only taken charge of the *Saratoga* months earlier, was expecting to be relieved by another ship by month's end and was looking forward to home leave after boring months in the harsh Nicaraguan climate. He studied the approaching vessel with a spyglass. She was the ocean steamer *Fashion*, a smallish side-wheeler that had operated on the Atlantic Coast for years. Counting fifteen men on her deck, Chatard hailed her as she drew near, asking her business. All he could make out from the reply was the word "Transit."[24] Chatard had orders to prevent the landing of fili- busters, "those glorious regenerators who go with the torch of enlighten- ment to weak countries to commit all kinds of outrages," as he'd described them in a July letter to a friend.[25] But Chatard knew that Cornelius Van- derbilt was anxious to reclaim Transit Company interests in Nicaragua, and assuming the *Fashion* had been sent by Vanderbilt, Chatard gave the passing ship a friendly wave.[26]

The *Fashion* dropped anchor off Punta de Castilla. Her boats ferried men ashore. Casually observing from the *Saratoga*, Chatard frowned: There were a heck of a lot of these fellows, and they were carrying rifles. And then he saw the unmistakable figure of William Walker stepping ashore. Chatard was devastated; Walker had outsmarted him, for the commander's orders prevented him from taking action against filibusters once they were on Nicaraguan soil. The very thing President Buchanan's secretary of state, Lewis Cass, and Cornelius Vanderbilt feared, and that Chatard had been posted here to prevent, had just taken place—right under Chatard's nose. Walker had returned to Nicaragua to reclaim his presidency.

On Punta de Castilla, Walker made camp and ran up his lone-star Nicaraguan flag. The *Fashion* had been chartered for him by U.S. support- ers, including Vanderbilt rival "Live Oak" George Law. On November 14, she had sailed out of Mobile, Alabama, with 270 well-armed regenerators aboard. Officers included stalwarts such as Anderson, Hornsby, Natzmer, and Fayssoux, and men racked by guilt after letting Walker down on the San Juan River—Rudler, Wheat, and Doubleday among them.[27]

Walker was unaware that the day after he sailed from Mobile, a newly elected Nicaraguan Constituent Assembly had itself elected a new president of Nicaragua—former Democratico general Tomás Martinez. Or that the Constituent Assembly had moved Nicaragua's national capital to Managua, halfway between Democratico León and Legitimista Granada. Not that Walker would have cared. He still considered himself president of Nicaragua and was determined to regain control of his republic.

Over subsequent days, Walker drilled his men on Punta de Castilla between rain squalls but made no attempt to go inland. He had no need to. Two days before arriving in San Juan Bay, in pouring rain that helped shroud the operation, Walker had secretly landed Frank Anderson and forty-five men farther south, at the mouth of the Colorado River, which joined the San Juan River several miles inland. Anderson's group had set off up the Colorado in three large rowboats. Their orders were to reach the San Juan, seize the first river steamer they encountered, then use that to reach El Castillo and surprise the Costa Rican garrison. It was a plan to equal Walker's most wily past tactics.

Despite the almost incessant rain, Walker and his men on Punta de Castilla remained in excellent spirits. Twelve days after their landing, a bungo had come down the San Juan, paddled by two disarmed Costa Rican soldiers while one of Anderson's men sat in the stern with a rifle trained on them. The regenerator brought news that Walker had been waiting for— El Castillo had been taken. As planned, Anderson's party had seized a river steamer, then steamed up to the El Castillo wharf, flying the Costa Rican flag. They had dashed up the hill and taken the castle before the garrison knew what was happening—the former garrison commander, George Cauty, Vanderbilt's man, had left the country in August.[28] What was more, Anderson had seized two more river steamers and a lake steamer at El Castillo. Walker now awaited the arrival of one of those river steamers to collect his main force. Once he headed upriver, he would dispatch the *Fashion* to New Orleans to collect reinforcements being assembled there by Charles Henningsen.

By December 8, the *Saratoga* had been joined by the USS *Wabash* and the elderly side-wheeler USS *Fulton*—after a despairing Commander Chatard had sent for Home Squadron commander Commodore Hiram

Paulding, at Panama: "I beg you, Sir, in the most earnest manner, to come here and advise me," Chatard had written.[29] Paulding, a teenage hero in the Battle of Lake Champlain during the War of 1812, had not come merely to advise Chatard. With two British warships now also anchored in the crowded bay, Paulding had come to take charge.

The ambitious Commodore Paulding wrote to his daughter that his action this day could either make him president of the United States or end his career.[30] It proved to be the latter. Even though the new Nicaraguan government would voice its approval of Paulding's actions against the man they considered an "incorrigible adventurer," President Buchanan would surprise many by subsequently removing Paulding from his command and forcing him into retirement for taking the offensive against Walker on December 8.[31] "Commodore Paulding was clearly not a politician," the *Atlantic Monthly* would remark when discussing the affair the following April.[32]

The commander of the British warships in port offered to combine with Paulding to expel Walker, but Paulding was neither prepared to share the limelight nor to let the British act against Americans. Without authority from the U.S. government to land armed forces on foreign soil, Paulding sent 350 marines and sailors ashore and surrounded Walker's Punta de Castilla camp, something Walker had not anticipated, for it contravened U.S. policy. Captain Frederick Engle, commander of the *Wabash*, apologetically read out a letter from Paulding calling on Walker to surrender, or be fired on from land and sea.

Walker listened quietly as Engle read. Realizing that Paulding, who was renowned for his aggressive nature, was in earnest, Walker responded: "I surrender to the United States."[33]

Anderson and his men were ordered to give up El Castillo and come back down the river to become prisoners of the U.S. Navy, along with Walker and the rest of the invaders. Despite the stunning initial success of Walker's return performance on Nicaraguan soil, the show was very soon over.

THE SURRENDER

ORNELIUS VANDERBILT LOOKED UP FROM A NEWSPAPER. THERE WAS a Mr. Charles Morgan outside, Lambert Wardell announced, wondering if the Commodore might be so kind as to see him. Vanderbilt, smiling, opened the single drawer in the table that served as his desk; he took out a Cuban cigar, bit off the end and spat it away, then jammed the stogie in his mouth. With deliberate slowness he lit the cigar. He took several puffs, then thoughtfully studied the glowing tip.

It was the spring of 1858. And still Vanderbilt had not won back control of the Nicaraguan Transit. William Walker did not concern him now. As far as the Commodore was concerned, his war with Walker was won. According to the press, Walker was talking about yet another tilt at the proverbial Nicaraguan windmill, having been returned to the United States in December following his second surrender in seven months and removal from San Juan Bay by Commodore Paulding. With the press now less inclined to laud him, and with the governments of both the United States and Great Britain having signaled they were prepared to act to prevent Walker's return, many men who had previously been prepared to follow the filibuster president back to Nicaragua had walked away. And importantly, moneyed supporters such as George Law had deserted him.

Having beaten Walker—even *Harper's Weekly* had come out and declared that the gray-eyed man of destiny owed his defeat to Vanderbilt and his employee Sylvanus Spencer—the Commodore still had to overcome other competitors and win over the Nicaraguan government.[1] On December 13, the Martinez government of Nicaragua had, to Vanderbilt's consternation, advised the U.S. government of the conditional granting of the Transit charter to a new competitor with an old name—the American Atlantic and Pacific Ship Canal Company.[2]

Over the past few years, Vanderbilt's former partner, lawyer Joseph L. White, who had since fallen out with him, again, had combined with Wall Street trader H. G. Stebbins to quietly buy up Canal Company stock for a pittance, until they had a controlling interest. When the new Nicaraguan government appointed the Washington ambassador of Guatemala and El Salvador to temporarily represent its interests in the United States following Walker's initial surrender, White and Stebbins had given that ambassador, A. J. De Yrisarri, five thousand dollars in cash and eighty thousand dollars' worth of Canal Company stock—which he reputedly passed on to the new government in Managua.[3] And this had purchased the Canal Company its provisional charter. Vanderbilt had not stood for that. He had fought too hard and invested too much money in his war with Walker to allow White and Stebbins to whip his charter from his grasp at the last moment. He would soon fix them. Even if it meant going to war again.

And then there were Mr. Morgan and Mr. Garrison, who claimed to still hold the charter. With the war in Nicaragua terminated, they had been prepared to resume operations on the Transit Route and had reemployed their agent C. J. Macdonald to bribe Vanderbilt's agent in Costa Rica to work for them. The Vanderbilt agent was, of course, William R. C. Webster. His colleague Sylvanus Spencer had since come back to New York and collected his fifty-thousand-dollar prize from Vanderbilt, but Webster had set his sights on larger rewards and was soon inveigled into the Morgan-Garrison fold to win Costa Rica's President Mora to their side—with Costa Rican troops still occupying the San Juan River, Mora intended to maintain Costa Rican control of the Transit, even if it meant going to war with Nicaragua.

"God damned rascal!" Vanderbilt had exclaimed when he learned that his man Webster had allowed himself to be seduced by Morgan and Garrison.[4] Vanderbilt had sent son-in-law Daniel B. Allen to Costa Rica with his bags bulging with a hundred thousand dollars in cash, to buy back Webster's loyalty, a task he had succeeded in doing. But then Walker had landed at Punta

de Castilla, and the ease with which he had retaken El Castillo had frightened President Mora into quickly signing a treaty with Tomàs Martinez's
new Nicaraguan government, a treaty in which both governments vowed to
work together against foreign invasion. In the same treaty, Mora had given
up the Costa Rican claim to southern Nicaragua and the San Juan River.

This meant that Vanderbilt had to then forget the Costa Ricans and con-
centrate on winning over the Nicaraguans. Morgan and Garrison's agent
Macdonald, meanwhile, had been told by President Martinez that the
Nicaraguan government would never contemplate allocating the charter to
Morgan and Garrison, because of their past connection with William
Walker. Now, while Vanderbilt was determined to continue the fight, Mor-
gan and Garrison were tossing in the towel. And that was why Charles
Morgan was waiting in the Commodore's anteroom.

Morgan had come to do a deal with the Commodore on behalf of his San
Francisco partner and himself. In that deal, Morgan and Garrison would
surrender all interest in the Nicaraguan Transit and the proposed Nicaragua
canal. In return, Vanderbilt would cease competing with Morgan in the Gulf.
Morgan would buy the Vanderbilt Gulf line and its ships. Vanderbilt would
buy the brand new SS *Queen of the Pacific* from Morgan—she had been idle
since being launched in New York on April 8 for the now defunct Nicaragua
service. The Commodore could put her to good use on the transatlantic run.
Vanderbilt would also be offered Morgan's half interest in each of the San
Francisco–based Morgan and Garrison Line steamers *Orizaba* and *Sierra
Nevada*—making the Commodore an owner of the *Sierra Nevada* for the
third time in her existence. If Vanderbilt agreed to the deal, Morgan and
Garrison would never trouble the Commodore again. But after the way he
had curtly dismissed Garrison when he had ventured into this office to offer
a deal, there was no guaranteeing that the Commodore wouldn't do the
same to Morgan.

Vanderbilt may not have ruined Morgan and Garrison as he once fa-
mously promised to do, but he had beaten them, just as he had beaten
William Walker. In July of the previous year, former Secretary of State
William L. Marcy had passed away, but not before learning to his satisfaction that Walker and his followers had been ejected from Nicaragua. More

than thirty years before, it had been Marcy who had coined a saying: To the victor belong the spoils of the enemy. And if he so chose, Cornelius Vanderbilt could now enjoy the spoils of his Nicaraguan victory. Or he could tell Charles Morgan to go to blazes.

Vanderbilt took another long puff on his cigar, slowly exhaling the smoke, watching it curl up to the ceiling. And then he looked down to Lambert Wardell waiting patiently at the door and told him to send Mr. Morgan right on in.

EPILOGUE

CORNELIUS VANDERBILT DID the deal with Morgan and Garrison. And then he won back the Nicaragua Transit charter that White and Stebbins had briefly pirated. Vanderbilt had paid Domingo de Goicuria to lobby leading Nicaraguan figures on his behalf, and when Dr. Maximo Jerez, the limping general, came to Washington as Nicaragua's new ambassador to the United States in the summer of 1858, Vanderbilt pampered and flattered him, winning the ambassador over. When White and Stebbins announced that the SS *Washington* would sail to Nicaragua to resume the Transit Route as a result of their provisional acquisition of the charter, Jerez placed a notice in the press warning that his government could not guarantee the safety of anyone who traveled to Nicaragua on the *Washington*. Not surprisingly, the sailing was canceled for lack of clientele. And soon after, as a result of Jerez's endorsement, Vanderbilt was awarded the Transit charter by the Nicaraguan government, which also gave him back the right to build a Nicaragua canal. But unlike the previous contract, this one would expire in just three years. Vanderbilt had finally won his war.

Even though he had wrested back the charter for the Transit Company, the Commodore sent no steamers back to Nicaragua. He simply used the regained charter as a means of keeping others from using the Nicaraguan Transit Route. Instead, he partnered with the U.S. Mail Line to create the new Atlantic and Pacific Steamship Company, which immediately monopolized the Atlantic run to Panama and which went into fierce, price-cutting competition with Aspinwall's Pacific Mail Line on the Pacific run to Panama, even though both put their passengers on the Panama railroad, which was owned by Aspinwall.

That situation changed in September 1859, when the U.S. Mail contracts to and from California finally came up for renewal. Both the East Coast and the West Coast contracts were awarded to the little-known Wall Street trader Daniel H. Johnson, who claimed he would use the Nicaragua Route to carry the mails. Shortly after, it was revealed that Johnson was acting on behalf of Joseph L. White. Vanderbilt complained to Postmaster General Joseph Holt that Johnson did not have the ability to carry the mails across Nicaragua. The Commodore offered to match Johnson's offer for the ocean carriage of the mails, if the government arranged their transport on the Panama railroad. On this basis, Postmaster General Holt transferred the contracts to Vanderbilt, giving the Commodore the lucrative mail contracts after which he had lusted for a decade. This transfer to Vanderbilt seemed highly suspicious, but a House of Representatives investigation of the matter found no evidence of graft or corruption on the part of Vanderbilt or Holt. The "damned old sea pirate," as Joseph L. White described Vanderbilt, had won again.[1]

George Aspinwall continued to try to compete with Vanderbilt on the Pacific run, despite losing the mail contract to him. But before a year had elapsed, Vanderbilt had done a deal with Aspinwall, and the pair merged their East Coast and West Coast shipping concerns. Several of Vanderbilt's ships joined Aspinwall's Pacific fleet, and Vanderbilt became a major shareholder of Aspinwall's Pacific Steamship Company. All California traffic was cornered by the partnership, which continued to use Panama. The Nicaraguan Transit Route lay dormant.

William Walker, meanwhile, had not given up on his dream of empire in Central America. In his own words, his return to Nicaragua obsessed his every waking and sleeping thought.[2] In December 1858, within months of being returned to the United States by Commodore Paulding, Walker had dispatched Frank Anderson and 111 men in the schooner *Susan* to establish a bridgehead on the Mosquito Coast. In the last stages of a Neutrality Act trial in New Orleans—he would be exonerated—Walker planned to soon follow Anderson with more men. But on December 14, when the *Susan* became stuck fast on Glover Reef off the coast of Belize, the mission had to be abandoned. Walker stubbornly launched a fourth venture in the summer of 1860. British settlers on the Caribbean island of Roatan had not been happy with the British government's plan to transfer the island to Honduras and had approached Walker in New Orleans to help them gain their independence, after which, they promised, they would help him regain Nicaragua.

In June, shortly after the publication of his hastily written memoirs, *The War in Nicaragua*, which he had penned in the third person in emulation of Julius Caesar's *Commentaries* and which quickly became a U.S. best seller, Walker and 130 other men sailed for Roatan aboard two schooners loaded with arms, leaving Fayssoux in New Orleans to organize reinforcements. But one vessel was caught by British forces waiting at Roatan—it is possible that the whole operation was set up by the British government to entrap Walker. After Walker and most of his men escaped on the second vessel, instead of returning to the United States, Walker proposed to land in Honduras, from where he would continue the struggle to regain Nicaragua. "With us there can be no choice," he had written in his memoirs. "Honor and duty call on us to pursue the path we have entered."[3]

Ninety-one of his men voted to go with Walker, who planned to link up with crusty old Democratico leader Trinidad Cabanas, who was fighting a guerrilla war against President "Butcher" Guardiola in Honduras. Walker planned to help Cabanas defeat Guardiola, then, supported by Cabanas's forces, march into Nicaragua. On August 5, Walker, his deputy Anthony Rudler, and their band landed at Trujillo. At dawn the next day, they attacked a Honduran fortress built by Cortes, taking it after a short, bloody fight.

But on August 12, the British steam frigates *Icarus* and *Gladiator*—two of fifteen British warships scouring the Western Caribbean for Walker—dropped anchor in the bay off Trujillo. After the Royal Navy's Captain Norvell Salmon demanded Walker's surrender, Walker, leaving his wounded at the fortress, escaped up the coast with 64 men. Ambushed by 150 Honduran troops, Walker struggled on until forced to surrender to a British lieutenant leading 40 Royal Marines. To the horror of Walker and his survivors, the British captain then handed them over to the Hondurans. Both Walker and Rudler were tried and sentenced to death, although Rudler's sentence was commuted and he was repatriated to the United States through the intercession of the state of Alabama. Just a dozen of Walker's followers lived to return home.

At first light on September 12, 1860, slight thirty-six-year-old William Walker was led onto the beach at Trujillo, escorted by seventy Honduran soldiers. As a firing squad lined up on the sand in front of him, the officer in charge read the death sentence aloud. Then, holding a crucifix, having converted to Catholicism prior to this last, ill-judged venture to Central America, a composed Walker addressed the Hondurans in Spanish. According to Honduran tradition, Walker apologized for making war on the Honduran people and said that he faced death with resolution and with the hope that it was for the good of mankind. He was still speaking when his executioners fired. The officer in charge then walked to Walker's fallen body, put a pistol to his face, and fired at point blank range, so that the corpse could never be recognized. Walker's naked body was buried in the sand. Requests from supporters in the United States for the return of his remains were denied by the Honduran government, which later relocated them to the Trujillo graveyard; the name on the tombstone was misspelled.

In New York, Cornelius Vanderbilt had forgotten all about William Walker; the Commodore's attention was now focused on beating competitors on the transatlantic route. Eighteen days after Walker's execution, Costa Rica's President José Rafael Mora was executed by firing squad at Puntarenas in Costa Rica. Deposed by his former business partner José Maria Montealegre, Mora had led a failed countercoup. His brother-in-law, General José Canas, was executed by Montealegre's troops the following day. Eighteen months later, President José "Butcher" Guardiola of Honduras was assassinated by his own bodyguard. General Ramon Belloso, former commander in chief of the Allied army, died in 1858 from cholera. His successor as Guatemalan commander in the war against Walker, General Geraldo Barrios, became president of Guatemala in 1859, only to be deposed and executed by firing squad six years later. After the war with Walker, the governments of Central America never again combined in a common cause.

William Walker, during his short life, was the most talked-about man in the United States. Yet news of his violent death in 1860 excited little interest when it came. One or two newspapers lamented that it was a pity he had not used his obvious talents in aid of his country, rather than trying to create one of his own. But mostly the press passed over his end or, like the New York *Tribune*, dismissed him as "insane."[4] President Buchanan, in an address to Congress in December, described Walker's death as "a happy change."[5] The United States had moved on, and no longer did the subject of Central America animate Americans. The nation's attention was fixed on matters closer to heart and to home, matters that were turning the component parts of the United States into the disunited states. Within months of Walker's death, on December 20, 1860, South Carolina seceded from the Union. The following year, ten more Southern states followed its example, and the American Civil War began—the War of the Rebellion, as it was called in the North; and the War of Northern Aggression, as it was labeled in the South.

Estimates of the number of Americans who had fought for Walker in Nicaragua ranged between twenty-five hundred and ten thousand, with all accounts agreeing that at a minimum, half of those who joined his Army of the Republic of Nicaragua died in Central America from wounds or disease. Walker's Nicaraguan War veterans served on both sides during the U.S. Civil War. Men who fought for Walker were valued for their experience, particularly by the South. Henningsen became a Confederate brigadier general. Birkett D. Fry, as a Confederate colonel, commanded Archer's Brigade and survived Pickett's Charge at Gettysburg and was taken prisoner. Wheat led his own Confederate battalion, the First Louisiana, or "Wheat's Tigers," calling the battalion's A Company "the Walker Guards." He was killed at the Battle of Gaines Mills, Virginia, in 1862. Robert Harris, one of Walker's artillery men in Nicaragua, took over command of Wheat's battalion. Rudler, a Georgia Infantry colonel, was seriously wounded at the Battle of Missionary Ridge. Tom Green was colonel of the Second Texas Cavalry; Sam Lockridge was his deputy. Other Walker veterans served in the U.S. Army during the Civil War. Charles Doubleday was a brigadier general of Union cavalry. Theodore Potter served as a captain with the Minnesota Infantry. James Jamison also fought for the North. The one-armed Parker French spent time in Boston's La Fayette federal prison as a Confederate spy, then turned up in the Confederacy as a Northern agent. Henry Titus lived to have a town in Florida, Titusville, named after him following the Civil War.

Both Jamison and Doubleday survived the Civil War. Jamison always remained loyal to Walker but disputed his claim, in *The Nicaraguan War*, that all his officers were proslavery; Jamison named several officers who, like himself, had never supported slavery. Doubleday sailed on Walker's second and third Nicaraguan ventures, but not the fourth, having lost faith in Walker's cause by that time. Though not in favor of slavery, he still considered Walker a great man.

In 1863, even while the Civil War was raging, the Accessory Transit Company was wound up, and investors holding worthless Transit Company scrip sued Vanderbilt for mismanagement. His acceptance of bribes to keep the Transit Company ships off the Panama run was declared immoral, but the investors never saw any of the millions that the Commodore reaped from those deals.

From late in 1862, an attempt was made to revive the Nicaragua route by Marshal Roberts, who had been Vanderbilt's partner in the Atlantic and Pacific Steamship Company only to later fall out with him. For a few profitless seasons, Roberts and New York shipbuilder William Webb ran several trips a year to San Francisco via Nicaragua; business was not aided by the Civil War. After the war, in 1867, John and Elizabeth Hollenbeck, of the El Castillo hotel renown, bought the aging Nicaraguan lake and river steamers for a song, only to go broke trying to make money from the Transit.

Nicaragua, which enjoyed decades of peace following Walker's brief reign, never again saw Americans thronging along the San Juan, over the lake, and down the Transit Road. There was talk of a Nicaragua railroad, like the Panama railroad. Joseph L. White even visited the country to look into railroad possibilities, only to be shot and killed while there on that visit. It was indeed a railroad that finally sealed the fate of the Nicaraguan Transit and ended the heyday of the Panama steamers—in 1869, the intercontinental railroad opened, linking California and the East Coast via Chicago. By the 1960s, U.S. interests still held the rights to build a canal across Nicaragua, and the route had been freshly surveyed.[6]

A canal was built across Central America, but in Panama, not Nicaragua. A French company began construction of the Panama Canal in 1879. Financial difficulties caused a collapse of the enterprise ten years later. In 1904, the United States acquired the rights, and after many problems and much loss of life due to accidents and disease, the Panama Canal opened in 1914. In 2000, the Republic of Panama assumed control of the canal and, in 2006, embarked on a $5.25 billion project to significantly increase the capacity of the waterway. In the early 2000s, the Nicaraguan government floated a proposal to build a series of locks on its San Juan River to improve navigation.

Both of Vanderbilt's former Nicaragua Transit rivals Cornelius Garrison and Charles Morgan went on to invest in railroads. Garrison moved to New York in 1859, initially to run Vanderbilt's Atlantic and Pacific Steamship Company, of which he had become a director. But before long, Garrison found himself sidelined by Vanderbilt, so he sold his interest in the line's ships to the Commodore and became heavily involved in the Missouri Pacific Railroad, only to lose a $5 million lawsuit connected to the line and die without assets and heavily in debt. Morgan owned railroads in Texas and Louisiana and died a rich man in 1878, but his wealth was never in the same league as that of Vanderbilt.

Vanderbilt had seen the future of railroads well before many others. Despite having been nearly killed in a railroad accident in New Jersey in 1833, he would accumulate controlling interests in sixteen key lines. During the Civil War, he chartered a number of his steamships to the U.S. government, which converted them into warships, but after the war, he consolidated his shipping interests and concentrated on the iron rail, buying up railroad after railroad. His crowning glory was the construction of New York City's first Grand Central Terminal. His statue stands outside Grand Central Station to this day. Steamships had made Vanderbilt wealthy, but railroads made him the richest man in America.

Many people in the United States today will recognize the Vanderbilt name and will associate it with wealth and success. Ask anyone in Central America, and most will not have heard of the Vanderbilts. But mention William Walker, and Central Americans will tell you all about the king of the filibusters. Throughout Central America today, Walker's name ranks with that of Hitler and Stalin. In Costa Rica, their national day is April 11, in celebration of the defeat of Walker's filibusteros at Rivas—since 1865, they have called it Juan Santamaria Day, in honor of the drummer boy who gave his life to set fire to Guerra's Inn. And the hacienda of Santa Rosa in Guanacaste, scene of the rout of Louis Schlessinger's Corps of Observation, is a Costa Rican national monument. Luis Pacheco, who also gained fame on April 11 and later helped George Cauty put an explosive end to the filibuster attempt to reopen the San Juan River, was, in his sixties, given a gold medal by his government and made a general for his part in defeating Walker.

In Nicaragua, they have two national days, September 14 and September 15. The latter commemorates the day Nicaragua wrested its independence from Spain in 1821. The former celebrates the day in 1856 that Colonel José Estrada's Nicaraguans defeated Walker's Yankee filibusteros at the San Jacinto ranch—the hacienda is today a Nicaraguan national monument. Yet the day was to come when Nicaraguans and Americans fought side by side. Graduates from the José Estrada military school led the Nicaraguan Army contingent, which, in 2004, joined the American-led Coalition in Iraq and served alongside U.S. troops.

What did Vanderbilt think about Walker? Vanderbilt had no moral objections to Walker or to filibustering. To begin with, when the Commodore regained control of the Transit Company, he had supported Walker's regime—until Walker disenfranchised his company. And after Walker's death, Vanderbilt went into an ultimately unsuccessful partnership with filibusters aiming to overthrow the government of Peru. Vanderbilt was only interested in two things—making money and winning. Often, he temporarily subjugated the need for the former to achieve the latter. Vanderbilt had an unquenchable thirst for conquest—at the card table, driving his horses, in his countless business deals, and, reputedly, in the bedroom with numerous mistresses. There was nothing he would not do, short of outright murder, to conquer. He probably cheated at cards and was even compelled to beat his own son at harness racing.

Vanderbilt and Walker were alike in several respects. Both were opportunists, and both were prepared to suffer through short-term adversity to achieve long-term victory. Both Vanderbilt and Walker were loyal to those who were loyal to them, attracting lifelong allegiance from their closest associates. But there the similarities ended. Walker, because of his limited resources, was prepared to give his trust too readily to achieve his ends, giving that trust to men who turned out to be liars, braggarts, and fools—the likes of Parker H. French, Louis Schlessinger, Domingo de Goicuria, and Henry Titus. The cunning Vanderbilt was a much better judge of character. And here is where the two men differed most—if you crossed Walker, he would banish you from his world; if you crossed Vanderbilt, he would set out to conquer you, no matter how long it took. Ultimately, that conquest would be signified by a surrender, and that surrender would usually take the form of a deal.

At one time or another, Vanderbilt got into bed with all his enemies—if they were prepared to submit to him, and most, being businessmen, were. George Law, William Aspinwall, Marshall Roberts, Cornelius Garrison, Charles Morgan, and many others fought Vanderbilt, lost the battle, and surrendered on his terms, ending up doing business with him. The exception was William Walker. He was not a businessman. He achieved his short-lived successes using war and the law as his tools. And unlike Vanderbilt's other adversaries, Walker was not afraid of the Commodore, when he should have been.

After Walker's enforced return to the United States in the summer of 1857, *Harper's Weekly* had suggested that it would be a good thing for Walker and for Central America if he could do a deal with Commodore Vanderbilt and the Transit Company and, in so doing, resume his Nicaraguan presidency. But Walker would not contemplate going cap in hand to Vanderbilt, as he must if such a deal were to be consummated.

Besides, Vanderbilt had already attempted that course, agreeing to Domingo de Goicuria's proposal that he loan Walker's government $250,000 in exchange for the return of the Transit charter. But Walker had flatly rejected that deal, one that made great commercial sense but meant going back on his agreement with Morgan and Garrison. Walker, driven by joint fixations with loyalty and the law, had dismissed an eminently suitable solution and dismissed its proponent, Goicuria, making firm enemies of both Goicuria and Vanderbilt. As a consequence, the former would prove a nuisance, the latter, Walker's nemesis.

Vanderbilt seems never to have forgotten that the "tin sojer boy" refused to deal with him and never forgave that slap in the face. Via Spencer and Cauty, Vanderbilt brought about Walker's defeat in Nicaragua, but Walker never surrendered to Vanderbilt, and that seems to have rankled the Commodore. Walker was the one who got away. It would also have rankled Vanderbilt that after the Civil War, there was still a deal of residual admiration

in the American South for William Walker, a Southerner who became president of Nicaragua. At the same time, there was a simmering dislike of Vanderbilt in the South, for his having engineered Walker's downfall and for
supporting the Union during the Civil War. The admiration for Walker was
greatest in his home state of Tennessee and greatest of all in his hometown
of Nashville. To this day, there is a historical marker honoring Walker outside the Nashville house where he was born and grew up.

Until late in his life, unlike many other wealthy Americans, Cornelius
Vanderbilt had no record of philanthropy. Though the recipient of countless
approaches for donations for one cause or another, he'd had a lifelong aver-
sion to charity. "What's the use of giving folks money?" he is reported to have
said. "It's the lazy ones beg."[7] In his latter years, he spent fifty thousand dollars buying Mercer Street Presbyterian Church in Manhattan for the Reverend Charles F. Deems, who had become his confidante and adviser.
Deems renamed it the Church of the Strangers. Up until 1873, that was the
extent of Vanderbilt's munificence. So, it was a great surprise to many when,
in that year, just four years prior to his death, Vanderbilt acceded to the
approaches of a Methodist bishop and gave a million dollars to endow a university. This was a huge donation—the single largest philanthropic endowment in the United States to that time. Just how huge can be judged by the
fact that Charles Morgan had given fifty thousand dollars to build the Morgan School in his hometown of Clinton, Connecticut.

The lucky bishop in question was Holland McTeyeire, a nephew by mar-
riage of Vanderbilt's second wife. First wife, Sophia, had died in 1868, and
a year later, seventy-three-year-old Cornelius had eloped to Canada to marry
thirty-year-old distant cousin Miss Frank Crawford. In 1873, Bishop
McTeyeire went to New York City for a medical procedure, after which he
spent some weeks recovering at 10 Washington Place as the guest of the
Vanderbilts. This gave McTeyeire plenty of time in which to tell the Commodore all about the new Central University that he was planning for his
hometown. The college's charter had been drawn up the previous year, and
the bishop had chosen the site. All that was lacking was a little finance. A
stunned McTeyeire returned home with a half-million-dollar check. He
would receive a further five hundred thousand dollars from Vanderbilt over

the next few years, in several installments.[8] Cornelius Vanderbilt's endowment came with just one condition—the university must bear his name. McTeyeire hastily agreed and wasted no time changing the charter, renaming his new college Vanderbilt University.

Was it purely coincidence that the new Vanderbilt University was located in Nashville, William Walker's hometown? At the age of fourteen, Cornelius Vanderbilt had slaved from dawn till dusk on his father's Staten Island farm, whereas at the age of fourteen, William Walker had graduated from the University of Nashville. By the 1880s, Walker's old college was being rapidly eclipsed by the affluent new Vanderbilt University across town in Nashville. Before long, Vanderbilt's university, the richest in the United States apart from several more established colleges in the Northeast, took over the older Nashville University's medical and teacher colleges, and in 1909, the struggling University of Nashville, Walker's alma mater, went out of business altogether and ceased to exist. Vanderbilt University thrives to this day.

Why did Vanderbilt, a man who never stepped inside a university and had no time for book learning, give a million dollars to establish Vanderbilt University? Was the Commodore's mind affected by the syphilis that a recent Vanderbilt biographer claims was diagnosed by Vanderbilt's physician in 1839? Perhaps. Yet, the Commodore was sufficiently in command of his faculties in his last few years to stipulate that a large part of his gift to the university be in the form of first mortgage bonds of his New York Central and Hudson River Railroad.[9] There may be another explanation.

Was this massive and totally out-of-character largesse Vanderbilt's ultimate revenge against Walker? Was his staggering generosity—to a distant Southern city he had never even visited—aimed purely at making Vanderbilt's name in Nashville and overshadowing Walker's lingering hometown fame? Did this give Vanderbilt the sense of conquest that Nashville's son had denied him all those years before?

This, it would seem, was the final triumphant act in this wily tycoon's war with the gifted yet stubborn, misguided, and ultimately maniacal adventurer from Tennessee.

THE PROTAGONISTS' MOTIVES

EVER SINCE WILLIAM Walker's death, many authors, academics, and historians have ascribed his motive for invading Central America to an intention to reintroduce slavery there. Yet, close analysis of Walker's short life reveals that this was not his original intent.

On the contrary, until he went to Nicaragua, Walker was against the spread of slavery. He had grown up in a house where slavery was abhorred; his deeply religious father had in fact retained several paid black employees. During his newspaper days in New Orleans, Walker wrote in favor of phasing out slavery and penned biting editorials against slavery advocates such as former U.S. vice president John C. Calhoun.

The slavery issue did not feature in any of Walker's rhetoric leading up to his arrival in Nicaragua in 1855 and never raised its head during his first eighteen months in the country, not even when he became president of Nicaragua. Just as the chameleon Walker led U.S. ambassador John Wheeler to believe that he agreed with the North Carolinian's bigoted views of Central Americans, all the while numbering colored locals among his closest allies, he allowed Southern slavery supporters such as William and Jane Cazneau to believe he shared their proslavery view. It was only when Louisiana's Pierre Soule arrived in Granada in the summer of 1856 and made it clear to Walker that he and other wealthy Southerners would only invest heavily in Nicaragua if Walker permitted them to use slave labor on their properties that he issued the infamous Slavery Decree, repealing the 1838 Nicaraguan law banning slavery.

Even then, Walker, highly intelligent and trained in the law, attempted to play fast and loose with his Southern supporters. As he himself was to write, his decree, quite deliberately only "gave the appearance" that slavery had been reintroduced, to fool backers such as Soule. In fact, it would have taken a second decree to physically reintroduce slavery, a decree Walker never made. This ploy was his way of salving both his conscience and his moneyed Southern supporters.

But Walker was too clever for his own good, and in the end, he was hoist on his own petard. The appearance of the reintroduction of slavery, while enough to cement his support in the Southern states of the United States, was also enough to lose him significant support in the North. So much so that, after his ejection from Nicaragua in 1857, he based himself in the American South and largely confined his personal appearances and speaking engagements to Southern cities as he went about the task of raising money for a fresh invasion of Nicaragua.

By the time Walker published his autobiography, *The War in Nicaragua*, in 1860, he had capitulated to circumstances. Having lost the sympathy of the North, he realized that if he was to overcome Cornelius Vanderbilt, the man behind his initial defeat in Nicaragua, and win the moral, financial, and manpower support he needed, he would have to embrace the South and all that it stood for, including black servitude. And so he wrote his self-serving book as if he were slavery's greatest champion and declared that "on the reestablishment of African slavery there (Nicaragua) depended the permanent presence of the white race in that region," a claim he had never made prior to going to Nicaragua nor during his two years there.

Walker's real motive for going to Nicaragua was clearly one of empire-building, as he spelled out to follower Charles Doubleday in 1855 within months of entering the civil war in Nicaragua. That he was indeed bent on the creation of a Central American empire, with himself at its head, is supported by the fact that one of his first acts as president of Nicaragua was the dispatch of a letter to all the heads of government of the surrounding Central American nations seeking a conference to discuss the reestablishment of the old Central American federation of states. In the end, slavery, or the appearance of slavery, became one more tool employed by an increasingly desperate Walker in his failing attempt to create that empire.

At the same time, it is clear that even before he landed in Nicaragua, Walker had perceived the importance, strategically and financially, of the Nicaraguan Transit Route to any Nicaraguan government. Prior to departing California, he had approached William Garrison offering to play a role in ending the difficulties existing between the Accessory Transit Company and the then government of Nicaragua, only to receive short shrift from Garrison. Subsequently, just weeks after landing in Nicaragua, Walker was able to convince naive Provisional Director Don Francisco Castellon to sign a contract that gave Walker the power to settle differences between the Transit Company and the Nicaraguan authorities. Later, once Cornelius Vanderbilt resumed control of the Transit Company, at the expense of Garrison and Charles Morgan, Walker was able to negotiate the deal that took the Transit charter from Vanderbilt and gave it to Garrison and Morgan.

In doing so, Walker brought the wrath of Cornelius Vanderbilt down upon himself and ultimately sealed his own fate. Yet there can be no doubt that Walker's stripping of the charter from the Commodore was not personal. To find a shipping company that would pay the Nicaraguan government a fair and honest share of its Nicaraguan Transit profits, he would have taken the contract from whoever was running the Accessory Transit Company at the time.

On the other hand, Cornelius Vanderbilt took the loss of the Transit charter very personally indeed. It caused him to launch a very personal war on William Walker, a war that he would fight tooth and nail, to the bitter end—as only a tycoon as pragmatic, powerful, and unprincipled as Cornelius Vanderbilt could.

BIBLIOGRAPHY

Books

Adam-Smith, P. *Heart of Exile*. Melbourne: Nelson, 1986.

Allen, W. P. *William Walker, Filibuster*. New York: Harper & Brothers, 1932.

Bauer, K. J. *Zachary Taylor: Soldier, Planter, Statesman of the Old Southwest*. New Orleans: Louisiana State University Press, 1985.

Baughman, J. P. *Charles Morgan and the Development of Southern Transportation*. Nashville: Vanderbilt University Press, 1968.

Bell, H. *Early Times in Southern California*. Los Angeles: Yarnell, Caystile & Mathes, 1881.

Bolanos-Geyer, A. *William Walker: The Grey-Eyed Man of Destiny*. St. Charles, MS: privately printed, 1992.

Brockett, L. P. *Men of Our Day*. Philadelphia: Ziegler & McCurdy, 1872.

Burke, L. H. *Homes of the Department of State, 1774–1976*. Washington, DC: Department of State, 1976.

Cardenal, E. *With Walker in Nicaragua and Other Poems*. Middletown, CT: Wesleyan University, 1984.

Carr, A. Z. *The World and William Walker*. New York: Harper & Row, 1948.

Choules, J. A. *The Cruise of the Steam Yacht North Star*. New York: Gould, Lincoln, Evans & Dickerson, 1854.

Conrad, H. C. *History of the State of Delaware*. Lancaster, PA: Wickersham, 1908.

Crapol, E. P., ed. *Women and American Foreign Policy: Lobbyists, Critics, and Insiders*. New York: Greenwood, 1987.

Croffut, W. A. *The Vanderbilts and the Story of Their Fortune*. Chicago: Belford, 1886.

Crook, G. *General George Crook: His Autobiography*. Norman: University of Oklahoma Press, 1946.

Davis, R. H. *Real Soldiers of Fortune*. New York: Scribner's, 1911.

Doubleday, C. *The Filibuster War in Nicaragua*. New York: Putnam's, 1886.

Dufour, C. L. *The Gallant Life of Roberdeau Wheat*. New Orleans: Louisiana State University Press, 1957.

Famous Fortunes: Intimate Stories of Financial Success. Freeport, NY: Book for Libraries Press, 1968.

Geron, A. C. *Fatal Corner*. San Antonio: Watercress, 1982.

Gordon, J. S. *The Scarlet Woman of Wall Street: Jay Gould, Jim Fisk, Cornelius Vanderbilt, the Erie Railway Wars, and the Birth of Wall Street*. New York: Weidenfield & Nicolson, 1988.

Greene, L. *The Filibuster: The Career of William Walker*. Indianapolis: Bobbs-Merril, 1937.

Hanna, A. J., and K. A. Hanna. *Florida's Golden Sands*. Indianapolis: Bobbs-Merrill, 1950.

Hayens, H. *Under the Lone Star.* London: Nelson, 1896.

Houghton, W. R. *Kings of Fortune; or, the Triumphs and Achievements of Noble, Self-Made Men.* Chicago: Davis, 1886.

Howden Smith, A. D. *Commodore Vanderbilt: An Epic of American Achievement.* New York: McBride, 1927.

Hoyt, E. P. *The Vanderbilts and Their Fortune.* New York: Doubleday, 1962.

An Illustrated History of Los Angeles County, California. Chicago: Lewis, 1889.

Irvine, L. H., ed. *A History of the New California, Its People and Resources.* New York: Lewis, 1905.

Jamison, J. C. *With Walker in Nicaragua.* Columbia, MO: Stephens, 1909.

Klepper, M., and R. Gunther. *The Wealthy 100: From Benjamin Franklin to Bill Gates, a Ranking of the Richest Americans, Past and Present.* New York: Citadel, 1996.

Lane, W. J. *Commodore Vanderbilt: An Epic of the Steam Age.* New York: Knopf, 1942.

Manfut, E. *History of Nicaragua.* Managua: José Dolores Historical, 2000.

McCabe, J. D. *Great Fortunes and How They Were Made.* Cincinnati: Hannaford, 1871.

McGowan, E. *The Strange Eventful History of Parker H. French.* Los Angeles: Dawson, 1958.

Medberry, J. K. *Men and Mysteries of Wall Street.* Boston: Fields, Osgood, 1870.

Melendez-Obando, M., and G. Bolanos-Zamora. *Luis Pacheco Bertosa, el Heroe Cartigo.* San José, Costa Rica: Archiva Historica Arquidioccena, 2000.

Miles, W. *Journal of the Sufferings and Hardships of Capt. Parker H. French's Overland Expedition to California.* Chambersburg, PA: Valley Spirit, 1851. Reprint, New York: Cadmus Book Shop, 1916.

Miller, D. H., ed. *Treaties and Other International Acts of the United States, 1776–1863.* Washington, DC: U.S. Government Printing Office, 1931–1948.

Miller, J. *The Complete Poetical Works.* New York: Arno, 1972.

Minnigerode, M. *Certain Rich Men.* New York: Putnam, 1927.

Montufar, L. *Walker en Centro America.* Guatemala: La Union, Typografia, 1887. Reprint, Alajuela, Costa Rica: Museo Historico Cultural Juan Santamaria, 2000.

Oliphant, L. *Patriots & Filibusters, or Incidents of Political and Exploratory Travel.* Edinburgh: Blackwood, 1860.

Renehan, E. J. *Commodore: The Life of Cornelius Vanderbilt.* New York: Basic, 2007.

Robinson, H. *Latin America.* London: Macdonald & Evans, 1961.

Roche, J. J. *Story of the Filibusters.* London, 1891. Reprinted as *Byways of War,* Boston: Sherman Freich, 1907.

Rosengarten, F. *Freebooters Must Die! The Life and Death of William Walker, the Most Notorious Filibuster of the Nineteenth Century.* Wayne, PA: Haverford House, 1976.

Ryan, W. R. *Personal Adventures in Upper & Lower California.* London: Shoberl, 1850.

Scroggs, W. O. *Filibusters and Financiers, the History of William Walker and His Associates.* New York: Macmillan, 1916.

Shuck, O. T. *Historical Abstract of San Francisco.* San Francisco: Shuck, 1897.

Stasz, C. *The Vanderbilt Women: Dynasty of Wealth, Glamour, and Tragedy.* New York: St. Martins, 1991.

Sugden, J. *Nelson: A Dream of Glory, 1758–1797.* New York: Holt, 2004.

Travis, I. D. *The History of the Clayton-Bulwer Treaty.* Ann Arbor: Michigan Political Science Institute, 1899.

Walker, W. *The War in Nicaragua.* Mobile, AL: Goetzel, 1860. Reprint, Tucson: University of Arizona Press, 1985.

Warren, T. R. *Dust and Foam, or, Three Oceans and Two Continents.* New York: Scribner, 1858.

Watterson, H. *Marse Henry.* New York: Doran, 1919.

Wheeler, J. H. *Reminiscences and Memoirs of North Carolina and Eminent North Carolinians.* Columbus, OH: Columbus Printing, 1884.

Williams, M. W. *Anglo-American Isthmian Diplomacy, 1815–1915.* 1916. Reprint, Washington, DC: Smith, 1965.

Wilson, J. G., and John Fiske, eds. *Appleton's Cyclopedia of American Biography.* New York: Appleton, 1887–1889.

JOURNAL ARTICLES

Absalom, S. "The Experience of Samuel Absalom, Filibuster." *Atlantic Monthly,* vol. 4, December 1859, pp. 653–656.

Amero, R. W. "The Mexican-American War in Baja California." *Journal of San Diego History* 30, no. 1 (1984): 49–64.

Bourne, K. "The Clayton-Bulwer Treaty and the Decline of British Opposition to the Territorial Expansion of the United States, 1857–60." *Journal of Modern History* 33, no. 3 (September 1961): 287–291.

Doll, G. "Tales of the Commodore. " *Vanderbilt Magazine* 77, no. 3 (summer 1994): 6–9, 11.

Lacayo, A. D. "La Guerra Nacional." *El Nuevo Diario,* September 18, 2003. Available at http://archivo.elnuevodiario.com.ni.

Rodriguez, M. "The *Prometheus* and the Clayton-Bulwer Treaty." *Journal of Modern History* 36, no. 3 (September 1964): 260–278.

Van Alstyne, R. W. "Great Britain and the United States: A History of Anglo-American Relations, 1783–1952." *Mississippi Valley Historical Review* 42 (September 1955): 363–364.

———. "British Diplomacy and the Clayton-Bulwer Treaty, 1850–1860." *Journal of Modern History* 11 (June 1939): 149–183.

Wyllys, R. K. "The Republic of Lower California, 1853–1854." *Pacific Historical Review* 2, no. 2 (June 1933): 194–213.

NEWSPAPERS AND MAGAZINES

American Heritage Magazine (Forbes Inc.), 1998.

Atlantic Monthly, New York, 1857–1860.

Daily Alta California, San Francisco, 1849–1857.

El Nuevo Diario, Managua, Nicaragua, 2003–2008.

Frank Leslie's Illustrated, New York, 1855–1857.

Harper's Weekly, New York, 1857.

Herald, New York, 1850–1858.

London Daily News, 1853.

Nashville Gazette, 1856.

New Orleans Daily Picayune, 1850–1857.

New York (Daily) Times, 1849–1861.

New York Express, 1855–1857.

Panama Star, Panama, 1851–1857.

Putnam's Monthly, 1857.
Times, London, 1848–1860.
Tribune, New York, 1850–1858.
United States Democratic Review, 1856–1857.

REPORTS
Commission de Investigacion Historica de la Campana 1856–1857. "Proclamas y Mena-jes" no. 3, Impresso en Editorial Aurora Social Ltda, San José, Costa Rica, 1954.
New York State Assembly, 90th sess. Senate Committee Report, 1867, II, December 19.

LETTERS AND OTHER DOCUMENTS
Admiralty, Captains' Logs (to 1853). ADM 51/1851, National Archives, UK.
Admiralty and Ministry of Defence, Navy Department, Ships' Logs (1849–1850). ADM 53/1851 (1849–1850); ADM 53/5295 (1851–1852); ADM 53/5296 (1852), National Archives, UK.
Callender I. Fayssoux Collection of William Walker Papers. University of Mississippi Libraries, Lafayette, MS.
Central American Miscellaneous Documents. Bancroft Library, Berkeley, CA.
Chatard Papers. University of Notre Dame Archives, Notre Dame, IN.
Jane Cazneau Papers. Barker Texas History Center, University of Texas at Austin.
Secretaria de Relacions Exteriores, Paquete 8, *Asuntos Historicos,* Expediente 23, 1853. Mexico City.

NOTES

INTRODUCTION

1. *The Vanderbilt News,* 1857, company newspaper, quoted in Carr, *The World and William Walker.*
2. Klepper and Gunther, *The Wealthy 100.*
3. *New York Daily Tribune,* March 23, 1878.
4. "Diplomatic and Consular Posts, 1781–1997," and "Department Personnel, 1781–1991," accessed at www.state.gov, under "State Department History."
5. Croffut, *The Vanderbilts.*
6. Howden Smith, *Commodore Vanderbilt: An Epic of American Achievement.*
7. Croffut, *The Vanderbilts.*
8. Howden Smith, *Commodore Vanderbilt: An Epic of American Achievement.*
9. Carr, *The World and William Walker.*
10. Ibid.
11. Ibid.
12. Lane, *Commodore Vanderbilt.*
13. Ibid.
14. Miller, *Treaties and Other International Acts.*
15. Lane, *Commodore Vanderbilt.*
16. Palmerston to Abbot Lawrence, December 24, 1851, confirmed that he had issued this instruction to Green on October 31. UK Foreign Office, FO 5/538.
17. Lane, *Commodore Vanderbilt.*

CHAPTER 1: GUN-BARREL DIPLOMACY

1. Lane, *Commodore Vanderbilt.*
2. Croffut, *The Vanderbilts.*
3. Crook, *General George Crook.*
4. Lane, *Commodore Vanderbilt.*
5. Ibid., description by Peter Stout, a passenger in the first Transit party, who passed this way six months later, in July 1851.
6. Passenger list published in *New Orleans Daily Picayune,* June 16, 1850.
7. Crook, *General George Crook.*
8. Shuck, *Historical Abstract of San Francisco,* gives details of all the Californian duels fought by Walker, Graham, and Nugent described here.
9. Ibid.
10. *New York Daily Times,* December 2, 1851.
11. James Green to Lord Palmerston, January 6, 1852.
12. *New York Daily Times,* December 2, 1851.
13. Ibid.

14. Robert Coates to James Green, undated. Quoted in Rodriguez, "The *Prometheus* and the Clayton-Bulwer Treaty."
15. James Green to William Fead, January 9, 1852, FO 53/30.
16. Admiralty, Captains' Logs, ADM 53/5295, July 2, 1851, to June 4, 1852; ADM 53/5296, June 5, 1852 to July 3, 1852.
17. *New York Daily Times,* December 2, 1851.
18. Ibid.
19. Ibid.
20. Lane, *Commodore Vanderbilt.*
21. All times shown have been taken from the log of the *Express:* Admiralty, Captains' Logs.
22. *New York Daily Times,* December 2, 1851.
23. Lane, *Commodore Vanderbilt.*
24. *New York Daily Times,* January 31, 1852.

CHAPTER 2: DOWN BUT NOT OUT

1. Lane, *Commodore Vanderbilt.*
2. Choules, *The Cruise of the Steam Yacht* North Star.
3. Croffut, *The Vanderbilts.*
4. The figures for 1854, a year when passenger numbers suffered a decline due to the *Cyane* incident, were 13,128 westbound passengers and 10,461 eastbound.
5. Davis, *Real Soldiers of Fortune.*
6. Antonio Campuzano to Manuel Maria Gandara, July 3, 1853. Secretaria de Relacions Exteriores, Paquete 8, Mexico.
7. Warren, *Dust and Foam.*
8. Walker, *The War in Nicaragua.*
9. Lane, *Commodore Vanderbilt.*
10. Ibid.
11. Ibid.
12. Walker, *The War in Nicaragua.*
13. *Daily Alta California,* December 8, 1853.
14. Davis, *Real Soldiers of Fortune.*
15. *Daily Alta California,* January 12, 1853.
16. Lane, *Commodore Vanderbilt.*
17. Davis, *Real Soldiers of Fortune.*
18. Walker, *The War in Nicaragua.*
19. Ibid.
20. Carr, *The World and William Walker.*
21. New York State Assembly, 90th sess., 1867, II, Doc. 19.
22. Lane, *Commodore Vanderbilt.*

CHAPTER 3: ENTER THE COLONEL

1. Some accounts give his name as Livingstone.
2. Doubleday, *Filibuster War in Nicaragua.*
3. Walker, *War in Nicaragua.*
4. Ibid.
5. Ibid.
6. Doubleday, *Filibuster War in Nicaragua.*
7. Doubleday's quote is from ibid.
8. Ibid.

9. Walker, *War in Nicaragua.*
10. Doubleday, *Filibuster War in Nicaragua.*
11. Walker, *War in Nicaragua.*
12. Ibid.

CHAPTER 4: LANDING BEHIND ENEMY LINES

1. Walker, *War in Nicaragua;* and Jamison, *With Walker in Nicaragua.*
2. Walker, *War in Nicaragua.*
3. Ibid.
4. Doubleday, *Filibuster War in Nicaragua.*
5. Walker, *War in Nicaragua.*
6. Ibid.
7. Doubleday, *Filibuster War in Nicaragua.*
8. Ibid.
9. Walker, *War in Nicaragua.*
10. Doubleday, *Filibuster War in Nicaragua.*
11. Ibid. In Walker's briefer account, there was no sentry.
12. Walker, *War in Nicaragua.*
13. Ibid.
14. Ibid.
15. Doubleday, *Filibuster War in Nicaragua.*
16. Walker, *War in Nicaragua.*
17. Doubleday, *Filibuster War in Nicaragua.*
18. Ibid.
19. Ibid.
20. Walker, *War in Nicaragua.*

CHAPTER 5: THE BATTLE OF RIVAS

1. Walker, *War in Nicaragua.*
2. Doubleday, *Filibuster War in Nicaragua.*
3. Walker, *War in Nicaragua.*
4. Doubleday, *Filibuster War in Nicaragua.*
5. Ibid.
6. Ibid.
7. Walker, *War in Nicaragua.*
8. Ibid.
9. Doubleday, *Filibuster War in Nicaragua.*
10. Ibid.
11. Montufar, *Walker en Centro America.*
12. Walker, *War in Nicaragua.*
13. Doubleday, *Filibuster War in Nicaragua.*
14. Ibid.
15. Doubleday, *Filibuster War in Nicaragua.*
16. Montufar, *Walker en Centro America.*
17. Doubleday, *Filibuster War in Nicaragua.*
18. *Daily Alta California,* September 3, 1851.
19. Crook, *General George Crook.*
20. Walker, *War in Nicaragua.*
21. Ibid.

22. Ibid.
23. Doubleday, *Filibuster War in Nicaragua*. Dewey, accused of burning down the barracks in San Juan del Sur that night, was shot the next day on Walker's orders.
24. Walker, *War in Nicaragua*.
25. Ibid.
26. Bell, *Early Times in Southern California*.
27. Walker, *War in Nicaragua*.

CHAPTER 6: VICTORY AT LA VIRGEN

1. Walker, *War in Nicaragua*.
2. Montufar, *Walker en Centro America*.
3. Walker, *War in Nicaragua*.
4. Ibid.
5. In 1850, an act proposed in the California legislature to ban Mexicans from the state was actually called the Greasers Act.
6. Doubleday, *Filibuster War in Nicaragua*.
7. Ibid.
8. Ibid.
9. Ibid.; the entire exchange is recorded by Doubleday.
10. Ibid.
11. Ibid.
12. Davis, *Real Soldiers of Fortune*.
13. Doubleday, *Filibuster War in Nicaragua*.
14. Walker, *War in Nicaragua*.
15. Doubleday, *Filibuster War in Nicaragua*.

CHAPTER 7: WALKER'S SECRET PLAN

1. Walker, *War in Nicaragua*.
2. Ibid.
3. Ibid.
4. Ibid.
5. Doubleday, *Filibuster War in Nicaragua*.
6. Walker, *War in Nicaragua*.
7. Miller, *The Complete Poetical Works*.
8. Walker, *War in Nicaragua*.
9. Doubleday, *Filibuster War in Nicaragua*.
10. Walker, *War in Nicaragua*.
11. Doubleday, *Filibuster War in Nicaragua*.
12. Walker, *War in Nicaragua*.
13. Ibid.

CHAPTER 8: TAKING GRANADA

1. Walker, *War in Nicaragua*.
2. Ibid.
3. *Frank Leslie's Illustrated*, February 21, 1857.
4. Walker, *War in Nicaragua*. Walker spelled the priest's name *Vigil*, but all other sources give it as *Vijil*.
5. Ibid.
6. Ibid.
7. Ibid.

Chapter 9: The Walker Way

1. *Daily Alta California,* January 12, 1853.
2. Unless otherwise noted, all quotes in this chapter are from Walker, *War in Nicaragua.*
3. Absalom, "Experience of Samuel Absalom, Filibuster."
4. Davis, *Real Soldiers of Fortune.*
5. Montufar, *Walker en Centro America.*

Chapter 10: Closing In on the Prize

1. Croffut, *The Vanderbilts.*
2. Medberry, *Men and Mysteries of Wall Street.*
3. Lane, *Commodore Vanderbilt.*
4. Ibid.
5. Walker, *War in Nicaragua.*
6. Montufar, *Walker en Centro America.*
7. Ibid.
8. Ibid.
9. Ibid.
10. Jamison, *With Walker in Nicaragua.*
11. Joseph S. Fowler, introduction to *Reminiscences and Memoirs of North Carolina and Eminent North Carolinians,* by J. H. Wheeler (Columbus, OH: Columbus Printing, 1884).
12. Ibid.
13. Walker, *War in Nicaragua.*
14. Ibid.

Chapter 11: On a Collision Course

1. *Daily Alta California,* May 1, 1855.
2. Jamison, *With Walker in Nicaragua.*
3. Register Book, New Orleans Agency of the Nicaraguan Emigration Company, Supreme Government of the Republic of Nicaragua, in Callender I. Fayssoux Collection of William Walker Papers. University of Mississippi Libraries.
4. Jamison, *With Walker in Nicaragua.*
5. Bell, *Early Times in Southern California.*
6. Jamison, *With Walker in Nicaragua.*
7. Lane, *Commodore Vanderbilt.*
8. Walker, *War in Nicaragua.*
9. Ibid.
10. Lane, *Commodore Vanderbilt.*

Chapter 12: Blindsiding Vanderbilt

1. Walker, *War in Nicaragua.*
2. Carr, *The World and William Walker.*
3. Jamison, *With Walker in Nicaragua.*
4. Ibid.
5. Ibid.
6. Bell, *Early Times in Southern California.*
7. Ibid.
8. Ibid.

9. *Daily Alta California,* December 26, 1850, reported the arrival of twenty-three aboard the barque JS *Jeserum* in San Francisco and recounted the story of the Overland Express, as told by one of them.

10. In a list of the French party from New York, the *New Orleans Daily Picayune,* May 26 included a "Sylvester Spencer." It's probable this was Sylvanus Spencer.

11. New York *Herald,* December 23, 1855.

12. Walker, *War in Nicaragua.*

13. *New York Tribune,* December 25, 1855.

14. Ibid.

15. Ibid.

16. Ibid.

17. Ibid.

18. *New York Morning Express,* December 26, 1855.

19. Ibid.

20. Ibid.

21. *Daily Alta California,* January 20, 1856.

CHAPTER 13: THE GATHERING STORM

1. *Daily Alta California,* January 3, 1856.

2. Ibid.

3. *Daily Alta California,* January 6, 1856.

4. Walker, *War in Nicaragua.*

5. Lane, *Commodore Vanderbilt.*

6. Walker, *War in Nicaragua.*

7. Ibid.

8. Ibid.

9. Ibid.

CHAPTER 14: GOING TO WAR WITH WALKER

1. Montufar, *Walker en Centro America.*

2. Walker, *War in Nicaragua.*

3. Thomas Meagher to Smith O'Brien, December 1849, in *Heart of Exile,* by P. Adam-Smith (Melbourne: Nelson, 1986).

4. According to *Putnam's Monthly,* vol. 9, April 1857, p. 432, Meagher became a supporter of Walker, with a letter from him being read out at a New York City public meeting in early 1857 in which the Irishman called for "instant aid" to be sent to the embattled Walker in Nicaragua.

5. Walker, *War in Nicaragua.*

6. *Frank Leslie's Illustrated,* March 1856.

7. Greene, *Filibuster.*

8. Commission de Investigacion Historica de la Campana 1856–1857.

9. *New York Daily Times,* June 10, 1856.

10. Ibid.

11. Ibid.

12. Thomas Lord to Hosea Birdsall, April 8, 1856, quoted in Walker, *War in Nicaragua.*

13. Ibid.

14. Montufar, *Walker en Centro America;* and Bolanos-Geyer, *Grey-Eyed Man of Destiny.*

15. *New York Daily Times,* June 10, 1856.

CHAPTER 15: THE BATTLE OF SANTA ROSA

1. Carr, *The World and William Walker*.
2. Walker, *War in Nicaragua*.
3. Ibid.
4. Ibid.
5. Ibid.
6. Ibid.
7. Ibid.

CHAPTER 16: COURTS-MARTIAL AND FIRING SQUADS

1. Bell, *Early Times in Southern California*.
2. Walker, *War in Nicaragua*.
3. Ibid.
4. Ibid.
5. *New York Daily Times*, April 30, 1856.
6. Williams lived to old age, becoming a leading journalist and author.
7. Manfut, *History of Nicaragua*.
8. Ibid.
9. Jamison, *With Walker in Nicaragua*.
10. Ibid.

CHAPTER 17: A KILLING OR TWO

1. Walker, *War in Nicaragua*.
2. Jamison, *With Walker in Nicaragua*.
3. Walker, *War in Nicaragua*.
4. Ibid.
5. Ibid.
6. Ibid.
7. *New York Daily Times*, March 6, 1856.
8. Carr, *The World and William Walker*.
9. Walker, *War in Nicaragua*.
10. Jamison, *With Walker in Nicaragua*.
11. *New York Daily Times*, April 9, 1859.
12. New York *Herald*, March 17, 1856.
13. *New York Daily Times*, April 9, 1856.
14. *Nashville Gazette*, June 13, 1856.
15. Walker, *War in Nicaragua*.
16. *New York Daily Times*, April 30, 1856.
17. Walker, *War in Nicaragua*.
18. *New York Daily Times*, April 30, 1856.

CHAPTER 18: THE SECOND BATTLE OF RIVAS

1. Jamison, *With Walker in Nicaragua*.
2. Walker, *War in Nicaragua*, says that there was only one cannon. Jamison, *With Walker in Nicaragua*, says two and is backed up by Costa Rican sources.
3. Jamison, *With Walker in Nicaragua*.
4. Ibid.
5. Montufar, *Walker en Centro America*.

6. Jamison, *With Walker in Nicaragua*. Walker, *War in Nicaragua*, does not mention this incident, but Montufar, *Walker en Centro America*, gives full details, and Jamison covers it briefly.

7. Jamison, *With Walker in Nicaragua*.

8. Ibid.

9. Ibid.

10. Ibid.

11. Ibid.

12. Walker, *War in Nicaragua*.

13. Jamison, *With Walker in Nicaragua*.

14. Walker, *War in Nicaragua*.

15. Jamison, *With Walker in Nicaragua*.

16. Melendez-Obando and Bolonas-Zamora, *Luis Pacheco Bertosa*.

17. Jamison, *With Walker in Nicaragua*.

18. Winters sailed from New York to Nicaragua on the SS *Star of the West* on May 20, 1854.

19. Myron Veeder sailed from New York to Nicaragua aboard the SS *Prometheus* on January 5, 1852.

20. Jamison, *With Walker in Nicaragua*.

21. Ibid.

22. Ibid.

23. Ibid.

24. Montufar, *Walker en Centro America*.

CHAPTER 19: PRESIDENT WALKER

1. Walker, *War in Nicaragua*.

2. Ibid.

3. Ibid.

4. Ibid.

5. Carr, *The World and William Walker*.

6. Walker, *War in Nicaragua*.

7. Ibid.

8. *Nashville Gazette,* June 13, 1856.

9. Carr, *The World and William Walker*.

10. Davis, *Real Soldiers of Fortune*.

11. *New York Daily Times,* June 10, 1856.

12. Lane, *Commodore Vanderbilt*.

13. Walker, *War in Nicaragua*.

14. Carr, *The World and William Walker*.

15. Palmerston to Clarendon, December 31, 1857, in Van Alstyne, "Anglo-American Relations."

16. Carr, *The World and William Walker*.

17. Ibid.

18. Ibid.

19. Walker, *War in Nicaragua*.

20. Carr, *The World and William Walker*.

21. Fowler, Introduction, Wheeler, *Reminiscences and Memoirs*.

22. Walker, *War in Nicaragua*.

23. Ibid.
24. Spencer description based on a painting of his father.
25. Lacayo, "The National War."
26. Walker, *War in Nicaragua.*
27. Jamison, *With Walker in Nicaragua.*
28. Walker, *War in Nicaragua.*

CHAPTER 20: BATTLES ON ALL FRONTS
1. Lane, *Commodore Vanderbilt.*
2. Ibid.
3. Ibid.
4. *New York Daily Times,* June 10, 1856.
5. Lane, *Commodore Vanderbilt.*
6. Ibid.
7. *New York Daily Times,* June 10, 1856.
8. Lane, *Commodore Vanderbilt.*
9. Ibid.
10. Ibid.
11. Ibid.
12. Howden Smith: *An Epic of American Achievement.*
13. Lane, *Commodore Vanderbilt.*
14. Howden Smith: *An Epic of American Achievement.*
15. Bolanos-Geyer; Manfut.
16. Manfut, *History of Nicaragua.*
17. Walker, *War in Nicaragua.*
18. Ibid.
19. Manfut, *History of Nicaragua.*
20. Ibid.
21. While Walker, *War in Nicaragua,* felt the battle was only brief, Manfut and Bolanos-Geyer, quoting Colonel Estrada, say it lasted much of the morning.
22. Manfut, *History of Nicaragua.*
23. *United States Democratic Review,* July 1857.
24. Jamison, *With Walker in Nicaragua.*

CHAPTER 21: NEW BATTLEGROUNDS
1. Walker, *War in Nicaragua.*
2. Ibid.
3. Carr, *The World and William Walker.*
4. Andres Castro recovered from his wound, married his nurse, and bought a house near Managua hospital. In his forties, Castro was killed in a bar fight.
5. Walker, *War in Nicaragua.*
6. Lane, *Commodore Vanderbilt.*
7. Carr, *The World and William Walker.*
8. Davis, *Real Soldiers of Fortune.*
9. Walker, *War in Nicaragua.*
10. Jamison, *With Walker in Nicaragua.*
11. Ibid.
12. Ibid.

CHAPTER 22: WHEELING AND DEALING

1. Gordon, *Scarlet Woman of Wall Street*.
2. Lane, *Commodore Vanderbilt*.
3. McCabe, *Great Fortunes*.
4. Howden Smith, *An Epic of American Achievement*.
5. Ibid.
6. Carr, *The World and William Walker*.
7. Croffut, *The Vanderbilts*.
8. Carr, *The World and William Walker*.
9. Ibid.
10. Lane, *Commodore Vanderbilt*. As a result of the falling out between Walker and Goicuria, most of the fifty Cuban fighters taken to Nicaragua by Goicuria deserted Walker's ranks; the Cuban Guard was never heard of again.
11. Walker, *War in Nicaragua*.
12. *Putnam's Monthly*, April 1857, p. 425.
13. Ibid.
14. Geron, *Fatal Corner*.
15. Montufar, *Walker en Centro America*.
16. Ibid.

CHAPTER 23: HERE WAS GRANADA

1. Walker, *War in Nicaragua*.
2. Ibid.
3. Ibid.
4. Jamison, *With Walker in Nicaragua*.
5. Walker, *War in Nicaragua*.
6. Jamison, *With Walker in Nicaragua*.
7. *Putnam's Monthly*, April 1857.
8. Jamison, *With Walker in Nicaragua*.

CHAPTER 24: CLOSING NICARAGUA'S BACK DOOR

1. That cell would nave been at Fort San Carlos.
2. Carr, *The World and William Walker*.
3. New York *Herald*, December 25, 1856.
4. Absalom, "Experience of Samuel Absalom, Filibuster."
5. Miller, *Complete Poetical Works*.

CHAPTER 25: OPERATION SAN JUAN

1. Doubleday, *Filibuster War in Nicaragua*.
2. Walker, *War in Nicaragua*, says the number was ten, but Doubleday, *Filibuster War in Nicaragua*, who was on the spot, put the number at twenty.
3. Oliphant, *Patriots & Filibusters*.
4. Doubleday, *Filibuster War in Nicaragua*.
5. Ibid.
6. Walker, *War in Nicaragua*.
7. Absalom, "Experience of Samuel Absalom, Filibuster."
8. Doubleday, *Filibuster War in Nicaragua*.
9. *New York Daily Times*, February 23, 1857.

10. Doubleday, *Filibuster War in Nicaragua.*
11. Ibid.
12. Walker, *War in Nicaragua.*
13. Ibid.
14. Carr, *The World and William Walker.*
15. Sugden, *Nelson.*
16. Hanna and Hanna, *Florida's Golden Sands.*
17. Ibid.
18. Ibid.
19. New York *Herald,* March 12, 1857.
20. Robinson, *Latin America.*
21. Hanna and Hanna, *Florida's Golden Sands.*
22. Walker, *War in Nicaragua.*
23. Ibid.

CHAPTER 26: TO THE VICTOR, THE SPOILS

1. New York *Herald,* March 17, 1857.
2. Doubleday, *Filibuster War in Nicaragua.*
3. Ibid.
4. Ibid. says more than one ton of gunpowder; Sites, New York *Herald,* March 17, 1857, said two tons.
5. New York *Herald,* March 17, 1857.
6. Doubleday, *Filibuster War in Nicaragua.*
7. Ibid.
8. New York *Herald,* April 17, 1857.
9. Doubleday, *Filibuster War in Nicaragua.*
10. Walker, *War in Nicaragua.*
11. Doubleday, *Filibuster War in Nicaragua.*
12. New York *Herald,* April 17, 1857.
13. Walker, *War in Nicaragua.*
14. Carr, *The World and William Walker.*
15. Walker, *War in Nicaragua.*
16. Ibid.
17. Carr, *The World and William Walker.*
18. Walker, *War in Nicaragua.*
19. Carr, *The World and William Walker.*
20. Walker, *War in Nicaragua.*
21. Ibid.
22. Ibid.
23. *Atlantic Monthly,* April 1858.
24. Carr, *The World and William Walker.*
25. Frederick K. Chatard to William Seton, July 20, 1857, Chatard Papers, II-1-a.
26. Carr, *The World and William Walker.*
27. Norvell Walker disappeared overboard while sailing from Panama to the United States via Cuba in mid-1857.
28. Cauty returned to England, where he married in 1859. The 1881 British Census found Cauty in London. Aged fifty-five, he was listed as an unemployed clerk, having long ago spent the spoils from his Nicaraguan exploit.

29. Carr, *The World and William Walker*.
30. Ibid.
31. A. J. de Yrisarri to Secretary Cass, December 13, 1857, reprinted in *New York Daily Times,* January 31, 1858.
32. *Atlantic Monthly,* April 1858.
33. Carr, *The World and William Walker*.

Chapter 27: The Surrender
1. Carr, *The World and William Walker*.
2. Yrisarri to Cass, December 13, 1857.
3. Carr, *The World and William Walker*.
4. Lane, *Commodore Vanderbilt*.

Epilogue
1. Lane, *Commodore Vanderbilt*.
2. Walker, *War in Nicaragua*.
3. Ibid.
4. Carr, *The World and William Walker*.
5. Ibid.
6. Robinson, *Latin America*.
7. Howden Smith: *An Epic of American Achievement*.
8. Renehan, *Commodore: The Life of Cornelius Vanderbilt*.
9. Ibid.

INDEX